AN A–Z OF HELLRAISERS

Robert Sellers is the author of the bestselling *Hellraisers*, *Hollywood Hellraisers* and *Don't Let the Bastards Grind You Down*. He has also written biographies on Tom Cruise, Harrison Ford and Sean Connery, *Always Look on the Bright Side of Life*, a history of the George Harrison/Monty Python film company HandMade, and the controversial *Battle for Bond*, which for a time was banned by the family of Ian Fleming. He was a regular contributor to *Empire*, *Total Film*, *Independent*, *SFX* and *Cinema Retro* and has contributed to a number of television documentaries, including Channel 4's *The 100 Best Family Films*

D1494254

ALSO BY ROBERT SELLERS

Hellraisers: The Life and Inebriated Times of Richard Burton, Richard Harris, Peter O'Toole and Oliver Reed

Hollywood Hellraisers: The Wild Lives and Fast Times of Marlon Brando, Dennis Hopper, Warren Beatty and Jack Nicholson

Don't Let the Bastards Grind You Down: How One Generation of British Actors Changed the World

An A-Z of HELLRAISERS

A Comprehensive COMPENDIUM of Outrageous INSOBRIETY

ROBERT SELLERS

arrow books

This paperback edition published by Arrow Books 2011

10 9 8 7 6 5 4 3

Copyright © Robert Sellers 2011

Robert Sellers has asserted his right to be identified as the author of this work under the Copyright, Designs and Patents Act 1988

First published in Great Britain in 2011 by Preface Publishing

20 Vauxhall Bridge Road
London SW1V 2SA

An imprint of The Random House Group Limited

www.randomhouse.co.uk

Addresses for companies within The Random House Group Limited
can be found at www.randomhouse.co.uk

The Random House Group Limited Reg. No. 954009
A CIP catalogue record for this book is available from the British Library

ISBN 978 1 84809 246 4

Typeset in Dante MT by Palimpsest Book Production Limited,
Falkirk, Stirlingshire

The Random House Group Limited supports The Forest Stewardship
Council (FSC®), the leading international forest certification organisation.
Our books carrying the FSC label are printed on FSC® certified paper.
FSC is the only forest certification scheme endorsed by the leading
environmental organisations, including Greenpeace. Our
paper procurement policy can be found at
www.randomhouse.co.uk/environment

Printed and bound in Great Britain by Clays Ltd, St Ives PLC

'I hate to advocate drugs, alcohol, violence, or insanity to anyone, but they've always worked for me.'

Hunter S Thompson

'I'm on a whisky diet. I've lost three days already!'

Tommy Cooper

'Ah, beer . . . the cause of, and solution to, all of life's problems.'

Homer Simpson

Contents

Contents

Introduction

According to the *Oxford English Dictionary* a hellraiser is a person who causes trouble by violent, drunken, or outrageous behaviour. A bit of a no-brainer, but that's the official definition.

Hellraisers are very different from your plain average drunks or your common or garden alcoholics. They're hedonistic, and therefore much more dangerous. They're anti-heroes, really. They're the opposite of a role model, in that they seem to want to sink to a level that's more abhorrent and disgusting than anyone else. There's a world of difference between walking back from the pub late Friday night and pissing against a wall and pissing on the Alamo and getting arrested at gunpoint, as happened to Ozzy Osbourne. Both are obnoxious and anti-social, but there's something of the grand theatrical gesture about Ozzy's act: it's defiant at the same time as being just plain bad.

Hellraisers are people who capture the imagination as much for their colourful personal lives as for their artistic talents, be they in front of the camera, on the stage, in a recording studio, typing at a keyboard or holding a paintbrush. I guess the fascination is to see the flaws in these iconic people: even someone who has attained celebrity and wealth can be just as much in the crapper as the rest of us – in fact more so; they've got further to fall and it hurts worse when they land.

But shouldn't this behaviour be condemned, rather than glorified? At some point in our lives haven't we all wished we could behave as outrageously? Isn't there a grudging admiration for some of their antics? And do we not extract some ghoulish pleasure when eventually they pay for their sins through incarceration or ruination or – in many cases – premature death?

I don't seek to moralise in the following pages; the facts, variously hilarious and tragic, speak for themselves. As for the subjects, they range from the legendary to the obscure, both current and historical. I've cast my net far and wide; I do hope you judge the haul to have been worthwhile.

A

ART ACORD (1890–1931: Actor)

He was the cowboy's cowboy, rough, unbullshitable, built like a Sherman tank with barely a patch of hide on him that didn't have a knife wound or gunshot scar. By the time Art Acord strolled into Hollywood in 1909, finding work as a stuntman and extra in the fledgling movie business, he was spoken of in revered tones as the greatest all-round rodeo champ America had ever seen, able to throw a steer in twenty-four seconds.

Art learned the ways of the west early. Born to Mormon parents in Utah, he was just nine years old when he hitched up as a full-time wrangler on a local ranch. It was that authenticity that saw him rise through the ranks to become a top cowboy star with Universal. But his drinking was a major problem. He'd go on booze binges and be missing for days at a time, causing a shutdown in film production. Or he'd indulge in mindless bar-room brawls. On set Art always insisted that the coloured water normally used to fill whisky bottles contain the real thing. Time and again studio bosses sacked him, only to be forced to reinstate the actor due to his popularity.

One thing Acord despised at Universal was the dreaded studio tour, which existed even back then. One day as the usual herd of blue-rinsed heifers floated by on a special bus Acord, having sucked liberally from a bottle of whisky stashed behind some scenery, began hurling abuse at Mexican actor Ortega, a mean bastard no one messed with. As Ortega went for his knife, Acord whipped out his .45 and fired, hitting the Mexican in the shoulder. But Ortega was made of stern stuff and pounced, plunging his knife deep into Art's chest with repeated thrusts until his own blood mingled with the cowboy's.

By this time the set had completely cleared of actors and technicians. It had also dawned on the tourists that this was no movie scene they were watching but an actual fight to the death and amid screams of terror they scattered for cover.

Viciously slashed, Acord managed to stumble to his feet and offload three more bullets into the prone Mexican before succumbing himself in a crumbled, bloody heap. Silence. The tour guides hurried their charges back onto the bus and roared away as heads of actors popped up from their hiding places. The eerie hush was suddenly broken by the raucous laughter of the two 'dead' men. Acord and Ortega got up, all smiles. It was a spectacular hoax to rid the set of tourists. When the guides discovered the truth they vowed never to take another tour onto an Art Acord set.

Such was his international appeal that Art often appeared in Wild West shows and rodeos around the globe. One incredible story has him performing in a large sports arena in Argentina in the mid-twenties. According to rodeo showman Milt Hinkle, amongst the spectators was none other than Butch Cassidy, this several years after he was supposed to have been blasted to hell by Bolivian cavalry troops. Many historians have suggested that Butch did not die in that 1908 shootout but lived on into moderate old age. So here he was, according to Hinkle, and after the show joined Acord and the other cowboy stars for a massive booze-up. Large quantities were obviously consumed because it was decided that Butch reform the famed 'Hole in the Wall' gang for one last nostalgic act of thievery. Off everyone rode to some wilderness town and committed an outrageous daylight, and drunken, bank robbery.

Back in Hollywood Art continued to get rat-arsed and brawl; he was even arrested for bootlegging. In his drunken rages he'd fight with anyone who marginally pissed him off, breaking the nose of Victor Fleming, future director of *Gone with the Wind*, for daring to suggest he wasn't a real cowboy, and picking a fight with one of Hollywood's toughest stuntmen Yakima Canutt, who gave him something of a pasting. Acord later apologised to Canutt, who readily accepted after seeing the damage he'd inflicted on his face. The two men made up over a drink.

In the end Art's alcoholism and self-destructive persona cost him three marriages and most of his colleagues' respect and friendship. Barely thirty, he looked positively clapped out and when Universal, finally tired of this horsing around, cancelled his contract Acord was left to dig around for morsels with the smaller B-movie studios. He even went to the elaborate length of orchestrating his own kidnapping as a publicity stunt. As a last desperate throw of the dice he headed to Mexico to hunt for gold, where his propensity for brawling almost got him killed when he was stabbed in a vicious bar fight.

It was in Mexico where Art met his inglorious end, in a room at the Palace Hotel in the town of Chihuahua. The police listed his death as suicide; that he'd drunk himself to death. But friends were convinced he'd been murdered by a local senior politician who'd caught the cowboy *in flagrante* with his wife. Acord's body remained in Mexico for some eight years after his death until it was returned to the United States for internment.

Alas, nearly every one of Acord's silent movies is lost to posterity. At least his contribution to the western genre is recognised with a deserved star on the Hollywood walk of fame.

ALEXANDER THE GREAT (356–323 BC: *Warrior King*)

The Macedonians were a people of legendary drinking habits, unlike their more civilised neighbours the Greeks, who diluted their wine with water. Like Brits on holiday in Ibiza, they drank for no other purpose than to get smashed. Drinking contests were an accepted and everyday part of life in Macedonia and it was not uncommon for the winner to end up dead from over-indulgence.

Alexander the Great was a Macedonian, born in the shadow of Mount Olympus, home to the gods. Tutored under Aristotle, as a youth he shied away from getting blotto, indeed looked scornfully upon his father King Philip, a habitual drunkard who thought nothing of going into battle troll-eyed. An inveterate womaniser to boot, Philip claimed seven wives, getting the hots for Alexander's mother, Olympus, when she was just twelve years old. A rare beauty, Olympus was addicted to weird religious cults; legend has it that she slept with snakes. A tremendous schemer, she also made sure that when her husband was assassinated in 336, Alexander, already an outstanding warrior, was the obvious heir to his throne, and the 40,000 troops that went with it. Though barely twenty, the new king set his sights on the Persian Empire, then the largest on earth. His conquests would span twelve years and cover the territories of what are now Turkey, Lebanon, Egypt, Iran, Iraq, Afghanistan and Pakistan.

As he vanquished, becoming the most powerful man alive, Alexander turned increasingly to alcohol, perhaps to anaesthetise himself against the constant fighting and killing. There was also his worship of Dionysus, the god of intoxication: wine was his gift to man and by pouring the stuff down his throat Alexander was paying homage, wasn't he? Wine was certainly his beverage, one he took every day, which leads one to speculate that Alexander must have lived much of his adult life intoxicated to various degrees.

As commander in chief Alexander often staged great feasts of drinking for his closest allies. The most memorable, which must go down as history's ultimate booze bender, took place in the conquered city of Persepolis, one of the treasures of the Persian Empire. The whole thing degenerated into a riot, with revellers going on the rampage, razing much of the city to the ground. Alexander himself led the way by throwing the first firebrand into the royal palace. Back home, Macedonians shook their heads in dismay that such a wondrous city had been destroyed by their king during a grand piss-up, then turned to the barman and said, 'Same again.'

Another time Alexander organised a mighty drinking contest, offering a gold crown to the victor. A young nobleman by the name of Promachus took first prize, managing to quaff some fourteen quarts of wine. Then a wind blasted through the camp, by the end of which Promachus and some forty of his fellow competitors lay dead, felled by a combination of the cold and plain drunkenness.

As dependency on the wicked brew increased so Alexander's character changed. An affable sort of chap when not putting nations to the sword, it was drink that sent him over the edge, made him, 'offensively arrogant and descend to the level of the common soldier', according to a contemporary. His drinking became so pronounced that he'd need to sleep the whole of the next day to recover from his wild binges.

Friends began to grow weary of Alexander's unpredictable nature. Without much judgement he could suddenly perpetrate acts of heinous violence. He once dragged an enemy general behind his chariot until he was dead. Then there was the fate of Cleitus, one of Alexander's most loyal friends and soldiers. It was during a celebration, which inevitably turned into another drunken orgy, that the two men clashed, Cleitus angry that Alexander was favouring his new Persian courtiers over his old Macedonian troops. Angry words were batted to and fro, tempers were raised, and then suddenly Alexander, too much wine swilling in his belly, took a javelin and rammed it through his old friend, killing him. Like most stinkos he quickly regretted what he'd done, retiring to his tent where he spent the rest of the night weeping uncontrollably.

Ominous clouds were beginning to hover above Alexander. His officers, missing home after so many years on the march, grew unruly, and the king's own strength began failing him. His mind, too, started wandering as he believed himself to be no mere man, more a god with a thirst to conquer yet more lands. An assassination attempt made on him by those fearful of his growing despotism failed; ironically because of drink. The plot was to kill the king as he lay sleeping in his tent, but that night Alexander indulged in one of his now quite common marathon drinking sessions and never retired. The conspirators, all teenagers, were found the next day and tortured to death.

The omens were coming thick and fast. Hephaestion, Alexander's closest friend, whose capacity for booze rivalled his own, drank a half-gallon of chilled wine for breakfast one morning and promptly dropped dead. Alexander threw himself on the body where he remained the whole day until his guards dragged him away. It was an eerie foreshadowing of his own death barely twelve months later.

There are many rumours as to exactly how Alexander perished. He may have been poisoned by enemies or succumbed to some disease, perhaps malaria, that his battered immune system had no chance of defeating. Or was it the booze that got him? In those final months he was consuming insane quantities and was probably by this time of his life an alcoholic. At the end of a drinking bout in Babylon that lasted two days and nights, Alexander insisted on drinking the health of every person in his presence and so called for the cup of Hercules, the capacity of which was legendary. After downing the whole thing he collapsed in a heap and was taken to bed where he developed a fever and died several days later.

So, dead at thirty-two, his military achievements unparalleled in history, but it was a sad decline, from strapping youth with the world literally at his feet, to a paranoid aggressive 'see you, Jimmy' drunk.

KINGSLEY AMIS (1922–1995: Author)

Over the course of four decades Kingsley Amis produced a steady flow of novels and journalist prose that established him as the leading British comic writer of his generation, resulting in a knighthood in 1990. What fuelled him was booze, a subject he took extremely seriously, arguing, for example, that proper drinkers should own a separate refrigerator for their stock: 'Wives and such are constantly filling up any refrigerator they have a claim on, even its ice-compartment, with irrelevant rubbish like food.'

Amis was born into blinding middle-classness in Clapham, London. Didn't like it at all and entertained much the same attitude towards his snobbish parents. Banned from having friends if they emanated from the working classes, Amis was the classic only child, pampered and obsessively fussed over by his mother, even down to being fed by hand until the age of thirteen. Is it any wonder that the adult Kingsley was hopeless unless there was a woman around to look after his every need.

At school he excelled in English and won a scholarship to Oxford, where he encountered alcohol for the first time, getting smashed on cheap sherry, an enlightening experience, despite the sour final note of throwing up in a chamber pot. Amis's drinking career had begun. Unable to afford a connoisseur's palate as a meagre student, he paid particular attention to the empties left behind by tramps in the park, a good clue as to what got you wasted on a modicum of outlay. Back then Kingsley's idea of a good night out was getting plastered on three barley wines and a pint of rough cider, all for five old shillings.

In 1942 Amis joined the army and ended up serving as a radio operator in Normandy, looking not so much for Nazis as girls and booze. He found a few of each, sleeping in the same evening with a prostitute and a waitress, contracting scabies, and discovering burgundy and Calvados. Demobbed, he returned to Oxford, setting his sights on not working if he could help it. There he met and fell in love with Hilary Bardwell, an art student, who disappointingly turned out, 'not nearly so depraved as I had hoped'. Even so they married and began a family, but you couldn't trust old Kingsley as far as you could throw him and he soon had a nice little harem going, some members of which included friends of his wife. What do you expect, though, from a man who described himself as 'selfish, self-indulgent, lazy, arrogant and above all inextinguishably promiscuous by nature'?

Between the bed-hopping Kingsley managed to get his degree despite publicly declaring that his dons had less dignity than a, 'procession of syphilitic, cancerous, necrophilic shit-bespattered lavatory attendants'. Landing a job lecturing at the University College of Swansea, Amis's drinking and whoring continued unabated – increased, in fact. He more or less made a pass at all attractive females. So frequent was the procession of crumpet that it got terribly confusing on occasions. At one weekend gathering Kingsley had to be on his best behaviour to every lady at the breakfast table, since he'd juice-looped so much the previous night he'd forgotten which one of them he'd banged.

Hilary knew, of course, about her husband's frequent trouser-dropping activities, and indulged a few times herself. One liaison was serious enough to threaten the marriage. 'Having one's wife fucked is one thing,' wrote Amis. 'Having her taken away from you, plus your children, is another, I find.' The marriage survived, as did Hilary's exasperation: witness the time on holiday when Amis lay sprawled asleep in the sun and she took out her lipstick and wrote on his back: 'One fat Englishman. I fuck anything.'

It was 1954 when Amis made his name as a writer with his debut novel *Lucky Jim*. With his remarkable powers of recovery, no matter how much liquor had been consumed the previous evening, Amis was able to sustain a highly disciplined approach to his career, always at his typewriter promptly each morning. The afternoon was another matter, usually entailing a liquid lunch that somehow always spread into the evening and beyond.

Novelist Elizabeth Jane Howard was upper class and sexy with it. Amis was hooked. It was the affair that spelled the end of his marriage. Together they moved into a country mansion where Kingsley saw his duties as never stretching beyond the mixing and serving of drinks at parties. As for bringing up his two sons, Philip and Martin, he'd always looked upon the job of parenting as a vocation rather than a true calling; when they became teenagers he gave each of them a generous stockpile of condoms.

Kingsley and the countryside did not get on at all well – not enough pubs where they lived, for a start – and so it was back to London. Jane did most of the packing; Kingsley's part in the operation consisted of polishing off the remnants of liquor bottles secreted around the house so they didn't need to pack them.

According to Jane, Kingsley was drinking more heavily now, often getting through a bottle of whisky a day. He once got so wired to the tits that he had to crawl upstairs to bed on all fours, being unable to make it standing up. Worryingly, it was beginning to impinge upon his mental capacities. One time he argued all day with Jane about the guests she'd invited to a previous evening's dinner party; only there'd been no such party, except in Kingsley's own bedraggled mind. He knew he was a drunk, of course he did, rejecting out of hand the word 'alcoholic'. Wrote reams about it, paraded his drunkenness at functions and pubs. He had all these vile recipes for hangovers; Bovril beef paste and vodka for one, or try a tumbler of Grand Marnier for breakfast. Son Martin called him, 'the laureate of the hangover'.

For the more physical type, try these Amis hangover remedies: 'If your wife or other partner is beside you, and (of course) willing, perform the sexual act as vigorously as you can.' Or, 'Go up for half an hour in an open aeroplane, needless to say with a non-hung-over person at the controls.'

He had a drink for every occasion; for example Milk Punch (one part brandy, one part bourbon, four parts milk, plus nutmeg and frozen milk cubes); this was to be drunk, 'immediately on rising, in lieu of eating breakfast'. He felt it bolstered one for a particularly hard day ahead. He also extolled the virtues of sangria: 'You can drink a lot of it without falling down.' But his first love was Scotch whisky, even though he was consuming rather too much of it, resulting in that common ailment of the true drunk: not remembering how the hell he got home. Amis said that if the day ever came when he had more money than sense he'd employ servants to carry him around.

Drink played a major role in Jane leaving him in 1980. 'You are not going to stop drinking,' she wrote in her farewell letter. 'And I cannot live with the consequences.' She did offer to take him back if he gave up the sauce but Kingsley swiftly vetoed that notion, even if the thought of suddenly being left alone at fifty-eight petrified him. After a period of 'dad-sitting', as his sons called it, Amis moved in again with Hilary, now remarried, who nevertheless assumed her old role of 'looking after the poor old sod'. It was an arrangement that lasted till his death.

Back in a cosy environment Kingsley continued with his writing, becoming a much in demand newspaper columnist, coming over as the original grumpy old man, or 'curmudgeonly old shit'. In one article he argued for the execution of Nelson Mandela. His reactionary views were for the most part designed to shock. Hilary recalled how if they were driving about and he spied a pensioner or disabled person crossing the road he'd order, 'Go on, run the bugger down.' And there was a famous dinner party with the novelist Julian Barnes and his wife, the literary agent Pat Kavanagh, who grew up in South Africa. The conversation turned towards that blighted nation and Kingsley spurted out that what was needed was, 'To shoot as many blacks as possible.' Pat is said to have fled to the loo in tears and a major row ensued. Plain mischievousness or was it the drink talking? 'He was rude about everybody,' said Jane. 'No holds were barred.'

Though he might get depressed reading the obituary of a friend, one less drinking companion, Kingsley was still knocking it back, drinking in his final years a whole bottle of single malt by mid-morning before progressing to tequila, gin and Campari. 'He was fairly hell-bent on destruction,' Jane believed. 'He was on a kind of motorway, and there weren't any exits.'

It is generally agreed that alcohol did warp his brain box by the end, robbing him of his wit as well as his health. He began to fall over with alarming regularity. 'To hear my mother tell it,' Martin Amis wrote, 'some of these collapses performed in his rooms at home sounded like a chest-of-drawers jettisoned from an aeroplane.'

In 1995 Kingsley suffered a severe fall and hit his head hard on a concrete floor. It was quickly apparent things were wrong, he'd mix up words when talking and in scenes reminiscent of *The Shining* would finish a session at the typewriter only to produce pages with the single word 'seagulls' littered all over it. Physically he was a wreck, overweight, his face puffy and blotched; the carefree, dashing author of *Lucky Jim* who had philandered his way through much of middle-class womanhood a distant memory.

He was admitted to hospital, but even then Amis refused to stop drinking, taking his medication washed down with whisky. The children nursed him, painfully aware the end was close. One day he screamed at Philip, 'Kill me, you fucking fool!' He died not long after that.

ANDRÉ THE GIANT (1946–1993: Wrestler)

A contender for all-time champ of boozy sportsmen, André the Giant was a physical monolith, coming in at 7' 4" and weighing 500 lb; this is a guy who once snapped his ankle just getting out of bed. Dubbed 'The Eighth Wonder of the World', beer cans were swallowed up in his palm and his colossal head resembled a hairless King Kong. Truly he was a giant exiled from a fairy tale. Kids ran away from him in the street and viciously trained guard dogs were known to turn tail and head for cover.

One evening André was enjoying drinks in a bar when four men approached and started taking the piss out of his size. He ignored them at first, hoping to avoid trouble, but they wouldn't let up. Exasperated, André chased them out into the street where they jumped inside their car and locked the doors. His blood up, André reached down and flipped the car upside down, trapping the idiots inside before fleeing. When a policeman arrived he found it difficult to swallow the men's story that a real-life angry giant had turned their car over.

Born in a small French village not far from Paris, by the time André was twelve he stood over six feet tall and was so strong he performed the work of three men on his father's farm. It was inevitable that he'd become a wrestler, either that or the world's most formidable doorman.

It's debatable whether anyone has consumed more alcohol in their lifetime than André; 7,000 calories' worth every day. He also holds the dubious record of drinking more standard bottles of beer in a single session than any human in history – 119 of them in just six hours. Afterwards he crashed out just feet from his hotel room. His drinking colleagues, unable to budge him, found a piece of tarpaulin and simply draped it over his snoring hulk and he remained in the corridor until morning.

One time in Kansas City after a wrestling show André retired to a local bar. When the owner hollered last orders, André took this as a personal insult. Preferring retainment of his front teeth, the barman told the big fella he could stay just so long as he kept drinking, figuring that after a while André would give up and leave. No, André went through forty vodka and tonics and was still drinking at five in the morning.

What's truly impressive is that all this alcohol had little or no effect on him; friends rarely saw André slurring or staggering around completely banjoed. One time, though, coming out of the Savoy Grill in New York after a marathon drinking session, André actually felt mortal for once and needed to puke. Such was the force and quantity of vomit that it shot out into the road hitting the front of a passing taxi, covering the windshield. Unable to see anything, the driver slammed on his brakes to come to a stop. As for André, he just smiled. 'Feeling better,' he said and walked off.

Everywhere he went André was a hit with wrestling fans. Japan treated him like a deity, and in liquor terms he acted like one. During one visit local sponsors presented him with a case of plum wine. It took him a mere four hours to polish off the sixteen bottles. Amazingly, even with all that fermented juice swilling around his innards André was still able to step straight into the ring and wrestle three matches. He finished off the evening ploughing through a case of beer.

Despite his popularity André always felt uneasy in Japan. Everything was just too damn small, making him feel like Gulliver in Lilliput; hotel beds became cribs, rooms resembled closets. As for taking a crap, he often resorted to ripping the door off the bathroom, his huge legs sticking out into the main room. General travelling was always a problem, necessitating the booking of two first-class airline seats to accommodate his girth. As a young man André drove around Paris with his head sticking out of his car's sun-roof.

The seventies and early eighties saw André at the peak of his popularity, when he was the highest paid WWF wrestler in the world, a true mega-star of his sport. But people were asking why he needed to drink such elephantine quantities. Unbeknown to his fans André had been diagnosed with acromegaly, a rare glandular disease which had caused his growth hormones to go haywire, meaning he would never stop getting bigger. Sufferers of the condition rarely reached their forties and there was no cure. André also hid the truth from his family and close friends, but far from sinking into depression, intended living what little time he had on earth to the absolute max, and to hell with the consequences.

One mighty piss-up took place in 1977 between André and fellow wrestler Dusty Rhodes. After polishing off 100 beers in André's favourite Manhattan watering hole they decided to return to their hotel. Unable to stand, let alone walk, they were in dire need of transportation. Up ahead was a pair of horse-drawn carriages. André and Dusty hauled both drivers to the ground and galloped off like some mad re-enactment of the chariot race from *Ben Hur*, racing through the streets, narrowly avoiding cars and pedestrians who had the gall to be in the way. Back at the hotel they ditched the carriages and hit the bar and that's where the cops found them, sipping brandy as if nothing had happened.

On tour with the WWF wrestling guys, André would finish off a case of beer every day on the bus, crushing each dead can in his hand and lobbing it at the back of Hulk Hogan's head. Every few hours he'd yell, 'Piss stop!' A reporter travelled with André for a week and noted that his average daily consumption was two bottles of wine, between six and eight shots of brandy, half a dozen Bloody Marys and Screwdrivers, the odd glass of Pernod and the obligatory case of beer.

This perpetual boozing was equalled only by André's ravenous appetite.

He loved to tell the story of when he visited a restaurant and the waitress was particularly condescending, asking in a loud voice if a bowl of soup and a cracker would be enough. 'No,' André answered, 'I'm hungry.' So he ordered the entire menu and demanded each dish be brought to him separately. It took him four hours to eat it all.

Another thing he liked to do was pass wind. These were toxic farts capable of felling seagulls at 200 yards. When he was being hassled by persistent autograph hunters who wouldn't take no for an answer, André would assume the position and let rip, scattering all intruders as if it was a First World War gas attack.

Considering his size you'd think people, even tanked up, wouldn't be stupid enough to test their mettle against him. – Wrong! On these admittedly rare occasions André only used his strength as a last resort, such as the time in a bar when a big lumberjack tapped him on the shoulder demanding they go outside for a fight. André grabbed him by the neck and belt and smashed him into the wall, breaking the guy's ribs.

By the mid-eighties the disease André had ignored for years was beginning to ravage his body, but he refused to quit wrestling or modify his drinking. Appearing in the cult fantasy film *The Princess Bride* (1987) as, inevitably, a giant, André took the cast out drinking most nights; they'd show up next morning on set suffering hangovers from hell. When he left the crew's hotel after a month's stay his bar bill was north of $40,000.

By 1992 even André's most ardent fans sensed that his wrestling skills had greatly diminished and ultimately he was forced to quit the sport he loved. André was literally buckling under his own weight, every movement required painful effort; sometimes he could barely walk. He retired to a 200-acre ranch in North Carolina, revelling in the peace and quiet, able to look back proudly at the wrestling accomplishments that proved he'd been something much more than just a freak.

News reached him that his father had suddenly passed away. Flying home for the funeral, André decided to hang around the village for a while, visit old friends, reminisce and take in the landscapes of his childhood. Going to sleep one night his heart just gave up and he was found dead the next morning. He was forty-six. Cremated, his ashes were scattered over his beloved ranch.

B

FRANCIS BACON (1909–1992: Painter)

Numbered amongst the most accomplished British painters of the twentieth century, Francis Bacon's artwork is unique, famous for its austere, homoerotic and nightmarish imagery, as if David Lynch had eaten lobster thermidor for dinner, taken an LSD tablet, then thrown up on a canvas.

A celebrated bohemian and boozer, Bacon once fell down the stairs of a pub and knocked his right eye half out of its socket and merely pushed it back in. Bacon was a magnetic fellow, his mere presence could either bring happiness to an occasion or plunge it into hellish darkness; part of the fun of being in his company was in not quite knowing where the evening was going to take you. It was a rollercoaster ride with Francis, the wheels lubricated by endless glasses of champagne. 'I'm essentially optimistic,' he used to say. 'Always grateful when I wake up each morning and discover I'm still alive.'

He was born in Dublin to English parents, his father a veteran of the Boer War, a somewhat fierce individual who not surprisingly got rather agitated when he noticed his son beginning to come over far too mincing for his liking. There's a story that when he took to training race horses he instructed his stud-farm grooms to horsewhip the lad. Things really hit the fan when Francis was caught wearing his mother's underwear and preening himself in front of a mirror. The thrashing that he received if anything brought him closer to his father and he'd slip on the odd piece of lingerie to elicit further beatings. When that didn't work he indulged in affairs with the grooms whose job it was to whip him raw; combining pleasure with pain.

At sixteen his father entrusted Francis to an uncle in order to put a bit of spunk into him, instructions that were applied all too literally. Carefree weeks were spent travelling Europe, places like Berlin, then at its most depraved with its gay bars and filthy cabarets. A trip to an exhibition of work by Picasso in Paris spurred Bacon on to become a painter himself. Never attending art school, something he took enormous pride in, Francis struggled at first, destroying nearly all of his early paintings. In 1945 he shocked the art world with his first masterpiece, *Three Studies for Figures at the Base of the Crucifixion*, nightmarish images of deformed hybrids; it set the course for Bacon's career.

For much of his life Francis spent most afternoons at The Colony Room, a notorious Soho drinking club; a sign outside insisted: 'This Is Not a Brothel'. He was one of its founding members when it opened in 1948, virtually adopted by the proprietor, a formidable lady named Muriel Belcher who hired him at £10 a week and all he could drink for free (which was quite a lot) to bring in a better class of clientele. As a result The Colony Room became the prerequisite non compos artists' hangout for the next several decades.

Francis was now at the epicentre of a bohemian world of non-stop boozing and gambling till dawn. The British painter Michael Wishart believed Bacon had two major ambitions, to be one of the world's best painters and to be one of the world's leading alcoholics. He was well on his way to achieving both in record time. As a struggling artist he'd always somehow managed to pay for endless bottles of champagne for friends. With the money rolling in the champagne continued to flow; only it was a better vintage.

Bacon's powers of recovery from a night of boozing were staggering, he seemed indestructible and generally immune to bodily disaster. Crossing a street in Paris a car ran over his foot but Bacon just shrugged it off; the next day it was so swollen he couldn't walk. Ailments, too, meant a mere trifle to Francis. After he had a kidney removed he said, 'When you've been drunk since the age of fifteen, you're lucky to have even one kidney!' Celebrating his fortieth birthday in a restaurant with friends he announced that his doctor had told him that his heart was in such a decrepit state of repair, his ventricles gone on a permanent tea break, that a single drink could kill him. Waiting for the news to sink in, Bacon beckoned over a waiter and ordered the first of a succession of bottles of champagne.

In this strange and bacchanalian world that Francis inhabited he mixed with a mad bunch of drinkers such as John Deakin, a portrait photographer. Going into his local one morning, Deakin asked for his usual, a large glass of white wine, which he drained in one enormous gulp. Next moment he was flat on his back on the floor. The new barman had accidentally served him a dose of Parozone bleach, which was kept behind the bar in a wine bottle. Oops! A lesser mortal might have died instantly, but these Soho drinkers were made of stern stuff. Rushed to hospital, Deakin had his stomach pumped and was back in the pub that afternoon demanding a refill on the house.

Bacon's lovers were the oddest bunch of all. Take Peter Lacy, well Francis obviously did, few others would have, since the former Battle of Britain fighter pilot when filled with drink was borderline psychotic. He kept a cottage where Bacon spent a lot of time in various states of bondage. Once, out of control on booze, Lacy hurled Bacon through a plate glass window. His face was so badly damaged that his sight was saved only by having his right eye sewn back into place. Bizarrely the incident made Francis even fonder of Lacy and he reprimanded friends who dared chastise him. When Lacy moved to Tangier it probably saved Bacon's life, even though he continued to love and visit him until his death from an overindulgence of booze that resulted in his pancreas exploding.

In 1964 Bacon began a relationship with an East End bit of rough called George Dyer, whose intimates included the Kray Twins. Bacon enjoyed telling the tale that they met when Dyer was in the course of robbing his flat. It was a predictably stormy relationship, ending when the tortured and alcoholic Dyer committed suicide in 1971 on the eve of a Bacon retrospective in Paris.

While his reckless affairs informed his paintings, Bacon's laissez-faire approach to life also informed his working practices. When moving studios or rooms, he sometimes left paintings in cupboards or simply destroyed them. Years later Bacon was wandering down Bond Street when he saw a familiar image in the window of a gallery; it was a painting he'd left behind in Tangier after a holiday. The asking price was £50,000. Unruffled, Bacon paid for it, took it outside and smashed it to pieces.

Perfectly at home in the Ritz or the gutter, Bacon's character was one of deep contradictions; he was a loner who loved parties, a man of terrific fellowship who could spurn you in an instant. He was no respecter of reputation either. At a glittering high-society ball Princess Margaret surprised everyone by taking to the stage, halting the orchestra and grabbing the microphone to perform a Cole Porter song. Getting quite carried away she was, thanks to polite applause from the sycophants. Then from the back of the room somewhere came loud solitary booing. It was Bacon. Margaret broke off mid-lyric, went bright purple and was led away by her ladies-in-waiting. Bacon later explained his breach of protocol: 'Her singing was really too awful. Someone had to stop her.'

Artist Peter Beard witnessed another drink-induced Bacon outburst, this time directed at the model Jerry Hall in a gay disco in Paris. He'd been very happy to meet Mick Jagger, then her paramour, but when Jerry turned up Bacon let fly. 'You fucking old cow,' he powder-puffed. 'You grotesque cunt, you hideous bloody witch.' The acerbic bile wouldn't cease flowing. 'The rest of us went down into some dark pit behind the dance floor and hid,' recalled Beard.

The Bacon vitriol could strike at any moment. One afternoon he was drinking at The Colony when the place was suddenly overtaken by unbearable American tourists. Bacon turned to his friend Jeffrey Bernard. 'Jeffrey, what woman do you fancy most in the world?' Bernard thought it a daft question and refused to answer, instead asking who Francis most fancied. 'D'yer know,' Bacon replied, in as loud a voice as possible. 'I think I'd really like to be fucked by Colonel Gaddafi.' The Americans quickly finished their drinks and were gone.

In the seventies Bacon continued to paint successfully and frequent the seedy drinking dens and bars of Soho, but as the years wore on his alcoholism got worse, leading to even darker and more savage moods. He died of a heart attack in Spain where he'd gone to visit his new lover, a trip his doctor had advised him not to take. As usual Francis didn't listen, doing his own thing was much more important than mere survival.

TALLULAH BANKHEAD (1902–1968: Actress)

Hailed as 'the most thoroughgoing libertine and free-swinging flapper of the age', Tallulah Bankhead's acerbic wit was matched only by her wild zest for life and sensory overload. She bedded men, and women, recklessly and could match anyone for drinking, reputedly able to down a whole bottle of bourbon in thirty minutes. 'I'm the foe of moderation,' she once said. 'The champion of excess.'

Incongrously for someone who labelled herself 'divinely impossible', Tallulah was born into a prominent Alabama political family with close links to the US Senate. When her mother died some weeks after giving birth to her, Tallulah's father sought refuge in the bottle and she and her sister were farmed out to their grandparents. An unruly and rebellious child, Tallulah was capable of diva-like tantrums when she didn't get her own way. Her grandmother usually met these head-on by throwing a bucket of water in her face to calm her down.

Aged fifteen, Tallulah announced ambitions to become a Broadway actress and wasn't in New York long before the great John Barrymore invited her into his dressing room, revealing from beneath his gown his famously rigid member. Tallulah fled in panic. It was probably the last large cock she'd ever flee from.

Consumed by a fever to be famous, even infamous, Tallulah indulged in drink and drug binges and flaunted her bisexuality, not to demonstrate a liberated worldview but merely for the pleasure of the shock it caused. At parties she'd blurt out to total strangers, 'I'm a lesbian. What do you do?' Or pick out the plainest-looking woman in the room, throw her arms around her and whisper, 'Surely, you must know by now that I'm mad about you.' These early lesbian encounters, she claimed, were the fault of her father who warned her about the dangers of men and booze, but never said anything about women and cocaine.

Yet to taste theatrical success in New York, Tallulah's fortunes turned round when she was invited to perform in London, where her intoxicating, exotic presence wowed audiences. Off stage she busily worked her way through the bulk of London high society, from lords to Italian aristocrats to . . . well, anyone, really. On moving into a new apartment one of the first things she did was knock down the bedroom wall to make the area big enough to accommodate her gigantic bed. And there were parties, endless parties. Tallulah rarely went to bed sober. At one a young man rather boldly approached Tallulah and blurted out that he wanted to make love to her that very night. 'And so you shall,' she replied, not batting an eyelid, 'you wonderful old-fashioned boy.'

Running out of specimens in London, Tallulah turned her attention to that wellspring of learning, Eton, narrowly avoiding a major scandal. MI5 were called in to investigate stories that Tallulah had seduced at least half a dozen pupils. To save the reputation of the school the whole thing was hushed up.

It was back to Hollywood and a lucrative contract at Paramount, but somehow Tallulah's personality, given full rein on the stage, seemed diminished by the movie camera and she didn't prove popular. She continued her regime of drink and drugs, though, not to mention a five-pack-a-day nicotine habit, and defended cocaine with this classic quote: 'Cocaine, habit-forming, dahling? Of course not, I ought to know. I've been using it for years.' There are also tales that she sometimes got her pet dogs pie-eyed.

Even though she was one of its lesser stars, Hollywood did have its compensations: non-stop partying and yet more seductions, including a romp in the swimming pool of the Garden of Allah Hotel with Johnny (Tarzan) Weissmuller, after which Tallulah claimed to be 'a very satisfied Jane'. The infamous Garden of Allah was a wild hang-out for Hollywood's most notorious drinkers, not least because the hotel bar stayed open twenty-four hours a day.

In every way Tallulah was a sexual creature, totally uninhibited about nudity, again another shock tactic. She'd strip at parties and perform erotic dances or leap onto the nearest grand piano wearing nothing but her pearls. When she starred in Alfred Hitchcock's *Lifeboat* (1944) she shocked fellow actors by not wearing underwear. One surely sympathises here, since to get to the lifeboat set they all had to climb a ladder and Tallulah, of course, always insisted on going first.

Then there was her unusual habit of leaving the bathroom door wide open while she went to the toilet. Eleanor Roosevelt was invited to tea once, along with a young actor friend. They were discussing the politics of the day when Tallulah suddenly rose to her feet. 'Wait a minute. I've got to pee. But I don't want to miss a word of this.' The toilet was at the end of the corridor, and in full view Tallulah pulled her pants down, squatted and relieved herself. After Miss Roosevelt left, the actor turned to Tallulah aghast. 'Do you know what you did? You peed in front of Eleanor Roosevelt!' 'Oh don't be ridiculous. Eleanor Roosevelt has more important things on her mind than my bathroom habits. I'm sure she didn't even notice. She pees herself, you know.'

But it was her man-crazy antics that proved her undoing when she was hit with a life-threatening case of gonorrhoea that required emergency surgery. Leaving the hospital unbowed, she told doctors, 'Don't think this has taught me a lesson!' For once her bravado hid an awful truth, the hysterectomy had left not only psychological scars but physical ones, and Tallulah claimed she could never again attain an orgasm.

Perfect conditions, then, for married life, when you generally don't need to. John Emery was a mediocre actor who bore a curious resemblance to Barrymore, and not just facially. One of Tallulah's party tricks was to escort guests to her bedroom where Emery was asleep, fling back the covers from the bed and crow, 'Did you ever see a prick as big as that before?'

More ignominies rained down on poor Emery. Soon Tallulah was telling friends, 'Well, dahling, the weapon may be of admirable proportions, but the shot is indescribably weak.' Not surprisingly it was a short-lived union.

Still drinking heavily, when America entered the Second World War a feeling of patriotism took over and Tallulah announced that not a drop of alcohol would pass her lips until Hitler was defeated, a vow she was never really likely to keep! Attending a party one night, while supposedly on the wagon, Tallulah got into a heated argument with someone and to emphasise a point delivered the man a severe kick in the ass. Watching all this was an elderly guest who stopped a passing butler to ask, 'Will you please find out what it is that Miss Bankhead isn't drinking and bring me one of those.'

When Hitler was finally dispatched, Tallulah's drinking became a major problem, one she faced head-on with her characteristic humour, telling a friend that her doctor had advised her to eat an apple every time she had the urge to drink: 'Really, dahling, sixty apples a day!' When it came to one-liners, Tallulah was the equal of Dorothy Parker. One classic example has Tallulah in a lift with a friend who looks over askance at her. 'Tallulah! Did you fart?' Tallulah just smiles, 'Why of course, dahling. Do you think I always smell like this?'

Approaching her mid-forties Tallulah's cravings remained strong, as Eugenia Rawls, a young actress she befriended, later wrote: 'Tallulah could be savage, her appetites of mind and body wild and sometimes gross, as if everything had to be possessed and devoured and destroyed.' Actress Patsy Kelly said that having Tallulah for a friend was like 'waltzing with an atomic bomb'. Such quotes only added to the myth, to the legend that Tallulah herself was only too aware of. 'Nobody can be exactly like me,' she once boasted. 'Sometimes even I have trouble doing it.'

As the 1950s beckoned, Tallulah resurrected her stage career, memorably performing with a new up-and-coming actor called Marlon Brando. She interviewed him personally at her home. When he arrived she was well tanked up and in some haste to grope at the bulge in his jeans. When the play opened Brando proceeded to upstage the diva at every opportunity: he picked his nose, scratched his balls and leered at the audience, even mooned them. Then he ate garlic before their big love scene: 'Avoiding Tallulah's tongue as best I could.' He drove the poor woman nuts and was fired when one night he stood at the back of the stage and pissed against the scenery. 'The next time Miss Bankhead goes swimming,' Brando declared, 'I hope that whales shit on her!'

During another Broadway production Tallulah turned her attention to Marlene Dietrich's daughter Maria Riva, who revealed that, 'she was usually blind drunk and completely naked, and liked chasing me down hotel corridors'.

Although her star had now dimmed to a sort of pallid rusty orange, Tallulah still behaved like a supernova in exile at her New York mansion, surrounding herself with a retinue of young gay men who fetched her food and mixed her drinks, even lit cigarettes for her. Rather more eccentrically she had a menagerie of animals including a rescued monkey and a pet lion cub called Winston Churchill, which she used to smuggle into hotels. Eventually it had to be given to the Bronx Zoo when it grew too big and started biting the ankles of Tallulah's guests.

More mundanely she kept dogs and a parrot. Dolores, her Maltese, usually slept beside her mistress in the bedroom. One night a servant smelled smoke and rushed in to see the poor mutt on fire; Tallulah had flicked her cigarette ash onto the animal before nodding off.

'Tallulah, Dolores is on fire!' He yelled.

'Well, for chrissakes, put her out,' she replied and went back to sleep.

As she passed fifty, Tallulah began to drink more heavily than before, something like a quart of bourbon a day, together with a dangerous mixture of Tuinal, Benzedrine, Dexedrine, Dexamyl and morphine. Not surprisingly, with all that whizzing round her system there were several psychotic episodes. One colleague observed her in a hotel corridor acting like 'a wild woman, like a caged chimp'. She was literally flailing at the walls screaming, 'Where am I?' It got so bad that Tallulah's maid resorted to binding her wrists together with adhesive tape at night to reduce the risk of her taking an overdose of pills.

All this took a huge toll on her body and looks. From an exotic creature she had degenerated into something resembling Bette Davis's ugly aunt. Orson Welles called Tallulah 'the most sensational case of the aging process being unkind'. The sad thing was she knew her face had crumbled, but amazingly could still laugh at herself. When people on the street asked, 'Aren't you Tallulah Bankhead?' she'd answer, 'I'm what's left of her, dahling.'

During her last few years she rarely strayed from her home. Her routine was not to get up before 4 p.m. and then spend the remainder of the day watching TV and drinking gin and bourbon, a cigarette forever bracketed between her lips. An insomniac most of her life, evenings saw friends sitting on her bed, keeping her company until she drifted into unconsciousness. She couldn't stand the thought of being alone at night.

The summer of 1968 Tallulah spent with her sister Eugenia, who if anything was worse than Tallulah in the man-grabber department, having married seven times! They spoke of the past and Tallulah confessed that life had ceased to be interesting and that every night she prayed she wouldn't wake up in the morning.

It was a nasty strain of Asian flu that finally did Tallulah in, her immune system, battered over decades by drink and drugs, was pitiful against it. Hooked up to a ventilator, she quietly slipped into a coma that she never woke up from, but not before asking for one of her favourite tipples, codeine and bourbon.

In characteristic good humour Tallulah once told a reporter, 'If I had my life to live again, I'd make the same mistakes, only sooner.' Not a bad epitaph for a woman who called herself, 'as pure as the driven slush'.

JOHN BARRYMORE (1882–1942: Actor)

Clown prince of America's royal family of actors, with a penchant for alcohol and chorus girls, John Barrymore's self-destructive rollercoaster career went from the zenith of his Shakespearean performances to the nadir of self-parody in Hollywood B movies. A massive drinker, who after a particularly strenuous binge actually slept through the great San Francisco earthquake of 1906 (after waking up he must have thought it the worst hangover of all time), it's been estimated that during his forty years in show business Barrymore consumed 640 barrels of hard liquor. As he once so eloquently put it: 'You can't drown yourself in drink. I've tried, you float.'

He was born in Philadelphia to theatrical parents, his father Maurice a dashing leading man. When he was aged eleven John's mother died of tuberculosis and with undue haste his father married again, this time to a much younger woman who thought nothing of seducing her step-son when he was just fourteen years old. It may have been this event that turned Barrymore to alcohol as he felt pangs of guilt for years afterwards. He'd get expelled from boarding schools for drinking and smoking and generally raising hell. It may also have left him with a skewed opinion of women; he'd subsequently marry four times and have innumerable mistresses.

When Barrymore was twenty he witnessed his father suffer a nervous breakdown on stage. The ravings grew so violent that his son had little choice but to cart his father off to the nearest loony bin. The cause of the illness was blamed on syphilis. Maurice really was quite barmy, strangling his own daughter Ethel when she paid him a visit. He died five years later, never quite recapturing all his marbles.

Eschewing an early interest in art to go into the family business, Barrymore established himself on Broadway with dynamic portrayals of Richard III and Hamlet. Critics proclaimed him one of the greatest actors alive, but drink had already taken him over. During a shitfaced performance of Hamlet he momentarily had to leave the stage in order to vomit.

The inevitable defection to Hollywood was not long in coming. There Barrymore quickly became infamous for his drunken off-screen antics, such as engaging in a ten-minute fist fight with producer Myron Selznick. Barrymore emerged the worse for wear, sporting two black eyes. He saw films primarily as a necessary evil, a way to make money, nothing more, and screen acting as a lowly art form. 'There are lots of methods,' he declared. 'Mine involves a lot of talent, a glass and some cracked ice.'

According to Adolph Zukor, movie mogul and founder of Paramount Pictures, Barrymore deliberately instigated bust-ups on his film sets, storming out in a huff just so he could have a crafty drink. He was trouble all right. 'His beginning a picture was a signal for us to go on the alert,' said Zukor. Often Barrymore went missing altogether during filming and Zukor would send assistants to check every saloon and bar in town and bring him back. One time he couldn't be traced at all, no one had seen him. Director James Kirkwood volunteered to scout around and finally unearthed Barrymore drinking at the famous actor's club The Players. 'I've got him,' he told Zukor over the phone, 'and he's coming back with me.' Barrymore did indeed agree to return to the studio to make Kirkwood's picture, but on one condition, that he join him for one last drink. Well, that last drink led to another and another and another . . . Three days later both men finally appeared on set, Kirkwood considerably wiser.

Hired to play Captain Ahab in a movie adaptation of *Moby Dick*, studio head Jack Warner and director Lloyd Bacon paid Barrymore a visit at his hotel suite. Opening the door, Barrymore's eyes were glazed, his complexion like that of a corpse, his hair a tangled heap upon his scalp, and it looked like he hadn't shaved since Christmas. 'That's a great make-up job, John, you'll make a tough-looking Ahab,' said Warner innocently. 'That's not make-up,' Bacon argued. 'It's a hangover.'

Warner then needed to use the bathroom but was shocked to find the bathtub full of champagne bottles. 'My God, Barrymore, what's all that stuff for?' The actor smiled. 'Hair rinse, care for some?'

By the early 1930s Barrymore's reckless drinking and mercurial disregard for his personal well-being had got so bad that his wife Dolores insisted he enter a hospital for treatment, but all that resulted in were violent attacks on nurses who refused to bring him alcohol. Her next plan of action was a quiet cruise off Canada, a dry one. It proved too much for poor Barrymore, so desperate for anything to drink he downed his wife's perfume and mouthwash. When they dropped anchor at Vancouver Barrymore made a bolt for shore, hoping to lose himself in a waterfront bar, but his nurse and wife both grabbed hold of him. In the ensuing skirmish the nurse had her nose broken, and Dolores was hurled violently to the deck.

Barrymore's last spouse was actress Elaine Barrie, thirty-five years his junior. They appeared in one play together, *My Dear Children*, which included a scene where Barrymore held her in his lap and roundly spanked her. Their relationship scandalised Depression-hit America, as Barrymore's amorous activities usually did. One night, while suitably curried and mashed, he accidentally went into the women's restroom and proceeded to relieve his bladder in a potted plant. A woman standing nearby reminded him that the room was, 'for ladies exclusively'. Turning round, his penis still exposed, Barrymore responded, 'So, madam, is this. But every now and again I'm compelled to run a little water through it.'

By the mid-1930s, after years of hard living, Barrymore's matinee looks had given way to haggard disillusionment; his body was battered by numerous alcohol-related illnesses, his psyche the harbinger of chronic spells of near insanity. No longer able to remember his lines, underlings were hired to hold large blackboards with his dialogue on them just out of camera range. It was pitiful. Once acclaimed as the greatest living actor, Barrymore in the end could scarcely find work except in bargain basement tosh, having thrown away his promise with drinking and whoring. 'The trouble with Jack,' said Charlie Chaplin, 'was that he had a naive, romantic conception of himself as a genius doomed to self-destruction which he eventually achieved in a vulgar, boisterous way by drinking himself to death.'

When a doctor suggested that he abandon 'wine, women and song', Barrymore asked if he had to quit everything at once. 'No, you can taper off,' was the advice. 'Then I shall quit singing,' said Barrymore.

In the last few years of his life Barrymore got pally with Errol Flynn, after arriving at the actor's house unannounced following an argument with the wife and asking for a bed for the night. The three weeks he ended up staying were the most harrowing Flynn could ever remember, worse than fighting crocodiles in the depths of New Guinea. One of the more unsightly habits that Barrymore excelled in was urinating out of the window, sometimes splashing passers-by. Worried that Barrymore's 100-per-cent-proof piss was washing the varnish off his window sills, Flynn complained, 'For God's sakes, can't you do it somewhere else?' Barrymore looked suitably admonished, 'Certainly, m'lad.' So he took to pissing in the fireplace and some-times even in wardrobes.

He was on a runaway trolley to hell, basically. At night he'd wake up screaming, or wander about pixillated with no sense of where he was. Once he stumbled into the clothes closet and couldn't get out. Screaming, he felt things jabbing and tickling the back of his neck. 'Bats,' he exclaimed as Flynn came rushing in. 'Your house is full of bats.' Flynn had to explain that what he'd felt were coat hangers.

Unable to take any more, fearful that his house might not be standing this time next week, Flynn urged Barrymore's wife to take him back.

Like the great actor he was, Barrymore took numerous curtain calls before finally succumbing to the inevitable final performance. More than once he'd be rushed to hospital with friends convinced this time he was actually going to die. He'd be in comas, coming out of them just long enough to ask a nurse to fetch him a drink. Those who'd fall for his charms and accede to his wishes were fired. He was a rascal, right to the end.

After emerging from one particular coma that lasted three days, Barrymore opened his eyes and beheld quite the ugliest, roughest-looking female nurse the American medical profession could rustle up. Wondering what kind of hell he'd woken up in Barrymore murmured, 'God!' then paused, looked at her again and said, 'Well . . . get in anyway, honey.'

There's a story of a close-to-death Barrymore, sick in bed, legs grotesquely swollen with fluid his body couldn't pass, asking his twenty-one-year-old daughter Diana to fetch a prostitute for him. Diana herself would succumb to alcohol and drug addiction, killing herself aged thirty-eight.

Then the final collapse; bronchial pneumonia, hardening of the arteries, haemorrhaging ulcers, cirrhosis of the liver, he had the lot. For ten days he faded and rallied, drifting in and out of consciousness. 'Die?' he roared. 'I should say not. No Barrymore would allow such a conventional thing to happen to him.'

When his friends, including Errol Flynn and director Raoul Walsh, heard of Barrymore's passing they gathered at a bar to commiserate and celebrate the old duffer. Walsh left early, claiming he was too upset. In fact he and two friends went to the funeral home and bribed the undertaker to lend them Barrymore's body. Transporting it to Flynn's house, it was propped up in a chair facing the door. Errol was 12-gauged when he arrived, but after putting the light on he very quickly got sober, staring as he was into the face of Barrymore. It was a Hammer horror moment. Letting out a delirious scream, Flynn ran out of the house into Walsh and his cohorts. Relieved it was a prank and that Barrymore hadn't risen as one of the undead, Flynn retired to bed. 'My heart was still pounding. I couldn't sleep the rest of the night.'

Before he died Barrymore left specific instructions that he be cremated, but his brother and sister insisted his remains be buried. In 1980 Barrymore's son, John Drew, decided to grant his pop his final wish and roped in his own son to help remove the body. As they entered the crypt it was obvious that the casket had cracked some years before and bodily fluids had leaked out to form a sort of gluey substance on the floor. They hauled the coffin into a waiting van and drove the short distance to the crematorium. As preparations were being made John couldn't resist taking a peek inside at the old devil. He soon wished he hadn't. 'Thank God I'm drunk,' he told his son. 'So I'll never remember it.'

ROY BEAN (1825–1903: Old West Judge)

The Wild West has produced a veritable plague of legendary characters, but few can match Judge Roy Bean, a true American folk hero and self-confessed scallywag who set up his own courthouse in a saloon bar along the Rio Grande, dispensing law and whisky with equal enthusiasm.

Born in Mason County, Kentucky, as a teenager Bean travelled far and wide seeking adventure, joining a wagon train bound for Mexico, where he opened a saloon bar in the town of Chihuahua. It's a wonder the place ever turned a dollar, since Bean was his own best customer, seen most nights pouring the profits down his throat – that's when he wasn't picking fights with his customers. One brawl ended with Bean killing a man and before the law got wind of it he'd loaded his remaining booze stock onto a mule and beaten a hasty retreat.

He ended up in San Diego, California, working as a bartender, again drinking most of the stock and behaving like a lunatic, traipsing round town waving a pair of six-guns in the air. Inevitably he shot someone dead and was sentenced to hang. Left dangling on the end of the rope, Bean was rescued and fled town, a permanent burn mark on his neck the only reminder of his close shave with mortality.

On the move again, Bean purchased ten fifty-five-gallon barrels of whisky and set up a saloon in a small town near a railroad construction site employing 8,000 thirsty workers. The region was full of desperadoes, gunslingers and thieves so crime was rife and the nearest courthouse a week's ride away. Despite having little formal education, and not a shred of legal training, Bean decided he was the man to dispense law and order and after promising free booze to the local commissioners was duly appointed Justice of the Peace. His workplace now served a double purpose, as watering hole and part-time courthouse, with the butt of his pistol as a gavel. One of Bean's first acts was to wreck the saloon shack of a Jewish competitor.

'Hear ye! Hear ye! This honourable court is now in session,' he'd start proceedings by bellowing. 'And if anybody wants a snort before we start, step up to the bar and name your poison.' It was not unusual to see drinks being served from the bar that was situated at the back of the court before, during and after trials. Bean also hand-picked the jury, good citizens of the town who also happened to be his best customers. Teetotallers were frowned upon.

As judge, and often executioner, inspiring respect for the law with his two six-shooters, Bean's method of dispensing justice was unorthodox to say the least. When Carlos Robles stood before him, caught red-handed cattle rustling, Bean solemnly passed sentence: 'Time will pass and seasons will come and go; Spring with its sweet-smellin' flowers, sultry Summer with her shimmerin' heat-waves, Fall with her yeller harvest-moon, and finally Winter with its bitin' wind. But you won't be here to see any of 'em, Carlos Robles, not by a dam' sight, because it's the order of this court that you be took to the nearest tree and hanged by the neck till you're dead, dead, dead, you olive-colored son-of-a-billy-goat!'

When a railroad worker stood accused of shooting dead a Chinese labourer, the man's friends threatened to destroy Bean's saloon if he was found guilty. That may have coloured Bean's thinking as he trawled through his law books from cover to cover before turning the culprit loose, remarking that he'd be damned if he could find any actual law against killing a Chinaman.

After a few years Bean relocated to the town of Langtry, Texas, opening a saloon called the Jersey Lily, named after the British actress Lillie Langtry, whom he idolised, spinning tales that one day she would accept his invitation to visit and perform in the local theatre. His saloon mostly sold home-made whisky, a concoction of 100-per-cent-proof alcohol, water, tobacco and God knows what else. For some cowboys even this lethal brew wasn't strong enough. One tale has a hobo entering the saloon and spitting out what he derisorily called 'this rainwater' and demanding something stronger. 'Gimmie some real tarantula juice,' old western slang for strong whisky. Bean reached behind the bar where three dead tarantulas bobbed about in a jar of alcohol. 'There's your tarantula juice,' he said. 'And by God you'll drink it.' The cowboy is said to have taken one look at it and bolted. Another version of the story has him downing a glass and then dying in a convulsive fit.

Again Bean presided over the town as judge, using a tatty copy of the *Revised Statutes of Texas for 1876* as his legal guide. Occasional updates were sent to him; Bean used them to light cigars or wipe his arse. When he wasn't presiding over cases or serving drinks Bean spent most of his time sitting on the porch, with rifle handy. The Lily's only other occupant was a large black bear named Bruno who growled at customers, drank beer from a bowl and slept at the foot of Bean's bed.

His unique, shall we say, brand of justice continued unabated. There was the time he fined a dead man $40 for carrying a concealed weapon; the exact amount in the corpse's pocket. A twenty-year-old boy once stood before him accused of horse stealing. After interrogation the youth admitted his guilt and Bean passed the only sentence he could, hanging.

'If there's any last word, or anything, I'll give you a few minutes,' said Bean. Thanking the court, the lad took a pen and paper and began composing a letter of apology to his mother. Standing directly behind him, Bean could see every word written: 'In small part perhaps I can repay you for the money I have cost you in keeping me out of trouble. Enclosed is $400, which I've saved. I want you . . .'

Bean almost coughed his guts out. 'By gobs!' he exclaimed. 'Gentlemen, I got a feelin' there's been a miscarriage of justice in this case. I hereby declare it reopened. Face the bar, young man.' And so the prisoner wasn't hanged but fined $300 instead and sent happily on his way. Bean adjourned with the cash in his pocket and collapsed at the bar.

One evening Bean travelled to a nearby town and stayed up till dawn drinking. Returning home, he died peacefully in his bed the following morning. Some say he deliberately drank himself to death, unable to adjust to modern times. He saw that the old west was dying and felt he no longer belonged.

Ten months later a train pulled up at Langtry and out stepped the unmistakable figure of Lillie herself. On her way to San Francisco she'd insisted on finally taking up Bean's invitation and paid the town a visit. Sitting in the saloon, she listened as locals told her of the judge's numerous antics. It was a short visit, 'but an unforgettable one' she later wrote.

BRENDAN BEHAN (1923–1964: Poet and Dramatist)

'I am a drinker with a writing problem,' Brendan Behan once said, exaggerating not one jot – after all, did he not once drag a cello halfway across Dublin to a pawnshop that he knew would give him the price of a round of drinks? Behan was full of such self-mocking statements, like saying he only drank on two occasions, 'when I'm thirsty, and when I'm not'.

His plays and stories that so colourfully depicted the life of the ordinary working man led to Behan becoming one of the most famous Irish dramatists of his time, but also one of the country's most notorious personalities, a man ultimately better known for his escapades than his work. It was a public image that proved his downfall, too afraid of looking for the real Brendan, wrecked by alcohol abuse he clung to the legend instead. No longer in touch with his real self his work inevitably suffered and his startling talent was extinguished.

Behan was born in Dublin and lived his childhood in a squalid tenement block. He started drinking young, very young, just six when his grandmother first pressed whisky to his lips. There's a tale of them both returning home from the pub when Brendan was eight and a passer-by remarking: 'That's a beautiful boy. 'Tis a pity he's deformed.' Granny was most put out. 'The curse of Jaysus on you. That child is not deformed. He's just got a couple of drinks taken.'

The Behan family were staunch Republicans, his mother a personal friend of the famed Irish revolutionary Michael Collins. Loyalty to the cause was expected and Brendan joined the IRA youth wing (like the Sea Scouts only more violent), allegedly booted out for drunken behaviour, before joining the real thing aged sixteen. When he wasn't in the pub Behan was in jail; sentenced to three years in borstal for attempting to blow up a battleship in Liverpool harbour, he was later given fourteen years for the attempted murder of two detectives. He tasted freedom under a general amnesty in 1946.

For a time he lived in Paris, writing pornography and working as a pimp in the famous Harry's New York Bar until the owner caught on to what he was doing and threw him out. 'However,' recalled Behan, 'before leaving, each of the barmen insisted upon buying me a drink.'

Behan saw alcohol as an indispensable part of a writer's make-up, luckily he'd had years of practice, while remaining conscious of the fact that any success required an element of discipline. Throughout much of his career Behan would rise at seven in the morning and work until noon, just before the pubs opened. Often he'd simply turn up at bars with his typewriter and pound away at the keys while indulging in a few pints.

It was the play *The Quare Fellow* about prison life, obviously culled from his own experiences, that proved Behan's breakthrough. He sent it to theatre director Joan Littlewood who immediately sensed the potential, despite the beer stains over nearly every page, and invited him to London. 'He wired back saying he hadn't the fare,' Joan recalled. 'So we sent his fare and he drank it, saying, I'm not an alcoholic, I'm saving up to be one.'

Behan did get to attend rehearsals, sitting chain-smoking and coughing in the stalls, occasionally interrupting the actors, declaring: 'Did I write that? I'm a fucking genius.' When Joan staged another Behan play, *The Hostage*, he thrilled audiences by interrupting performances with severe heckling and breaking into song.

When *The Quare Fellow* transferred to the West End Behan was invited by Malcolm Muggeridge to be interviewed live on BBC television. The two men met beforehand for lunch at the Garrick Club, where much drinking went on, so by the time Behan arrived at the studio he was decently lubricated. The drinking continued in the green room, where he knocked back at least two bottles of whisky. A headmistress of a finishing school and some of her charges were also appearing on the programme. Walking into the green room to find Behan holding forth, they about turned and marched out again. 'Didn't I see a lot of pretty girls in here just now?' asked Behan with some anguish. Muggeridge explained that he had been dreaming.

As Behan grew increasingly lathered the show's producer began to wonder whether all this was a good idea, turning to Muggeridge to advise: 'If he uses the word cunt, don't laugh.' Propped up by Joan Littlewood, Behan at first dozed off and then slurred his words in front of an audience of millions. It was a disaster, though Muggeridge couldn't help but like the Irishman. 'Except that, like all drunks, he was a bore. Drunkenness is a device to avoid having to think of anything to say.'

More squiffy appearances on television would follow. On a US chat show Brendan was beamed in live from a studio in Ireland, but his conduct was so incoherent and vitriolic he was cut off mid-broadcast, leading the New York *Daily News* to say: 'If the celebrated author was not pickled, he certainly gave the best imitation of rambling alcoholism you ever saw.' Then on a 1962 edition of *This Is Your Life* a mullocked Behan caused a ruckus behind the scenes and almost came to blows with the show's host Eamonn Andrews.

The opening of *The Quare Fellow* on Broadway provided Behan with international recognition. More plays and books followed, including his first volume of autobiography, *Borstal Boy*, a huge seller, except in Ireland where it was banned. Behan didn't mind: 'The number of people who buy books in Ireland would not keep me in drink for the duration of Sunday opening time.'

By now Behan was on course to becoming a full-blown alcoholic. His wife Beatrice believed he used alcohol 'as a shield against life, against things that upset him'. In their early years together she never presumed to tell him to lay off the booze, seeing it as a problem only when it began to seriously affect his health and mind.

She took great comfort in the periods, however short, when he abstained. A friend met Brendan in Dublin one day and was surprised to see him for once not resembling third place in a scarecrow competition. 'Heavens above, Brendan,' he said, 'have you given up the drink altogether?'

'NO!' he replied. 'I've joined Alcoholics Anonymous. I'm drinking under an assumed name!'

Believe it or not, a London temperance league invited him to be guest speaker at their annual meeting. Behan accepted and hired a suitably grand dinner jacket from Moss Bros. Come the evening of the event Behan managed to get as far as the first pub en route and was still sleeping off his hangover in the gutter come morning, his Moss Bros suit smeared with vomit and other even more unpleasant bodily fluids. No amount of dry-cleaning was going to render it inhabitable again, so Behan dug a hole in his garden and buried it. A few months later when Moss Bros requested the suit back, Behan had no choice but to dig it up again.

Beatrice soon began to worry where her husband's drinking would take him. He was now so afraid of the night that he preferred sleeping during the day and going out on binges in the evening; poor Beatrice would sometimes have to undergo search-and-retrieve missions.

Behan came to believe that the staggering, incoherent artist was what the public wanted, and he gave them exactly that. 'There's no bad publicity except an obituary.' His fame grew as his body deteriorated with the alcohol bashing it received. Diabetic comas and regular seizures sent him to hospital; unconcerned he'd creep out when the nurse wasn't looking and go to the pub. He looked bedraggled, like an unmade bed; if Tracey Emin had knocked him up in half an hour and put him on show at Tate Modern she'd have won the Turner Prize.

By the end he was a caricature, the stereotypical bladdered Irishman. 'I ruined my health by drinking to everyone else's.' Landlords were now booting him off their premises. In New York a Judge banned Behan from the 1963 St Patrick's Day parade for being a 'drunken disgrace'. His roistering also got him thrown out of the Algonquin Hotel.

Behan's lifelong battle with alcoholism ended in a Dublin bar. Enjoying a few too many drinks with friends, he collapsed and was rushed to hospital suffering agonising pain in his liver. He pulled through, as he'd done before. Then someone smuggled in a bottle of brandy and – bang – Behan was in a coma, a coma from which he never returned. He was forty-one. Before slipping into final unconsciousness, so legend has it, Brendan spoke to the nuns who sat at his bedside. 'God bless you, and may your sons all be bishops.'

BIX BEIDERBECKE (1903–1931: *Jazz Musician*)

He's been called the best cornet player of the 1920s, an undisciplined talent and a true child of the jazz age, whose sensitive and introspective style of playing foreshadowed the 'cool' jazz sound of later decades. But Bix Beiderbecke was also a self-destructive alcoholic who drank himself into the ground with illegal prohibition liquor by the age of twenty-eight.

Bix never learned to read music; he didn't need to, having an instinctive ear for it, learning tunes by himself with a beat-up second-hand cornet. Raised in Davenport, Iowa, in comfortably off middle-class surroundings, his parents disapproved of his passion for jazz, this 'degenerate music born in the brothels of New Orleans'. It was a rebellious act, a slap in the face of their bourgeois lifestyle. Especially galling was his lack of interest in anything else, resulting in poor grades at school.

A worse shock was to come when Bix, who'd just turned eighteen, was arrested for what amounted to abducting a five-year-old girl and locking her in a garage where he committed an act deemed, 'lewd and lascivious' by the police; although no charges were ever brought.

Discreetly, one suspects, Bix was shunted off to an exclusive boarding school outside Chicago, his parents obviously unaware that the city was a jazz hotspot, ruled by Al Capone and populated by fast cars and flappers. Bix soon formed a combo of like-minded musicians who sneaked out of school to play, and drink, in speakeasy clubs. When the education authority found out, the band were grounded. As revenge they got rat-arsed on the only alcohol they could find on school property, a bottle of face lotion that was a potent 85 per cent proof.

After further misdemeanours Bix was expelled, and only too happy to be so. Now he had the freedom to pursue his career in jazz, a decision his parents apparently never forgave him for. First he joined a few local bands before graduating to orchestras with more nationwide appeal. He also enrolled in the University of Iowa to further his musical education, but was kicked out after getting into a drunken fight in a bar. Bix's college career lasted exactly eighteen days.

By now Bix had developed a taste for hard liquor. As early as 1924 he was drinking large measures of neat gin in lieu of breakfast. Even in a profession where getting plastered was a statutory requirement, Bix's boozing was legendary. When he couldn't get his hands on whisky or gin, he was reported to drink pure alcohol mixed with lemon drops.

Bix's drinking coincided with prohibition and you were risking more than just a hangover pouring bootleg liquor down your neck. A sample of this stuff sold in the streets of Harlem was once taken to a lab for analysis and found to contain wood alcohol, benzene, kerosene, nicotine, formaldehyde, iodine, sulphuric acid and soap. No wonder suckers who got hooked on it suffered blackouts, advanced aging, partial blindness and paralysis.

Playing one time in Indiana, Bix bought home-made whisky off a couple of old bootleggers. After drinking all day with some band members, the stock ran out. 'I just remembered,' said Bix, 'I got a spare gallon buried up on the hill.' They sneaked out of rehearsals with Bix leading the way like a frontier scout, across fields, over a railway line and lastly a barbed-wire fence. Bix started digging and sure enough came across his stashed jug of booze. Heading back, someone got stuck on the wire and while the others helped him off Bix sat down on the railway tracks for a breather. Just then a fast-moving train came hurtling round the bend. The group screamed and hollered, but Bix paid no attention, thinking it a practical joke. Only at the last second, with the train a mere 100 feet from him, did Bix sense the danger and roll off the track in time.

One night a cornholed Bix left the bandstand in too much of a hurry and fell down the stairs, knocking out a front tooth. Now, teeth being a pretty important element in playing the cornet, Bix visited a dentist and had a new one fitted, but sometimes during gigs it would pop out, causing Bix to fly off his chair and begin crawling up and down the stage in search of it. On one memorable occasion he roped in half the orchestra to hunt for the damn thing, while the other musicians carried on playing and the audience watched dumbstruck.

When his tooth wasn't making dramatic escape attempts from his mouth, Bix was frequently falling asleep during gigs, due no doubt to little helpings from the bottle of gin he kept in a bucket of ice under his chair. One bandleader, Paul Whiteman, came up with a novel way to make sure Bix was ready for his solo, scribbling on the music score a special direction for the second trumpeter a few beats before Beiderbecke was on. It read: 'Wake up Bix'.

Whiteman's Orchestra was the most popular band of the 1920s and Bix enjoyed the prestige and money of playing with such an ensemble, but it didn't stop his drinking. In 1929 he suffered from delirium tremens and had a nervous breakdown, he literally went to pieces and smashed up a hotel room, a full forty years before the Rolling Stones.

In a bid to recover Bix returned to the home of his parents, with Whiteman promising the musician that there would always be a place in his orchestra for him. But Bix was destined never to rejoin them. The next couple of years saw a marked decline in his health and a deterioration of his once youthful body. He began to have trouble walking, had strong nocturnal cramps, convulsions and shakes that disturbed his sleep. Several stays in rehabilitation centres attempting to dry out never worked as he'd just fall into old bad habits. A friend recalled driving Bix home from a jazz club one evening when he started shivering and yelling, 'I have to have it! Pull over!' Down some squalid alley was a bootlegger's and Bix disappeared into the gloom. A few minutes later he was back in the car holding a half pint of booze that he said he was going to take to bed with him.

In New York Bix recorded some tunes with his friend Hoagy Carmichael, and then disappeared into his own dark nightmarish world, holed up in a rooming house in Queens where he drank himself into regular stupors. Throughout the spring and summer of 1931 Bix had a continual cold and was weak to the point of exhaustion.

One evening the landlord heard strange noises and yells coming from his lodger's apartment. He rushed in to find Bix in a state of hysteria, his body trembling violently, and insisting that two Mexicans were hiding under his bed with long daggers. The landlord tried to reassure him there was nothing there when Bix suddenly staggered forward and fell as a dead weight into the man's arms. His body had finally had enough.

JOHN BELUSHI (1949–1982: *Comedian / Actor*)

'You know what I like to do? Get fucked up.' In the mouths of others this statement would appear cocky, so much hot air; coming from John Belushi it was sheer understatement.

He was a haze of contradictions, a solid professional who'd turn up for work paralytic, a generous, lovable guy who alienated friends by preferring the company of hell-bound drug dealers. The image left behind by his untimely, if totally expected, early death is that of a wild man, a self-destructive comet wracked by his own insecurities. Belushi was the Keith Moon of comedy.

The eldest son of Albanian immigrants, Belushi was born in Chicago and became a star athlete at high school. What's more he neither smoked, drank nor did drugs. You couldn't find a more strait-laced kid. Keen on dramatics, Belushi formed his own comedy group when he left school and word of his talent spread; in 1971 he was invited to join Second City, a leading comedy theatre in Chicago. Though part of an ensemble, it was Belushi who stood out, Belushi that the punters queued up to see. But already he could get dangerously out of control on booze, which he'd recently been introduced to and was making up for lost time. Movie critic Roger Ebert knew Belushi around this time. 'To put it cruelly, you'd put drinks into him like quarters into a jukebox, and he'd entertain everyone in the room.' Fun for a while but eventually Belushi's behaviour got him barred from most of his local pubs.

Another new comic joining Second City was Dan Aykroyd and the two men discovered an immediate rapport. Often Aykroyd took Belushi to a bar he owned in Toronto, Club 505, an after-hours speakeasy. Belushi loved the low-rent atmosphere of the place, and many a night they knocked back the bootleg booze till dawn. Belushi loved sensations; loved toting on whisky or cognac, and the sweet relaxation of smoking dope. Things got darker when he upped the ante and started dropping amphetamines and progressing to cocaine, the drug that took him over, the habit he'd never kick.

The defining period in Belushi's career was his epoch-making appearances as one of the original cast members on *Saturday Night Live*, along with Aykroyd and Chevy Chase. A massive success and launch pad for subsequent generations of American comics, those early days on *SNL* were hectic, with Belushi often doing drugs on the office floor or sleeping off booze benders on the couch, then going out to do the show live in front of millions. One time a frantic assistant told *SNL*'s producer Lorne Michaels that Belushi was in bad shape. 'We're on live at eleven-thirty,' yelled Michaels. 'He's not allowed to die until after the show!'

SNL made Belushi a household name and he was personally chosen by Jack Nicholson to play a seedy Mexican bandit in his film *Goin' South* (1978). People knew that the cocktail of drink and drugs Belushi was consuming altered his personality dramatically, but no one expected the sight that greeted them when he arrived late for the shoot, looking as if he hadn't slept for days. Shown his hotel room, Belushi insisted on staying with Jack in the more luxurious bungalows up in the hills. 'The hotel is suck-o, man,' he grumbled.

Back in the production office producer Harold Schneider had the unenviable job of calming Belushi down. It didn't work; he continued to talk in an incoherent fashion and then picked up a large kitchen knife which Schneider feared he intended to cause damage to himself with. Co-producer Harry Gittes arrived and was taking no crap from a TV comic. 'You're acting like a complete asshole,' he blasted. Belushi seemed not to be hearing this; instead he collapsed in a convenient chair and fell asleep. 'What's this?' snapped Jack, as he walked in. 'A crash pad? Get him out.' Easier said than done. Stirred from his audible slumber, Belushi was wild and abusive and a furious Schneider would surely have belted him one if he hadn't been restrained.

It was a coy and still rather hung-over Belushi who emerged on set the next day full of apologies. Jack was having none of it. 'If Paramount top brass had been here, your career in movies would be totally fucked.' He got another chance with *Animal House* (1978). Belushi was a screen natural, his face giving the permanent impression of demented anger lurking barely beneath the surface, although his wild reputation preceded him and he was socially quarantined in a house miles away from the rest of the cast. He still managed to put in one hellraising appearance at a local college. Introduced at assembly, he arrived on stage with a chainsaw and sliced the podium in half.

Meanwhile his friendship with Aykroyd deepened. As all-night booze and drug binges became an increasingly common part of Belushi's life, Aykroyd now rarely indulged, his tastes more sedate, happy with a six-pack of Moose Head Canadian lager and maybe a joint or two. They looked out for each other, too, though Aykroyd tended to do the majority of the looking. Belushi had a habit of just nonchalantly walking out into the road, and more than once Aykroyd pulled him back in the nick of time from an onrushing vehicle. 'He's Mister Careful and I'm Mister Fuck It,' Belushi said.

It was inevitable that the unique chemistry the two men shared would be exploited in the movies and *The Blues Brothers* (1980) was the perfect vehicle, if ultimately a fraught production with a spiralling budget and a manic Belushi. Shooting the famous car chase in the shopping mall, come 3 o'clock in the morning the crew had set up the final shot but Belushi had gone AWOL. Everyone was out looking for him. Aykroyd walked into a neighbouring street, every house was dark save for just one, and he'd nothing to lose so knocked on the door. 'I'm looking for John Belushi.' The guy who answered said, 'Oh yeah, he's asleep on my couch.' He'd walked into a complete stranger's house, said, 'Hey, I'm Belushi, I'm shooting this movie, I'm hungry, got anything?' raided the guy's fridge and then crashed out.

Another day on set Belushi point blank refused to come out of his trailer. Director John Landis stormed inside to find a war zone, Belushi near-comatose in a chair, the floor covered in a mixture of spilled cognac and piss, and a huge pile of cocaine on a table begging to be snorted. 'John, you're killing yourself,' yelled Landis, sort of stating the obvious. Belushi lurched to his feet and staggered across the room like a reanimated corpse. Something snapped inside and Landis hit him full in the face.

Belushi knew he had a problem; he was taking booze and Quaaludes, a deadly combination that could have landed him in a coma – or worse. He submitted to a guard looking after him twenty-four hours a day, while Aykroyd must have flushed enough coke down the pan to pay off

Colombia's national debt. Doctors too were telling Belushi that his craving for drinks and drugs would kill him. But he ignored it all; money for cocaine was even built into some of his business deals.

In the last few years of his life the self-destruct button was hit big time. Going out on the town had to be an invasion, not just a quiet, relaxing evening. Heading to a new punk club in LA he emptied two champagne bottles just on the drive over in the limo. Once inside he hit the gin and then switched to Jack Daniel's. He was out of control, his life ruled by his addictive personality. Where other friends had experimented with drugs and managed to give them up, Belushi never discovered how to stop.

After a couple of box office bombs his career was also in steep decline and he sought refuge not with friends but with drug vermin. Booking into a bungalow at the Chateau Marmont Hotel on LA's Sunset Strip, Belushi hooked up with addict and drug dealer Cathy Smith, who later described the actor's mental state then as 'like a train going 9,000 miles an hour heading for a brick wall'.

Whether Belushi actually intended to kill himself or go as far out as he could to prove some kind of macho immortality bullshit thing, who knows. What's clear is that on his last night on earth he drank to excess at the Roxy nightclub on the strip before returning to his bungalow. In the course of Belushi's descent into hell comedian Robin Williams, a drug addict himself at the time, popped by to snort a few lines but left utterly creeped out by the druggie friends Belushi had there. 'If you ever get up again, call,' were his last words to Belushi. Robert De Niro also came by, leaving for much the same reason. Turning to Cathy, Belushi asked her to administer a 'speedball', that's a hit of coke and heroin. Thinking he'd merely passed out, Cathy left only to return a little later to utter pandemonium; Belushi's naked body had been found in the foetal position on the bed. 'I'm going to die young,' he'd told a journalist just a few weeks before. 'I just can't stop destroying myself.'

Aykroyd was alone in his office in New York working on the script of *Ghostbusters* that he hoped Belushi would star in alongside him when he took the call and learned that his friend was dead. He was shaken to the core and for months afterwards racked with guilt that maybe he could have done more to help; 'That maybe I should have taken two or three of my friends and handcuffed him and put him in an institution just to turn him around, clean him up.'

Belushi wanted a Viking funeral, his body set aflame and floated out to sea. In the end it was more conventional, though not by much. Aykroyd organised the Bluesmobile and all the boys were packed into it. They'd been drinking and as they pulled into the cemetery, with people weeping and looking suitably solemn, everybody got out and relieved themselves in full view.

For years, whenever Aykroyd drove by that cemetery in Martha's Vineyard, he honked his car horn long and loud, just on the off-chance Belushi might hear his old friend passing through. But the pain and loss never healed. As one obituary read: 'His tragedy came in never realising that drugs aren't rebellious, a common flaw in counterculture heroes.' Belushi died a messy death just like any other junkie.

ROBERT BENCHLEY (1889–1945: *Writer*)

Numbered amongst America's best-known humorists whose often absurdist jottings influenced many other comedy writers, Robert Benchley was a true one of a kind. Not only did he enjoy a wildly varied career as columnist, drama critic and actor, but he could bullshit with the best of them. He loved to mislead and plain confuse, claiming, quite madly, that he was born in 1807, wrote *A Tale of Two Cities*, married Princess Anastasia of Portugal, died in 1871 and was buried at Westminster Abbey.

But behind the sophisticated, urbane image, the boozy nonchalance of a man holding a dry Martini with an acid-laced quip always at the ready, the master wag, was an utter drunkard, 'a walking series of contradictions', according to his grandson Nat Benchley. 'A finger-shaking teetotaller who drank himself to death,' and a family man who spent most of his later years 3,000 miles away from his wife and sons.

He was born in Worcester, Massachusetts, to a nice middle-class family and wrote extensively for *Vanity Fair* and the *New Yorker*, as well as undertaking freelance assignments. His output was prodigious, considering he claimed to be intensely lazy. There is a story that he submitted a magazine piece titled 'I Like to Loaf' two weeks after deadline. His explanatory note: 'I was loafing.'

He was certainly a great wit and immensely quotable, once saying, 'I have tried to know absolutely nothing about a great many things and I have succeeded fairly well.'

And then, no doubt with a Martini in his hand: 'A puritan is one who sits around all day worrying that someone else is having a good time.'

One year Benchley received notice that his income taxes were being audited. The IRS requested he fill out a detailed form outlining every cent made and spent over the last decade. He eyed the document, scrawled, 'Don't be silly' across it and sent it back. Two Treasury Department agents arrived the next morning to interrogate him.

An early advocate of prohibition, would you believe, by his early thirties Benchley was a boozer of some distinction, indulging in all-night benders with boozy chums. 'The only cure for a real hangover is death,' he once said, with the voice of bitter experience. Caught in a rain shower one afternoon, he arrived home soaking wet and called to his butler, 'Get me out of this wet suit and into a dry Martini!'

Leaving a particularly swank nightspot he eyed a well-uniformed gentleman at the door whom he commanded to summon him a taxicab. The man looked scornfully at Benchley and announced that he was an admiral of the United States Navy. 'All right, then,' said Benchley, 'get us a battleship.'

At *Vanity Fair* he worked with the redoubtable Dorothy Parker; they made quite a mischievous team. When the staff were ordered not to discuss their respective salaries Benchley and Parker paraded around the office with home-made signs strung from their necks proudly announcing their pitiful earnings. And when management introduced a policy requiring all employees to fill out a form even if they were just a few minutes late, Benchley took great exception. One morning he was eleven minutes late and scrawled in the tiniest handwriting imaginable his excuse, that on the way to work a herd of elephants from a nearby circus had escaped and, fearing pandemonium, he had chased the beasts up Fifth Avenue to Central Park, where he managed to ride them, à la Tarzan, back to the big top and safety. Benchley was never asked to fill in another late form.

Together with Parker, Benchley was a leading member of the renowned Algonquin Round Table, or the Vicious Circle, as they called themselves. Other notables included playwright Robert Sherwood and Harpo Marx. They would regularly meet for several hours of witty banter and scathing gossip. They really were New York's smart set.

Benchley's brilliant humour soon gained the attention of Hollywood and he was brought over to make a series of comedy shorts, besides playing several film roles, notably in Alfred Hitchcock's *Foreign Correspondent* (1940). His grandson Peter would decades later make an even bigger splash in movies when his novel *Jaws* was turned into a box-office sensation. But Benchley felt awkward and adrift in Hollywood. When the classic film about alcoholism *The Lost Weekend* was being shot in Hollywood, an exact duplicate of a Third Avenue bar was erected on a sound stage at Paramount. Every afternoon at five o'clock, without fail, the door of the set would open, a man would walk up to the bar, order a straight bourbon, chat about the weather, pay his fifty cents, and stroll out. It was Benchley, homesick for New York.

In his private life Benchley admitted not being the perfect husband, and a largely absentee father to his sons. He even voiced disappointment that he never pursued a career as a serious writer. But he was loved so deeply by friends that when he was diagnosed with cirrhosis of the liver and lay in hospital haemorrhaging to death, forty people showed up to volunteer to give blood. His condition, however, continued to deteriorate and Benchley passed away. As he once admitted, 'I know I'm drinking myself to a slow death, but then I'm in no hurry.'

JEFFREY BERNARD (1932–1997: Journalist)

One of London's great modern characters and a chaotic drinker whose stomping ground was the pubs and drinking dens of Soho, his tattered frame a permanent feature, sometimes obscured by clouds of smoke from the ever-present fag in his gob. Jeffrey Bernard was an irascible old bugger, completely feckless, self-destructive, irresponsible, a walking, talking object lesson in dissolution. He once told an interviewer that getting blitzed was an awful accident that he found happening to him every day of his life.

He was born in Hampstead from artistic stock, an architect father, who died when Jeffrey was still quite young, and opera-singing mother. He submitted to public school with scarcely concealed loathing, eventually expelled for gambling, smoking and/or drinking – take your pick. His comfortable middle-class upbringing also repelled him: one afternoon he launched a rocket down the chimney into the drawing-room where his mother's bridge club were enjoying a quiet evening and felt betrayed when his mother set the police on him.

After going AWOL from military service, Bernard settled in Soho, seduced by its lurid glamour and the bohemian low life lurching in every pub, café and drinking club. 'It was like walking out of Belsen into Disneyland.' He worked odd jobs but seemed always to be skint, cadging free drinks and 'loans' off the rich old queens and artists who littered the place. Still potless and moving to the countryside for a short time, with no car, Bernard saved money on taxis to the village pub by regularly sending letters to himself: when the postal van came miles out of the way to deliver them he'd wangle a lift back.

By this time drink had already got its hooks tight into his flesh. Intensely shy, Bernard used the booze initially as a crutch; he was afraid of being perceived as boring in social circles and drink gave him courage. As early as 1965 came his first attack of acute pancreatitis; predictably he ignored doctor's advice to give up drinking.

One great story has Bernard on the town with Tony Hancock in the late fifties. Hancock is absolutely soused so it takes some time to find a taxi that will take him home, the cabbies' reluctance due in no small part to the fact that Hancock has quite obviously wet his pants. As he is about to leave Hancock offers Bernard his card and the words, 'If you ever need my help, just call me.' Looking at the urine-soaked clown with incredulity Bernard replies, 'Why on earth should I want help from you?' Hancock smiles benignly. 'Because I think you may have a drink problem.'

Then there's the occasion Bernard appeared wankered at the window of a second-floor cocktail party atop a ladder. The guests stood gaping at the apparition as Bernard announced loudly that the host was a, 'FUCKING CUNT!' then darted off before anyone could catch him.

Bernard took up journalism and began writing a racing column for the *Sporting Life* in 1970. General drunkenness got him sacked, though not before he managed to vomit spectacularly in front of the Queen Mother at Ascot.

Serious attempts were made to lay off the sauce since he'd already developed diabetes as a result of a ruined pancreas, but he always went back. 'I've never met such boring people as my friends when I'm sober, never been so miserable or so lonely.' Booze was his first loyalty, that's why marriage to him was impossible. Drink was the other woman. He did, however, manage to tie the knot four times, all too fleeting moments of domestic bliss, bulldozed by meandering hormones. A friend he was drinking with one night suddenly blurted, 'All right, Jeffrey, I know you've fucked my wife, haven't you?' Bernard held his hands up, 'Yes, and your mother and daughter as well.'

He was quite simply irresistible to women, a great charmer before the booze ruined his features by middle age. Women enjoyed mothering him and looking after him, even though he was often known to fall asleep during intercourse, or accidentally set fire to wherever he was staying. In the end all his wives made the same devastating mistake of thinking they could change him.

In 1976 Bernard began his now classic column at the *Spectator*, funny musings about low life in Soho and horse racing, but also glimpses at the man behind the tatty typewriter, a peek into the chaotic, murky world of an alcoholic, a column described by one critic as, 'A suicide note in weekly instalments.' They were a roaring success not least because, said Bernard, 'people like to read about someone who is deeper in the shit than they are'. His politically incorrect view on life was further reason to become an addict. Of one girlfriend he wrote, 'I am going to lend her to a farmer to frighten the cows.'

By the eighties Bernard had become a permanent fixture at the Coach and Horses public house in Greek Street, Soho, always arriving a few minutes after opening time and taking his seat on a tall stool at the far end of the bar. The establishment was presided over by Norman Balon, self-styled rudest landlord in the West End. He once barred a well-known writer, snatching away his lunch and throwing him out for being, 'fucking boring'. There's also the tale of when a rugby team walked in and one of them ordered a snakebite and Balon responded indignantly, 'We don't do cocktails in here, get out!'

It's difficult to decide whether Bernard's life revolved around the pub, or the Coach and Horses revolved around Bernard. Either way he was as synonymous with the place as its naff furnishings. There's the story of him becoming enraged at the lethargic bar staff, going outside and ringing them from a borrowed mobile to bawl, 'ANY CHANCE OF GETTING A FUCKING DRINK?' Or when a new barmaid suggested he put his own ice in his drink, Jeffrey picked up a soda fountain and let fly at her ample cleavage.

One day as a doctor friend of his took a pew at the bar Bernard loudly announced, 'Oh, there's Neil. I'll ask him to come into the lavatory with me and look at my cock. I think I've got thrush.' Indeed he did and subsequently paid a rather urgent visit to his GP, a woman. She looked at his todger and remarked, 'Oh, that's interesting.' No one had quite put it that way before. Bernard felt like saying, 'Well, it's been in some interesting places.'

Inevitably such a lifestyle had an adverse effect on both his health and his work. It was not unknown for his usual column to be replaced by the sad, solitary sentence: 'Jeffrey Bernard is unwell', polite prose for 'Jeffrey got too pissed to fucking bother this morning'. Such behaviour would have seen lesser mortals hurtling out the door straight to the nearest dole queue; for Bernard it merely enhanced the myth. He was once observed writing his column in a pub, large vodka by his side and fag in hand. After struggling with a few sentences he crashed comatose upon the table until the cigarette burned down into his fingers, causing him to scream and sit bolt upright. Casually he lit up a fresh fag and resumed writing.

For years now Bernard's life had resembled some kind of warped Whitehall farce. How strange, then, and apt, that he be approached by Keith Waterhouse to turn his demented life story into a stage play: *Jeffrey*

Bernard is Unwell. At the time Bernard was writing in the *Daily Mirror* and he informed his readers that the play was packing them in: punters were literally hanging from the rafters. Later that day Waterhouse had to call Bernard to tell him, 'Jeffrey, we haven't opened yet. We open in six weeks.' Drunk out of his head the previous night, Bernard had gone to bed, dreamed the whole thing was a tremendous hit and woken up to write his column.

Of course the production did go on to tremendous acclaim and success, with Peter O'Toole inspired casting, having known Bernard for some forty years. Most nights of the run Bernard would visit O'Toole in his dressing room, drink his vodka, then totter off to his seat in the stalls where he'd fall asleep before the end of the first act. In the intermission he'd struggle over to the theatre bar where he gladly accepted free drinks from delighted audience members, something more heartening than his royalty cheques which were taken by the Inland Revenue in lieu of unpaid taxes.

In the last few years of his life Bernard became a walking, talking casualty unit. His regime of fifty cigarettes a day and vodka at breakfast was taking its toll, combined with his ongoing diabetes. ('My thigh is like the triple twenty on a dart board.') He also had to contend with agonising pancreatitis, failing eyesight, insomnia and eczema. Every time he was rushed to hospital friends would say, 'This is it.' Invariably, once installed in a ward he'd try to get one hand up the skirt of a nurse while cracking open a bottle of vodka with the other; the staff always had one at the ready, realising it did him more good than harm.

In 1994 one of his legs grew gangrenous from the complications of diabetes and had to be amputated below the knee, the stump becoming merely another talking point at the pub, where he'd wave it around. He even asked a nurse to buy him a parrot to put on his shoulder. The humour hid a depressing reality, that he was now confined largely to his flat high up in a tower block, save for the odd occasion when his helper wheeled him over to the Groucho Club or the Coach and Horses.

To the bitter end he kept writing, alone in his few rooms, surrounded by the paraphernalia of his life; he'd lost almost everything else: women, friends, health, good looks and money. Even booze was denied him after the leg came off. He hated life without it, though. Once asked what it was like not drinking he replied: 'Awful. It's like being half dead.'

Pretty soon he was completely dead, after refusing to undergo any further kidney dialysis treatments. His death came as no surprise to anyone, since he'd been given a year to live some three decades previous. With his passing Soho lost perhaps its last great character, or pain in the arse, depending on your point of view.

It was almost a dereliction of duty that Bernard never wrote his life story proper. He was approached by publishers on more than one occasion and even sent this request to a newspaper: 'I have been commissioned to write an autobiography and I would be grateful to any of your readers who could tell me what I was doing between 1960 and 1974.'

He got a reply, too, which read: 'On a certain evening in September 1969, you rang my mother to inform her that you were going to murder her only son. If you would like further information, I can put you in touch with many people who have enjoyed similar bizarre experiences in your company.'

Yours Sincerely,

Michael Molloy

Editor

Daily Mirror.

GEORGE BEST (1946–2005: Footballer)

He was a symbol of his age, the first 'celebrity' footballer, the most gifted of Saturday heroes whom even Pelé said was the best he ever saw. Sadly the Greeks couldn't have scripted his fall from grace any better, George Best's life was classic tragedy: a man brought to ruin by a tragic flaw, an addiction to alcohol.

A typical evening out drinking would end like this, Best staggering back to his hotel slurring to the receptionist that he wanted a wake-up call. 'Of course, Mr Best. What time?

'Seven, *hic*, a.m., please.'

The receptionist would look puzzled. 'Er, it's a quarter past seven now, Mr Best.'

Such is the almost surreal life of the alcoholic, though for the most part Best seemed to enjoy playing the role. It had its rewards. As he once so memorably observed: 'I spent a lot of my money on booze, birds and fast cars, the rest I just squandered.'

Best was the first of six children born to a shipyard worker in Belfast and brought up on a housing estate. Football mad since he could walk, his incredible skill was spotted by Bob Bishop, Manchester United's chief scout in Ulster, who rang United's manager Matt Busby and proclaimed: 'I think I've found a genius.'

The teenage Best arrived at Old Trafford at a propitious moment in the club's history. The glory days before the Munich air crash were a bittersweet memory, Busby was in the process of building another team and Best was to be the catalyst to United's glorious revival. Quite early on, however, there were hints that Best's fun-loving impulses might get the better of him. Even though initially he'd begun drinking partly in an effort to overcome his inherent shyness, booze helped a very private young lad lead a very public life.

Going out to parties and boozing after the Saturday match soon became regular occurrences. Choosing a nice quiet pub near the ground, once word spread that George Best drank there the place was swamped with fans and punters. Fame when it arrived was a double-edged sword for George, not sure how to handle it, but wallowing in it at the same time. No one quite knew how to deal with this strange new phenomenon; suddenly a footballer was on the front page of a newspaper, unheard of before. He was attracting the same kind of screaming adulation as The Beatles. Today's players receive professional advice on how to cope with all the adulation and media intrusion, but for George this was uncharted territory. He was the Christopher Columbus of football celebrity.

Although essentially a loner, Best loved the convivial atmosphere of pubs; he saw them as places that functioned as a home for those who didn't belong anywhere else. His own home had become a goldfish bowl and he a permanent exhibit in it, fodder for lurid glares and the intrusive photo lens – no wonder he drank some nights until five in the morning so he wouldn't have to go back.

Best's life grew ever more chaotic; going on benders that lasted days he'd suffer blackouts, unsure where he'd been or what he'd done. This is an occupational hazard for alcoholics, but Best was a long-term sufferer. In the eighties he was drinking in his local when the landlord told him he was wanted on the phone. 'George, I've tracked you down at last.' Turned out the guy ran a classic-car repair firm in Dublin and wanted to know 'what to do with the Mercedes'. 'What Mercedes?' asked Best, who had no idea who the man was. 'The one you brought in here for repairs two years ago.'

At least on the pitch he remained an inspiration, and because of his tremendous fitness levels able to disguise his wayward drinking habit. On the night he won the 1968 European Footballer of the Year award, Best picked up a bird and went back to her flat. Five winos gone he stood swaying in her bedroom as she stripped off. Intending to sit on the bed, he missed it by four feet and collapsed on the floor. 'Some player of the year,' the girl groaned as he fell soundly to sleep. 'I woke up still clutching my award and staggered out of the flat. I hadn't a bloody clue where I was.'

The drinking and hellraising may initially have been an up-yours gesture to his stern Presbyterian background. Best knew he had been born with a great gift, and that it came with a destructive streak. 'Just as I wanted to outdo everyone when I played, I had to outdo everyone when we were out on the town.'

Ironically, Best's fame had the hardest impact on the family he left behind in Belfast, notably his mother Ann, who couldn't handle the press scrutiny, the prying eyes trying to peek through the lace curtains. An intensely shy and private woman, and a staunch teetotaller to the point that she never allowed alcohol in the house, Ann took to drink aged forty-four as a way of dealing with the insurmountable pressure she and her family were under. Sadly, within a short time she was a full-blown alcoholic, hiding bottles in the garden shrubbery and turning up at home after work hours late and covered in bruises.

By the early seventies Best was starting to arrive for training still smelling of drink from the night before, exasperating United's strait-laced captain Bobby Charlton. Then, when Busby retired, Best led his managerial successors a merry dance with his unscheduled absences. Still a great player, he grew frustrated and increasingly angry that he was carrying what had become a mediocre team. It led to depression and more drinking. At a time when he should have been reaching his peak as a footballer Best left United, a hasty and acrimonious decision that must have rankled with him his whole life.

Best's football career wasn't over, far from it, but in the eyes of the public and the media it played second fiddle to his sex life and drinking. Scoring goals had given way to scoring babes in the tabloids. He'd fly in a girl from Australia, for example, and after a couple of weeks, when he got bored, send her back again. On his chat show Michael Parkinson asked: 'What was the nearest to kick-off that you made love to a woman?'

Best: 'Er, I think it was half-time actually.'

He'd a particular penchant for bedding Miss Worlds, getting his leg over at least four of them. There is the classic story about the porter who entered his hotel room with breakfast and caught George in bed with the current Miss World, a magnum of champagne and several thousand pounds of cash won from a night's gambling. The youth exclaimed, 'George, where did it all go wrong?'

For a while he played in the American soccer league, facing the likes of Pelé and Franz Beckenbauer. He also got married, to Angela, a model and former Playboy bunny, arriving stewed for the ceremony in Las Vegas, forgetting the ring and spending his wedding night gambling. It was during this period that he seemed to hit a brick wall, stop for once and face his addiction. His mother had recently died just short of her fifty-sixth birthday of alcohol-related heart disease and Best was devastated, yet still going on binges that lasted four or five days, sometimes a week, during which his wife wouldn't know where he was. (She probably had a good idea, but there were a lot of gutters in California.) He searched out solutions and cures, listened to the advice of doctors. 'I might go to Alcoholics Anonymous,' he said. 'But I think it would be difficult for me to remain anonymous.' In the end he knew no one else could decide for him.

The lowest point came when he was sitting in a bar one day, desperate for a drink but out of cash. Next to him was a lady, a complete stranger. When she got up to use the bathroom Best quickly trawled through her handbag, located her purse and took some money. He got his drink but lost his self-respect. 'I had to look at myself and say you're a mess, you're a disaster area and that's the hardest part, to say you're no good.' He obviously didn't look hard enough. The real tragedy of Best was that here was an articulate, intelligent guy utterly incapable of resisting drink despite the fact that he knew it was killing him. 'There are dark moods and demons,' he said. 'And you just need to go off and get wrecked.' After months on the wagon he hit the bottle again and his marriage collapsed.

At thirty-three Best shocked the football world by signing for Hibernian in the Scottish league, a development akin to Led Zeppelin playing Butlins at Bognor Regis. In a match against Rangers a beer can was thrown at him, skidding to a halt at his feet. Best bent down, picked it up, raised it to his lips and toasted the crowd.

As usual it wasn't long before he pressed the self-destruct button. Before Hibs were due to play a cup tie Best engaged in an all-night drinking session with the French national rugby team, who happened to be guests in the same hotel, and was proud to be the last man standing at the bar next morning, albeit barely. The team doctor tried desperately to revive him for the match. 'They gave George enough shots that would have brought Shergar back from the grave,' said a team-mate. 'But still he didn't flinch.' Best and Hibs soon parted company, as he did from football altogether.

From then on reporters invariably knew where to find Best: the Phene Arms near the Kings Road in London. It was a home, of sorts. He'd spend all day there sometimes, only seeing daylight to pop over to the betting shop. At night he'd stagger home, or fall unconscious on a bench and be picked up by the local fire brigade who had a regular bed for him back at the station.

His life was now more soap opera than reality. In 1982 he was declared bankrupt, although there was no shortage of fans happy to buy him a pint. In 1984 he spent Christmas in prison after failing to appear in court on a drink-driving charge and head-butting a policeman. Sent down, Best delivered a line worthy of any hellraiser: 'Well, I suppose that's the knighthood fucked.'

Then in 1990 there was the infamous appearance on the Terry Wogan TV chat show. Things didn't get off to a good start when Best hit the bar with Omar Sharif in the BBC hospitality room. 'I was that drunk I started thinking Omar was Sacha Distel.' The live interview turned into a public embarrassment, not only for Best, but for his family and close friends. Slurring his words and having trouble preventing himself sliding off the chair, Best looked a pitiful spectacle, like a once great gladiator humbled in the arena. One good thing did come out of it, 'Omar Sharif and myself became engaged that evening.'

He needed direction and purpose back in his life and was handed a golden chance in 1995 when he married Alex Pursey, a former air hostess almost half his age. Alas, the relationship went in much the same direction as all the others, down the toilet. Alex would tell of how their rows escalated to the point where she was left with black eyes and broken arms. Once she even had her hair hacked off in the night by a drunken Best.

Seemingly happy to be labelled Britain's most high-profile alcoholic, Best probably thought he was invincible, going on one marathon booze binge after another. He no longer drank beer, hadn't for years. His poison was white wine, reportedly four bottles a day when on a bender, supplemented with brandy chasers. On being made Footballer of the Century in 1999 he japed: 'It's a pleasure to be standing here. It's a pleasure to be standing up.' Then in March 2000 the inevitable happened, he collapsed with liver failure and spent five weeks in hospital. Warned that just one more drink could finish him off Best, wilfully it seemed, went back on the booze, resigned to his fate rather than endure a life on the wagon. Such macho bluster soon faded and Best was faced with a stark choice, life or death. 'People say you have to hit rock bottom and, I can tell you, almost dying is as rock bottom as it gets.'

When Best was controversially given a liver transplant in 2002 it sparked a nationwide debate. Considering his past history and the desperate shortage of donors, many believed that others more deserving should have been ahead of him in the queue. Still the operation went ahead, lasting ten hours during which he suffered a massive internal haemorrhaging and required forty pints of blood.

What little public sympathy Best might have had evaporated barely twelve months later when he was spied knocking them back at his local. Friends and fans were dismayed; Alex was convinced her husband 'was on a mission to self-destruct'. Best, though, remained defiant, he planned to be around for a long time yet, but privately felt searing guilt that he'd let the public down so badly.

His last three years were marked by more binges and the collapse of his marriage. And people couldn't have been very surprised when his emaciated body was carried into a London hospital under the mournful glare of the world's media. By his side was Best's eighty-six-year-old father who for decades had endured the public spectacle of his son's alcoholic slide, and now he watched on helplessly as George slowly faded away into nothing.

All that was left was a final image, a haunting photograph of his wasted frame that Best wanted to be seen as a warning to other potential alcoholics not to follow the same path.

And then there was the funeral, as if the people of Northern Ireland were putting some deity into the ground. It stirred up memories of the football demon swerving and scoring on the pitch, the world at his feet, but even back then his life of crap was preordained. Matt Busby saw it, recognised in the young man a darkness, believed that one day he'd top himself. For the next thirty years Best tried everything to prove his old boss right, a suicide note printed again and again in the tabloid press until it wasn't funny any more, just sad and stained in the vinegar of last night's fish and chips.

HUMPHREY BOGART (1899–1957: Actor)

Bogie loved his booze, once saying, 'I don't trust a bastard who doesn't drink.' Returning from a holiday in Italy he told reporters, 'I didn't like the pasta, so I lived on Scotch and soup.' That just about sums him up, he was totally his own man and refused to compromise on anything, traits that feature in so many of his best-known screen roles. As pal David Niven said, 'Bogart's life was either black or white – he had little patience with the greys.'

The quintessential anti-hero, Bogart was born in New York and was a rebel from an early age, being routinely expelled from school for poor marks and misbehaviour. Placed into a prestigious academy by his well-to-do parents, Bogie seemed more interested in pursuing girls and partying than study. He flunked out, ending up taking a succession of menial jobs, even working in a biscuit factory. To dull the hardship he soaked up the jazz age scene in Manhattan, touring illegal speakeasies and drinking till dawn or until he passed out under the table. It was in one of these bars that Bogart reportedly got his trademark lip scar and slight lisp, the result of a drunken brawl.

Getting work at a theatrical agency gave Bogie the acting bug, probably by osmosis. The lifestyle certainly appealed: go on stage a couple of hours a night, then spend the rest of the time drinking in clubs and cavorting with actresses who'd have trouble spelling the word morality. Small acting roles began to turn up, but Bogie would get himself fired for showing up so hung-over he'd forget his lines. He soldiered on and in 1926 married Helen Menken, an established Broadway actress. It didn't last, collapsing after just a year, and Bogart hit the booze and chorus girls again. Mary Philips, another actress, swiftly became wife number two. A boozer herself, the couple drank their way through much of the liquor supply of Lower Manhattan.

It was after one such hectic night on the tiles that Bogie appeared for an audition, hung-over, unshaven, looking like the worst kind of skid row veteran, actually just the look the producers were after for the role of a cynical gangster in the play *The Petrified Forest*. It changed Bogart's life. A huge hit, he was snapped up by Warner Brothers, who already had a roster of movie tough guys: Cagney, Raft and Edward G Robinson. Bogie joined them as a contract player making twenty-nine films over the next five years.

Having come to films late – he was now thirty-six – Bogie was determined to make the most of Hollywood. Ultra professional, he only drank a single can of beer for lunch. It was a different story after the director wrapped for the day; Bogie would walk into his dressing room where his well-trained hairdresser had already poured him a Scotch. He'd then leave the studio and pretty much carouse all night with pals. When he wasn't working Bogart felt free to flit from one drinking den to another. 'Bogie had an alcoholic thermostat,' screenwriter Nunnally Johnson remarked. 'He just set his thermostat at noon, pumped in some Scotch, and stayed at a nice even glow all day, redosing as necessary.'

His womanising hadn't diminished either. Mary was soon history, making way for wife number three in 1938. Bogart seemed to choose his women carefully and Mayo Methot was exactly what he was looking for, a fun-loving party goer and a two-fisted drinker who could hold her liquor. Together they were as volatile as TNT and their booze-fuelled rows became fodder for the press; even their wedding ceremony turned into a free for all. Dubbed 'The Battling Bogarts', matters reached the stage where many nightclubs simply wouldn't let them both in at the same time.

On screen Bogie had graduated from supporting roles to true stardom as private eye Sam Spade in *The Maltese Falcon* (1941), closely followed by *Casablanca* (1942). But Mayo's liver-lubed antics were getting out of control, spilling over into real domestic violence and wild jealousy. Waiting on a dockside for a ferry boat, Mayo caught Bogie eyeing up another woman. She decked him one and he fell in the sea. When Bogie announced he was going on a trip for a few days she produced a pistol and chased him into the bathroom. Locked out, she fired off a few bullets into her husband's suitcase. Bogie soaked himself in the tub with a cocktail.

On another night Bogie returned home late after a heavy drinking session. Convinced he'd been with a hooker, Mayo grabbed a kitchen knife and embedded it in his lower back; grounds for divorce, you'd think. A studio doctor had to be bribed to keep it a secret from the police. Besides, 'the knife only went in a little bit', excused Bogie.

Amazingly they remained a couple, despite Mayo slashing her wrists on several occasions and setting the house on fire. 'The Bogart–Methot marriage was the sequel to the Civil War,' said friend Julius Epstein. Their neighbours simply got used to the noise of crashing plates and screams of 'fuck you'. Rarely did their fights spill out into the street. Memorably there was the occasion when neighbours watched as Mayo ran across the top of the house with a noose round her neck and Bogie chasing behind yelling, 'I'm going to hang you.' Instead of calling the police they all stood laughing hysterically.

They even travelled to Europe together entertaining the troops during the Second World War. It was 'The Battling Bogarts' on tour. After one show the couple drank with GIs and borrowed a couple of revolvers. Back in their billet, the tottering pair started shooting holes in the roof until they were quelled by MPs. Bogie never drank with officers, only with the enlisted men, due to his contempt for authority. When a party he was throwing in his hotel got out of hand a general in the next room asked him to quiet it down. 'Go fuck yourself!' Bogie hollered back.

There was a dark side to Bogart, no doubt about it. Especially when he was shined up, he could turn angry and verbally abusive, threatening always to spill over into violence. Dave Chasen, owner of one of Bogie's favourite watering holes, offered this: 'Bogart's a helluva nice guy until around 11.30 p.m. After that, he thinks he's Bogart.'

As the rows with Mayo intensified and his drinking increased, for the first time in Bogie's career his work began to suffer as he'd arrive on set hung-over, or a few times still smashed. While shooting the war picture *Sahara* (1943), he sometimes refused to leave his dressing room until Mayo showed up with a thermos full of Martini. After knocking it back he'd walk on set and deliver his lines perfectly. Bogie always felt that the hallmark of a good drinker was someone who was absolutely blotto but those around him never knew it.

Take, for example, the time he was invited to speak at an Easter service at the Hollywood Bowl. Due to go on, Bogie was nowhere to be seen. A frantic search took place and he was found at a friend's house nearby, fried to the tonsils and smelling like a tramp's jockstrap. Once at the Bowl, however, he stepped on stage and recited the Lord's Prayer with such sublime emotion there was scarcely a dry eye in the house. Congratulated afterwards, Bogie's only comment was, 'Where can I puke?'

After what must have been a monumental night of drinking, Bogie turned up at the Warner Brothers studio still in his pyjamas, still obviously drunk, and refusing to work, instead riding around the lot on a bicycle shouting, 'Look, no hands, no hands!' Jack Warner was told and stormed out to see his star.

'It's time to go to work, Bogie,' he ordered.

'I don't feel like working.'

'You don't, huh?'

'That's right, I don't.'

'Well,' Warner said. 'There's a lot of people who feel like working and they get paychecks that are less than what you spend on Scotch.'

All of Mayo's jealous rages were ultimately justified when during the shooting of *To Have and Have Not* (1944) Bogart fell in love with his co-star Lauren Bacall, twenty-four years his junior. After their divorce Mayo really hit the skids, settling into a pattern of alcoholism and depression, dying in 1951 alone in a third-rate hotel in Oregon. Her body wasn't discovered for several days.

Following the alcoholic wars with his previous wives, Bacall was a calming influence on Bogie. Yes he still drank as much as ever, but his young bride never nagged about his late-night booze orgies or dreadful hangovers. And he was still up for making mischief. One night he and Peter Lorre got so stinko at Chasens they made off with the restaurant's immense safe, which they rolled out the door and abandoned in the middle of Beverly Boulevard.

Another time Bogart hit New York's chic El Morocco Club carrying a large stuffed panda as his drinking date for the evening. In the early hours of the morning two partygoing girls tried to make off with the toy, but Bogie was having none of it and fought back, resulting in the women landing on their arses and punches being traded with a boyfriend, whom unknown to Bogart was a real-life gangster.

The next day Bogie was hauled into court facing charges of assault. Asked by the press if he was 'stiff' during the altercation, Bogart replied, 'Who isn't at 3 o'clock in the morning? This is a free country, isn't it? I can take my panda any place I want to. And if I want to buy it a drink, that's my business.' As for punching out at the women: 'I didn't sock anybody; if girls were falling on the floor, I guess it was because they couldn't stand up.'

Despite his acquittal Bogart was banned for life from the El Morocco, adding to an impressive list of places at which he was no longer welcome. 'You got to hand it to him,' Bacall said. 'When he gets barred, he gets barred from all the right places.'

Bogart continued to raise hell, not giving a damn. When asked if he'd ever been on the wagon Bogie replied, 'Just once. It was the most miserable afternoon of my life.'

He seemed to attract similarly minded drinkers to share his misadventures; he and Richard Burton were great booze pals. 'He was my kind of man,' said the Welsh lush. 'If you challenged him to put his hand through a plate glass window, he'd do it. And keep on drinking with the other hand.' Bogie even formed his own drinking club that included the likes of Frank Sinatra. In Las Vegas for a wild week, on about the fifth day of debauchery, Lauren Bacall, announced, 'You look like a goddamned rat pack!' The name stuck. Asked what the purpose of the group was Bacall responded, 'To drink a lot of bourbon and stay up late.'

A heavy smoker all his life, getting through two packs a day, in January 1956 Bogart was diagnosed with cancer of the oesophagus and underwent nine hours of surgery. Out of hospital he went straight back on the bottle, happy to drink while his body wasted away. Everyone could see the diagnosis had been too late, that the cancer had spread. At the end Bogie was too weak even to make it down the stairs to greet the many guests who came to visit him for an hour each day. He solved the problem by crawling inside a dumb waiter and lowering himself down to the ground floor, where he was lifted into a chair and wheeled into the drawing room, a sherry glass in one hand and a fag in the other. Few in Hollywood could recall witnessing such courage before.

Just before he died, Bogart reflected upon his life and declared that things had gone downhill after a single bad decision. 'I should never have switched from Scotch to Martinis.'

JOHN BONHAM (1948–1980: Musician)

There have been technically better drummers than John Bonham, or 'Bonzo' as he was affectionately known, but few if any matched the sheer thunderous power and theatricality he was able to create. His contribution to music was revolutionary as the engine room of the greatest rock band in history – Led Zeppelin, a band that didn't just live rock hedonism, they invented it, and Bonham flew the flag of excess more enthusiastically than most.

He was the ultimate rock 'n' roll bad guy. In the middle of a flight one day in 1974, Bonham got so groggified he couldn't be arsed to pay a trip to the lavatory so simply relieved himself in his first-class seat. The squelching became too uncomfortable so he offered the seat to one of the roadies in economy. 'That's bloody nice of you,' the unsuspecting man declared. On another occasion Bonham got so annoyed with Zeppelin guitarist Jimmy Page's girlfriend he took a crap in her purse. Bonham sailed through life with the belief that he didn't have to abide by any social rules at all. As one critic suggested, his brief tenure on earth 'created an impact somewhere between Genghis Khan and the Kobe earthquake'.

He was born in Redditch, Worcestershire, and first learned how to play drums at the age of five, making a drum kit out of food tins. It wasn't until he was fifteen that Bonham finally got the real thing, a gift from his father. Still he never took lessons, preferring to seek advice from local musicians. After leaving school Bonham worked as a bricklayer before joining a succession of bands, developing a reputation as the loudest drummer in England. Some clubs refused to book any group featuring Bonham; he was manic. 'Just watch me tonight,' he'd say. 'I'm gonna totally demolish this drum kit.'

Bonham found his natural home in Led Zeppelin, recommended by lead singer Robert Plant. Their rise was meteoric, after two stunning albums and hard touring, Zeppelin were flying around in a personal jet, playing stadiums and raking in untold sums of money. They wrote the rulebook on rock excess, renting out entire hotel floors merely to cause maximum damage. They destroyed an entire room at the Tokyo Hilton and were banned for life from the establishment.

One album launch took place in the sedate environs of an art gallery in Copenhagen. Bonham, who had been drinking since breakfast, was in no mood for gentility and when a stuffy critic began pontificating about one of the paintings Bonham struck. 'Do you want to know what I think?' he asked. 'Oh yes,' replied the deluded critic. Without pausing, and ignoring the alarm bells ringing as he lifted the art treasure off the wall, Bonham smashed it over the critic's head. 'Are there any other paintings you'd like me to critique tonight?' Bonham asked.

Really 'Bonzo' could cause chaos pretty much anywhere. After both had been boozing at the Coach and Horses in Soho, he and a pal decided to invade the office of Chrysalis records, tie up an executive in sticky tape and leave him mummified on the pavement in Oxford Street. Then, in Arab robes hired from a theatrical costumier, they borrowed a Rolls-Royce and arrived at the Mayfair Hotel posing as Middle Eastern princes. Booking into the Maharaja suite they ordered champagne and fifty steaks, with which they began to decorate the room. In the ensuing mayhem a priceless statue was destroyed. Bonham would ultimately be banned from almost every West End hotel.

Still, there were always hotels in Los Angeles he could destroy. Zeppelin usually took over the entire sixth floor of the Hyatt House on the Sunset Strip. At Bonham's twenty-fifth birthday party, his present was a Harley Davidson which he tore up and down the corridors on. The next day he happily paid for the damage caused and told the management, 'Oh, and keep the bike.'

There's a story that Bonham handcuffed two groupies to a bed before leaving for a gig to ensure they would be there when he got back. Another classic tale has the mad drummer forcing a naked girl into a bathtub that contained an octopus. Zep's most notorious deed involves their stay at a Seattle wharfside hotel, where visitors could catch fish from their balconies. During one sex misadventure a naked groupie submitted to being prodded in various orifices by dead fish parts, caught by a drunken Bonham: which gives a whole new meaning to fish fingers.

As the band's tour schedules grew ever more hectic Bonham turned increasingly to alcohol. He hated being on the road for months on end, hated being away from his wife and young family; that's when the black moods and the violence reared their ugly heads. His favourite tipple was vodka, which he'd swig from the bottle like water. But really anything would suffice. Amazingly the drinking and the antics never got in the way of his job. No matter how much grog, women, or drugs he'd indulged in, Bonham always turned up to rehearsals and performances on time and ready to play. He was awesome, with his live drum solos reaching half an hour in length sometimes, which pleased Jimmy Page, who often took the opportunity to retreat to the band's dressing room with some groupies. During one indulgently long drum solo Page actually returned to the band's hotel!

Many who encountered the sober Bonham described him as the nicest bloke you could meet; it was the drink that made him cut loose and turn into a maniac. And when wozzled he would actually start to growl like some rabid Rottweiler, hence another of his nicknames – 'the beast'. In a Los Angeles bar one night, Bonham ordered twenty Black Russians, polishing off ten in rapid fire. A woman at a nearby table recognised him and smiled. Bonham walked over, his face glowering, 'What the fuck did you say?' The girl began to protest but got Bonham's fist in her face so hard the impact sent her sprawling to the floor. 'Don't ever look at me that way again.' Then Bonham turned round and went back to his drinks. Like most bullies Bonham felt comfortable picking on women or starting brawls he knew he could win, helped of course by the bruisers hired as the band's roadies. One of the few exceptions was when he picked a fight with a club bouncer who turned out to be a karate master and put the drummer in hospital.

For rock journalist Ellen Sanders her time following the band on tour in the States is forever seared on her memory. She compared it to being inside a cage at a zoo where 'you get to smell the shit first-hand'. There was the time the band, with Bonham at the helm, tore at her clothes in such a frenzy she feared that she might be raped. Zep's manager Peter Grant had to bodily pull Bonham off her.

Poor old Bonham drunk wasn't exactly the most tactful romantic. With girls constantly throwing themselves at him he got into the groove where he thought any piece of arse was his for the taking. Being part of Led Zeppelin gave him a false sense of power, of being invulnerable.

Aboard their private jet Bonham had drained a bottle of whisky and was on the prowl. Grabbing a stewardess, he bent her over in an arm lock, pulled up her dress and announced that he was going to 'have her from the rear'. Again it was Grant to the rescue, hauling Bonham off the terrified girl.

Away from touring and the booze Bonham actually lived quite contentedly in a farmhouse in Worcestershire, his only concession to the rock 'n' roll high life a vast collection of cars and motorbikes. He was a car salesman's dream, buying a Ferrari, a red AC Cobra and an Aston Martin without batting an eyelid. He even purchased a nearby village pub, which was remodelled so he could drive his motorbike behind the bar.

By 1977, with their best work behind them, Zep was becoming a spent force and it showed. Cracks in the band were becoming wider. Bassist John Paul Jones had grown so tired of all the debauchery he refused to be on the same hotel floor as the rest of them. Bonham's alcoholism was also worsening; to curb his excesses friends were putting Valium in his brandy to calm him down. And with the advent of punk, the music Zeppelin propagated was judged Jurassic in comparison. Bonham attended a London gig by the Damned and staggered boiled as an owl onto the stage, his presence there not altogether appreciated, as was evident by the shouts of 'fuck off' from the audience. Spying a film crew Bonham shouted, 'Who wants to see a TV camera get smashed?' He was ushered away. Later that night he was attempting to chat up a punk girl by bragging about his fame and fortune. She replied, 'I don't care who you are. Get your bleeding hands off me.' Times were a-changing.

In 1979 came the release of Zeppelin's final studio album followed by a low-key European tour. At one show in Germany Bonham collapsed and was rushed to hospital; it was claimed from overeating, but more likely it was his drinking and drug taking. Still, the decision was made to take the band on the road again in the States. One morning Bonham was picked up from his hotel for rehearsals at Bray film studios. He stopped for breakfast at a local pub; unfortunately his idea of breakfast was sixteen measures of vodka and a ham sandwich. The bingeing continued throughout rehearsals and deep into the night after the band retired to Page's country house. Around midnight Bonham passed out and was taken upstairs to bed. It was a roadie who found him dead the next morning. In the night he'd rolled over in his sleep and in a manner that seems especially popular amongst rock stars, choked on his own vomit. He was thirty-two.

Zeppelin's years of wild antics and hedonism had finally caught up with Bonham; it was a hefty price to pay. Out of respect to their fallen comrade, and because they'd been such a close-knit band, four equal members on stage, it was decided to call it quits. Apart from the odd resurgence, Zeppelin would never reform. How could they? Bonham was irreplaceable.

JUNIUS BOOTH (1796–1852: Actor)

It was hard to tell sometimes with Junius Booth whether he was just plain insane or merely out of his box on booze, so famed was he for his eccentric nature. One evening, while playing the title role in *Othello*, Booth prolonged his death scene for an absurdly long time, then had the audacity to jump back to 'life' and ask the audience, 'Well, how did you like that!?'

One night in Philadelphia, the theatre owner surmised Junius was more plastered than the scenery and requested that he 'finish the play as quickly as possible'. Booth walked to the front of the stage: 'Ladies and gentlemen, I have been directed by the manager to finish this as soon as possible, and so I'll finish it at once.' With that he threw himself on the floor and lay spread-eagled, gurgling in the death throes of his character's final scene. The curtain fell amid roars of laughter.

Booth was born in St Pancras, London, and dropped out of school at an early age, disappointing his father who'd hoped the lad might take up a position in his own profession, law. After leaving home Booth joined a troupe of travelling players, performing in tents pitched in village squares, then in professional theatres where his reputation as an actor of power quickly spread. 'He had the look of an uncaged tiger,' said fellow thesp

Joseph Jefferson, and when his belly was overflowing with liquor actors feared to play opposite him. Take, for example, the occasion he appeared as Richard III; pity the poor lad playing Richmond, for during combat on Bosworth Field Junius was apt in his excitement to believe himself in reality the king fighting for his life. During one of these 'lapses' Booth's face was disfigured by an imperilled actor who in self-defence delivered a blow that broke the bridge of his nose.

Booth's descent into alcohol as a young actor had much to do with the constant travelling from town to town, and missing his young wife. Also, leaving the stage and the high of a performance, he'd no one to relax with afterwards, so turned increasingly to the bottle for companionship. Sometimes he'd wander a fair distance from his lodgings in search of drink, and would fail to turn up the next day for rehearsal, or even miss performances altogether and be located several hours later roaming nearby woods in full costume. For one performance he put the last touches to his make-up, then staggered from his dressing room at curtain time to enquire, 'Where's the stage? And what's the play?' When he was broke and desperate for booze, he'd go into a pawn-broker's shop and literally pawn himself for money. On more than one occasion he was exhibited with a ticket stamped on him in the shop window, where he stood until he was redeemed by a friend or charitable actor.

On the London stage Booth was seen as the arch rival to Edmund Kean, then the foremost tragedian in Britain. Blistering were the occasions when they appeared on the same bill, with scuffles and rows erupting in the auditorium between rival sets of fans.

In 1821 Booth inexplicably deserted his wife and newly born son and went to live in the United States, setting up home in Maryland with a much younger woman who bore him ten children. For the next thirty years he embarked upon a distinguished, if erratic, acting career that saw him acclaimed as one of the leading Shakespearean actors on the American stage. Left to his own devices, in other words allowed to drink to excess, Junius wrought havoc. Performing Hamlet oiled one night he abandoned Ophelia and climbed a ladder, where he sat howling until he was coaxed back down again. Sometimes stage managers took the precaution of locking Booth up ahead of time to keep him sober for his performances.

Sometimes such behaviour could stray from the prankish to the darkly insane. In Boston, Booth began to shout, 'Take me to the lunatic asylum!' Hauled off, he was replaced by his understudy. Tearing off his costume Booth left the theatre and began to walk to the company's next venue, in Rhode Island some fifty miles away. He was spotted the next day striding along the side of a road in his stocking feet, naked save for his underwear, reciting poetry in an abrasively loud voice. Most alarming of all was the time his wife discovered him in the act of hanging himself. She cut him down in the nick of time.

Booth could get away with such madness on stage because his name continued to draw crowds, but it was decided that one of his sons, Edwin Booth, a budding actor, accompany his father on the road, babysitting the tempestuous genius, steering him away from trouble and the bottle. Often in his dressing room after a show Booth would attempt to swat Edwin away like an annoying fly, but the young man stood his ground. In Louisville, Kentucky Junius, desperate to find a drink, made a bolt for the door and high-tailed it out of the theatre, with Edwin in hot pursuit. There followed a race through the midnight streets of the city, one that only ended at the first signs of dawn when an exhausted Junius called a halt to their test of wills.

Given the amount of liquor Booth poured down his throat, it's ironic that it was a glass of water that finally killed him. Following a professional engagement in New Orleans Junius caught a steamboat down the Mississippi. Desperately thirsty, he ignored warnings and drank several glasses of polluted river water. With no physician on board or any medical supplies he succumbed to a high fever and delirium, dying after five wretched days.

Besides Edwin, other Booth children followed in their famous father's footsteps to become actors. John Wilkes Booth was one of them, but none of his theatrical achievements are remembered today; history has but one role for him, as the assassin of Abraham Lincoln.

LOUISE BROOKS (1906–1985: Actress)

An unrepentant hedonist, a pure pleasure seeker, Louise Brooks was the ultimate Jazz age flapper. Nicknamed 'hellcat' by her social set – and for good reason, she was once kicked out of a New York hotel for promiscuity – Louise was a woman born years ahead of her time in relation to her attitudes about sexual liberation and rebellious bent towards Hollywood. She pissed off studio heads and her directors with reckless abandon. 'I have a gift for enraging people,' she once said. 'But if I ever bore you, it'll be with a knife.'

A star in her twenties, incredibly Louise would be forgotten by the movie-going public for a quarter of a century while she destroyed her amazing beauty by becoming a gin soaked middle-aged woman living on the verge of destitution in a one-room apartment in New York before undergoing a remarkable redemption.

She was born in Cherryvale, Kansas, to loving parents who tragically could not save their daughter at the age of nine falling prey to a neighbour who carried out heinous acts of sexual abuse on her. The incident would have a profound effect on Louise's life, and screwed her up sexually without question; she'd later confess to sleeping with hundreds of men. On a film set an actor called her 'a cheap, drunken tramp', and poor Louise had to admit, 'He was right.' She did get married on two occasions, both failures that never bore children; Louise referred to herself as 'Barren Brooks' and once claimed she was incapable of real love.

At the age of fifteen Louise moved to New York dreaming of a career as a dancer and joined a professional troupe run by dance legend Ruth St Denis. Let loose in the big city, Louise drank and cavorted in clubs and speakeasies, careless behaviour that set her on a lifelong course of self-destruction and led to numerous showdowns with the puritanical St Denis, who desired that her dancers be pure and idealistic; cigarettes, drink and most especially sex were right out. When Louise's errant ways would not be tolerated any further she was sacked in front of the entire company.

Louise did not stay humiliated for long, landing a featured part in the famous Ziegfeld Follies on Broadway where she was talent spotted by Paramount Studios. It was Louise's extraordinary photogenic quality and naturalist approach to acting, vividly in contrast to the overly melo-dramatic style then prevalent in silent cinema, that made people talk about her in terms of being the next Garbo. Louise couldn't have cared less; she detested Hollywood, the rigid studio work schedules got in the way of drinking and sex. Very early on Louise forged a dangerous reputation as a rebel: she flouted the rules, swore like a sailor, sunk gin by the pint and slept around like an alley cat. Sexually liberated, she wasn't afraid to experiment, even posing nude for 'art' photography. She was not entirely 'loose,' exercising her own quaint moral code, refusing on principle to casting-couch approaches by studio heads but happy to fool around with a crew hand to relieve the boredom of hanging round on set.

After a string of pictures Louise stunned Hollywood by upping and leaving after a promised pay rise was not forthcoming. She travelled to Berlin to work for the great director G W Pabst, and wolfed up the deca-dence on offer, drinking and dancing all night in the Weimar cabarets, coming on the set next day bleary-eyed. Pabst was infuriated but knew he'd cast the right actress as his Lulu, the screen's ultimate femme fatale in *Pandora's Box* (1929), the film that would immortalise Brooks.

Next she went to Paris to make *Prix de Beauté* (1930), where her brazen drunkenness reached new heights. She'd start drinking cognac and cham-pagne early in the morning and didn't finish until late in the evening, then start again the next day. It was a constant booze cycle. Arriving at the studio she'd sit in a chair and fall asleep while they administered her make-up. When it came time to take Louise to the set they'd have to carry her bodily because she was so zonked out, necessitating some quite violent prodding to wake her up in order to shoot. On the last day she disappeared completely and the director sent the police on a desperate search to find her, which they did eventually at a friend's house where she was drunk, as usual. Louise certainly knew on what side her toast was buttered: during the whole of the production she was sleeping with her hotel bartender. Given the excessive drinking, everyone was amazed just how well she still looked on screen, even after suffering the most horrendous hangovers and her unorthodox method of sobering up – three shots of gin straight down.

In spite of her recklessness, Louise was begged to stay and make her career in Europe but she was homesick and returned to America and a frosty reception; Hollywood had still not forgiven her for walking out and she was essentially blacklisted, cast in small roles in inconsequential B pictures. After several years of this humiliation she quit altogether, later confiding to a friend that she'd been kicked out of Hollywood because 'I like to fuck and drink too much'.

Setting up home in New York, Louise slowly slipped into alcoholism and obscurity. Gin was her obsession; it was all she ever drank, so much so that the few visitors who came to see her could smell the boozy odour in the long corridor leading to her apartment door. And woe betide anyone who got in the way of it. One night when a concerned friend poured her bottle of gin down the sink, Louise almost killed him. She was a true alcoholic. One of her lovers recalled waking up next to her one morning and she was staring into his face with a furious, almost demented look. 'I finally figured out it was from her being an alcoholic – that thing of waking up without knowing right away who the person was who you were in bed with.'

Louise existed by working crummy jobs, a far cry from her glamour days as a Hollywood starlet, including as a sales girl in a store and even, according to some stories, resorting to prostitution when in dire financial need. These were desperate years when she grew utterly tired of living and would sometimes end telephone conversations to friends with the order, 'Bring a gun.' She did find time to write her autobiography but after reading it burned every page.

A financial lifeline was provided by one of her old lovers, William Paley, founder of CBS, a monthly allowance that continued until her death. This gave her a modicum of security, but she remained firmly rooted in her own private little world, hardly leaving her one-room apartment, where she spent most of the day in bed, her hour-glass figure now bloated, her once radiant beauty faded like a photograph left out in the sun too long. When she did leave it was usually to her favourite watering hole, Jimmy Glennon's saloon on Third Avenue, a place Bogart and Robert Benchley drank. She'd come in alone and sit at the end of the bar by herself and engage in conversation with precisely no one.

Then a miracle happened. In the mid-fifties her films were suddenly rediscovered and critics acclaimed her as a film icon, much to her amusement. Her presence was requested at film festivals around the world. But the old Louise hadn't gone away. In Copenhagen, a friend took her to eat in one of the city's grandest restaurants and as a treat ordered lobster thermidor. When it arrived Louise took one look at it and threw the whole concoction on the floor. The mess was cleaned up by a waiter who then returned with what Louise had wanted in the first place, a bottle of gin. Another time she was being driven back to New York and getting ever more drunk with secret nips from a bottle hidden in her coat. Suddenly without warning as the car was speeding along a highway she opened the door and tried to climb out. Miraculously the driver was able to pull her back in before she hit the tarmac.

A rediscovered celebrity, Louise was flooded with visitors. One journalist was told to take half a pint of gin with him when he called by and during the interview Louise sat with the drink and a glass of milk on the side, growing ever more inebriated as she spun tales about the golden era of Hollywood. When she sat for artist Don Bachardy, he described his subject as 'a dipsomaniac for sure, probably a nymphomaniac, and certainly a destructomaniac, she is driven to excess and helpless to resist'. Indeed, even as an old woman Louise hadn't lost any of her ability to shock or play around with her sexuality, boasting to critic and admirer Kenneth Tynan that she could still ejaculate clear across a room.

In her final years Louise moved to a quaint suburb in Rochester in upstate New York and became an accomplished and insightful film journalist. She also corresponded regularly with fans and film historians, but as ill health crept up on her even this simple pleasure was denied her due to arthritic hands. Finally unable to breathe properly due to emphysema, Louise succumbed to heart-failure and died, one of the few links to the flickering early days of Hollywood lost for ever.

GEORGE BROWN (1914–1985: Politician)

There is a story concerning George Brown, when he was Foreign Secretary, that may very well be apocryphal, but somehow typifies a man who staggered about the Labour Party for much of his career sloshed, to the extent that when he finally resigned there was an audible sigh of relief from cabinet colleagues. The story sees our hero arrive late, and well plastered, at a state gala in South America. As the orchestra starts playing Brown espies a beautiful robed figure in the distance and makes his approach: 'Beautiful lady in scarlet,' he begins, 'will you do me the honour of dancing with me?' 'Certainly not!' is the reply. 'Why not?' asks an offended Brown. 'For three reasons: Firstly, you are drunk. Secondly, the band is playing the National Anthem. And thirdly, I am the Bishop of Montevideo.'

Brown was born in a working-class housing estate in Lambeth, the son of die-hard socialists. It's said Brown delivered campaign leaflets for the Labour Party in the 1922 general election when he was eight years old; that's borderline child abuse, isn't it?

It was his strong association with the trade union movement that made Brown such ideal Labour material, that and his resentment of the privileged classes, and he won a role in the 1945 government, steadily rising in ministerial prominence until the Tories regained power in 1951. Brown remained in politics, becoming part of the shadow cabinet, but fostered a reputation for being rude to those who did not see eye to eye with him, famously indulging in a slanging match with Nikita Khrushchev during a private dinner at the Houses of Parliament, where the Russian leader was guest of the Labour Party.

What was supposed to be a nice cordial evening hit the buffers when a tanked-up Khrushchev got to his feet and launched into not so much a speech as a tirade, accusing Britain of making Hitler turn his sights on Russia during the war and saying that it was the Soviet Union who virtually won the bloody thing single-handed. Having stomached just about more than he could stand Brown muttered, 'God forgive you!' Khrushchev stopped abruptly. 'What did you say?' There was a bowel-loosening pause as Labour delegates panicked that Khrushchev might have brought the red button with him. Instead he roared in Brown's general direction: 'Don't be afraid. Say it again!' So Brown did, resulting in massive verbals between the two men.

The dinner was a disaster and the Soviet premier remained in a rage for days after, saying that if this was British socialism, he preferred to be a Tory. When they met again the next day Brown offered his hand, but Khrushchev curtly said 'Nyet' and walked away.

It was incidents such as this, plainly exacerbated by his excessive drinking, that lost Brown the Labour leadership contest with Harold Wilson, an election that MP Anthony Crosland called, 'a choice between a crook and a drunk'. Brown bitterly resented his defeat and relations thereafter between the two men, though never barbarous, rarely rose beyond what might be called a civilised level. The problem was respect; Brown didn't have an awful lot of it for Wilson, while the PM considered Brown a pain in the arse and his uncontrolled behaviour an embarrassment.

For years the public were none the wiser about Brown's snifters until a fateful appearance on television paying tribute to John F Kennedy on the day of his assassination. Rushed into the studio from a reception party, Brown had several dozen cocktails and Martinis swilling round him and in the hospitality room viciously rounded on fellow guest Eli Wallach for refusing to indulge in idle small talk with him. 'Why are actors so conceited?' he exclaimed. Much put out by this unwarranted abuse, Wallach went for the politician and was only just prevented from giving him a good pummelling by Associated Rediffusion's assistant controller of programming. 'I'll knock the shit out of you,' yelled Wallach as he was sternly led away.

Things didn't improve once Brown went on air and millions of viewers saw him slur his tribute. Other inadequate performances on television elevated Brown to national joke status. People would actually write to scold him for his excesses, while others came to accept him as a 'character'.

When Labour won the 1964 general election, Wilson gave Brown the new post of Secretary of State for Economic Affairs. Re-elected in 1966, Brown was reshuffled to become Foreign Secretary, an appointment that elicited amazement and concern in equal measure around the world.

Drink was becoming an increasingly important factor in his life; in fact he was a borderline alcoholic, a condition exacerbated by the pressure of top-ranking jobs. At work he wasn't immune to pouring generous slugs of whisky into his tea or coffee. Colleagues took to having the odd quiet word in his ear to ask him to rein back a bit; even his wife pleaded with his colleagues 'to keep an eye on him'.

Brown continued to drink, especially at lunchtime, and heavily, too. Denis Healey, then Defence Secretary, always met for an hour every week with Brown, but made sure such meetings were before noon otherwise there was the risk that the Foreign Secretary would be blotto. 'He was one of these people who would get drunk on the smell of the cork,' recalled cabinet colleague Barbara Castle. 'It wasn't that he drunk a lot, he just couldn't take drink.' He also suffered appalling hangovers which knocked him out for the rest of the following day.

Brown's younger brother Ron, a fellow Labour MP at the time, revealed that the family had a metabolic problem with processing alcohol, the reason he never drank himself. Good old George did not heed the family curse. Some say he needed to drink in order to boost his confidence to tell stuffy people where to get off.

One evening, no doubt walking home from the pub, Brown collapsed and fell into a gutter, helped to his feet by of all people a newspaper reporter. *The Times* the next day printed the opinion: 'George Brown drunk is a better man than the Prime Minister sober.'

Brown's alcoholism was now being openly lampooned, the main culprit being the satirical magazine *Private Eye* whose writers dreamed up the euphemism 'tired and emotional' to describe what seemed to be his regular condition. The phrase has since entered into common usage as a chiefly British term for being, well, pissed.

Brown indulged, too, in champagne socialism, trying to gatecrash the royal box at Ascot, that kind of thing. One year he went to the FA Cup Final, completely forgetting that he was supposed to be addressing a Labour Party rally in Wales that afternoon. His hosts weren't best pleased when they saw his cheery mug live on TV from Wembley stadium.

He also developed a fetish for either threatening to resign over policy difficulties or plain walking out of the government; this happened quite often, usually when he'd had one too many.

When the pound took a hammering early in 1968 following devaluation, Wilson convened an emergency meeting but couldn't locate Brown, his office staff reporting his condition as only 'so-so' when last seen. Incensed that the meeting took place without him, Brown stormed into 10 Downing Street, three sheets to the wind, and hurled incoherent abuse at Wilson, who, not standing for it, hurled a few home truths back. Brown stormed out and within twenty-four hours had left the cabinet, to much wiping of brows; 'because we knew that the whole government was in danger as long as George was on the loose', confessed Barbara Castle. 'You never knew when this explosive mixture was going to ignite.'

Out of politics, Brown couldn't keep out of the headlines. Once boasting that 'many Members of Parliament drink and womanise – now, I've never womanised', the old goat did just that in 1982 when he walked out on his wife of forty-five years to set up home with his distressingly young secretary. Three years later he was dead, not from nocturnal exhaustion but, rather predictably, cirrhosis of the liver.

CHARLES BUKOWSKI (1920–1994: Writer/Poet)

Few people's lives revolved quite so much around alcohol and drinking than Charles Bukowski's. Even his books and poems are saturated in it, exploring the life of a barfly, the lonely existence of an alcoholic. Not for nothing was he dubbed 'the poet laureate of skid row'. He saw drinking as a way of wrenching oneself out of the conservative box of sane living, a form of suicide where the drinker is reborn to begin all over again the next day. 'I guess I've lived about ten or fifteen thousand lives now.'

Born in Germany in 1920, the son of a GI and a Fräulein, Bukowski was just a kid when the family immigrated to the United States. Settling in Los Angeles, young Charlie suffered at the hands of his tyrannical father who continually whipped him with a razor strap for the slightest reasons, often invented. As he was later to say, without a hint of overstatement, 'I guess a twisted childhood has fucked me up.'

Adolescence was no better, an invasion of boils 'the size of apples' made him painfully shy around girls, so he hid his pain and awkward loneliness in cheap booze.

Aged sixteen he came home skinned one night and vomited on the living-room carpet, only to be grabbed by his father and like a dog made to rub his nose in it. Years of pent-up anger finally burst out and he decked the bastard. It was the end of his torment, the last time his father ever raised a hand to him.

Studying journalism at college, Bukowski left home in 1941 after his father finally read some of his stories and, not impressed, threw his son's possessions into the street. He bummed around, working menial jobs: dishwasher, labourer in a dog-biscuit factory and parking-lot attendant, jobs that gave him just enough money to rent a room, drink and write. After a dustbin-full of rejection slips he managed to get a story published, but instead of being spurred on Bukowski abandoned his writing ambitions for nearly a decade and hit the road, drinking, whoring, living in flophouses, lying arseholed in alleyways and spending nights in jail. 'I don't like jail,' he once said. 'They've got the wrong kind of bars in there.'

In 1955, at the age of thirty-five, Bukowski was rushed to hospital dying, ten years of cheap wine and hard living was haemorrhaging out of his mouth, fountains of blood coming out of his arsehole too. A priest was summoned to administer the last rites; 'Please go away and let me die,' he screamed. Thirteen pints of blood were pumped back into him and somehow he came out the other end still alive, but with a warning that if he touched alcohol again he'd be dead for sure. Bukowski walked out of casualty to the nearest bar and ordered a beer.

It had been a wake-up call, for sure, and, buying an old typewriter, Bukowski started to write again, this time the poetry that would make him a cult figure: poems of gritty realism, about low-life people struggling to survive in poverty and drunkenness, with striking titles like 'The Night I Fucked My Alarm Clock', 'I Have Shit Stains in My Underwear Too', and 'The History of a Tough Motherfucker'. John Betjeman, he wasn't.

Living in crummy apartments in LA, Bukowski produced more than forty-five books of poetry and prose, happily existing on the outer edge of American literature. He always refused to go on talk shows to plug his books, breaking his rule just once, appearing on live French TV in such a fried condition that the host ordered his eviction. The next day Bukowski naturally didn't remember a damn thing, but hordes of French students were clamouring to buy his books.

Bukowski drank when he wrote, always, drank when he recited his poetry, too. 'I do all of my creative work while I'm intoxicated.' The drink also served another purpose: it was a release, allowing this essentially shy, withdrawn man to be larger than life, to live up to the drinking, brawling legend he'd become, though one critic called Bukowski a one-man argument for the return of prohibition. He'd also get drunker than usual when faced with a social situation that he felt uncomfortable in. Take the occasion sometime in the mid-eighties when Hollywood hell-raising stars clamoured to bask in his vomit-spattered sphere, and Sean Penn invited him to a family party. He arrived and sat down with a drink. Not for long. 'He decided he was going to prowl around the room and steal everybody else's drinks,' Penn recalled. 'This was always the mode whenever you did go out with him, if there was no more wine to drink, it was mix everything and die!' Penn's mother decided she wanted to dance with Bukowski and being Irish/Italian she liked to drink too. 'And now his pants are coming off,' continued Penn. 'He's trying to take my mother's clothes off, who was in her late sixties at this point, and everybody is sitting back and saying, this is what he's supposed to do. It was the first time that they'd actually seen a legend behave like his legend.'

That legend, when he felt arsed enough, would read his poetry or give talks on university campuses. Appearing at a morning English class still hung-over from an all-night party, he was asked by a girl, 'Who are your three favourite contemporary writers?' He replied, 'Charles Bukowski, Charles Bukowski and Charles Bukowski.' Getting increasingly fed up, he enquired if anyone had a beer. 'Won't you read us one of your poems?' another girl asked. 'And that's when I got up and walked out.' Unsteadily he made his way across the campus; suddenly, bracing himself against a tree, he began puking. 'Look at that old man,' a couple of passing students said, 'he's really fucked up.' At other college poetry readings he'd regularly exchange insults with his audience, an atmosphere of unrestrained violence always pervading. These recitals usually ended the same way, with an ovation and Bukowski urging his audience, 'Now let's all go out and get smashed.'

If he hadn't been a drunk, Bukowski always claimed he'd probably have committed suicide. Note the use of the word 'drunk'. Bukowski refused to admit he was an alcoholic since, on occasion, he could always go dry, for twenty-four hours at least. He smoked like a chimney, too, preferring nasty-looking Bidi cigarettes, made in India and, 'rolled by lepers'. He smoked them so often his hands turned yellow. 'Oh, shit,' he'd say. 'What do my lungs look like? Oh Jesus!'

Just as important as booze and cigarettes were women. Bukowski claimed to have lost his virginity at the age of twenty-three to a woman he described as, 'A 300-pound whore.' Throughout his adult life Bukowski indulged in seedy one-night stands, had sex with low-life prostitutes who indulged in ripping flesh off his face with their fingernails when he was too crocked to fight back. His numerous affairs were tempestuous at best, full of drunken rows, evictions and fights. All this without being the most attractive man in the world; to put it mildly, he had the face of an Old Testament prophet who'd gone ten rounds with Mike Tyson.

In the early seventies Bukowski had an affair with poet Linda King, who recalled that he was a mass of rampaging conflicts. 'The first month I was with him the unknown enemy was coming out of the walls. He had a knife taped behind the door. He jumped up five times a night facing murderers. He couldn't sleep.'

In the mid-eighties Bukowski finally seemed to calm down after marrying a woman twenty-five years his junior, and ended his days in blissful comfort, in a house with a swimming pool and a BMW in the driveway, a long way from the skid row of his prose. As the *American Book Review* commented in 1986, 'Those who despised him as a drunken bum now despise him as a drunken rich bum.'

After a year-long bout with leukaemia Bukowski died aged seventy-four. Not a bad innings, given that doctors had warned him in his twenties to give up drinking or he'd die. His gravestone reads: 'Don't try.' But I prefer this as an epitaph from the man himself: 'Some people never go crazy, what truly horrible lives they must lead.'

RICHARD BURTON (1925–1984: Actor)

Few men have adored drinking more than Richard Burton. He loved the sheer sociability of booze, drinking in pubs, sharing stories with mates; he was a man who enjoyed life better with a drink in his hand. Even when he was working booze was never very far away. Shooting *The Spy Who Came in from the Cold* (1966), one scene required Burton to down a whisky. Given flat ginger ale, the movie's usual substitute for Scotch, Burton waved it away: he wanted the real thing. This simple shot took forty-seven takes. 'Imagine it, luv,' Burton bragged to a journalist later, 'forty-seven whiskies.'

Happily embracing that seemingly inbred Celtic desire to walk as dangerously close to the precipice as desirable, Burton scandalised the British stage and did it all over again in Hollywood. Many say he wasted his God-given talents – he could apparently recite every single one of Shakespeare's sonnets, all 151 of them – that he sold his soul for movie stardom. With Burton mere wealth wasn't enough, it had to be opulence; fame wasn't sufficient, it had to be notoriety. As he once confessed: 'I rather like my reputation, that of a spoiled genius from the Welsh gutter, a drunk, a womaniser.'

He was born into poverty in the small Welsh coal-mining village of Pontrhydyfen. In reaction perhaps to the crummy hand fate had dealt him Burton got into trouble early on, fighting other kids and smoking Woodbines at the age of eight. By his teens he was a rugby playing big bastard who'd developed a fearsome taste for beer, often reeking of the stuff when he returned to school after lunch. Undisciplined and rebellious, he wasn't above striking out at teachers and there's a story of him pissing out of a carriage window as the train roared by a station platform filled with commuters.

Academically he was borderline genius and in 1944 won a place at

Oxford University. Everyone drank amongst the student fraternity so Burton fitted right in and out-drank the lot of them. He could down two pints of college beer in ten seconds, a record that's never been beaten. 'I had never met anyone like him before or since,' recalled fellow student and actor Robert Hardy. 'Put half a dozen hellraisers in a room with him and he would be their chief in ten minutes.'

Appearing in several Oxford stage productions, Burton was talent spotted and soon making his West End and Stratford debuts, hailed by the press as the heir to Olivier's crown. Certainly he had no equal when it came to carousing. Challenged to a drinking bout by a fifteen-strong rugby team, all Welsh miners, Burton downed nineteen boilermakers. Alas, the next day he was in no fit state to remember who won the contest. During rehearsals for *Henry V* at Stratford, dressed in full armour, Burton whiled away the hours drinking eighteen bottles of pale ale. As the battle of Shrewsbury approached he was overwhelmed by a desire to urinate, but the director refused him permission to leave the stage. 'Right,' said Burton. 'Watch this.' An incredulous cast stood gawking as Burton relieved himself and eighteen bottles' worth of pale ale seeped through his costume and collected in a large puddle on the floor.

Whisked off to Hollywood, Burton made a slew of rubbish movies but did become a film star. In between copious amounts of shagging, 'knocking off everything in sight', he also earned a reputation as something of a madman, riding a horse into a restaurant and physically destroying a whole set because he couldn't remember his lines. But it was his scurrilous public adultery with Elizabeth Taylor on *Cleopatra* (1963) that enhanced his mythic status. 'I have achieved a sort of diabolical fame,' Burton said.

Battered by the public spotlight over the affair, Burton proceeded to give his body a good battering too. Drinking Bloody Marys at 10.30 in the morning, he'd be on to his second bottle of vodka by the afternoon. Throughout his thirties and early forties Burton pushed his body almost to breaking point, but his powers of recovery seemed unimpaired. He always considered his acting talent a gift, so too his ability to withstand alcoholic punishment and the endless boozing. Burton once revealed that up until the age of forty-five he never had a single hangover. After that his hangovers were sometimes so severe that he couldn't even get out of bed.

Certainly he never allowed his boozing to interfere with his work. Appearing on Broadway in *Camelot*, Burton would arrive some nights completely off his face, the director convinced his star was incapable of going on, but once on that stage something mystical happened and Burton always delivered the goods. Shooting *Night of the Iguana* (1964) in Mexico Burton was drinking so heavily that crew members began joking that the recipe for a Richard Burton cocktail began: 'First, take twenty-one tequilas'. This derived from the day he drank twenty-one straight tequilas and then dived fully clothed into the sea after a friend swore he'd spotted a shark.

The Burton and Taylor media circus, for that is what it was, more circus than marriage, lasted the whole of the sixties and into the seventies. It was a rough ride for all concerned. They were gloriously mismatched. He was a rough Welsh working-class hero, she a Hollywood starlet, pampered since childhood. It was the ultimate example of opposites attracting and the textbook case of can't live with her, can't live without her. There were endless rows, many turning violent with blows being mutually exchanged. In truth, Elizabeth could be every bit as uncontrollable as Burton. Many friends attest to the fact that she was the heavier drinker. Burton enjoyed boasting that he could drink any man under the table, but not necessarily Elizabeth, who scarcely showed any ill effects from her boozing. 'I had a hollow leg,' Liz said once about those days. 'My capacity was terrifying.'

By the time they came to make the American TV movies *Divorce His* and *Divorce Hers* in 1973, the wheels were off completely. Burton was known for bedding his nubile co-stars, and when he escorted a young actress back to his dressing room one afternoon Elizabeth was waiting for him. Jumping out from behind the sofa, she chased Burton around the room with a broken bottle. In Hollywood they quarrelled outside a restaurant and Elizabeth spent the night away from the marital bed. The next day she turned up at the Beverly Hills Hotel, walked up to Burton in the bar and punched him in the face. Their eventual split made world headlines, temporarily knocking Nixon and Watergate off the front pages.

To cope with the collapse of his marriage Burton dived into the nearest bottle and took whatever movie was going. On the set of *The Klansman* (1974) he was drinking like a man possessed, three bottles of vodka a day. Doctors informed the actor that he only had three weeks left to live if he carried on the way he was. 'I'm amused you think I can be killed off that easily,' Burton answered back. But director Terence Young was seriously concerned that Burton might not be able to finish the picture. He was getting progressively more ill and having to force his whole body just to speak a line of dialogue. His complexion was white, sometimes blue, and then yellow. When Young shot Burton's death scene in the film he complimented the make-up man, 'You've done a great job.' The make up guy replied, 'I haven't touched him.'

Young quickly finished the scene and organised Burton to be raced to hospital, where he received an emergency blood transfusion. He was on the edge for about a week but pulled through. By getting him to hospital so fast Young was convinced he'd saved Burton's life. He stayed in hospital for six weeks as doctors fought to repair his battered system and wean him off alcohol. During the drying-out process Burton had to be fed through a tube, he was shaking so much. Eventually he recovered, even getting back into some semblance of shape, but he would never be quite the same man again, spending the remainder of his life in various states of pain. Suffering from severe back trauma he underwent a major operation; when the team of top surgeons opened Burton up they discovered that his entire spinal column was coated with crystallised alcohol, which had to be scraped off before they could rebuild the vertebrae in his neck.

After further marriages, including a short-lived encore with Elizabeth Taylor, Burton settled down for the last time with film production secretary Sally Hay. 'I think it was the only one of my weddings at which I have been sober,' Burton admitted. But at fifty-eight he looked old and frail, unable even to put on his jacket without assistance. One crew hand on his last movie, *Nineteen Eighty-four* (1984), remarked: 'He's like a wild beast whose spirit has gone.'

Not long after finishing the movie Burton was out boozing with co-star John Hurt. Returning home he complained to Sally of a headache and retired to bed early. In the morning Sally noticed he was breathing very heavily and that he couldn't be woken. Something was wrong. She called an ambulance and at the hospital it was discovered that Burton had suffered a cerebral haemorrhage. Despite emergency surgery he could not be saved. The great Burton was no more. A distressed Sally returned to the home she'd shared with Burton and noticed on a night-stand his personal notebook. The last jotting was a line from Shakespeare's *The Tempest*: 'Our revels now are ended.'

Not long before his death Burton was asked to look back over his life and sum it up if he could. 'Much of it has been a circus,' he admitted, 'Played out in full view of the public. And, to be honest, I've loved every terrible minute of it.'

C

CALAMITY JANE (1852–1903: Wild West Heroine)

She was many things in her life: an Indian guide, a gambler, a sharp-shooter; she could chew tobacco and drink even the toughest cowboy under the table. Her name was Martha Canary, but legend knows her better as Calamity Jane. She was a hellcat in leather britches, ranking amongst the lowest of harlots, without a trace of feminine refinement. As one historian put it, 'Her temper was so violent that when she went on a tantrum the population took to the woods.' It was also one of her boasts that she never went to bed sober or with a penny in her pocket.

Born in Princeton, Missouri, the oldest of six children, Calamity's early years are clouded in mystery, save that she loved adventure and by the age of thirteen could already cuss as fiercely as any man and had learned to like the taste of whisky. When her parents died she was thrown upon the world to make her own way and as a young woman quickly set herself apart from others of her sex by dressing in buckskins and smoking cigars. She could out-fight and out-drink most people; even hardened frontiersmen were terrified of her.

Having gained a reputation for daring horsemanship and skill with a rifle, Calamity worked as a scout during the military conflicts with the Indians. There's a tale – doubtless propagated by Calamity herself, few were better at spinning yarns than she, especially when cadging drinks in saloons – of when a small group of cavalry were ambushed by Apaches. Fighting desperately for their lives, the officer was hit by an arrow and fell off his horse. Into this mêlée rode Calamity who dismounted, lifted the captain onto her saddle, and dashed out again.

Years later, in another daring feat, she rescued a stagecoach when it was attacked by marauding Indians. The driver had been killed and none of the male passengers had the guts to take the reins. It was Calamity who mounted the driver's seat and, dodging arrows, got them all out to safety.

Her desperation to be accepted as the equal to the tough frontiersmen she worked with, drinking and playing hard with them, would prove Calamity's downfall as she slowly sank into alcoholism, going on binges that often resulted in her arrest for being drunk and disorderly. Her drinking became so renowned that in one saloon they renamed their whisky 'Calamity water'. She was a celebrity of a kind, swaggering into a bar and hailing, 'I'm Calamity Jane and this drink's on the house.' But the booze ultimately made her a homeless outcast, arriving in a new town, she'd go on the wagon for several weeks then hit the bottle with a vengeance, get fired from whatever menial job she was doing and have to move on. It wasn't unusual to see her begging or even resorting to prostitution to pay for board and booze. One shudders at the thought, she was hardly the most appetising sight, more Sid James in drag than Doris Day, who played her in the famous Hollywood musical. One commentator called her, 'About the roughest looking human being I ever saw.'

Bartenders came to tremble when Calamity walked into their saloons; she could drink whisky all day and all night and got violent and obnoxious with it. One householder found Calamity sleeping off one of her many hangovers in his wood shed and asked her to leave. 'I'm Calamity Jane,' she roared. 'Get the hell out of here and let me alone.' Such was her reputation that when she arrived in a town in Wyoming and registered in a hotel, the local newspaper wrote whimsically that, 'the management were polishing up their guns and imploring the marshal for protection'. The township of Cheyenne went one better, actually arresting Calamity on a trumped-up charge of theft just to get rid of her. The judge, however, saw through this ruse and let her off. Calamity walked out of the courthouse a free woman, promptly bought a bottle of whisky, stole a wagon and horses and galloped out of town. Such was her walloped state that Calamity passed right through her intended destination without noticing and ended up ninety miles away. During the journey she was set upon by Sioux Indians who fled in terror at her wild dishevelled appearance and use of profanities.

In 1876 Calamity settled in the small gold-boom town of Deadwood, falling in love with the equally legendary Wild Bill Hickok. She doted on him and was his occasional drinking partner in the town's many saloons, but her love was unrequited and then unachievable when a gunman put a bullet through his brain.

Deadwood took Calamity to their hearts following a smallpox epidemic during which she nursed several quarantined sufferers without concern for her own safety. Miraculously Calamity never succumbed, perhaps the alcohol stored in her system staved off any viral attack. As reward the locals organised a benefit to raise cash in order for Calamity to send her daughter (from a brief marriage to a Texan), to a convent school. Taking all the money she promptly walked into the nearest saloon and spent the lot on drinks for everyone and got roaring drunk.

After Hickock's death Calamity acted as a pony express rider carrying the US mail over rough and dangerous terrain, then spent a year prospecting for gold before heading east. Arriving in New York, she discovered that dime novelists had popularised her as a gun-toting heroine of the Wild West and she was invited to star in western extravaganzas, wowing audiences by shooting targets with a rifle from the back of a trotting horse.

This celebrity did not sit well with Calamity. In the city she was expected not to spit and chew tobacco and her drunkenness was frowned upon by snooty ladies in fancy hats. More than once she caused uproar by walking into a classy restaurant carrying a six-shooter and as dizzy as a goose.

After a few years of this Calamity wanted out and headed back to her beloved old west. She continued to drink and would howl like an animal until some punter volunteered to carry her home and put her to bed, a bottle of whisky by her side to keep her quiet for the night.

Yearning in the end to settle down, that blissful existence alluded poor Calamity, never able to fend off her raging alcoholism, she couldn't keep a steady job and so spiralled ever downward, always on the road, in between bouts in the poor house. Aboard a train passing through South Dakota, Calamity indulged in her last drinking binge. When she complained of feeling ill, the conductor carried her off and she rented a room at a nearby hotel. She died there alone the next morning. Her passing was ascribed to inflammation of the bowels and pneumonia. Amongst her pathetically scant possessions was a bundle of letters to her daughter that now would never be posted.

In accordance with her dying wish, Calamity was buried in Deadwood alongside the man who had spurned her love all those years before, Wild Bill Hickok.

GRAHAM CHAPMAN (1941–1989: Comedian/Writer and Python)

At his alcoholic peak Graham Chapman was consuming three pints of gin a day. He once told author Douglas Adams that, growing irritated at the slow service in his local pub, he'd taken to slapping his penis against the bar to attract the attention of staff.

A bit of an eccentric, then, who when presented with a showbiz award at some swish function crawled to the stage on all fours, clasped the prize between his teeth, squawked, then returned to his table. This was not normal behaviour, even for a comedian. On another occasion he was invited to speak at the Oxford Union and arrived dressed as a carrot, stood at the podium in utter silence for ten minutes, then left.

Chapman was born in Leicester into a solid middle-class family. He attended grammar school, performed in Gilbert and Sullivan amateur productions and was determined to go to Cambridge, ostensibly to learn medicine, but also to join the Footlights comedy troupe. At his audition he met fellow Footlights wannabe John Cleese, forming one of Britain's most significant comedy writing partnerships.

Chapman always blamed his medical training for his drinking, that's where it all started. As a trainee doctor at Bart's hospital, slogging his guts out all day, he'd retreat after-hours to the bar which conveniently stayed open until three o'clock every morning and drink copious amounts of alcohol, mainly because it subdued his natural shyness and made him more socially outgoing. 'People liked this new improved Chapman that wasn't quite so reticent, but I just went a bit too far over the next few years and it gradually took over.'

After graduation Chapman ditched a planned career in medicine to concentrate on showbiz, working with Cleese on comedy material for several well-known shows including *That Was the Week That Was*, before the advent of Monty Python. By now Chapman was struggling with the early stages of alcoholism. His fellow Pythons knew he drank a lot but initially didn't see it as a problem, indeed his alcohol intake merely added to his quirky personality. At BBC functions he'd pretend to be a dog and rub himself affectionately against the legs of executives and lick the feet of their wives. 'I think the alcoholism probably gave Graham the courage to behave as badly as he did,' said Terry Gilliam.

He was also notoriously unpunctual. Michael Palin would often pick Chapman up in the morning to drive him to the BBC studios where *Monty Python's Flying Circus* was recorded, park outside his house and toot the horn to let him know he was there. Invariably a male's head would pop out, 'He'll be down in a minute,' followed by another mysterious personage from a different window, 'Yes, he won't be long,' leaving Palin to imagine what on earth had been going on upstairs. Chapman would then arrive apologetically and get in, the vodka on his breath all too evident. Only later did Chapman admit that he couldn't start the day without a couple of shots.

It was only a matter of time before the dependency on drink began to affect his work; he'd hide glasses of gin or vodka behind the sets on the Python series and surreptitiously take a hit during camera set-ups. He began cocking up his lines during recordings; one complete sketch had to be abandoned and was never shown because he simply couldn't get the lines right. Cleese was particularly irritated. 'I remember feeling, what's the point of writing these sketches if he's going to fuck 'em up.'

Still no one confronted him about his boozing; either the Pythons still considered it nothing to worry about, or they simply refused to see what was plainly staring them in the face. Things finally reached a head when the group toured Britain in a live stage show in 1973. Suffering acute stage fright, Chapman drank more than usual and sometimes missed his cue to go on stage. After a week of this Cleese could take no more and gave his partner, in Palin's words, 'a real big bollocking' in front of the rest of the group. A BBC doctor also had a quiet word with him, but Chapman went ballistic. 'Nobody tells me what to do,' he hollered. 'I'm a doctor myself, I'll deal with it.'

The drinking continued, including revelries with famous boozer pals like Harry Nilsson and Ringo Starr. Another close friend was the Who's drummer Keith Moon. Staying in the top-floor suite of a London hotel, actually the only one which would allow him to stay at it, under the name Rupert Wild, Moon invited Chapman over. Alas, Moon was out of gin, Chapman's drink, so called down to room service to ask for some to be sent up. After fifteen minutes none had arrived and Chapman had been making do with beer, which wasn't really strong enough for his needs. Moon picked up the phone. 'Listen, if the gin doesn't arrive within the next ten minutes then your television set's going to arrive on the pavement.' Time dragged on and still no gin. A restless Keith got up and walked out of the window, onto a balcony Chapman presumed, except there was no balcony, just a ledge about four inches wide. There was no mess on the pavement and Chapman heard no blood curdling scream, so assumed Keith must have crawled along outside the building somehow. Anyway, he sat down and about ten minutes later Moon reappeared with a bottle of gin and plonked it down on the table, 'There you are Graham.' He'd gone next door and burgled their drinks cabinet.

On the first day of shooting *Monty Python and the Holy Grail* (1975), Chapman was a drunken sot, forgetting his lines and too smashed to make it across the Bridge of Death, over the Gorge of Eternal Peril, so the assistant cameraman had to double for him. He got the shakes, a bad case of DTs, but still managed to turn in a terrific performance as King Arthur. Warned that if he continued on the sauce he'd be dead within a year, having already suffered liver damage, Chapman decided to go cold turkey. It was desperate, he suffered sheer torment, hallucinations, seizures and after three days keeled over at home. But he was determined to face down his alcoholism and in the end beat it through sheer guts.

It was a fit and healthy Chapman who delivered a career best performance as the false messiah in the Python classic *Life of Brian* (1979), a performance that's all the more tragic since Chapman's fate was to be the most underachieving and overlooked Python member. There would be no *Fawlty Towers*, no *Ripping Yarns* or *Rutles* for Chapman. Instead he got involved with the Dangerous Sports Club, a group of adventurers and extreme sports pioneers. Chapman's inaugural stunt, a noble failure, was an attempt to hang-glide over a volcano in Ecuador. This was followed by a trip down a ski-run in a gondola that ended in predictable disaster when Chapman and his co-pilot suffered an unplanned exit midway down the route and ended up skidding on their arses pursued by their sturdy craft. Chapman said farewell to extreme pursuits by being catapulted into the air in Hyde Park with the same elastic that's used to launch fighter planes from aircraft carriers.

Chapman embraced his sexuality early on in his career, becoming a founder member of *Gay News* and an active campaigner for gay rights. He outed himself in the mid-seventies during a television interview, one of the first celebrities to do so. He loved to shock, to spring surprises, and embodied everything that was tasteless and just plain silly about Python. There was the time all of them were invited to Germany to write a TV show. Arriving at Munich airport, each was greeted with a huge stein of beer and whisked around Bavaria on a brief tourist trip. The last stop was Dachau. As the party pulled up at the gates, the camp was just closing. 'No you cannot come in,' said the guard. Graham couldn't resist it, 'Tell them we're Jewish.' They were admitted.

In November 1988 Chapman was diagnosed with throat cancer which swiftly spread to his neck and spine, symptom of a thirty-year smoking habit. He endured prolonged and painful treatment, but it proved incurable and he died, Cleese and Palin by his side.

At his memorial service Cleese offered this fine, well-meaning eulogy: 'Graham Chapman, co-author of the Parrot Sketch, is no more. I guess that we're all thinking how sad it is that a man of such talent, of such capability for kindness, should now so suddenly be spirited away at the age of only forty-eight, before he'd achieved many of the things of which he was capable, and before he'd had enough fun. Well, I feel that I should say: nonsense. Good riddance to him, the freeloading bastard, I hope he fries.'

WINSTON CHURCHILL (1874–1965: Statesman)

The phrase, 'cometh the hour, cometh the man' might have been coined for Winston Churchill, who saved our bacon in the war and kept Blighty afloat while the rest of Europe sank beneath the jackboot of Nazism. Glorious pisshead, as well. He believed it to be his inalienable right to smoke cigars and partake of alcohol before, after and during all meals, and the intervals between. Pol Roger champagne allocated a large amount of its stock for Churchill's personal consumption in gratitude for the liberation of France. After a lifetime of drinking Winston was able to survey a landscape of discarded whisky and wine bottles and conclude that he had 'taken more out of alcohol than alcohol has taken out of me'.

It's not difficult to see where Winston derived this love of liquor from. His famous father, Lord Randolph Churchill, was a keen boozer in his youth, tragically dying aged forty-five, reportedly from syphilis, while his American mother, so legend has it, invented the Manhattan cocktail.

Winston's favourite tipple was champagne, of which he imbibed a pint a day. 'I could not live without champagne,' he once declared. 'In victory I deserve it. In defeat I need it.' In 1929, when he was informed that Scotland Yard had learned of a plot to kill him, Churchill ordered some lackey to quickly fetch him a bottle. 'I had better go first and make plans against these plots,' said the servant. 'First things first,' said Winston. 'Get the champagne.'

He also had a hankering for whisky, a habit formed during his 1899 visit to South Africa. 'The water was not fit to drink, to make it palatable we had to add whisky. By diligent effort I learned to like it.' The twenty-five-year-old Churchill was then a war correspondent covering the Boer War. Sent out to the front line he took with him thirty-six bottles of wine, eighteen bottles of ten-year-old Scotch and six bottles of vintage brandy. On his triumphant return to England he entered the world of politics and was viewed by some as nothing but a cock-eyed embarrassment. Walking along the corridors at Westminster he was accosted by a disgruntled female MP. 'Mr Churchill, you are drunk.' Which elicited the now classic riposte, 'And you, madam, are ugly. But I shall be sober tomorrow.'

The drinking inevitably led to the occasional social gaffe. After a formal dinner at Buckingham Palace, Churchill was trying very hard to make the Prime Minister of Pakistan (a devout Muslim) take a whisky and soda. Flabbergasted when he refused, Churchill asked, 'Why not?'

'I'm a teetotaller, Mr Churchill.'

'What's that you say?'

'I'm a teetotaller!'

'A teetotaller? Christ! I mean God! I mean Allah!'

When the head of the Mormon Church paid a visit to Churchill's home at Chartwell, again poor old Winston was confused by his refusal of a beverage. 'Mr Churchill, the reason I do not drink is that alcohol combines the kick of the antelope with the bite of the viper.' Churchill is said to have looked forlornly heavenward and replied: 'All my life, I have been searching for a drink like that.'

Lady Astor was giving a costume ball and Winston asked what disguise she would recommend for him. 'Why don't you come sober, Mr Prime Minister?' These two seemed to have enjoyed, if that's the right word, a combustible relationship. Staying at Blenheim Palace one weekend, hurling brickbats at each other, Lady Astor said, 'Winston, if I were your wife I'd put poison in your coffee.' Quick as a flash Winston replied, 'If I were your husband I'd drink it.'

Churchill made frequent trips to America, a land and people he truly loved. During one visit in 1933 he was taken to a speakeasy. 'I went of course in my capacity as a social investigator.' During stays at the White House he'd pull all-nighters, accompanied by snifters of brandy and hefty cigars. President Roosevelt ruggedly engaged in the Brit's benders, or what his staff called, 'keeping Winston hours'. It was noted that afterwards Roosevelt slept for ten hours a night, three nights in a row to recuperate.

Actually in the early part of the Second World War Roosevelt and other prominent Americans did voice concerns about Churchill's drinking, but the British leader refused to moderate his intake, believing the citizens of Europe liked heads of state who could hold their liquor. If anything this regimen of regular alcohol may have been the fuel that kept him going, when other ministers flaked out. His usual day consisted of sleeping long into the morning, just so long as there were no meetings of the War Cabinet. Over lunch he'd partake of a bottle of champagne, followed by a brandy. After a siesta in the afternoon, he'd take command of vital meetings accompanied by iced whisky and soda. Dinner would follow with more champagne and brandy, fortification for discussing vital war planning sometimes until three in the morning.

It has been said that Winston used alcohol as a prop to his persona, rather like the cigars and pet bulldog, and that he rarely got monkey-arsed, or reached the falling-down, slurred-words state. Total inebriation was something he abhorred, which says much for what must have been a steel constitution. Certainly he was dependent on alcohol, but was Churchill an alcoholic? Professor Warren Kimball, author of a Churchill biography, maintains that he was not – 'No alcoholic could drink that much!' When Winston was knocked down by a car in New York in 1931 and taken to hospital, the attending doctor actually issued a medical note that Churchill's convalescence 'necessitates the use of alcoholic spirits, especially at mealtimes'. That leads to only one conclusion, that he must have had a genetic predisposition to booze. Once asked at a function if he wanted or needed a post-lunch liqueur Winston replied, 'I neither want it nor need it, but I should think it pretty hazardous to interfere with the ineradicable habit of a lifetime.'

After retiring from politics Churchill seemed to drink more than ever. 'There was always some alcohol in his blood,' wrote biographer William Manchester. 'And it reached its peak late in the evening after he had two or three Scotches, several glasses of champagne, at least two brandies, and a highball.' Quite an achievement. Lord Butler shared many a dinner with the aging Churchill, 'the dinners being followed by libations of brandy so ample that I felt it prudent on more than one occasion to tip the liquid into the side of my shoe'.

Finally at the age of seventy-six, Churchill succumbed to doctors' orders and tried to cut down on his intake. 'I have knocked off brandy,' he said. 'And take Cointreau instead.'

And when the end drew near Churchill declared that he was ready to meet his Maker. 'Whether my Maker is prepared for the great ordeal of meeting me is another matter.'

ERIC CLAPTON (b. 1945: Musician)

He was a drug addict, a serial womaniser, a smasher-up of cars and a Beatle-wife-snatcher, add to that chronic alcoholic and you have the perfect rock star. Eric Clapton was all that, and a little bit more, once confessing that his memory of the late sixties right through until the early eighties was, at best, 'severely hampered'. He once had an epileptic fit because he hadn't fed his body any alcohol for a day.

Once in Honolulu he saw a band mate score with a girl and take her back to his hotel room. Time for a jape, thought Clapton. Tucking a ceremonial samurai sword that was a present from Japan into his pyjamas, Clapton scaled the outside of the hotel, edging along ledges, climbing between balconies until he'd reached the thirtieth floor, whereupon he jumped into his mate's room and scared the hell out of them. By the time they saw the funny side of it there was a loud rap at the door. Clapton opened it and stood facing two cops with guns pointing at him. A guest had spotted Clapton's nocturnal mountaineering and believing him to be some kind of ninja assassin had called the police. It took quite a lot of persuasion to get rid of them.

Clapton was born in Ripley, in Derbyshire, his mother just a girl of fifteen when she got pregnant after an affair with a Canadian serviceman who shipped off back home to his wife at the close of hostilities. Clapton was raised by his grandparents, kept in the dark throughout his childhood about his real parentage. He was nine when he discovered the truth that his older sister was in reality his mother.

Clapton coped with all this emotional confusion by losing himself in music. He got his first guitar aged thirteen and struggled through hours of painful practice to play like the great blues guitarists he so revered.

Alcohol became a feature of his life pretty early on, too; getting blind drunk gave him the courage to approach girls and by the time he was an art student he was regularly sinking ten pints of stout at the pub.

Thrown out of art college, Clapton played with local bands, then rose to public consciousness with the Yardbirds, followed by the supergroup Cream, establishing himself as the people's guitarist, inspiring the scrawled graffito 'Clapton is God' on a subway wall in 1967. Such a reputation became a burden.

Like nearly everyone in the rock business Clapton took marijuana and cocaine. Then came a nasty predilection for heroin. Friends tried to rescue him from this twilight world and eventually he agreed to accept treatment and managed to kick the habit. Unfortunately Clapton merely swapped one addiction for another – hard liquor. Perversely, drinking felt much better; with heroin he never left his room, would stay zonked out in front of the TV, but at least alcohol came with the added bonus of a social life, it got you out of the house and into the pub with your mates.

For much of the early seventies Clapton coveted George Harrison's wife Pattie Boyd; he'd write 'Layla' and 'Wonderful Tonight' in homage to her. The ex-Beatle, not averse to playing around himself, was only too well aware of the infatuation and often invited Clapton to his home, Friar Park, a sprawling madhouse where he and Pattie lived in a surreal private world fuelled by alcohol and cocaine. Clapton arrived one evening, minced on brandy, and was no sooner through the door when he was handed a guitar and an amp by Harrison. For two hours, with scarcely a word spoken, they duelled. Clapton was declared the winner. Even pissed he couldn't be beaten.

He also seemed to have nine lives, blessed with an unerring knack of walking away from accidents with nary a scratch, like the time he returned home plotzed from Friar Park in his Ferrari, took a corner too fast, hit a fence and flipped the car over on its roof. He wasn't even bruised. In another Ferrari, and again consummately shitfaced, he hit a van head-on at something like 70 mph and had to be cut from the mangled wreckage by rescue services. Badly concussed and with no real clue where the hell he was for two weeks, by all logic he should have been dead.

In 1974 Pattie finally left Harrison for Clapton, flying with the guitarist to America where he was on tour, a gruelling twenty-six shows. Without the crutch of heroin, Clapton drank himself to oblivion and back again in order to cope. He'd start in the morning with his favourite tipple, Courvoisier and 7-up; by four an assistant would begin the task of sobering him up in time for that evening's show, replacing his Courvoisier with iced tea, Clapton being so whacked out by this stage he never noticed. It didn't always work; during one show Clapton was so far gone he played guitar flat on his back, singing into the microphone lying next to him. Other times he simply walked off stage, unable to continue, and a roadie would have to push him back out.

Clapton was now in the throes of total alcohol addiction; his regular nightcap was a pint of brandy. Conveniently there was a pub at the end of his country mansion's driveway and most lunch times he'd be in there, then drive back the 300 yards home, usually sliding into a ditch or making contact with a tree. Pattie believed he drank because at the time he didn't much care for who he was; drink and drugs changed him into someone he felt was more acceptable to other people and also allowed him to act the image of the rock star.

Not surprisingly his intake began to seriously affect his personality, sweet and charming one minute, hostile, dangerous, a loose cannon the next. On holiday in Spain Pattie and friends left a drunken Clapton alone in their rented villa. When he awoke and panicked that there was no one around he left to look for everyone – except he'd no clothes on! In Greece, Clapton got so Picassoed he fell off a boat in the harbour. The fact he couldn't swim a stroke combined with the alcohol resulted in him sinking like a stone. Pattie fished him out, probably saving his life.

Recovering alcoholic Anthony Hopkins bombarded Clapton with messages offering help and support; they were ignored. He was in complete denial. Thing was, Clapton never believed he was an alcoholic because in his frazzled brain he thought he was handling the situation and could quit any time. He was as much a prisoner of his own delusion as he was of drink. This was a man who as soon as he checked into a hotel room located the mini bar and drained it dry in thirty minutes.

Drink loosened Clapton's inhibitions to such a degree that his larks grew ever more outrageous and embarrassing. At a dinner party once he stood up and very loudly asked the wife of the host if she'd take a bath with him. 'There was always this mad man inside of me trying to get out,' he later said. 'And drink gave him permission.'

Flying into Tulsa, Oklahoma to play a gig, a whiffled Clapton became so abusive that the police were waiting for him at the airport and threw him in jail. 'Do you know who I am?' asked Clapton defiantly. When the police didn't believe him Clapton asked for a guitar to prove it. He did and was let out.

In 1980 Clapton complained about severe back pain during another US tour. Downing handfuls of painkillers washed down with brandy, he battled through the pain barrier until after a few nights it became so intolerable he was rushed to hospital. Doctors found he had five enormous ulcers, one very close to exploding into his pancreas. It was estimated that he was less than an hour away from death. The time had come to curb his drinking, if he could. Doctors advised that he needn't lay off completely, but maybe it wasn't a good idea to drink a bottle of brandy a day. So Clapton ditched brandy and took up whisky instead, not giving a damn about his health. Roadies grew so concerned they put a baby alarm in Clapton's hotel bedrooms and took turns to check he was still alive.

At his darkest moments Clapton contemplated suicide, but never carried it out simply because of the realisation that if he were dead he wouldn't be able to drink any more.

Instead he checked into rehab in 1982, emerging six weeks later hardly cured, indeed bitter and angry that the thing he really enjoyed doing most in life, drinking, was being denied him, so he dived back into alcoholism just as recklessly as before. In LA recording an album he'd drink and take cocaine all night, but try and stay sober at the studio. He thought he was keeping his drinking a secret from everyone until he saw that some of the crew had made up a fake license plate for his rental car: CAPTAIN SMIRNOFF.

Meanwhile his marriage was falling apart. 'There were times when Eric was more like an animal than the loving husband I'd known,' Pattie later recalled. She was genuinely terrified that in one of his black booze moods he might kill one of them. Finally she couldn't even tolerate sharing the same bed, a situation not helped when Clapton got one of his lovers pregnant. Then one morning he suffered a complete meltdown and burst into Pattie's room in a drunken rage, telling her to get out, that she wasn't a proper wife, and hurling all her belongings out of the window onto the drive. Divorce was the only conceivable route now.

Unrepentant, Clapton carried on drinking until on tour in Australia he got the shakes so badly it affected his playing. 'I'd reached the point where I couldn't live without a drink and I couldn't live with one.' He was a mess and went back into rehab, this time coming out the other side cured. As a result of his experiences Clapton founded his own alcohol and drug addiction treatment centre in Antigua, West Indies, so you can go cold turkey and top up your tan at the same time.

MONTGOMERY CLIFT (1920–1966: Actor)

Along with Marlon Brando and James Dean, the brooding and vulnerable Montgomery Clift was the kind of actor Hollywood had never seen before; he reflected the changing mood of fifties America, the loss of innocence of the post-Second World War generation. He had it all, astonishing beauty, talent and intelligence, and scaled the heights of achievement, but away from the camera lens Clift lived an isolated and tortured existence, a closeted gay man whose life ended in tragic decline as an alcoholic and drug addict, uninsurable, a liability, an actor no one would hire.

Clift was born into privilege in Omaha, Nebraska, the son of a stockbroker. Aged thirteen Monty discovered he had a gift for theatrics, but was pampered and spoiled by an overbearing mother who sought to control every aspect of his life, from the neighbourhood kids he played with to the girls he dated. By the age of seventeen Clift was an established star juvenile on the Broadway stage, loved by all who knew him as a zany individualist with a keen love of life, someone with seemingly no angst or neurosis, and someone who neither smoked nor drank.

Inevitably Hollywood began to sniff around the youngster and he made his film debut opposite John Wayne in *Red River* (1948). By the time *A Place in the Sun* was released in 1951 Monty was a genuine film star, chased in the streets by fans. Sadly, his life would never be the same again.

Away from the influence of his mother, Monty had begun to take gay lovers as well as indulging in numerous affairs with women. He'd known since childhood that his sexual preference was for men. Born a twin, his sister had arrived first, followed an hour later by Monty. In later life Clift pondered whether there'd been some mix-up in the womb, that in fact he should have been the girl and his sister should have been the boy. Of course, any hint of homosexuality would have killed his career instantly, so Monty kept his gay lovers a secret, secluded at home. It was a huge burden, essentially living a double life, and he suffered terribly from the guilt and took comfort first in drink and then drugs. 'He wanted to love women,' according to actress Deborah Kerr. 'But he was attracted to men, and he crucified himself for it.'

Friends began to notice a disturbing change in Monty, the carefree guy of a few years before was gone, replaced by a daredevil recklessness, a thirst to go as close to the edge of danger as possible. 'He'd try anything,' recalled close colleague Kevin McCarthy. 'I remember when we were staying in a hotel in Florence and Monty would get out onto the balcony and literally hang there, seven floors above the street, by his fingertips, dangling, and then pull himself up.'

He'd throw sudden tantrums in public, act up during film shoots. There are tales of him eating raw meat, sometimes right off the floor. 'When Monty drank he seemed to lose his identity,' said director Fred Zinnemann. 'He'd melt before your eyes.' Making *I Confess* (1953), at the end-of-picture party director Alfred Hitchcock, intrigued by Monty and aware of his problem, encouraged the actor to drink and watched, fascinated, as his suave and charming exterior cracked to reveal the raving neurotic drunk beneath. After Clift had consumed plenty of hard liquor Hitch poured him a large tumbler of brandy and dared him to drink it in a single gulp. Monty did, and fell flat on his face.

Somehow Clift was able to maintain his film career. On *From Here to Eternity* (1953) he became great friends with Frank Sinatra; they'd go out together and drink long into the night. Returning to the hotel they'd throw beer cans out of windows and Monty would blast the bugle he plays in the film, waking up half the guests. Twice studio executives had to intervene to keep them from getting thrown out.

While filming *Raintree County* (1957), Clift attended a party at the home of Elizabeth Taylor. Feeling tired, and maybe a little tipsy, he left early but had trouble negotiating a tight bend in the road and smashed his car into a telephone pole. Told of the crash, Liz raced to the scene. It was a mess, the force of the impact had hurled Clift under the dashboard and his face was a bloody pulp, hanging off. He had to be dead, but no, there were stirrings. Crawling inside, Liz cradled Monty's head in her lap and noticed some of his teeth had been knocked out; two were lodged in his throat. Reaching down his gullet she pulled them out, saving him from choking to death.

Miraculously Clift survived, but his face required reconstructive surgery and would never look the same again. Although he continued to act, Monty was so devastated by the loss of his beauty that for months afterwards he hid himself away, black drapes over the windows and every mirror removed from his house. The accident itself was never mentioned again, not by him and certainly not by friends who knew never to bring up the subject, yet its aftershocks were catastrophic and what followed has been described as the longest suicide in show-business history.

Monty's drinking intensified; indeed he became a true alcoholic. To get away from things he rented a cabin out in the Maine countryside. When an estate agent arrived to check the inventory a week later what greeted him was a pigsty, furniture upturned and empty bottles strewn everywhere, and in the middle of it all a naked and blasted Monty. He was dragged outside and a blanket placed over him. Coming to, he screamed and ran back in, put some clothes on, leaped into his car and sped off.

Besides the drink Monty was taking amphetamines to dull the pain of the injuries he'd received in the accident and sedatives to make him sleep. Still, he was prone to sleepwalk and at least twice was found wandering nearby streets naked. He carried round with him his own private pharmacy, an enormous supply of uppers and downers that he'd hand out as if they were candy. On film sets he used a hip flask containing a potent blend of vodka, orange juice and crushed Demerol.

When Marlon Brando starred with him in *The Young Lions* (1958), he labelled Clift a tormented soul. Going out drinking together in Paris, Monty downed fifteen large gin Martinis and danced a jig on a car roof before sliding down onto the bonnet. Brando had to put him to bed. Often Marlon would pull his friend and acting rival to one side and warn him that he was destroying himself, but Monty insisted he wasn't an alcoholic and could give it up any time he wanted. He was deluding himself; Clift was now at the stage where he couldn't make it through a few hours without taking a drink.

Some friends began drifting away, unable to cope with his manic behaviour. He'd turn up unannounced at their homes howling drunk in the early hours of the morning or arrive at dinner parties insisting on cooking for everyone; once, beating eggs for an omelette, he repeatedly spat in the mixture. When Monty held his own parties invariably he'd drink until he collapsed on the floor, where he'd stay for hours because he never wanted to be touched or helped up. One evening actress Maureen Stapleton was so distressed she turned to Roddy McDowall, one of Clift's closest friends, asking, 'There must be something we can do.' Roddy looked at her forlornly and replied, 'There's nothing anybody can do, except hold his hand to the grave.'

Other loyal friends stood by him, like Elizabeth Taylor, who used her star power to win him a supporting role in *Suddenly, Last Summer* (1959). But Monty was his own worst enemy; unable to stop drinking, he was visibly shaking on the set in London. Director Joe Mankiewicz and producer Sam Spiegel wanted to fire him but Taylor and co-star Katharine Hepburn threatened to quit if they did. Hepburn reportedly spat in their faces at how they were treating Monty. But he was a loose cannon, no question. Actress Mercedes McCambridge told the story that every morning she'd ride to the studio in the same car as Clift, who always insisted the driver stop by Wormwood Scrubs prison, so he could scream out the window at the convicts within.

On the set of *The Misfits* (1961), again Monty drank heavily, indeed was hospitalised prior to filming for ten days for alcoholic hepatitis. Frank

Taylor was more guardian angel than producer, saving Clift from getting pummelled in a bar brawl and from sleepwalking naked in a hotel corridor. At least Monty found some emotional solace in the equally neurotic Marilyn Monroe. They became close buddies almost instantly, understanding each other's addictions and flaws. Tellingly, Marilyn was to describe Monty as, 'The only person I know who is in worse shape than I am.'

Back in LA after filming, Monty invited Marilyn out to dinner but arrived at the restaurant poleaxed, insisting on feeding her with his feet. He'd taken off his shoes and socks and dipped the hors d'oeuvres in the sauces and Marilyn, being the damaged angel that she was, played along with the fun and ate them. It was so sweet and understanding of her. She knew they were both doomed and not long for the world of the living.

Physically Monty was falling apart, suffering from arthritis, a long-undiagnosed hypothyroid condition which affected his balance, worsening eyesight and liver disease, in fact so many health issues that Universal Studios sued him for production delays on his film *Freud* (1962). The action failed. But the damage had been done; Monty didn't work for four years, ostracised by the industry that had made him a star. Depression took over. A friend found him one night on the roof of his New York town house, in his pyjamas, drunk and on pills, literally staggering along the parapet.

It was Liz Taylor who came through again, insisting that Monty be her next leading man. He never made it. A servant found his body one morning lying naked on top of his bed; dead at forty-five from a massive heart attack. Few were surprised to read his obituary. Alfred Hitchcock perhaps summed him up better than most: 'Montgomery Clift always looked as though he had the angel of death walking along beside him.'

PETER COOK (1937–1995: Comedian)

The most dazzlingly brilliant comedic wit of his generation, Peter Cook had succeeded in the West End, on British television and Broadway by the time he was just twenty-eight. Like Alexander the Great, he wept when he saw there were no more worlds to conquer. Really, there was nowhere else to go but down after all that, or at best flat line. The next thirty years were sometimes painful to watch and left no end of casualties, including two broken marriages, as Cook became a semi-recluse, severely addicted to alcohol, happy, or so it seemed, to spurn his talents and give the public mere whiffs of the comedic power he possessed.

He was born in Torquay, Devon, the son of a distinguished colonial civil servant, and with a view to joining the diplomatic corps went to Cambridge, where he instead fell into writing and performing with the prestigious Footlights Club. Alongside fellow graduates Jonathan Miller, Alan Bennett and Dudley Moore, Cook starred in *Beyond the Fringe*, a revue show that changed the landscape of British comedy and was a hit on both sides of the Atlantic; it was the devilishly prickly mind of Cook that lay behind much of the show's brilliance. During this period Cook could do no wrong. He was like an Exocet missile of mirth, opening his own comedy venue, the Establishment Club in Soho, thus igniting the 1960s satire boom, and becoming the chief shareholder of *Private Eye* magazine.

Like most of his social circle Cook smoked and drank, but never to excess; he feared total inebriation since it meant losing self-control. Even at university he rarely drank, save for one night of debauchery at a dining club whose members were obliged to wear seventeenth-century costume. Driving home less steadily than Stevie Wonder in an out-of-control dodgem car, he was stopped by two policemen. Stepping out in powdered wig all askew and fancy britches, Cook excused, 'But officer, I swerved to miss a cat which ran across the road.' Incredibly, he got off.

As the satire balloon burst Cook formed a new alliance with Dudley Moore for the popular BBC television show *Not Only . . . But Also*. Their partnership was an instant hit, branching out into movies, notably *Bedazzled* (1967), a cult comedy version of the Faust story. With his star in the ascendancy, a socialite wife, Wendy Snowden, and beautiful young daughters, there was the first of what would become numerous, and sometimes quite avoidable, disasters. Cook began an affair with swinging sixties model and actress Judy Huxtable, in between screwing the obligatory Swedish au pair. It was curtains for his marriage and the divorce ruptured him emotionally as he lost custody of the children. Filled with guilt, Cook turned to drink and popping pills, as if they would scrub out the misery he was in. In November 1970 he got himself arrested, bollocksed behind the wheel of his car. His work grew erratic, haphazard. The BBC gave him his own chat show; it was an unmitigated disaster. Kirk Douglas was a guest one evening and Cook rose unsteadily to his feet to ask the obvious, 'How are you?' Unfortunately it came out as, 'Who are you?'

It was to Dudley Moore that Cook clung like a lifebuoy. Together they took a new sketch show, *Behind the Fridge*, out on tour, hitting Australia first. Early performances in Sydney saw Cook so jackassed he needed to hold on to the furniture for support, sometimes even Dudley, lest he fall over. Worse came in New Zealand, with Cook well lubricated for the entire run. For Moore it was like acting alongside a grenade with the pin pulled out. Taking revenge, he got himself plastered one evening and as the curtain fell Cook went ballistic. 'That's the worst performance you've ever given.' Moore looked smug, 'Now you know what it feels like.'

Back at their hotel Cook retired to bed, out of his head, while his wife and others stayed in the bar to listen to Dudley at the piano. In the early hours of the morning the lifts were seen going maniacally up and down; it was Cook in his underpants, too chateaued to find the right button to get him to the lobby to fetch Judy.

When the show came to London Peter was struck by nerves and hit the bottle again. On opening night with a packed auditorium he passed out backstage. Coffee was forced down his throat, while Dudley tried to slap him back into the world of the living. No luck. The inevitable chorus of 'why are we waiting' wafted in from the audience. 'I'll tell you why we're fucking waiting,' raved Dudley from behind the curtain. 'The cunt is drunk. He's out of his fucking mind.' Somehow Cook came round and the show could begin. Dudley walked out to thunderous applause and waited for Peter, who should have followed. He didn't. He'd frozen in the wings. 'I can't do this. I can't fucking do this.' He began to cry, miserable tears. The director felt little sympathy and pushed the bugger on.

For the Broadway run Cook agreed to reduce his alcoholic load, aware of the trials of hell he'd put poor Dudley through. Wife Judy was even hired to measure his drinks so he couldn't indulge before the show. All these good intentions went out of the window, of course. For one performance Cook didn't show up at all; crew hands had to literally break down the door to his apartment and drag him out. A minder was hired to ensure Cook's punctuality, but he ended up roped in as the comedian's drinking companion.

When the show closed on Broadway and Moore decided to stay on in America, essentially calling an end to the partnership, Cook seemed lost, adrift without him. Even more painfully he had to endure the spectacle of Moore becoming a movie star and sex symbol with films like *Ten* and *Arthur*.

Meanwhile Cook's marriage to Judy was strained beyond belief. She could barely live with his wild mood swings and seemed forever to be walking on eggshells; at any given moment he could fly into violent rages or be as depressed as death. It was all caused by his drinking; he was apt to pour red wine down his throat until he passed out. Finally Cook relented and entered a detox clinic, complaining immediately that his private nurse was too fat and ugly. When he got a slimmer model, and blonde to boot, he promptly seduced her.

He also continued to drink and fall over. At a dinner party at the house of singer Lynsey de Paul he slipped off his chair and passed out on the floor. The horror-stricken guests were reassured by Judy, 'Leave him. He'll come round in half an hour.' And so he did, confused and bewildered, trying to take in the strange surroundings, 'Where am I? What the fuck am I doing here?' It was getting worse at home; he'd fall down and was often too gibbled to get up again without assistance, assistance Judy was growing tired of giving him.

By the 1980s Cook had added cocaine use to his numerous vices. And his antics were getting increasingly outrageous. When someone parked an open-topped Rolls-Royce outside his Hampstead home, blocking the entrance, Cook threw the contents of his dustbin all over the seats. Attending a celebrity golf tournament in Spain he got incredibly wasted and punched a German tourist. Buying a new car, he promptly drove it into a police car on a zebra crossing. Later, a guest at Rolling Stone Ronnie Wood's wedding, he drank vulgar amounts of champagne and tried to seduce the bride!

Drink had sadly become for Cook 'not a pleasure but a necessity'. He enjoyed triple vodkas for breakfast and maintained, shall we say, a robust social life that was geared to enjoying himself at the expense of doing very much. 'I ran out of ambition at the age of twenty-seven,' he once said. The one constant in his life was *Private Eye*, though even here he was seldom seen, popping in just for the occasional meeting. He was far more visible during those frequent occasions when the magazine was sued, usually by Robert Maxwell. Cook enjoyed turning up at court waving his chequebook at the newspaper magnate. Then there was the splendid time he mounted a raid on the Daily Mirror building. 'It was our equivalent of *The Guns of Navarone*,' recalled *Private Eye* editor Ian Hislop. Maxwell had managed to get *Private Eye* taken off every news-stand in Britain, replacing it with his own amateur rag called *Not Private Eye*, produced by *Mirror* journalists. Hislop and co. sat depressed in their cramped office unsure of their next move. Suddenly Cook perked up. 'I bet they don't want to do this magazine, I'll send round a crate of whisky.' This he duly did. An hour later Cook called to see how they were getting on. Raving drunk was the answer. 'Let's go down and join them,' suggested Peter. Crowding into a taxi they alighted outside the Mirror building. 'We're going to Mr Maxwell's office.' The doorman took one look at them and said, 'Yes, of course Mr Cook, up you go.'

With stealth worthy of a commando brigade, they got inside Maxwell's private office and there flat out on the floor were three journalists. Hislop spied the dummy copy of Maxwell's magazine and swiped it. 'Let's go, Peter,' he urged. 'Oh no,' replied Cook. 'I haven't had half enough fun yet.' He got on the phone to the catering department and ordered a case of champagne. Up it came and the *Private Eye* boys indulged heartily. 'Can we go now, Peter?' said Hislop, imagining walls that had bars in them. 'Why don't we get the *Mirror* picture desk to take a picture of us drinking champagne?' was Cook's next suggestion. After that was accomplished Cook picked up the phone and called Maxwell in New York:

'Guess where we are!' It was at that moment security burst in and threw them all out.

In 1989 Cook's marriage to Judy collapsed; he was alone and at the mercy of his demons again. Living as a shambling alcoholic, his house resembled the blitz on a good day. Unpaid bills jostled for space on the carpet with strewn vodka bottles and cigarette butts. Blu-Tacked on the wall were his passport and driving licence so he could find them quickly amid the clutter. One of his daughters moved in not too far away and sat outside on the doorstep, aware her dad was inside drinking himself insensible and pleading to be let in. 'It seemed he was too ashamed for them to see him as he had become,' said ex-wife Wendy.

He'd changed physically, too. No longer the handsome bounder of his youth, the physical deterioration was such that he was now more like something two nutty aunts would keep locked up in the attic. But his charm, when he was wont to deploy it, could still be intoxicating and he married for a third time, to Lin Chong, who managed to bring some order back into his life, although they lived in separate houses 100 yards apart. On doctors' orders Cook reined back on the drinking and there was a sudden burst of activity, his now classic appearance on the Clive Anderson chat show, also a series of spoof interviews with humorist Chris Morris. On the day of recording Morris feared Cook would appear, 'A boozy old sack of lard scarcely able to get a sentence out.' Indeed he did stumble into the studio carrying a Safeway's bag full of Kestrel lager and duty-free quantities of cigarettes, but then proceeded to mine comedy gold.

Just when there appeared to be a Cook revival taking place, an emotional bullet hit him between the eyes: the death of his mother, to whom he was very close. It devastated him and predictably his escape route was once again alcohol; he himself would be dead just a little over a year later. Suffering from a liver complaint, Cook collapsed at home and was rushed to hospital where he fell into a coma after throwing up blood. He never returned from the darkness and six days later was dead from an internal haemorrhage. The first person Lin called was Dudley in America. Coming off the phone, dumbstruck, he called Cook's answering machine, 'Just to hear his voice once again.'

The simplistic and often-made observation about Peter Cook was that he never fulfilled his early promise and preferred sloth to ambition for the remainder of his life. Cook himself couldn't give a toss; he was arrogant perhaps about his comedy genius because it was all achieved so easily, the way Brando resented acting because he didn't have to try as hard as everybody else. There were periodic flashes of it down the years, enough to influence practically every subsequent generation of comedian. Yet behind the eyes there was a painful sadness, the guilty hint of an unfulfilled talent that perhaps Cook himself was never able to truly forgive himself for squandering.

ALICE COOPER (b. 1948: Singer/Songwriter)

He was the face of shock rock whose on-stage antics of beheadings and chopping up baby dolls seemed deliberately primed to piss off the likes of Billy Graham and Mary Whitehouse. Drawing heavily on the horror films he loved as a kid, Alice Cooper is the bastard offspring of Morticia Addams and Elvis and has been a hugely popular musical figure since the seventies. But it's all an act; the Alice on stage is radically different from the man who appears after the make-up is smeared off. Although of course, when his creator was an alcoholic there was a very blurred line indeed. 'I didn't know where Alice began and where I stopped.'

Born Vincent Damon Furnier in Detroit, Michigan, the son of a preacher, it was in high school where he assembled his own rock band, naming them, so the legend goes, after an experience with a Ouija board that told him he was the reincarnation of a seventeenth-century witch named Alice Cooper. Wacky, but not as wacky as how he avoided being drafted to Vietnam. After drinking a bottle of whisky before his physical and passing out, he told the psychiatrist how he wanted to lock his audience in a concert hall, shock them with electricity, lower spiders on their heads and let monkey semen out of the ventilation system. The psychiatrist's written assessment of Cooper was blunt and to the point: 'A homicidal transvestite capable of mass murder; a megalomaniac.' Perfect credentials for rock stardom.

Ready to take on LA, still seeped in late-sixties psychedelia and hippie-love bullshit, Cooper and his band's type of music embracing death and depression was met with about as much enthusiasm as a proctology examination. At one early gig they managed to empty the entire venue of patrons after playing for just ten minutes.

The band caused a near riot at the 1969 Toronto Peace Festival, low down on a bill that featured John Lennon and the Doors, when some guy in the audience hurled a live chicken on stage. Being a city boy, Alice figured that since chickens had wings they could fly, so he grabbed it and threw it back. It no more flew as plummeted, into a mass of scrambling hands and was torn asunder. The next day newspaper headlines screamed: 'Alice Cooper rips chicken's head off, drinks blood.' The record label called him: 'Whatever you did, keep doing it.'

The release of the group's breakthrough album, *Love It to Death*, saw the flowering of the full Alice persona – goth make-up and fake blood galore, the image that would prove so influential. He'd also begun to hang out with the likes of Jim Morrison, Jimi Hendrix and Keith Moon, so not surprisingly began to drink heavily; Janis Joplin introduced him to Southern Comfort. 'I was the new kid on the block, and they were my big brothers and sisters. Everybody I knew was like, you know, the worst of the worst.' Pretty soon he was drinking beers by the case, but fine with it, never missed a show. 'Alcohol to me was like speed, it was like energy, it wasn't a depressant. I would drink a six pack before I went on stage and just fly.'

And the hits kept coming – 'School's Out', 'Elected', 'No More Mr Nice Guy' – while on stage Cooper ratcheted up his shocking antics, coming on with a live boa constrictor wrapped round his arm. Staying at the Marriott Hotel in Knoxville, Tennessee one time, Alice put the snake in the bathtub and went to sleep. Predictably in the morning it wasn't there, having escaped down the toilet and into the pipes. After he'd informed the manager, 'My snake's gone!' workmen tore down the walls, but there was no sign of the reptile. Two weeks later Cooper was amused to hear that country and western singer Charley Pride got the shock of his life staying in that room when he came face to face with a boa constrictor emerging from his toilet.

Other antics on the road included the time Cooper decided to pull a prank on his band mates by hauling down his pants and pretending to be humping the television in his hotel suite as they entered. When the door opened, instead of his musicians he was greeted by a maid and the hotel detective.

Such was Cooper's reputation in early seventies Britain that Mary Whitehouse, doyen of the nation's scruples, and several MPs led a campaign to ban him from performing in the country for 'peddling the culture of a concentration camp'. Ever the showman, Cooper sent Whitehouse flowers to thank her for the publicity. But the endless touring, combined with their frenetic lifestyle, took its toll on the band. Lead guitarist Glen Buxton's drinking habits actually caused his spleen to explode. Amazingly he survived, but the band broke up at their peak in 1974 and Alice Cooper went solo with a stage show more theatrically demented than ever. However, his drinking could make things more dangerous than they needed to be, like the time he put a sword through his leg or the time in Vancouver when he tripped over a footlight and plunged twelve feet into the audience. Bloodied and dazed, with his ribs busted, fans thought it was all part of the show and grabbed his blood-matted hair until he was saved by security and hauled off to hospital. Cooper was able to carry on with the tour, though. 'I was anaesthetised,' thanks to plenty of Buds, mixed with Seagram's VO.

He even formed his own celebrity drinking club called the Hollywood Vampires, who'd meet upstairs at the Rainbow Bar & Grill on Sunset Boulevard. In order to join you had to outdrink the other members, who included Ringo Starr, Harry Nilsson, John Belushi and Keith Moon, who invariably arrived in one of a variety of get-ups: as a nun, a French maid or Hitler. Whenever John Lennon was in LA, he'd usually drop by and he and Cooper would drink all night. It was manic, all of them knew they had a drink problem but were having way too much fun to give a damn; it was like, hey we're rock 'n' rollers, what do you expect?

In London Cooper and his band were invited to a drinking contest by the Who.

It was held at a private club and everyone sat at a long table, facing their challenger. Alice was matched with Pete Townshend, whose tipple was Rémy cognac; Cooper had his trusty Seagram's VO. The deal was each drank half a bottle, then swapped over, so Cooper had to finish the remaining Rémy, Pete had to gulp down the rest of the VO. Everything was going swimmingly until Cooper's record producer Bob Ezrin joined in. He'd just come from eating a huge steak dinner. After polishing off a bottle of whisky Ezrin involuntarily decided to do an impersonation of Linda Blair from *The Exorcist*; large projectiles of vomit rocketed across the table splattering members of the Who, who just sat there, slightly miffed, calling for more drinks.

By the time of his 1977 US tour Cooper was in dire need of help with his alcoholism; at its peak he was rumoured to drink two cases of Budweiser and a bottle of whisky a day. No longer fun, he was drinking to survive, drinking to get to the next day. Sometimes he'd throw up blood in the morning, 'which is OK on stage but when it's just the Holiday Inn maid seeing it, it loses its impact'. It was a sign that his body was rebelling against the lifestyle imposed on it. And doctors confirmed it; a few more months of this and he'd be dead without the aid of a guillotine.

It took the strength of his wife Sheryl and his manager to commit him to a sanatorium. At the time he didn't want to admit he had a problem. 'Of course I can stop drinking if I want to,' he'd say. But take the booze away and 'I couldn't walk from my bed to the door'. Checking in, Cooper could barely sign his name, he had tremors so bad. With a lack of proper rehabs back then, Cooper found himself in a lock-down ward with drug addicts, criminals and the mentally disturbed. Three months later he came out clean. Maybe he figured that since the people he used to hang out with – Hendrix, Moon, Joplin – were all dead he should heed the lesson that you don't have to die to be a legend. Actually one music magazine ran a mock obituary taken as fact by so many fans that Cooper had to issue a formal statement: 'I am alive, and drunk as usual.'

Abstinence seemed to suit Cooper, for a while. Then during a meal with Sheryl he casually partook of a sip of wine and that was enough for his body to start its cravings again. Soon he was stashing bottles of whisky around the house and going on all-out benders. As for the four albums he produced around this time, Cooper can't recall writing or recording any of them; touring them is a bit of a blur, too.

Fearing for both his sanity and his marriage, Cooper readmitted himself into hospital in 1983 and went cold turkey. He left after a month, found the nearest bar, sat down – and had a Coke. Not a drop of alcohol has passed his lips since. This was no mere cure, but a miraculous healing. God's fingerprints were all over his recovery. 'People say there are no miracles and I go, oh, yes there are. I'm a walking miracle because I was the worst alcoholic you could imagine.' Since then Cooper has counselled other rock musicians battling addiction problems who often turn to him for help.

Without drink Cooper channelled his neurosis and dark side into the persona of Alice during his blood-soaked vaudevillian stage shows, even roping in his daughters when they were old enough, one dressing up as Britney Spears, cue decapitation, the other as Paris Hilton, whose throat is torn out by a Chihuahua. Such visuals, though, looked like kindergarten kitsch against the antics of his progeny, Slipknot and Marilyn Manson. Cooper's children had taken over the asylum.

RUSSELL CROWE (b. 1964: Actor)

Notorious for his fiery and unpredictable temper, Russell Crowe has carved out a reputation as a Hollywood hard man both on screen and off. Spending most of his time, 'telling people to fuck off and get out of my life' was an attitude that detracted hugely from his talents as an actor. The words brawl and bar became synonymous with Crowe, there were madcap stories of him biting a chunk out of a man's neck and spitting it back in his face during a fight in a Sydney bar, or beating up his own bodyguard. Then there was the time he had to be rescued by Mounties after sparking a fight in a bar in Alberta by dismissing ice hockey as a game for wimps. Crowe certainly knows how to live dangerously.

Born in Wellington, New Zealand, the son of movie-set caterers, Crowe was raised mainly in Australia. Leaving school to chase his dreams of rock stardom or acting, Crowe appeared in several stage musicals, and when work was hard to find busked on the streets to pay his rent and bar tab.

In 1988 he landed his first big break, playing the lead role in the Australian stage production of Willy Russell's musical *Blood Brothers*. As usual with Crowe, friction was inevitable. In one scene he had to throw a prop gun to the floor, except it usually ended up bouncing off the nut of his co-star Peter Cousens. Fed up, Cousens marched into Crowe's dressing room and called him an arrogant amateur. Crowe head-butted him, breaking his nose. The director demanded each actor apologise in writing to the other. Crowe refused and within the week was fired.

Many believed that marked the end of his career, that he was just too much of a trouble maker, but Crowe persevered by working on television until he was cast as a neo-Nazi skinhead in *Romper Stomper* (1992), the film that brought him to the attention of Hollywood. *LA Confidential* (1997) was another important stepping stone in his rise to stardom. He was playing a hard-nosed cop, and author James Ellroy told Crowe that his character abstained from drinking. 'Come on,' bugged Crowe. 'This is 1953. He's a blue-collar bloke, a cop. You're telling me he doesn't sit around with the boys after his shift and have a beer?' And Ellroy said, 'Absolutely not.' It was a hammer blow for Crowe, but true to his method actor instincts, he never touched a drop for the five-month shoot. 'It's probably the most painful period of my life.'

By the time he made *Mystery, Alaska* (1999), Crowe's reputation as a heavy drinker was firmly established. When Burt Reynolds was invited out on the lash with him the veteran star took special precautions. 'Russell is an animal. I do love him but this guy is a badass.' Reynolds instructed the barman to alternate each of his vodkas with a plain tonic, and as the evening progressed Crowe was genuinely puzzled that oldie Burt was keeping up with him. 'At our fourteenth drink, Russell said, "Let me sip your drink, mate." Thank God it was the vodka.'

Crowe's propensity for violence was now making headlines. In 1999 there was a brawl outside a nightclub in Coffs Harbour, the coastal town near Crowe's 1,400-acre cattle ranch in northern New South Wales. Well liquored up, Crowe had sauntered over to the DJ informing him that his show was crap. 'So are most of your movies,' he'd replied. The great one did not take kindly to this burst of the Barry Normans, and told the DJ's wife exactly what he was going to do to her husband, nay punch his lights out. The fists were soon flying and in jumped some hefty secur-ity guards, which if anything made matters worse. One eyewitness told *People* magazine that Crowe was, 'kicking, punching and biting like a wild man'. The blurry CCTV footage that captured the incident saw Crowe biting the neck of a bouncer.

Little surprise, then, that Ridley Scott cast Crowe as a fighting machine in *Gladiator* (2000). Performing a lot of the stunts himself, Crowe sustained numerous injuries like having the tendons of both biceps pop out of their shoulder sockets. Getting up one morning he looked in the bath-room mirror and thought, 'Gee, what's that? And I started playing with it and I realised that it was part of my insides. So I had a little shot of Jack Daniel's and I stuck it back in place and it's been fine ever since.'

On set he bonded immediately with Richard Harris, cast as a Roman general, the pair becoming firm drinking buddies and close friends. Harris saw in Crowe something of his old hellraiser self, tipping the star to carry on his bad-boy ways. 'Russell's a top bloke. He will carry the baton on. He irritates the hell out of the Hollywood bigwigs but he's too good for them to ignore.'

Crowe was in London attending the BAFTA film awards when he heard that Harris was terminally ill. During a speech he offered the poem 'Sanctity' by Patrick Kavanagh as way of tribute, but was later furious when he heard the BBC had cut it out of their television broadcast. Hunting down the show's director Malcolm Gerrie at the post-awards dinner at London's Grosvenor House Hotel, Crowe slammed him against the wall and with his face mere inches from Gerrie's called him everything from a 'cunt' to a 'motherfucker'. Venting further frustration, Crowe smashed three chairs before storming off. Forced to apologise, Crowe shrugged: 'He's not battered, he's not bruised but I'm quite sure his ears are still ringing.'

That same evening a fan who took Crowe's picture received a similar volley of abuse. 'How dare you take my fucking picture,' he screamed. 'Who gave you fucking permission?' Harris would have smiled.

Such was the two men's rapport that Crowe flew 5,000 miles to attend Harris's memorial service when he passed away. In a pub afterwards Crowe leaped on top of the bar to raise a pint of Guinness to his fallen comrade. It was a grand night and a fitting send-off; staff had to call out for more Guinness as the revellers drank the place dry.

Certainly Crowe had inherited Harris's dark side, which tipped over into sudden acts of violence when lubricated. Filming *Master and Commander* (2003) in Mexico, he challenged a group of drinkers in a bar to a fight. In the resulting mêlée Crowe had to be rescued by his personal trainer, a female karate champion. When Crowe was involved in a drunken fight in a London restaurant with Eric Watson, the multi-millionaire owner of the New Zealand Warriors rugby league side, it predictably made headlines round the world. According to reports a boozy Crowe had been throwing plates and champagne glasses around all evening, but as the hours wore on and the drinking got worse the behaviour turned aggressive. Turning on the women, he licked one of them down the side of her face. In his sozzled mind this might have constituted foreplay, but the girl in question was unmoved, film star or not, further put off by his dishevelled appearance, clothes that carried on them a disturbing array of stains and that smelled as if they hadn't been changed for days.

It was when Crowe hit the toilets that his fracas with Watson got out of hand. A supporter of a rival rugby team, Crowe was said to have described the Warriors as 'a bunch of coconuts' and 'darkies'. Watson was having none of it and blows were exchanged. Quickly the scrap spilled out into the main bar area and it took ex-EastEnders actor Ross Kemp to leap in and separate the pair before security staff called police.

Such bust-ups merely obscured Crowe's highly driven work ethic. It was an odd paradox, the brawling boozer and the perfectionist, who takes himself and his 'art' perhaps a little too seriously. Known for his obsessive intensity, to play a role in *The Insider* (1999) Crowe put on 80 lb in two months with 'a medically controlled diet of bourbon and cheeseburgers'.

Following his marriage in 2003 to actress Danielle Spencer, quickly followed by the birth of a son, it was hoped that Crowe might mellow, calm down a bit; er, no. In 2004 he decided to knock seven bells out of the person hired to protect him from bodily harm by others – his own bodyguard! The altercation took place at a drinks party when Crowe mistakenly believed the former Australian rugby league player was spreading malicious gossip about him. Pretty dented by the end, Crowe still managed to bite into the chest of his bodyguard, who was trying to smother him at the time. They were all smiles the next day.

In June 2005 Crowe hurled a telephone at a New York hotel concierge who had to be treated for facial lacerations. Hauled away in handcuffs, Crowe was held for six hours before being charged with second-degree assault and possessing a weapon – the said telephone. Days later a humbled Crowe went on live TV to apologise for what he described as 'possibly the most shameful situation that I've ever gotten myself in, and I've done some pretty dumb things in my life'. He blamed the outburst on the sheer frustration at not being able to place a call through to his wife. Asked if he intended to apologise in person to the concierge Crowe said he did, 'but at the moment he's not answering his phone'.

Funny, but by now the formula of exploding into rage where people got hurt, followed by a fit of remorse, was becoming a cliché. Theoretically Crowe faced a maximum penalty of seven years in prison over the phone assault, but that was never going to happen and the whole thing was settled out of court.

Perhaps more than any other it was this incident that made Crowe realise what booze was doing to him, spirits in particular, and he made a conscious decision to lay off certain drinks. 'Tequila and I are still good friends, and vodka and I still get on. It's just the dark drinks that don't seem to bring out the best of my personality.' He'd no future plans to become completely sober, then. Filming a Robin Hood film in England, Crowe was spotted downing pints of real ale in numerous country pubs, even reportedly managing to get himself banned from one after arguing that it should stay open after closing time so he could continue drinking.

Then came the bombshell. In September 2009 Crowe took the extraordinary step of releasing an open letter to his fans apologising for his bad behaviour over the years, accepting full responsibility for the embarrassment it had caused to loved ones and the adverse impact upon his career. It was a bold decision and took balls, but a damn shame, really. In the tradition of Flynn, Mitchum, Marvin and all the rest, Crowe just might be Hollywood's last true hellraiser.

D

SIR FRANCIS DASHWOOD (1708–1781: Founder of the Hell-Fire Club)

Around the 1750s in England, principally London, men of wealth, power and influence were drawn to the attractions of fashionable gentlemen's clubs where every grubby vice could be satisfied. The most infamous of these was undoubtedly the Hell-Fire Club founded by Sir Francis Dashwood, an unashamed libertine, the godfather of Georgian debauchery. Indulging in drunken orgies, not giving a stuff what society thought, Dashwood was so dedicated to pleasure in all its many lurid guises that he became a figure of lurid legend, one whom many believed consorted with the very devil himself.

Born in London and educated at Eton College, Dashwood was sixteen when he inherited his family's vast fortune, and like most of his class around this time took to sampling the intellectual and cultural offerings of Europe on a Grand Tour. Well, maybe the odd museum was visited, Dashwood much preferred the atmosphere of continental taverns and risqué bordellos where his lively young spirit found expression. His personal mission was, 'to taste the sweets of all things'. In Rome he played an outlandish prank on those pious worshippers who visited the Sistine Chapel on Good Friday to flagellate themselves symbolically as a sign of penitence. Dashwood managed to smuggle in a prize English horse whip and ran about the place really letting the snivelling buggers have it. They fled in terror screaming, 'Il Diavolo! Il Diavolo!' believing the evil one was amongst them; maybe he was. Cardinals politely explained to Dashwood that his presence in perpetuity was not required at the Vatican.

Back at his ancestral home in West Wycombe, Buckinghamshire, Dashwood devised history's most ribald garden, with streams, shrubbery and plantations arranged in such a way as to represent the curvature of the naked female form. The pièce de résistance comprised two mounds each topped with a circle of red flowers, then lower down a triangle of dark shrubbery. Dashwood once took a local priest to the roof of his tower to glance at the handiwork, and then signalled for his gardeners to release fountains which shot out milk into the air from the horticultural breasts. The poor minister fainted and had to be revived.

Over the years Sir Francis had founded several clubs that catered for the hard-drinking and womanising habits of wealthy rakes. He himself was said to have had a ravenous sexual appetite; dipping his wick into aristocratic ladies and whores off the streets alike. Still, he managed to surprise many of his friends by eventually marrying a pious widow.

In 1751 he formed The Hell-Fire Club, who met at the secluded Medmenham Abbey situated by the River Thames near Marlow, not too far from London. No expense was spared turning the place into a Butlins of debauchery; murals depicted obscene acts, hedges were sculpted into huge erect penises, while carved above the front door was the motto: 'Do What You Will', an invitation to unrestrained excess if ever there was one. The abbey was well supplied with fine wines, claret and port and its library stocked with books ranging from the Bible to occult literature and pornography. Dashwood owned one of the earliest copies in the English language of the Karma-Sutra. Had video been around then you'd have bet he'd have had the first import version of *Debbie Does Dallas*.

Some of the most powerful men of the day, prominent members of Parliament and the establishment, began to show up for the notorious late-night ceremonies: the Prince of Wales, Sir John Montagu, Earl of Sandwich, John Wilkes (the Reformer), William Hogarth and Thomas Potter, MP and son of a former Archbishop of Canterbury. Clad in masks and costumes, like extras in a bad Hammer horror film, pseudo black-mass rituals were carried out over the writhing naked bodies of willing aristocratic young ladies. Once that was over, top-class prostitutes brought down the Thames from London in barges were let loose and the good men ruling our country fucked, ate and got well pissed up.

Despite attempts to keep their doings a secret, rumours of supposed Satanism circulated through the English establishment and the brotherhood was demonised, probably by those who'd been refused membership. Actually nothing worse than mock 'pagan' ceremonies took place and the worshipping of Venus and Bacchus, the god of wine; one doubts if the Duke of Queensberry ever summoned up the horned one.

Such gossip, however, did little to hinder Dashwood's political career. Undoubtedly the Hell-Fire Club's inner circle wielded great power, between the throwing up in the vestibule and deflowering of recorked Holborn tarts, and certainly favours were exchanged. When the Earl of Bute, a member, was elected Prime Minister in 1762 he made Sir Francis his Chancellor, a flagrant show of favouritism and one of the maddest political appointments in history, since Dashwood was a numerical dunce, by his own admission sums over five figures began to seriously impair his brain stem, yet the nation's finances were entrusted to him. He was predictably useless, heavily taxing cider and thereby alienating producers and consumers alike, resulting in his ousting from office within the year.

With the Hell-Fire Club becoming too hot to handle, Dashwood relocated it to a series of caves and catacombs beneath his family seat in West Wycombe, but such dank surroundings didn't have the same ambience as the old place and the club slowly wound down as members died off, though most lived to a ripe old age, paying into the Georgian equivalent of BUPA, no doubt. Dashwood himself remained a jovial and enthusiastic libertine for the rest of his life, happily fathering illegitimate children well into his seventies.

As for the Hell-Fire Club itself, poet Paul Whitehead kept records, but before he died made sure to destroy them, ensuring that the rituals of the order would stay a secret for ever.

F

FRANCES FARMER (1913–1970: Actress)

One of the most tragic figures in cinema history, a luminous actress of depth and sensitivity, Frances Farmer will be forever remembered for her dramatic and harrowing fall from grace rather than her relatively brief career when she starred opposite such leading men as Cary Grant, Bing Crosby and Tyrone Power. She was a rebel when it wasn't fashionable to be one. Born out of time, Frances would have been more suited to the era of people like Jane Fonda. Instead, as a free-thinking woman during the dictatorial studio system of the thirties and forties, her anti-social behaviour, driven by drink, landed her in the nuthouse from hell.

Born in Seattle, Washington, Frances demonstrated a gift for writing and performing at school and caused a scandal with a prize-winning essay provocatively titled 'God Dies'. Local Baptist ministers singled her out as evidence of 'rampant atheism' in schools. 'If the young people of this city are going to hell,' one told his congregation, 'Frances Farmer is surely leading them there.' It was her first taste of notoriety, 'and when they began calling me the Bad Girl of West Seattle High, I tried to live up to it'.

Dreaming of a career as a Broadway actress, Frances was spotted by a talent scout and signed to Paramount, but her creative sensitivities were at odds with the Hollywood machine. This was an age when the studios dictated every facet of a star's life and Frances simply refused to play the fame game, and resisted the one-dimensional, glamorous roles assigned to her. To combat her frustrations, and heal the wound of a disastrous love affair with playwright Clifford Odets, she turned to drink.

Studio big wigs made Frances pay for her rebellious attitude by offering her third-rate scripts, and her career began to lose momentum. Her heavy drinking had also given rise to chronic depression, leading to bouts of erratic behaviour; cast in one movie, she simply never showed up. By 1940 she was considered so unstable Paramount cancelled her contract. Frances went into virtual hiding. Isolated and bitter, she felt herself 'beginning to slip away' while consuming ever increasing amounts of alcohol and with an emerging dependency on amphetamines, which she used to control her weight. In October 1942 Frances was stopped by a police officer in Santa Monica for driving with her headlights on full beam in a wartime blackout zone. Unable to produce a driving licence and noticeably tanked to the uvula she was arrested on the spot after turning violent and abusive. She was sentenced to 180 days in jail, suspended.

In a bid to dampen any bad publicity friends whisked Frances out of Hollywood, getting her a job on a low-budget movie shot in Mexico. Things didn't quite work out when Frances was seen roaming a hotel corridor completely naked and spraying people with a seltzer bottle. After fights and other acts of lewd behaviour she was deported and never made the film.

A few months later Frances was given another chance, this time on a B-picture melodrama called *No Escape*. On the first day of filming she arrived on set trashed and hit a studio hairdresser so hard she fell backwards and busted her jaw. The incident was reported to the police and when detectives caught up with the actress at a Hollywood hotel she fled into a bathroom, only to reappear in the nude. At police headquarters, Frances listed her occupation as 'cocksucker'.

The next morning Frances appeared in court looking like a bag lady who'd been run over and dragged fifty yards by a Greyhound bus. She was as defiant as she was bedraggled, replying to the judge's question whether she'd been drinking, 'Listen, I put liquor in my milk, I put liquor in my coffee and in my orange juice. What do you want me to do, starve to death?' Ordered to now serve her original 180-day sentence, Frances yelled 'fine', as she was taken to a cell. At that moment she broke loose, felling a policeman with a swift right to the jaw, nobbling another and wounding an attending matron for good measure. Forced into a strait-jacket, she was then unceremoniously hauled away, her last words echoing round the courtroom: 'Have you ever had a broken heart?' It was as dramatic as anything she'd committed to celluloid.

Frances spent the night in jail, spitting in an officer's face, before being examined by a psychiatrist who pronounced the actress mentally ill and transferred her to a sanatorium. It was a minimum security facility and Frances managed to escape, running back home to her mother Lillian for sanctuary. But relations between the two women, strained for years, quickly developed into bitter recriminations and arguments. When Frances physically attacked Lillian, she complained to the authorities of being unable to control her daughter and asked the courts to designate her 'an insane person'. As a result Frances was committed to Western State Hospital near Seattle, where she received electric shock treatment two or three times a week for three months in a bid either to cure her symptoms or break her rebellious and defiant will. When this didn't work she was stripped naked and thrown into a bath of freezing water.

'It's all been like a terrible dream,' Frances told reporters upon her release after several months, with doctors satisfied that her anti-social behaviour had been modified. She even spoke of her hopes of returning to acting. It wasn't to be. Just a few weeks later she was arrested for drunken vagrancy and handed back to the custody of her mother, who had her recommitted. This time Frances wouldn't see daylight for another five years.

Western State Hospital was a pretty dismal place back in the 1940s, overcrowded and understaffed, and there are some hellish claims about what happened to Frances within those walls. That she was strapped into straitjackets, chained in padded cells, prostituted out to soldiers from the local military base and raped by orderlies. The most extreme rumour was that she underwent a transorbital lobotomy, an excision of the nerves which control aggressive behaviour. Whatever the truth, the strong-willed Frances continued to fight and buck the system, but her spirit couldn't last the distance and when eventually released she was a mere shell of the vibrant artist and firebrand individual she had once been.

Once out Frances bought a one-way bus ticket to California, as far away as possible from the institution and her parents, whom she never saw or spoke to again. She worked menial jobs and told reporters she'd given up alcohol. There was even an attempted comeback with a few TV dramas and theatre productions, but work soon dried up and she ended up presenting on a local television station in Indianapolis; a far cry from her early Hollywood years when gossip columnist Louella Parsons predicted she'd be the next Greta Garbo. The old demons returned, too. Sometimes she'd arrive for work too squiffy to go on air, changing from the elegant, sensitive lady her co-workers knew most of the time into a raging harridan, screaming obscenities at her bosses and storming out. The station's general manager finally had enough and fired her.

Most of her new friends knew little about her past, since Frances never raised it. All they saw was a woman capable of bursts of fiery temper when drunk and the odd flash of delinquency, such as the time she'd been drinking heavily and rammed her car into the local jail. After her release, Frances attended a party where, not surprisingly, the guests were too embarrassed to discuss the incident. Finally Frances, a glass in her hand, announced, 'Would anyone like to see my impression of Frances Farmer drunk?' It certainly broke the ice.

A heavy smoker all her life, Frances died of throat cancer just shy of her fifty-seventh birthday, the once glamorous star all but forgotten and penniless, her soaring spirit battered and torn. Towards the end of her life Frances found God and became a dedicated church goer, but often in the long, lonely hours of the night her mind wandered back to those hellish years in the asylum and asked, 'I didn't know where God was. Didn't He hear me at all?'

W C FIELDS (1879–1946: Comic Actor)

Making movies, W C Fields was never very far away from his trusty thermos flask, which he maintained was filled with pineapple juice, and not by any stretch of the imagination Martini. When one of the crew hands discovered the truth and swapped the contents Fields was heard to roar, 'Somebody put pineapple juice in my pineapple juice!' On another occasion he bemoaned, 'What contemptible scoundrel has stolen the cork to my lunch?'

Fields knew he was a soak of the highest order. 'Drown in a cold vat of whisky?' He said. 'Death, where is thy sting?' When Harpo Marx turned up at his home for lunch one day Fields took him up into the attic which was filled with hundreds of cases of liquor. 'What's with all the booze?' Harpo asked. Fields smiled. 'Never can be sure Prohibition won't come back, my boy!'

Fields was born, appropriately enough, above a bar that his father James managed in Philadelphia. Many a night the little WC was kept awake by the sound of clunking tankards, boisterous singing and general revelry. It must have sounded like fun. James could knock it back a bit, too. Accosted years later by a reporter – 'Say Mr Fields, I heard that you consume two quarts of liquor a day. What would your father think about that?' – Fields replied, 'He'd think I was a sissy.'

His mother did not approve, though, and made her husband quit the bar, it being no proper place to raise a family, but life after that was pretty tough and there are tales of Fields running away from home aged eleven to escape a father who'd become an abusive alcoholic, who used to hit him on the head with a shovel. How much volition one puts upon these events is debatable, the savage years living rough, stealing food and clothes to survive, because Fields enjoyed embellishing stories about his youth. What's known for sure is that he became an expert pool hustler and juggler in his teens, doing well in vaudeville and burlesque with an act that progressively leaned towards comedy.

The drinking began quite innocently enough. Travelling a lot on the road, from gig to gig, Fields found himself staying alone in dreary boarding houses, listening to the sound of laughter coming from the other rooms where his fellow entertainers were partying. As a juggler he never touched alcohol, for fear of ruining his dexterity, but over time he began to travel the vaudeville circuit with a trunkload of booze, just so his fellow vaudevillians would come to his dressing room and he'd have company. Pretty soon he was crawling into that trunk himself, and never really came out again.

By the time he started working in film Fields had developed a chronic alcohol problem that informed his screen image, that of a lecherous, child-hating, mean-spirited, but somehow lovable old duffer. He was happiest working with directors who understood his special needs, allowing him to come to work when he wanted to and after he got plastered, usually in the late afternoon, letting him go home again.

Fields came late to film, by the time he established himself as a star he was approaching his mid-fifties, and drinking more heavily than ever, despite protestations to the contrary. 'I certainly do not drink all the time, I have to sleep you know.'

Crossing the border into Mexico one time, Fields spent several days in a fleapit hotel drinking himself into a stupor. One morning his dozing was disturbed by the nightmare scenario of a brass band tuning up. Taking on the role of critic, Fields stood on his balcony and relieved himself over the rail into the square below, missing the horn blowers but claiming a direct hit on a medal-strewn local politician about to deliver a speech. Fields was kicked out.

During another particularly blinding hangover a waiter graciously offered to fetch Fields some Bromo-Seltzer. 'No-o-o-o,' came the reply. 'I couldn't stand the noise!'

His drink-inspired witticisms were now becoming as much a part of his legend as the famous bulbous nose. 'Reminds me of my safari in Africa,' he once informed a flock of reporters. 'Somebody forgot the corkscrew and for several days we had nothing to live on but food and water.'

Besides being a walking billboard for the liquor industry – 'I exercise extreme self-control,' he once observed, 'I never drink anything stronger than gin before breakfast' – Fields was a man of quite eccentric character. During dinner he enjoyed nothing better than unnerving his despised mother-in-law by keeping a lit cigar or a beer bottle balanced atop his head. He was fond of dressing up his mistresses as Chinamen and wore a hideous clip-on false moustache that looked like a crushed beetle simply because all his friends loathed it. He also once tried to kill a swan with a golf club until the fowl outmanoeuvred him and chased him back into his house.

When a close friend died of alcoholism, Fields halted the sauce for a year, but the habit proved too irresistible. His willpower was never the strongest. 'I only drink to steady my nerves,' he once remarked. 'Sometimes I'm so steady I don't move for months.' It all got too much and he checked into hospital suffering from the DTs. Even here legend has it that he drank two bottles of gin – smuggled past the nurses by friends – every day. The road to recovery was slow and painful but he eventually returned to the movies, joking, 'It's hard to tell where Hollywood ends and the DTs begin.' He hired a doctor to personally halt his drinking; it was a battle of wills. Seemingly recovered, Fields offered to teach the medico how to play golf. Once on the course Fields explained that the secret behind the game was to always stare intently at the ball and count to ten slowly before striking it. 'Now count,' said Fields as he softly stepped back. 'One . . . two . . . ,' the doctor began. 'Much slower,' Fields instructed. 'One . . . two . . . ' 'Still slower,' said Fields. 'And don't take your eye off the ball.'

Unbeknown to the doctor, Fields had come prepared, his baggy tweed suit secreted with numerous small bottles of whisky. Every time the doctor took a swing, Fields downed one. This deception lasted for several days, after which the doctor announced, 'I must say, after a week without a drink Fields you're looking better already!'

Fields's darkest nemesis wasn't the bottle, but Baby LeRoy, a child star who often upstaged him in his films. Once, asked how he liked kids, Fields replied, 'Parboiled.' During a break in shooting Fields once spiked the three-year-old LeRoy's milk bottle with gin, so when the director called 'action' the poor little bugger was too soused to perform. 'Walk him around, walk him around,' Fields advised, before adding: 'That kid's no trooper. Send him home!' Production was halted until the child could sober up.

There were clashes with other colleagues, too. His co-star on *My Little Chickadee* (1940) was the fearsome Mae West, who insisted that Fields stay sober. 'Don't worry, my dear. I'm on the wagon.' But Fields's idea of being on the wagon was trading sherry for gin. When Mae discovered his true state he was physically carried off the set by crew members and suspended from the film. On his return Fields called Mae 'a plumber's idea of Cleopatra'. When the director was asked what it was like directing these two great stars he replied, 'I'm not directing, I'm refereeing.'

Living across the street from Fields was the distinguished director Cecil B DeMille, whom the comedian accused of tossing empty whisky bottles onto his front lawn, revenge for property damage caused by Fields firing his BB gun at imaginary prowlers. One evening Fields collected the bottles in a bag and hurled the lot through DeMille's windows, bellowing, 'Take that and that, you sanctimonious knave!!'

After the commercial failure of 1941's *Never Give a Sucker an Even Break* and bouts of illness brought on by his drinking, Fields drew back from film work. But his humour never dimmed. 'My illness is due to my doctor's insistence that I drink milk, a whitish fluid they force down help-less babies.' And the classic: 'I never drink water, fish fuck in it.' He sought comfort in the camaraderie of his friends, a close-knit group that he shared a bottle or two with: painter John Decker, writer Gene Fowler and fellow actor John Barrymore. Not long after the Japanese attack on Pearl Harbor and America's entry into the war the boys were discussing world affairs over several drinks when they came to the conclusion that what the Allied effort needed was their immediate assistance. Fields stood up and decreed, 'Let's enlist.' Now Fields, not to mention Barrymore and the others, were already well advanced in years and hardly in prime shape, or to put it another way, they were geriatric drunks. Yet they turned up at the nearest recruiting centre with Fields intent on requesting duty as a commando. Looking over his desk the officer in charge said, 'Who sent you? The enemy?'

Fields's patriotism was unanswerable; well, maybe. He maintained something like twenty-one bank accounts across America, but liked to joke that he had $10,000 stashed away in a bank in Berlin, 'Just in case that son of a bitch Hitler wins.'

It was inevitable really that the booze would eventually claim him. His closest friends visited Fields in hospital and caught him reading the Bible. 'For Lord's sake, WC, you're an atheist and you're carrying a Bible, what are you doing that for?' Fields replied, 'I'm looking for loopholes.'

Fields's ultimate jest was to die on Christmas Day, a holiday he claimed to despise above all others. Pressing a finger to his lips, he just had time to wink at a nurse before he was gone. 'It was a woman who drove me to drink,' he once claimed. 'And I never had the courtesy to thank her.'

F SCOTT FITZGERALD (1896–1940: Author)

Although he wrote only a handful of novels, including The Great Gatsby, F Scott Fitzgerald ranks high amongst America's literary giants, his works eerily evocative of the roaring twenties, an age he and his wife Zelda embraced perhaps too enthusiastically. They were drunken pranksters of the highest order, jumping into the fountain at the Plaza Hotel, boiling party guests' watches in tomato soup, or the time both arrived in their pyjamas for a cocktail party, which Zelda had no compunction about removing and then dancing naked. Such innocent high jinks soon turned sour, however, leading to rampant alcoholism and madness.

The problem was Fitzgerald couldn't take his booze; it only required a few drinks to tip him over the edge. His friend Ernest Hemingway wasn't alone in his belief that Fitzgerald was destroyed by his weakness for alcohol; 'It was just poison to him.'

His rise to literary celebrity and self-inflicted collapse was truly shocking, this charming playboy writer who threw away his talent in endless partygoing and gin bottles. As Fitzgerald himself observed: 'First you take a drink, then the drink takes a drink, then the drink takes you.'

He was born in St Paul, Minnesota, to comfortably off middle-class parents. Academically bright, his first piece of writing to see print was a detective story in the school newspaper when he was thirteen. A handsome lad, Fitzgerald was thoroughly spoiled with a burgeoning ego the size of Mussolini's: 'I didn't know till fifteen that there was anyone in the world except me.'

It was at college where the drinking started. During one vacation at home he barged into a local church conducting a Christmas service, staggered up to the pulpit and casually said to the rector: 'Don't mind me, go on with the sermon.' Neglecting his studies, Fitzgerald took up a commission in the US Army in 1917, but never saw action, just as well perhaps, for he left the services as 'the world's worst second lieutenant'.

Beginning his writing career by supplying stories for mass-circulation magazines like the *Saturday Evening Post*, it was his debut novel, *This Side of Paradise*, published in 1920, that made the twenty-four-year-old Fitzgerald famous overnight. It gave him the courage to ask the love of his life, Zelda Sayre, a rebellious and reckless Alabama beauty who drank almost as much as he did, to marry him. Embarking on an extravagant life as new celebrities, getting off to a grand start on their honeymoon by being ejected from the New York Biltmore Hotel for rowdiness, both seemed to embody all the gaudy excesses of the roaring twenties, a decade Scott nicknamed 'the jazz age'. In New York he drank and fought with waiters, while Zelda danced on tables in restaurants. Arriving well bladdered at a Broadway play, they hurriedly reached the conclusion it was rubbish and made their criticism known by standing up and beginning to undress while giggling like schoolkids. They were kicked out. When Dorothy Parker first met the couple they arrived sitting on the roof of a taxi.

Wherever the Fitzgeralds chose to live one of their first tasks was to locate a reputable bootlegger and arrange for regular deliveries. Fitzgerald's preferred liquor was gin; he believed you could not detect it on the breath. Their parties became legendary amongst New York's high society, with house rules such as: 'Weekend guests are respectfully notified that invitations to stay over Monday, issued by the host and hostess during the small hours of Sunday morning, must not be taken seriously.'

But such a lifestyle came with a hefty price tag, as Scott became a confirmed alcoholic and their joint benders ended mostly in nasty domestic rows. This image as a gin-drenched dandy also crucially obviated his work as a writer. Nevertheless, the couple left America early in 1924 to swan round Europe, never staying in one spot for long: Capri, Rome and the Riviera, with regular trips back to the States. In Paris it was '1,000 parties and no work'. Fitzgerald went on ten-day benders and would arrive in places as far afield as Brussels wondering how the hell he got there. In Paris he stole a three-wheeled delivery cart and rode it around the Place de la Concorde pursued by angry gendarmes. While in Rome he got into a fight with a taxi driver and a policeman and spent the night in jail.

Fitzgerald was now drinking so much that a friend was convinced the writer was destined to die young in a garret. A nasty violent streak surfaced, bringing with it a belief that he could box the hell out of anyone; in fact the opposite was true, with bar brawls usually resulting in injury to himself. Once, a slaughtered Zelda encouraged him to take on a bouncer at a Manhattan speakeasy and he came away with two black eyes.

On the Riviera the Fitzgeralds made quite an impression with their dangerous habit of diving into the sea from thirty-five foot high rocks after returning mothered from late-night parties. Upset at not being invited to one Riviera high-society gathering, Scott stood behind a hedge and threw garbage at guests. At another Zelda kicked off her black lace panties and presented them to the host as a going-away present.

During these travels Scott sat down and wrote *The Great Gatsby*, which was not the success he'd anticipated. Meanwhile Zelda indulged in an affair with a French pilot and asked for a divorce; Fitzgerald's answer was to lock her up in the house until she saw sense and changed her mind. There were other rifts, exacerbated by their reckless drinking. Dining one evening on the terrace of a hilltop restaurant that overlooked a sheer drop of 200 feet, Fitzgerald spied the famous dancer Isadora Duncan. He left Zelda to introduce himself, sinking to his knees at her feet, always one for the dramatic gesture. Insanely jealous, Zelda stood on her chair and leaped into the darkness of the stairwell. Friends watched in stunned horror, convinced she'd toppled over the edge to her doom; instead she emerged minutes later bloodied and unbowed. During another fight, driving home as usual far too fast along winding roads, Zelda got out and lay prostrate under the wheels of the car and dared Scott to run her over. For a split second he started to move the car forward, and then stopped.

On returning to Paris Fitzgerald met the then largely unknown Ernest Hemingway. It was an odd first encounter, in a bar unsurprisingly, where Fitzgerald asked Hemingway whether he'd slept with his wife, before promptly passing out. If anything Hemingway couldn't abide Zelda, calling her insane, domineering and destructive.

The Fitzgeralds remained in France until the end of 1926, during which time Zelda's behaviour had become alarmingly nutty and Fitzgerald's alcoholic intake was out of control, sometimes more than a quart of gin daily. He considered the offloading of a case of beer within twenty-four hours as 'being on the wagon'.

There were long periods when Scott never touched alcohol, refraining from drinking while writing, for example, but his remarkably low tolerance for booze sometimes resulted in a personality change that influenced how he behaved. As Hemingway observed: 'No matter what Scott did, I must know it was like a sickness to him and try to be a good friend.' Sadly, petty professional rivalry got in the way. It was galling for Fitzgerald to see Hemingway's star in the ascendancy, under his support and mentoring, while he was heading in the opposite direction. 'My God I am a forgotten man,' he wrote.

In April 1930 Zelda suffered a mental breakdown and was admitted to a sanatorium where she was diagnosed as a schizophrenic. It marked the end of her life with Scott as she spent the rest of her days in and out of psychiatric hospitals. But her love never wavered, the tender letters she wrote to him filled with memories of happier days together.

While he did his best to support her financially, the strain was crippling. No longer commanding huge fees for his stories, Fitzgerald was wiped out. By his fortieth birthday he'd hit rock bottom and tried to commit suicide by drinking a bottle of morphine.

He was saved by an unlikely source – Hollywood. MGM gave him a lucrative screenwriting contract and he happily drank with the likes of Spencer Tracy and Errol Flynn, but hated the town itself and everything it represented. Estranged from Zelda, and on the wagon, he met movie columnist Sheila Graham and they became lovers, but he soon returned to the booze benders that left him paralysed in bed for days on end or hospitalised. His return to heavy drinking may have had something to do with the soul-destroying hack work he was undertaking in Hollywood: 'What I am doing here is the last tired effort of a man who once did something finer and better,' he lamented.

It was his drinking most likely that resulted in the termination of his MGM contract. Going freelance, Scott realised that few producers were prepared to take the risk of hiring him. Sheila had also grown tired of his drunken bouts, which were destroying their relationship. Finally, in January 1940, Scott sorted himself out for good and never touched alcohol again. But it was already too late.

Sober, he started work on a new novel, amongst the first to satirise the Hollywood system, posthumously published as *The Last Tycoon*, convinced it would elevate him back into the literary glitterati. But he was in poor health, years of gin and fags had hardened his arteries causing a mild heart attack. Leaving a movie premiere with Sheila he almost collapsed and had to be helped to his car. 'My God,' exclaimed Fitzgerald. 'They're all going to think I'm drunk.'

The next day, quietly relaxing in his apartment, Scott felt a massive bolt of pain streak across his chest. He shot up and flung himself at the mantelpiece, trying to stay on his feet, but gasped and fell like a stone to the floor. Sheila was hysterical, not sure what to do, so poured brandy into his mouth in an effort to bring him back. It didn't work. F Scott Fitzgerald was gone at forty-four. When she heard the news of his passing, old friend Dorothy Parker burst into tears then cried out, 'The poor son of a bitch.'

Tragically, Fitzgerald died believing himself a failure. By the 1960s, however, his gifts as a writer had been re-evaluated, his books finding a new appreciative audience and his status as one of America's finest writers assured.

As for Zelda, she continued to live in mental institutions until one evening in March 1948 when she was locked in a room, awaiting electro-shock treatment the next day, and a fire broke out. She numbered amongst nine women who burned to death as the flames swept through the building.

KEITH FLOYD (1943–2009: Cook and Restaurateur)

Putting it bluntly, Keith Floyd revolutionised the art of cooking on television, dispensing with the mock kitchen studio set he rustled up food guerrilla-style, on the run as it were, on a cliff edge or fishing boat knee deep in vomit, usually attired in a skewed bow tie and 'What-ho, Jeeves!'

blazer, with a bottle of wine always within easy reach. I don't think a photograph exists anywhere of Floyd without a glass of red wine in his fist. This is a man who once fired up his trusty portable gas stove to cook a meal inside a Tasmanian hotel room, setting off the fire alarm which resulted in six burly firemen barging through the door. Then there was the occasion he attempted cooking on the Thailand–Burma border, with bombs hurtling past courtesy of the Thai army waging combat against the Burmese drug warlords. It was one of the most interesting meals Floyd ever partook of. 'They opened the stomach of an ox, took out its still pulsating liver and presented it to me. Sometimes it's a pain in the arse to be an honoured guest.'

Floyd was born in Somerset to working-class parents who scrimped and saved to send him to public school. After that he joined the army after seeing *Zulu* but got kicked out for spending more time in the mess kitchens than in a tank. His path to culinary greatness began modestly enough in Bristol where he opened his first restaurant at the tender age of twenty-two. Floyd, however, quickly proved to be not your average restaurateur. Tired of one of his regular customers always finding something to moan about, Floyd served him up a large beer mat soaked in beer stock with mushroom sauce, and hung around to watch him eat it.

Sadly his business acumen was on a par with his diplomacy, the words 'liquidation' and 'taxman' loom large in the Floyd lexicon. With the Bristol bistro almost on its knees by the early eighties salvation arrived in the form of BBC producer David Pritchard. Over coffee, with the smell of garlic and Gauloises in the air, they chatted. Floyd's phrase 'cooking is the new rock and roll' inspired Pritchard to put this maverick chef on television and *Floyd on Fish* in 1985 was an instant ratings winner, although Pritchard had to reassure his bosses that they hadn't hired a complete wino. 'He's a bit like Dean Martin without the singing,' he excused.

More series followed, plus reams of books, including Floyd's own authoritative guide to hangovers. The fame got to him, it was all so sudden, so unexpected. Increasingly he found himself staying up all night, unable to sleep because he was worrying about the next day's shoot.

Alcohol now became his crutch, a companion that would help him through the hours from midnight to dawn. 'I drank just to anaesthetise myself. When I go in front of a television camera I have to perform, and after that performance there is nothing.'

Floyd became a national figure, teaching the British to cook continental-style, paving the way for that insufferable breed, the modern celebrity TV chef. Asked once what he'd do with the Ramsays and the Jamies and all the rest, Floyd replied, 'I'd like to napalm the lot of them.'

Political correctness just wasn't on the Floyd radar. Greenpeace wrote to him asking how he could cook an ostrich egg in front of its mother. 'Ostriches don't give a toss,' he responded. 'They are thick.'

Cursed with the casebook Jekyll and Hyde drunk personality, Floyd was amiable for most of the day. At night he became a, 'raging paranoid misanthrope who could clear a room with his ferocity', according to one journalist. Filming an episode up in the Orkneys, Floyd burst into a bar and screamed at the locals, 'You bunch of tossers!' When a member of the crew left a copy of Mary Shelley's *Frankenstein* on Pritchard's desk one day the inference was all too obvious. 'I think I've created a monster and it's time to load the gun with silver bullets,' admitted the producer. Theirs was always a rocky relationship, threatening to spill over into open warfare at any moment. Sometimes Pritchard wished he had a revolver instead of a camera pointing at the chef. When the shows finally ended the pair didn't speak again for sixteen years.

Away from the camera and the kitchen Floyd was equally passionate. He went through wives like Bluebeard on speed, four times divorced; 'Don't come to me for marital advice or financial services.' Wives one and two left because of his drinking and general grumpy demeanour, which clung to him with all the benevolence of a tank homing in on a Chinese student. He proposed to wife number three within four hours of meeting her in a pub, but that marriage quickly went tits up after he accused her of forgetting his birthday then throwing her and fifty fellow diners out of his restaurant. Next was food stylist Tess Smith, who upon learning that Floyd was listed as one of the ten worst husbands in Britain quipped, 'Why not number one?' When that marriage predictably landed in the divorce courts, with Tess citing his 'unreasonable' and 'abusive'

'I spent a lot of my money on booze, birds and fast cars, the rest I just squandered.' George Best enjoys a quiet night out.

A volcanic marriage: Ava Gardner drank champagne like soda water and once urinated in the lobby of the Hotel Ritz, Madrid, while Sinatra ('The Bourbon Baritone') drove golf carts through plate glass windows.

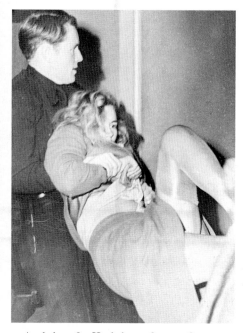

A rebel too far. Hauled out of court after one misdemeanour too many, Frances Farmer was thrown into the nuthouse from hell where she was reportedly lobotomised.

Tallulah Bankhead was the most thoroughgoing libertine of her age, bedding men and women with reckless abandon and able to down a bottle of bourbon in thirty minutes. 'I'm as pure as the driven slush, darling.'

Ernest Hemingway once said, 'a man does not exist until he is drunk,' and spent the rest of his life trying to prove it. When the booze so raddled his brain he couldn't write anymore he blew it apart with a 12-gauge shotgun.

Brendan Behan played the role of the stereotypical bladdered Irishman to perfection, seeing alcohol as an indispensible part of a writer's make up. He only really drank on two occasions, 'when I'm thirsty, and when I'm not.'

The leading comic writer of his generation, Kingsley Amis paraded his drunkenness at functions and pubs and was the laureate of the hangover - try Bovril and vodka or a tumbler of Grand Marnier for breakfast

John Belushi was the Keith Moon of comedy, a self-destructive comet with no brakes or iota of common sense. 'I'm going to die young,' he prophesied. 'I just can't stop destroying myself.' Yep!

Debauched, misanthropic, crude, alcoholic, just a few of the nicer things you can say about Serge Gainsbourg. French icon, too – who else could get away with singing a duet with their twelve-year-old daughter espousing incest or asking Whitney Huston to fuck him on live TV.

Described as, 'the most controversial woman in the history of rock' by *Rolling Stone* magazine, Courtney Love graduated from stripper to drug- and booze-addled rock bitch who tried to dent the skull of a reporter with Quentin Tarantino's Oscar for *Pulp Fiction*.

Tales of Shane MacGowan's drunken debauchery are so gobsmackingly unbelievable that they must be apocryphal – frighteningly most aren't. Like the occasion he fell out of his tour van at 50mph and survived and when he tried to ingest a vinyl LP of the Beach Boys' greatest hits.

The ultimate lounge lizard, Dean Martin's world revolved around booze, even his car number plate read: DRUNKY. He couldn't comprehend sobriety. 'Imagine getting up in the morning and knowing that's as good as you're going to feel all day.'

behaviour, Floyd lived up to his reputation by demanding his mother-in-law foot the court costs.

By his mid-fifties Floyd had gone to seed awfully, looking at least half a century older than he actually was. He began referring to himself as an 'old geriatric fart'. One wonders if he ever had the guts to walk past cemeteries. He continued drinking unapologetically, not giving a stuff. Asked what was his most memorable drink he replied, 'This one, because it could be my last.' He also continued to court financial problems, declared bankrupt once after personally guaranteeing an order for £36,000 of drinks.

The demon booze still held sway over him. He'd keep a bottle of Scotch on his bedside table, in the mornings partaking of a few large glasses before he even had the courage to go downstairs. Near Christmas 2004 Floyd was convicted for drink-driving after crashing his car while three and a half times over the limit, losing a lucrative deal to advertise champagne for Tesco as a result. Banned from driving for thirty-two months, he emerged from the magistrate's court issuing his own in-imitable festive warning to revellers: 'It's coming up to Christmas. Get pissed at home, don't drive – and have a great time.'

Floyd certainly followed his own advice, getting pissed at home and generally wherever he found himself. He claimed to have been blacklisted by the BBC in 2005 after appearing torqued on a political discussion programme, blaming the incident on a twelve-hour wait in a restaurant before filming.

Then in 2008 he collapsed at a pub – where else? – and was admitted to hospital. It was alleged he'd spent the preceding week swallowing whisky following the collapse of his fourth marriage. To all extents and purposes he was on his death bed. His son slept on the floor for two days keeping vigil, while his daughter held his hand, trying not to look at the green saliva trailing out of his mouth, and begged the comatose Floyd to give up the booze. When he emerged into the land of the living a doctor told him, 'Carry on drinking like you have been and you will die.' Floyd heeded the warning and drastically reined back on his intake, but the old rogue wasn't embracing sobriety just yet.

Floyd's eventual demise was both bizarre and fitting, a last night on earth enjoying a gourmet meal of champagne, oysters and partridge, then sitting down to watch a television documentary about himself, when he croaked it thanks to an ill-timed heart attack.

Whatever his faults and flaws, Floyd had a real passion for food, one that irresistibly translated itself to the watching millions. He was genuinely exciting to watch, and in the great tradition of English eccentricity, slightly crackers, and more than a little dangerous. And far from getting in the way, drink was an integral part of his image.

As he once said, 'I have dedicated my liver to my career.'

ERROL FLYNN (1909–1959: Actor)

A heavy drinker, an unapologetic womaniser, accused of murder and rape, Errol Flynn lived life to the full because he hated the alternative – mediocrity. Or as John Huston put it: 'Fighting, drinking, brawling and whoring featured in both his screen image and his everyday behaviour.' Take this typical Flynn anecdote. One time when flying to Chicago, Flynn's chartered plane put down to refuel in the middle of a prairie town. Jagged up, Flynn took a wander and found a pet store that was selling a female lion cub. He bought it on the spot. Landing in Chicago, Flynn and the beast, on a collar and chain, took a cab to his hotel. During the journey Flynn began to sober up and looked over at the cub, which suddenly seemed to be a lot bigger and more aggressive than he remembered; maybe this wasn't the most sensible purchase of his life. Arriving at his hotel for an appointment with his wife, Flynn wandered casually into reception and handed the desk clerk the cub. 'Check this in, will you, please; Mrs Flynn will call for it very soon,' and then bolted to the nearest bar.

He was born in the seaport town of Hobart, Tasmania, the only son of a distinguished marine biologist. 'A devil in boy's clothing,' in his own words, Flynn ran away from home when he was seven, sending his parents into hysterics for three long days and nights. He was eventually found miles away trying to find work on a dairy farm. Frequently he clashed with his disciplinarian mother; she once locked him in a back room for two days after one misdemeanour too far. The young Flynn never forgot the experience and was determined never again to be cooped up.

He was restless by nature and after leaving school plunged into the life of an adventurer, working as a slave trader, plantation owner and gold prospector in New Guinea, crossing crocodile infested waters, getting tried for murder when he shot a native in self-defence during an ambush and catching the clap for romancing too many native girls.

In the Australian outback he worked on a sheep ranch and takes the prize for the shittiest job of all time, sticking his face into the back end of a young sheep, amid the crap and flies, and biting its bollocks off, then spitting them out into a bucket. Even covered in blood and sheep shit his charm worked on the ladies, and he was soon bedding the ranch owner's daughter. When he was caught Flynn bounded out of the window and ran like hell pursued by shotgun-wielding relatives. He never looked back.

Arriving in England, his debonair demeanour landed him a job in repertory theatre where by chance he was spotted by a Warner Brothers representative and taken to America. Landing in New York, Flynn was shown the sights by a studio PR man. He expressly wanted to check out Harlem, so several hours were spent in seedy clip joints. Flynn spied a beautiful dancer and invited her over to his table. As he sat enraptured, his hand began to make steady travels up her thigh until he grabbed hold of what turned out to be quite a stiff cock. Turning to the Warner's guy Flynn said, 'Let's get out of here.' They bolted; no doubt with the sound of raucous laughter in their ears.

Flynn's debut lead role as *Captain Blood* (1935) rocketed him to stardom as the undisputed king of swashbuckler films, the new Douglas Fairbanks. A veritable conveyor belt of adventure pictures followed, including the classic *Adventures of Robin Hood* (1938). From his early days in Hollywood Flynn was set upon a hedonistic lifestyle. As he once boasted: 'If I have any genius, it is a genius for living.' With pal David Niven he shared a bachelor pad in Malibu nicknamed 'Cirrhosis-by-the-Sea'. He picked fights in bars for no other reason than perhaps to reinforce his manhood, working as he did in a profession that saw him speaking cod-Shakespeare dialogue mainly in tights. On the set of *The Charge of the Light Brigade*

(1936), a burly extra poked Flynn's horse with a lance, causing it to rear up and throw him in the dirt. As he and his fellow extras laughed Flynn dusted himself down, marched up to the guy, hauled him off the saddle and soundly thrashed him in front of the whole crew. Flynn was respected after that. The extra spent two days in hospital.

And there were the women, of course. 'I don't have to seduce girls,' Flynn once admitted. 'For Christ's sake, I come home and they're hiding under my bed.' His first mistake, in a veritable litany of boobs, was to get married; worse it was to neurotic French actress Lili Damita. The marriage got so bad that Flynn escaped to the Spanish Civil War, preferring a paella-fuelled bullet in the head to another bout of nagging. When she organised a surprise party to celebrate the anniversary of their first meeting, Flynn arrived an hour late. 'Happy anniversary, darling,' said Lili as Flynn came into the room, then smashed a bottle of champagne over his head. Before unconsciousness overtook him, Errol aimed a punch, connecting with his wife's chin and knocking out a tooth. Coming round in hospital he was apoplectic with guilt about punching a woman, even if it was his wife.

After reconciliation, things got back to normal and the Flynn household came to resemble downtown Beirut. Their arguments were mere preludes to Lili lobbing bottles and plates and anything else she could grab in Flynn's general direction. 'Only by great nimbleness of foot did I avoid a weekly fractured skull.' In the end Flynn took to staying away from home as often as possible, drinking with friends or going off on wild booze binges. He bought a yacht, the *Sirocco*, essentially a floating knocking shop; his crew all wore badges bearing their employer's emblem – an erect dick with testicles and the initials FFF – 'Flynn's Flying Fuckers'.

Flynn took ever more comfort in extramarital sex. When working in the studio he would leave his dressing-room door open while he changed, 'to enable the wenches to engage in a little window shopping'. When one director spotted Flynn starkers he screamed, 'For decency's sake, cover yourself.' Errol merely draped a handkerchief over his erection. Another time Flynn's father paid a surprise studio visit and came across his son giving a naked starlet a good seeing to against the wall of his dressing room. 'Take a seat, Dad. I shan't be long.'

After leaving Lili for good, Flynn built his own 'bachelor' pad up on Mulholland Drive. One of the features was a huge circular mirror on the ceiling above his bed. At parties select couples were invited to frolic in there, unaware that the mirror was two-way and that Flynn and his pals were watching from what was dubbed the 'jerk-off' room directly above.

Still a box-office draw, Flynn was starting to creak a bit. He'd already caused so much damage to his body that he was declared unfit for duty in the Second World War, so had to fight the Nazis and the Japanese on the back lot at Warners, a huge dent to his macho pride. The drinking was also getting desperate, despite his doctor telling him that his heart and lungs were irreparably damaged due to his hedonistic lifestyle and he had five years to live at best. If anything Flynn deliberately increased his alcohol intake. Banned from bringing booze on to any of his sets, Flynn went to extraordinary lengths to hide his habit. He'd pour bourbon into fake bottles of skin cleanser that he kept in his make-up case, or inject oranges with vodka, then enjoy tucking into the spiked fruit throughout the day without raising suspicion.

Ironically it wasn't the booze that was his comeuppance, but his predilection for seducing young women. Flynn's easy, irresistible charm was so captivating that he'd seemed always impervious to criticism. Then in 1942, in a case that stunned America and grabbed worldwide attention, two under-age girls accused him of statutory rape. Following a high-profile trial Flynn was acquitted, but the damage to his reputation was irreparable.

Still, it didn't dampen his ardour and he quickly married again, a young redhead he'd cheekily chatted up during the trial who worked at a tobacco kiosk at the courthouse. He'd no intention of being faithful and was quite brazen about it, installing his new bride in a separate house so as not to interfere with his sexual shenanigans. 'The Christian concept of monogamy is to me nothing more than a travesty of human nature,' he said. 'It doesn't work, never will.' Flynn got so obsessed with sex he briefly became addicted to opium, believing the drug heightened sexual pleasure.

By the late forties Flynn was combining booze with amphetamines and morphine, and had become a regular user of prostitutes. He was still starring in successful pictures but not the sort he wanted to make, ones that traded on his swashbuckling image and didn't challenge him as an actor. When the studio refused to vary the kind of roles he was being asked to play Flynn fell into a deep depression. More than once he stayed up all night, a bottle of vodka beside him and a loaded revolver in his hand, debating whether it was worth blowing his brains out.

Still he was drinking; directors coped by getting as many shots of him as they could in the morning before he got too blotto. He also kept a small bottle that he shoved up his nose at regular intervals. Most thought it was for blocked sinuses, not realising it was full of cocaine mixed with vodka.

Fed up with Hollywood, Flynn began to make films on the continent. His behaviour on *Adventures of Captain Fabian* (1951), filmed in France, performing scenes zonked, throwing tantrums and walking off set whenever he felt like it, was so bad that not one member of the French crew ever wanted to speak to him again.

While shooting *Crossed Swords* (1954), Flynn fell ill and checked into a clinic where he was told his liver had stopped working, literally. 'What happens now?' Flynn asked. 'You die,' was the reply. Certainly he should not touch a drop of booze ever again. Flynn somehow recovered and arrived back on the set with a tumbler of neat vodka ready to work. Tasmania certainly raises them tough.

He battled on, sailing round Europe on his yacht, continually on the run from creditors in America, alimony payments galore and the taxman, all the time drinking vodka till it ran out of his ears. He didn't give a shit, and why should he. He'd been Errol Flynn.

When they bothered, producers were now hiring him simply to play drunks and forgotten bums, which is what audiences had come to think he was. In *The Sun Also Rises* (1957) Tyrone Power was his co-star. They'd been drinking buddies in the old days but now Power was disturbed to see his friend a virtual empty shell of a man, unrecognisable from the Adonis he'd once been. He was even more shocked that Errol started the day with several tequilas for breakfast, and by eleven was well off with the fairies. Ironically, though, it was Power who was to die first.

The Roots of Heaven (1958) was filmed in French Equatorial Africa in stifling conditions, so hot, recalled its director John Huston, 'that whenever you relaxed you went into a coma'. The only social outlet for Errol was booze and drugs, supplied by a benevolent French doctor, who also made sure he had a nightly diet of local native girls.

So much drinking went on during that movie that pretty soon the unit's booze supply ran out and they had to airlift crates of the stuff in at regular intervals. 'In three months,' recalled actor Marc Doelnitz, 'we had drunk all the reserve whisky for Africa.' Flynn had been clever, bringing his own supply, twelve cases of vodka, which he managed to polish off and had to send for more. He was drinking the stuff at six in the morning in large tumblers; probably brushed his teeth in it, too.

Such was his financial plight that Flynn continued to live mostly on his yacht, sailing the world as a boozing bum, anywhere the IRS couldn't find him. He stayed in Kingston, Jamaica for a while, causing mayhem. So local legend has it, he released an alligator into the town's main street and drove his Cadillac into a swimming pool.

Keeping him scandalous company was a fifteen-year-old blonde called Beverly Aadland. 'I like my whisky old and my women young,' Flynn once said, and by God he was true to his word, you have to give him that. She was with him when he died. He'd arrived in Vancouver to sell his beloved yacht because he needed the money, as always, but was struck down by a heart attack just four months after his fiftieth birthday. The autopsy showed he had the body of a man fifteen years his senior, which considering what he put it through, isn't at all bad.

True to form Flynn was buried with six bottles of whisky in his coffin.

FREDERICK WILLIAM I (1688–1740: *Prussian Monarch*)

As potty European monarchs go, old Frederick was one of the more barking, not helped by his ravenous appetite for fine wine. Take, for example, his habit of carrying around a walking stick, not to aid him, rather that he might clout over the head any poor unfortunate who displeased him. Kings could do that in the eighteenth century. News of these indiscriminate whackings circulated around the kingdom. Enjoying a pleasant stroll one fine morning, Frederick noticed a peasant trembling behind a bush. Asked what on earth he was doing, the peasant replied that he was afraid of His Majesty.

'Afraid?' roared Frederick. 'You ought to love me and not be afraid; yes, to love me, I tell you!' To which accompaniment the peasant was roundly beaten with the stick.

He was a good old-fashioned tyrant; more than one of his servants was missing an eye due to his always carrying two pistols, loaded with rock salt, which he'd offload at anyone who startled him.

Despising the ostentatious reign of his father, Frederick I, Frederick William was more puritan in outlook, prone to ripping the 'extravagant finery' from the clothes of ladies in the street. At court he led a frugal, almost Spartan existence, paring down on royal expenses, sacking so many servants that the Queen had to help wash the dishes after dinner. He did have some redeeming qualities, however: he intensely disliked the French.

Nor did Frederick much care for democracy, running the country without any form of government. He'd just invite a small clique of cronies to discuss important affairs of state while drinking vast quantities of wine and beer.

One area in which Frederick showed no frugality whatsoever was his army, and under his rule Prussia became the third greatest military power on earth. On occasions when he was under the weather, or just plain depressed, Frederick would order a few hundred of his finest soldiers to march through his bedroom to raise his spirits. His own private regiment was populated exclusively with incredibly tall men recruited from across Europe. 'The most beautiful girl or woman in the world would be a matter of indifference to me, but tall soldiers – they are my weakness.' When insufficient volunteers were forthcoming agents were sent out to press-gang giants into service. After the scandal of an Italian priest being dragged from his altar mid-sermon and an imperial diplomat shanghaied, Frederick changed tack and began mating his lofty soldiers with freakishly tall local women, a principle that would reemerge two centuries later as Nazi party policy.

His military fanaticism extended to his family. Frederick wanted his eldest child Fritz to become a soldier, so every morning the poor little sprog was woken by a cannon firing outside his bedroom window. Unlike other children who had to make do with toy soldiers, at the age of six Fritz was presented with his very own regiment of 'live' children to drill.

Frederick often flew into dark rages, especially after a visit to the wine cellar, breaking noses and knocking out teeth with the force of his blows. Other times he would fall into deep depressions and sit alone weeping for hours. It's now known that the monarch suffered from porphyria, a hereditary disease that brought on killer migraines and episodes of delirium. Poor Fritz bore much of the brunt of his father's declining mental health. If the pair crossed paths in a palace corridor Frederick might grab his son by the throat and force him to kiss his boots, or he'd be beaten for merely using a silver spoon at luncheon or for daring to wear gloves on a wintry day.

It was no surprise to anyone when Frederick suffered a complete breakdown and had to be wheeled about the palace like a pathetic invalid. In his misery Frederick took even more to drink, and to directing increasingly malicious japes at his staff. Poor Jakob Paul Gundling, the King's privy counsellor, seemed to suffer more than most. His master once threw him into his bed, where he'd hidden a brace of ferocious bear cubs. Another time he had the door of Gundling's private chambers walled up so that the poor clot spent the whole night seeking his vanished room, disturbing half the servants.

One of Gundling's duties at court was to read the newspapers to Frederick, after which he was invariably thrown out of the window into the moat. During the winter months he'd bounce off the foot-thick ice, incurring some discomfort. On at least one occasion he was deliberately set alight. Is it any wonder that he twice fled the country in a vain attempt to escape his tormentor's clutches? Or that he became an alcoholic? Even in death, Gundling's ordeal continued: Frederick encoffined him in a wine casket that was pulled to the cemetery on a gun carriage by pigs.

Frederick still reserved the bulk of his temper for his unfortunate son. Summoned to his father's chamber, Fritz was flogged with a cane until Frederick had exhausted the strength of his arm. Still gripped with fury, he seized a curtain cord and proceeded to strangle the lad with it. Just barely able to scream for help, a chambermaid rushed in, possibly preventing the King extinguishing all breath from the future heir.

After he was publicly beaten at a military parade in Saxony, dragged along the ground by his hair and suffering other indignities, Fritz quite understandably legged it. His father had him captured and imprisoned, and pondered long and hard on the idea of execution; maybe that would teach him a lesson. In the end, no doubt swayed by some withering looks from the Queen, Frederick pardoned him.

As the symptoms of porphyria steadily grew more severe Frederick sought increasing consolation in the bottle, with the result that by the end of his life he'd swelled to the size of a hot-air balloon, was ravaged with gout and in constant pain. One morning he had himself wheeled into the apartment of the Queen, who had grown to despise the very sight of him, and announced, 'Get up! I am going to die today.' And he duly did.

G

SERGE GAINSBOURG (1928–1991: Singer/Songwriter)

'There's a trilogy in my life,' Serge Gainsbourg once said, 'of Gitanes, alcoholism and girls.' He was prodigiously expert at all three. Described at various stages in his life as debauched, irreverent, misanthropic, crude, genius, alcoholic, poet and national treasure, Serge sure knew how to push the buttons of the French bourgeoisie with his outrageous lifestyle. With his don't-give-a-fuck attitude, he numbered amongst the most important figures on the European music scene for over thirty years and was a cult icon to the youth; hell, he might even have been the first punk.

Born in Paris as Lucien Ginsburg, later changing his name to sound more French, he was from a poor Russian Jewish family, all of whom were forced to wear the yellow star during the Nazi-occupation and were lucky to escape deportation to the death camps.

Classically trained, Serge hoofed it as a piano player and crooner on the cabaret circuit before becoming a recording artist and songwriter, causing numerous scandals with his brazenly sexual lyrics. Take his 1966 song 'Les Sucettes' for petite teen idol France Gall, who realised too late that this seemingly innocent children's ditty about a girl who enjoyed sucking lots of lollipops was really a metaphor for oral sex. Then we have *Histoire de Melody Nelson*, Gainsbourg's 1971 concept album that tells the story of a wealthy, aging dandy who slams his Rolls-Royce into a fourteen-year-old English girl on her bicycle and watches her tumble on the ground doll-like, exposing her innocent white knickers. With indecent haste he whisks her off to some lurid hotel and deflowers her, their lovemaking reflected in the mirror above the rococo bed.

Terribly self-conscious about his looks, admitting that he resembled a toad nailed to a wall, Gainsbourg consoled himself by sleeping with as many women as possible. He had an affair with Brigitte Bardot (mandatory in France at the time for all over-sixteens) and years later at a film festival staggered onto the stage plastered to tell an obscene story about the actress and a champagne bottle before tottering off again and collapsing into a chair.

After Bardot he met English actress Jane Birkin, confessing to her that he'd been terrified of Bardot's titanic knockers so this flat-chested English ingénue was right up his alley. Ironically the two did not initially strike sparks, Birkin put off by Gainsbourg's arrogance. She soon discovered his cynical persona was a defence: when you feel weak, you attack. To break the ice Serge took Jane on a whistle-stop tour of Parisian nightclubs, finishing off in a transvestite bar. Then it was straight to the Hilton, where the desk clerk asked, 'Your usual room, Mr Gainsbourg?' In the end Jane's virtue remained intact when he collapsed in a drunken stupor and was out cold for the night.

An inauspicious start, then, but the pair quickly became inseparable, despite a twenty-year age gap. Together they recorded 'Je T'Aime Moi Non Plus', Serge's hymn to sexual liberation. It was an international hit and a seduction classic, with Jane's orgasmic moans giving the impression you were listening to two people actually shagging. Banned in numerous countries and by the BBC, Serge revelled in its notoriety, especially when The Vatican denounced it as obscene. Bullseye!

The couple moved into Paris's fashionable Left Bank, the apartment rooms painted black from floor to ceiling. He bought a vintage Rolls-Royce, even though he had no driving licence ('You cannot drink and drive and I have chosen'); he just sat in the front seat and smoked, using it as an expensive ashtray. It never left his garage.

Most nights the couple whiled away the hours at nightclubs drinking vats of wine, excursions that could often turn, as Jane later put it, 'barmy'. On one occasion Gainsbourg emptied the contents of her handbag on the floor of a restaurant. Furious, she retaliated by hurling her dinner at him, then storming outside and throwing herself into the Seine. She was rescued by an off-duty fireman.

In 1973 Serge suffered the first of two heart attacks, a sure sign that his hard-drinking, chain-smoking lifestyle was taking its toll. When they carried him to hospital he grabbed two cartons of Gitanes and smoked like a chimney during his stay, against regulations, covering himself in Old Spice deodorant to camouflage the fact.

He certainly continued to drink, mostly champagne, cocktails and liqueurs. Often he'd sit at hotel bars and work his way through all the different colours. Sometimes he'd drop by his local police station at 3 a.m. with a bottle of champagne for the gendarmes and invite them all back to sample some of Birkin's home cooking.

As the seventies drew on Serge continued to tread a thin line between musical genius and downright bad taste, releasing the single 'Nazi Rock' and recording a reggae album that included an ode to an under-age Rasta girl whose breasts are 'two spheres that I would give up two months' pay for, just to get to roll my poor joint between them'. But what really annoyed the French establishment was Serge's Rastafarian version of the national anthem 'La Marseillaise', which sparked death threats from right-wing groups.

Domesticity continued with Jane – the Serge way. They had a daughter together, Charlotte, but Gainsbourg continued his hedonistic lifestyle, even cajoling Jane into posing for erotic magazines. For the Christmas issue of one she was photographed chained to a radiator wearing suspenders.

After a thirteen-year turbulent relationship Jane finally left Gainsbourg, no longer willing to put up with his excessive behaviour, brought on by increased drinking. He was devastated and continued to write music for her and phone her every evening, depths of loneliness in his voice.

The 1980s resembled one long suicide note as Gainsbourg became a regular figure on French TV, usually turning up drunk, unshaven and smoking like a chimney. During one talk show Serge had a slanging match with Catherine Ringer, a singer who in the past had appeared in pornographic films. 'You're nothing but a filthy whore, a filthy, fucking whore,' Gainsbourg yelled at her. 'Look at you,' she angrily spat back. 'You're just a bitter old alcoholic. I used to admire you but these days you've become a disgusting old parasite.' Touché.

Then there was the Whitney Houston incident, arguably Gainsbourg's finest moment. Introduced to the American signing sensation by Michael Drucker, host of a live family TV show, Serge behaves at first like the perfect gentleman, standing up to kiss her hand. Sitting back down, he begins speaking in French to Whitney and admonishes the host for not translating him properly before switching to English himself, 'I said I want to fuck her!' Whitney's face is a picture; it's like, *I can't believe he just said that on live television*. The host, perhaps watching his pension going up in flames, tries to smooth things over, 'No, he says you are great.' But even he knows all is lost. 'Sometimes, he's a little bit drunk.' Serge takes exception to this. 'I'm not drunk!' he cries. 'I'm not drunk today.' Whitney looks on incredulously. 'Are you sure?' It's a great moment.

His Gaelic charm alone might have been enough in the past to gloss over such extremes of behaviour, but by his mid-fifties Serge looked like shit, his face and body utterly polluted from alcohol abuse, his persona edgy and unpredictable. Yet his public weren't repelled at all; they couldn't get enough of these public spectacles and Serge revelled in the company of his admirers, who would buy him drinks and listen enraptured to his reminiscences. Others, though, saw a beloved icon that had lost all self-control, a pathetic drunk heading for oblivion.

At least he hadn't lost his knack to scandalise and shock. Witness his 1984 cringe-making duet with his then twelve-year-old daughter Charlotte called 'Lemon Incest', which includes such lines as, 'the love that we will never make'. The video's even worse: father and daughter on a circular bed together, she in panties and a shirt, he bare chested, wearing jeans. Many scratched their heads trying to understand the reasoning behind doing this, save the obvious: to cause a scandal. The real point, Jane Birkin excused, was that Serge could only show love for his child if there was a camera there to record it. How sad.

In 1988 Gainsbourg began performing live again after years of absence, but his charismatic on-stage persona hid a fragile man whose health was rapidly declining. He was in and out of hospital with liver problems and his doctors insisted that he give up drinking immediately, it now being a matter of life or death. He ignored them and continued to get pissed, turning into something of a recluse, rarely leaving his apartment. When no one could raise him for two days the fire brigade broke in and discovered that Serge had died of a heart attack in his sleep. He was sixty-two.

His daughter was inconsolable and wouldn't allow his corpse to leave, keeping vigil beside it as it lay on the bed for five days. Meanwhile, outside people crowded the tiny street, singing his songs and leaving bottles of whisky and packets of Gitanes as tributes. Finally Charlotte handed over her father's body to be laid to rest at Montparnasse cemetery, amongst fellow artists like Man Ray and Jean-Paul Sartre. But she vowed to keep the house exactly the way it was on the day he died; cans of food lay unopened in the cupboards for years.

Not long before he died Gainsbourg appeared on a French TV show where sixty adoring children came on dressed as mini-Serges in jeans, all with little Gitanes in their mouths. He was so touched that he burst into tears.

AVA GARDNER (1922–1990: Actress)

She was one of the great screen goddesses, floating in front of the camera with a feline grace, exuding exotic charm by the barrel-load, but in private Ava Gardner was a sexual predator and borderline alcoholic, a gal who loved to have fun, who swore like a trooper and so intoxicated poor old Frank Sinatra with galloping hormones that he threatened suicide. 'My vices and scandals are more interesting than anything anyone can make up,' she once tantalisingly revealed, and how right she was!

Brought up on a tobacco farm in North Carolina with six other siblings, Ava enjoyed the classic rags-to-riches story. It was a simple modelling shot that was her passport to Hollywood, when a talent scout was knocked out by her sultry looks and signed her as an MGM starlet. After her screen test the director clapped his hands gleefully and yelled, 'She can't talk! She can't act! She's sensational!'

Heavily promiscuous, Ava cared nothing for protocol; she loved sex and wanted as much of it as possible, taking numerous lovers including Robert Mitchum and John F Kennedy. At a party she was propositioned by a visiting English actor. Looking up, she asked him, 'Do you eat pussy?' Women just didn't say things like that in 1940s Hollywood. This fascination with sex extended to nightly guided tours of brothels.

Inevitably Ava went through husbands with Liz Taylor-like abandon. Number one was Mickey Rooney, one of MGM's biggest stars. Rooney later recalled Ava's 'tremendous capacity for liquor', drinking champagne like it was soda water and mixing beer with Scotch. Actor and friend Howard Duff recalled the evening Ava asked him to mix her favourite cocktail – vodka, gin, Scotch, brandy and anything else that was to hand, 'Whammo, we were out on the carpet.'

Ava changed when she hit the booze, sober she was delightful company, breezy, vivacious and mischievous; wankered she was a bloody nightmare, and violent with it. During a row with Rooney she threw a heavy inkwell at his head while 'juiced on Martinis'. Another evening she brandished a kitchen knife and redesigned every piece of furniture in their home.

Essentially a loner, Ava learned early in her career to take hard liquor because it took the edge off her shyness at social functions. She also took a shot before a movie take to fortify her rampant nerves.

Looking for love after the collapse of her marriage to Rooney, Ava indulged in a brief dalliance with tycoon Howard Hughes. Again there were fireworks. When Hughes slapped her around during a row Ava retaliated by laying him out cold with a well-aimed hit from a marble ashtray. 'I thought I'd killed the poor bastard.' No, he recovered to propose marriage. Ava declined; they were too volatile. 'Our chemistry was the stuff that causes hydrogen bombs to explode.'

Her next husband was bandleader Artie Shaw, who worshipped Ava's body, 'She was a goddess. I would stare at her, literally stare in wonder,' but cruelly mocked her country bumpkin education. Unable to take it any longer she downed a bottle of whisky and drove to a friend's house somewhat erratically, drawing the attention of some cops who gave chase, lights flashing. Screeching to a halt, Ava ran to the porch but the cops beat her to it, their revolvers inches from her head. Instinctively she pushed the gun barrel aside and snapped, 'How dare you!' and rushed inside, slamming the door in their faces.

Making *My Forbidden Past* (1951) with Robert Mitchum, Ava predictably fell big time for the broad shouldered, ganja-puffing hunk and they began an intense affair. Mitchum was married and Ava pleaded with him to dump his wife and family for her. Mitchum said she ought to call his wife Dorothy about it, and Ava, the balls she had, did just that. 'You've had him for ten years,' she blasted down the phone, 'Give somebody else a chance.'

'What does Bob say?'

'He said to ask you.'

'OK,' said Dorothy, 'so you asked me. The answer is no.'

So many leading men, Ava must have thought, so little time. Years later on *Bhowani Junction* (1956) she laid siege to Stewart Granger's bedroom. 'I can't, Ava,' he pleaded. 'I'm too much in love with Jean Simmons.' 'Fuck Jean Simmons!' Ava yelled. 'I'd love to,' said Granger, 'but she's not here.'

In the late forties Ava met Frank Sinatra, thus beginning the most volcanic and tempestuous love affair of her life. Like Burton and Liz Taylor their passion was so intense, so electric, they simply couldn't live together. They drank hard and fought with wild abandon. One night after drinking and flirting in a nightclub they hopped into Sinatra's Cadillac with a bottle of liquor and roared off, passing the booze back and forth between them. Pulling up in a small town in the middle of nowhere, Sinatra pulled two revolvers from the glove compartment and together they blasted out the street lamps. Still swigging from the liquor bottle, Ava's aim was less good and she blasted up a hardware store. Two local police turned up and the pair were arrested on the spot. At the station a blotto Ava lay stretched out on a bench when in walked a studio fixer armed with a black bag that he handed over to the desk sergeant, no doubt for the police's benevolent fund. Ava and Sinatra were released, no charge, no publicity.

At the time of their marriage Ava was the bigger star, Sinatra's career was in a slump. During a press junket, some idiot questioned why she was with Sinatra, 'What do you see in this guy? He's just a hundred-and-nineteen-pound has-been.' Demurely Ava retorted, 'Well I'll tell you – nineteen pounds is cock.'

The marriage was predictably fiery, containing more left hooks than an Ali–Frazier fight, along with separations and reconciliations. When Ava became pregnant she made the harrowing decision to terminate it, even though she'd always dreamed of having children. 'We couldn't even take care of ourselves. How were we going to take care of a baby?'

Their fights were monumental, as if Cecil B DeMille were orchestrating them. At one party their shouting and screaming proved so disturbing to the other guests the couple were locked in the host's study to calm down. On holiday in Havana one row ended with a drunken Ava standing on the edge of the hotel balcony. 'Frank was afraid to go near me. He thought I was going to jump. God I was crazy. God almighty.'

Divorce was the only solution. It was painful and the scars never really healed on either side. Years later they both found themselves in Rome working and met up for dinner at the home of mutual friends. Ava would get juice-looped and stagger off to her room leaving Sinatra to mutter mournfully, 'She's the only woman I've ever been in love with, and look at her. She's turned into a falling-down drunk.'

Ava never remarried but was mightily aggrieved when Sinatra did, especially when it was to that stick insect Mia Farrow. 'I always knew Frank wanted to sleep with a guy.' She called Farrow 'a fag with a pussy'.

In the early sixties Ava left Hollywood and went to live in Madrid, bedding Spanish matadors to mop up her puddles of loneliness. She caused chaos round the place, invading restaurants with her mad coterie of revellers, gatecrashing parties and generally living it up. At a restaurant one evening Ava ordered every drink that her large party of friends were consuming. Eleven shots of hard liquor were lined up in front of her and she slugged three of them straight away, the rest following soon after.

Quite capable of drinking till dawn, if a paparazzo caught her unawares he'd get a glass of booze thrown in his face, and if he was especially unfortunate the glass itself would swiftly follow. 'She had gone from famous to infamous to notorious,' wrote friend and fellow MGM starlet Esther Williams, then a Madrid resident. 'And was now regarded as something of a menace to polite society.'

There were tales of abandoned lovers attempting suicide and car chases; she'd be found wandering at night in a local park dressed only in her bra and panties. Pretty soon bar owners and restaurants began recoiling in horror from the thought of Ava dropping by; then to alleviate the possibility of it ever happening banned her altogether. Most infamously of all she was banned from Madrid's Hotel Ritz when she drunkenly squatted down and urinated in the reception lobby in full view of horrified guests.

Past her prime as a screen beauty, Ava's film appearances became sporadic. On *55 Days at Peking* (1963) she was constantly drinking, turned up late and didn't know her lines. Worried about her performance, she approached co-star Paul Lukas and asked him how their scenes together could be improved. 'It would help, Ava, if you stop drinking before noon every morning.'

On *The Night of the Iguana* (1964), Ava found herself in sweltering Mexico City with Richard Burton. Director John Huston had come up with the interesting ploy of handing out pistols to the cast with bullets, one with each actor's name on it, his way of saying if tensions run out of control and you want to kill each other, use the designated bullet. It turned out a fun, if tough shoot. At the wrap party Ava water-skied in the dark, with a glass of tequila in her hand. Conscious of her fading beauty, Ava grew irritable at having her photograph taken, even by approved stills cameramen working for Huston. When she told one of them to stop and he carried on clicking she charged at him and swiftly kicked him in the stomach.

Moving to London, Ava lived out her final years in relative anonymity in a sumptuous flat near Hyde Park. But she could still indulge, turning up for a party with a big basket filled with bottles of rum, Scotch and gin which she poured all together in a big punch bowl, christening it 'Mommy's little mixture'. And working on *Tam Lin* (1970) she invited a very nervous young actor called Bruce Robinson (future director of *Withnail and I*) into her dressing room on the first day of filming. To relax him Ava said, 'Here, have some breakfast,' handing over a full glass of vodka.

With her looks spoiled by the booze and struggling against lung cancer and partial paralysis, the legacy of a stroke, Ava began to tell friends that she no longer wanted to live. She finally succumbed to bronchial pneumonia, passing off into the long night peacefully in her Chippendale bed, her loyal housemaid by her side but with no sign of the many husbands and men she'd won and lost.

In spite of the embarrassing episodes, the scraps, the temper tantrums – 'When I lose my temper, honey, you can't find it any place' – people couldn't help but love Ava. Her zest for life was irresistible. As she once said, 'I wish to live until 150 years old but the day I die I wish it to be with a cigarette in one hand and a glass of whisky in the other.'

PAUL GASCOIGNE (b. 1967: Footballer)

It's strange to think that the only British football player to come even close to the natural genius of George Best, Paul Gascoigne, shared almost exactly the same self-destructive qualities and propensity for boozing his talent away.

The Gazza legend was sealed at the 1990 World Cup with his tearful reaction to the booking that ruled him out of the final, should England have got there, which they didn't of course. It endeared him to the nation, along with his distinctively British sense of fun. Asked by a Norwegian TV camera crew if he had a message for their viewers as England's next opponents he replied, 'Yes. Fuck off, Norway,' and ran off laughing. He once turned up at his club's canteen after training wearing nothing but his socks and casually asked for lunch. He also met his friends at a London pub just one hour after playing for England, still in his full kit and boots.

Gascoigne was the second of four children and grew up in a cramped home in Gateshead, Tyne and Wear. Money was tight so his mother worked three jobs to make ends meet while his dad left for Germany to find employment as a builder. On his return he suffered a brain haemorrhage and never worked again.

There were demons playing around Paul Gascoigne's head from an early age; one can only imagine what scars were left behind after an innocent trip to the shops aged twelve ended in the horror of watching one of his friends killed in a road accident. A petty thief as a kid, stealing just for fun, he got plastered for the first time aged fourteen when he and a mate stole a bottle of vodka from a shop and drank it. He felt like shit afterwards and vowed never to touch a drop of alcohol again.

Football was his salvation and Gascoigne excelled at a local boys' club before joining Newcastle as an apprentice in 1983. Handed his senior debut in 1985, Gascoigne spent three more years at St James' Park before making a big-money switch to Tottenham, celebrating signing with the London club by holing up in a hotel with four mates and getting half-corned on champagne. In three days they managed to drink thirty-eight bottles of Dom Pérignon before the hotel threw them out for rowdiness.

It was at Spurs that Gascoigne's reputation for daft practical jokes and general larking about was forged. At a Christmas party he challenged one of the team's younger players to a drinking contest. Barely sober but still standing, unlike his opponent, Gascoigne threw his paralytic teammate into a taxi and took him to King's Cross Station, where he sat him on the first outward bound train, stripping him stark bollock naked first, of course. The unfortunate player woke up in Cambridge.

Gazza's fame was such that he attracted a fair share of hardcore fans, one of whom took to following him everywhere, even to training. One morning Gascoigne asked the guy if he didn't mind climbing on top of his motor home, since some silly sod had left a traffic cone up there. No problem. Once the bloke was on top Gascoigne raced into the cabin and revved the engine up, racing off down the A1 at blinding speed with his stalker hanging on for dear life screaming, 'Please, please, Gazza, stop! I'm a married man, I've got a family. You're going to kill me!'

From Spurs Gascoigne moved abroad to the Italian Serie-A side Lazio. Seconded in the relatively civilised environs of Rome, Gazza was still able to get up to drunken mischief. When a couple of mates arrived from England, one of them Jimmy 'Five Bellies' Gardner, Gascoigne organised a secret gastronomical treat: mince pies with the mixture scooped out and replaced with cat shit. After a night on the booze Gascoigne knew they wouldn't be able to resist the snack back at his flat, and sure enough they grabbed one each and put them in the microwave; the stench was unbearable but they were too drunk to notice and wolfed the pies down. What's more, they were fighting over the last one. When Gazza owned up to what he'd done, Jimmy immediately hurled in a toilet bowl, while the other mate declared they'd been the best mince pies he'd ever tasted.

Gazza was always playing such highly sophisticated japes on his buddies, the principal victim invariably 'Five Bellies', waking him up once from a drunken snooze by placing a lit cigarette lighter under his nose, setting him up with a 'girl' he knew to be a transvestite and driving his car towards Jimmy at 30 mph to scare him shitless. When he made contact and Gardner bounced off the bumper, Gascoigne thought he'd killed him. He could see the headlines: GAZZA RUNS OVER BEST MATE FOR LAUGH. Luckily Jimmy was unhurt save for an enormous lump on his nut that took a whole year to go down.

His Italian experience over, Gascoigne joined Scottish champions Rangers. He enjoyed his football there and the fans took to him, but it was at Rangers where Gascoigne's drinking steadily began to get out of control. After training he'd drink until he passed out; usually two bottles of wine would do it. Then he got into the habit of taking a nip of brandy before going out on the pitch; it relaxed him, lubricated the joints, but plunged him into a deep depression at the same time. One morning he came to training drunk. The manager Walter Smith took one look at him and knew. Picking Gascoigne up by the scruff of the neck, Smith blasted in his face, 'Get out, go home, and never come back.'

He was forgiven of course, but the problem wasn't going away. The absurd thing was Gascoigne never actually liked the taste of alcohol, he drank to feel numb; 'My main aim was always oblivion.' The drunker he got the more 'Gazza' took over from Paul Gascoigne and the more idiotic he became, doing mad stunts like jumping in front of buses; always a risk taker, drink made him bolder. It was also an anaesthetic from the dull, dead feeling of life away from the pitch. When he felt lousy he dived into the bottle to cheer himself up, 'to stop myself thinking about death and dying'.

At this juncture one must pause and sympathise with the poor woman who in 1996 decided it was a good idea to marry Paul Gascoigne. Her name was Sheryl Failes. It was probably a good idea at the time, but when the abuse started the fairy-tale turned from Disney into Grimms. On a family holiday they sat having dinner in their hotel, Gascoigne drinking recklessly, mixing champagne and whisky. They got into an argument and Sheryl left to go back to the room. Gascoigne followed and completely lost all common sense, if he had any to start with. His attack on Sheryl was brutal; he admits to head-butting her and throwing her to the floor where she broke a finger and screamed out in pain. 'I tried to click the finger back into place,' Gascoigne later recalled. 'And that made her really shriek.' Sheryl's two kids from a previous marriage, Bianca and Mason, aged ten and seven, were in the next room with a nanny listening. Bianca was so upset she contemplated taking a kettle of boiling water and pouring it over Gascoigne's head. 'Fortunately the nanny calmed her down.' Sheryl eventually had enough and called a halt to the marriage after just two years.

The drinking carried over to Gascoigne's next team Middlesbrough, where he was at his loony best, not least the time he noticed the team coach unattended, the doors open. It was too much of a temptation. With an eye to taking the lads into town to the bookie's, Gazza started the engine and off he went through a narrow gate, momentarily forgetting he was driving a coach and not a car and dragging most of the gate with him. Jumping out, he threw the keys to a wide-eyed security man, 'Quick, you take it,' and buggered off. Middlesbrough's manager Bryan Robson phoned his star player later that day. 'I know you're mad, but this is fucking too much.'

A mid-season trip to Dublin with Middlesbrough inevitably turned into a four-day drinking binge. Flying back, Gascoigne was well gone prior to getting on board having downed sixteen hot toddies, the equivalent of about thirty-two whiskies. Leaving the airport, he had to catch a train to see Regan, the child he'd conceived with Sheryl. It remains a vivid memory for Gascoigne, standing at Stevenage platform crying his head off about his wrecked marriage, about no longer being wanted for the England team, life in general, really. He arrived at the decision that he was going to throw himself in front of the next train. He waited, and he waited. A guard saw him and explained that the last train had already gone. 'Even when I was trying to kill myself I couldn't get it right.'

Frantically he called Sheryl: 'Please help. Please come and get me.' It wasn't the first time Sheryl had heard this sort of pleading, nor would it be the last. She took him to a nearby hotel and then called Bryan Robson, who arrived shortly after and personally escorted Gascoigne to the Priory, a leading private psychiatric hospital renowned for its star clientele. Here Gascoigne was confronted with the fact that he was an alcoholic, because the doctors told him so. He refused to believe it and left after three weeks, determined to show them he could lay off the booze. This was to be the first of numerous visits to clinics and attempts at detox; he was so adept at falling off wagons he could have starred in a remake of *Stagecoach*.

When he left football for good in 2002 there followed a humiliating search for a meaningful role. He tried his luck at management with lowly Kettering Town but that lasted barely a month before he was sacked by the club owners, citing his continuing alcohol problems. As a TV pundit for the 2002 World Cup, Gascoigne ran up an impressive London hotel drinks bill of just under ten grand over the course of three weeks.

Turning forty, Gascoigne's body appeared to be packing in, the fall-out from an injury-prone career; he underwent emergency surgery for a perforated stomach ulcer. His mind was also on the blink when he became so drunkenly deluded that he believed two toy parrots he'd bought were talking to him and were the only friends he had in the world. 'I started to think they were real and once ordered three pints – one for me and one each for the parrots.'

The year 2008 was certainly Gascoigne's 'annus horribilis', a wild period that began at the close of 2007 following a hip replacement operation when he hit the bottle hard, well actually several hundred bottles of wine and gin over a six-week period. Moving into a hotel in Gateshead, he carried on boozing with gusto, though frighteningly rarely if ever got truly stoned. It was drinking for the sake of it. Reportedly hotel staff and guests felt intimidated, especially when Gascoigne was said to have answered the door of his room naked and with the word 'mad' written on his forehead.

His family grew concerned, fearing he was close to suicide. It was his sister who called the police and Gascoigne was relaxing in his bath when five burly PCs burst in and dragged him out naked. Sectioned under the Mental Health Act, it was a humbling episode, from national hero to mental hospital patient. 'I'd never felt so embarrassed and ashamed.'

Like all alcoholics, Gascoigne takes each day at a time. From his drinking flowed all his other problems and behavioural disorders, an Argos catalogue worth – prescription drugs, depression, OCD, cocaine binges, you name it. It wasn't so long ago that he was drinking thirty cans of Special Brew every day. The body can only take so much; in rehab Gascoigne's heart stopped beating three times. He came back from the abyss and a nation, alternately repulsed and pitying, await the next drama.

GEORGE IV (1762–1830: English Monarch)

A libertine, whoremonger and boozer extraordinaire, George IV was the last reprobate monarch, the last profligate to sit on the English throne. As a prince he ran up huge debts gambling, stuffing his face and building ridiculous palaces, and it was always the poor put-upon British taxpayer who bailed him out. When Parliament was forced to agree to increase his allowance, his father the King lamented how it was, 'A shameful squandering of public money to gratify the passions of an ill-advised young man.'

By the time of his death poor old George waddled along the corridors of Windsor Castle a bloated recluse despised by his fellow countrymen, a decaying and decrepit specimen upon whom even his own servants were ordered not to gaze.

He was born, importantly, the first son of George III and Queen Charlotte. Five days later he was made Prince of Wales. Amongst a phalanx of private tutors whose job it was to educate and mould the lad to the highest office in the land was Dr Richard Hurd, Bishop of Lichfield, who upon leaving his post gave this report of his pupil's progress: 'He will either be the most polished gentleman or the most accomplished blackguard in Europe.'

By the 1780s George was a strapping young dandy but also an inveterate gambler and cherry merry. According to Hon. Augusta Barrington,

'He was very charming when he was not drunk, but he generally *was*.' At one ball he poured so many bottles of wine down his gullet that he vomited most capriciously in front of much of the landed gentry. At another social gathering his drinking gave way to mad merry-making as he assaulted various guests as they left, jumping out at them from behind a door like some deranged jack-in-a-box. When he spied the Duchess of Ancaster he grabbed her by the neck and planted a wet kiss on her lips, then attempted to pull Lord Galloway's wig off and knock out his false teeth. It was at this juncture that George was hauled away to his carriage.

For dinner one evening he invited some friends over to entertain and keep him company. When one guest conspicuously failed to do either, instead sitting silent all through the meal, George, irritated and not a little badgered, filled a glass with wine and threw it in his friend's face. 'Say something funny, can't you?' blasted the Prince. Without a pause the man threw his own glass of wine in his neighbour's face, saying, 'Pass His Royal Highness's joke.'

For the young Prince of Wales everything revolved around his own whims and caprices. He ran around with a motley band of like-minded rakes. One of these idiots once rode a horse into the house of George's mistress, up the stairs and into an attic. It took two blacksmiths to coax the animal back down again. Brighton was the scene of many of their frolics. They'd race down there from London in a coach, stopping along the way to rearrange signposts or scream 'murder, rape, unhand me villain' at startled passers-by. Upon reaching the seaside town they terrorised the populace by going about at night carrying a coffin and knocking on doors asking servants for their dead masters to be handed over.

As for his womanising, it knew no sane boundary; he cared not one jot for their station in society as he bagged ladies-in-waiting, friends' wives and aristocratic ladies with equal indiscretion, between trips to brothels. There was the occasion, the result of a drunken bet, when he entered the home of a lady he knew well and shrieked at the top of his voice, 'I must do it, I must do it.' When asked what it was he needed to do so badly, George got some of his colleagues to hold the woman down as he gave her a sound whipping.

In 1794 George agreed to marry if Parliament once again paid off his enormous debts. The bride in question was Caroline of Brunswick, a none too striking woman hailing from aristocratic German stock. When George first clapped eyes on her in the flesh he called immediately for a glass of brandy. She, on the other hand, found him, 'very ugly, and not as attractive as his portrait'.

It was obvious George's heart just wasn't in it, evidenced by the fact that he got off his pickle before the ceremony and almost passed out twice. While making his vows his hiccups rebounded off the chapel walls as he gazed longingly at one of his mistresses sat amongst the congregation. When the Archbishop of Canterbury asked whether anyone knew of any reason why the marriage should not take place George burst into tears. Afterwards he drank himself into a complete stupor and, according to Caroline, 'passed the greatest part of his bridal night under the fire grate, where he fell and where I left him'. The honeymoon was even less romantic, spent at the Prince's hunting lodge in Hampshire with his most loutish friends, who spent much of the time getting cabbaged and sleeping off their enormous hangovers.

One is hardly surprised to learn that Caroline was not altogether bowled over by her coupling with George, and as his rancid appetites began to play havoc with his external extremities she was repelled even more, refusing to have sex with him. Approaching his forties, George had come to resemble a leprous hippopotamus, with an alcohol consumption that was positively indecent; he'd taken to drinking neat gin in half-pint mugs. The Duke of Wellington observed, 'By God, you never saw such a figure in your life as he.'

At least there was some good news. His father George III, who'd shown signs of dementia for years, had gone authentically crackers and finally pegged it. The throne was George's. By the time of his coronation in 1821 the marriage to Caroline had deteriorated to such an extent that she was turned away from Westminster Abbey by guards; some of them hired prize fighters, even though by right she was Queen. Repeatedly she tried to gain entry, at one point standing gallantly while bayonets were held inches from her throat until the door was slammed in her face. That very evening she took ill and within weeks was dead.

Not a moment too soon for George. Some months previously when Napoleon had snuffed it and George was informed, 'Sire, your greatest enemy is dead,' he'd replied, 'Is she, by God!'

By the year of his ascension to the throne George weighed almost twenty stones and was obliged to wear corsets. By 1824 his waistline had expanded to fifty inches and his stomach hung down like a sack of melons. 'He has become enormous, like a feather bed,' commented Mary, Duchess of Gloucester, the King's favourite sister. It got so bad that George withdrew from public life altogether.

Yet he continued to drink and eat voraciously, as if the indulgence of all the sensual enjoyments was the sole purpose of his existence, which of course it was. Some of his breakfasts consisted of a pigeon and beefsteak pie, half a bottle of wine, a glass of champagne, two glasses of port and a glass of brandy. He was also now heavily addicted to laudanum and heading the way of his father into total lunacy. He began to tell people that he had been a soldier and fought at the Battle of Waterloo; complete and utter fiction.

Sulking away in Windsor Castle, George feared to leave the safety of its walls, so reviled was he by his subjects and ridiculed mercilessly in the press. The diarist Charles Greville wrote: 'A more contemptible, cowardly, selfish, unfeeling dog does not exist than this King.'

Finally he was put out of his misery. One morning George awoke to crushing pain and cried out for Sir Henry Halford, his physician: 'Sir Henry, Sir Henry! Fetch him – this is death!' And it was.

JOHN GILBERT (1897–1936: Actor)

Once the most popular star of the 1920s, the epitome of the 'matinee idol' who rivalled even Rudolph Valentino as the sex symbol of the age, lover of Garbo and Dietrich, boozer extraordinaire, a man who in the words of noted screenwriter Ben Hecht, 'drank with carpenters, danced with waitresses and made love to whores and movie queens alike'. So why is John Gilbert such a forgotten figure today?

Gilbert's childhood was Dickensian in its squalor and deprivation. His mother was a vaudeville actress whose husband abandoned her when she fell pregnant and Gilbert was born in a cheap rooming house in Utah. He spent his earliest years shepherded out to various relatives while his mother toured theatres and drank like a fish. She even dumped him for a year with a prostitute who told her customers to ignore the small child playing on the carpet.

When his mother returned to claim him she carried on as if he didn't exist. Moving from town to town, Gilbert hardly attended school, wasn't given toys or books, and was locked in closets for hours on end just to be kept out of the way. His mother also indulged in a string of love affairs, and every so often the child would be woken in the middle of the night to be introduced to his new 'daddy'. All this misery ended in 1913 when his mother died of alcoholism.

Gilbert moved to Hollywood as a teenager and slowly worked his way up in silent films from extra to leading man at MGM, establishing a reputation as a bit of a lad along the way, infuriating his boss Louis B Mayer. The two men despised each other: Gilbert considered Mayer a prude, Mayer thought his top star a whoremonger. Gilbert's habit of taking Mayer's right-hand man, the boy-wonder producer Irving Thalberg, to brothels didn't help.

In 1926 Gilbert made *Flesh and the Devil* with newcomer Greta Garbo. Sparks flew immediately and their intense off-screen romance made them the couple of the age. But the cool Swede gradually turned Gilbert into an emotional wreck as she took numerous female lovers. Repeatedly he asked her to marry him but each time Garbo said, 'I von't to be alone,' or words to that effect. Finally she relented, but on the big day Gilbert was kept waiting and waiting while 500 guests, comprising Hollywood's finest, all stood around looking at their watches. Garbo was a no show. Distraught, Gilbert escaped into the bathroom weeping. Mayer was in there and took one look at his prized asset and advised, 'Don't marry her. Just fuck her and forget about it.' Not the comforting words Gilbert required at that moment, far from it, and he let Mayer have it, a right hook that sent him flying on his arse. The mogul slowly got up off the tiled floor, seething rage showing in his reddened complexion. 'You're finished.' The words were like daggers in the air. 'I'll destroy you!'

Over the next few years Gilbert started to get rotten film projects that flopped at the box office. Combined with the Garbo fiasco it conspired to push him further into an alcoholic haze. Gilbert had always liked a good drink, hell, everyone did back then; his problem was he could never stop. He had to keep on drinking until he fell over unconscious. One night a young couple innocently parked their car below Gilbert's hillside home to look at the stunning views over LA. Gilbert grabbed one of his guns and started spraying the vehicle with bullets, the couple cowering inside terror-stricken. The incident was hushed up by MGM.

Gilbert was now out of control. Soberly challenged one night he paid a visit to Garbo's house, banging repeatedly on the door. When there was no answer he climbed up to the second-floor balcony only to get pushed off by Maurice Stiller, Garbo's Swedish mentor. The cops were called and Gilbert was arrested. This time Mayer had no intention of hushing it up and allowed justice to proceed. Gilbert was charged with drunk and disorderly conduct and sentenced to ten days in jail. But Mayer's plan backfired when a media circus descended on the prison, with drinking buddies showing up, aspirant actresses and fans galore. In the end Gilbert was let out after serving just a day and a half.

Still peeved, Gilbert got a gun and went looking for Stiller. Luckily his drink-induced erratic driving down Sunset Boulevard, almost careering off the road at one point, alerted a squad car and he was stopped from doing something he might have regretted.

With the advent of sound upon the motion picture industry Mayer took his final revenge on Gilbert. It has been alleged that Mayer deliberately sabotaged Gilbert's first talking films so that his perfectly adequate speaking voice was reproduced on screen as high pitched, almost feminine. Sure enough audiences greeted his squeaky, 'I love you's, during romantic clinches with howls of derision. It was the final ignominy.

Languishing at home, taking pity on himself, Gilbert drank and drank. He was only in his mid-thirties and his career was already dead. In just a matter of a couple of years he'd gone from the happy-go-lucky guy who'd wave at fans as he drove out of the MGM studio, to someone who wore a hat pulled down over his eyes to avoid contact with anyone.

He was also desperately ill. By 1932 he'd developed bleeding ulcers, even one stiff shot of alcohol made him intoxicated. But still he drank; in between getting married, four times altogether, all ending in divorce. Actress Virginia Bruce was his last bride. She adored him, calling Gilbert the most charming and exciting man she ever knew. 'There was no one like Jack when his spirits were up. But when he was down, it was like death.'

Sometimes Gilbert stayed up all night drinking and then asked Virginia to throw him into the swimming pool to sober him up. Other mornings he awoke throwing up blood until he fainted. His doctor would call round to inject sodium amytal into his veins in a bid to give him a restful night, that was until a vein collapsed and became infected.

It probably didn't help Gilbert's drinking that John Barrymore lived next door and they indulged in massive benders. Barrymore reputedly tried to get Gilbert into hard drugs. 'My God, no,' he said. 'I can't even hold my liquor.'

Just as offers of work were drying up, it was Garbo, now the biggest star in Hollywood, who was powerful enough to force MGM to bring Gilbert back as her leading man in *Queen Christina* (1933). He turned in a good performance but it was too late, his audience had long ago deserted him, his popularity a distant memory. And when Virginia finally walked out on him Gilbert grabbed the nearest bottle, sat down in his big empty film-star mansion and proceeded to drink himself to death.

His last film, *The Captain Hates the Sea* (1934), was a complete disaster. Director Lewis Milestone complained to Columbia Chief Harry Cohn that Gilbert was Newcastled all the time. 'It's too goddamn bad,' Cohn replied. 'But if a man wants to go to hell, I can't stop him. Shoot around him as much as you can. But keep the picture moving!'

This was easier said than done, since the film had been cast largely with drunks who happily supplied Gilbert with liberal samples from their private reserves and swapped bottles filled with coloured water for the real stuff in scenes. Filming was predictably a slow process. One day, Milestone received an angry cable from Cohn: 'Hurry up. The cost is staggering.' He promptly fired off an apt reply: 'So is the cast!'

Returning home, Gilbert continued to drink. The bleeding ulcers returned, with them fever and hallucinations. Marlene Dietrich was his final lover, but not even she could prevent the inevitable. Gilbert died suddenly at home of a heart attack. He was thirty-six years old. Some say he died of a broken heart, unable to comprehend the treachery of Mayer or deal with the bitterness he felt at being toppled from his pinnacle.

After his funeral Gilbert's effects were auctioned off. Dietrich acquired her lover's satin sheets, but alas the bed they had shared was snapped up by a motel who intended to use it in their honeymoon suite.

JACKIE GLEASON (1916–1987: Comic Actor)

'I'm not advocating that everybody should drink,' said Jackie Gleason when questioned about his monolithic booze habit on the Johnny Carson show. 'It just worked for me.'

Gleason's dad was a lush and as a kid Jackie peered through the saloon door of the local bar and watched with fascination how several jars turned this sullen and repressed man into a goofy joker. There was a darker side, lonely hours waiting for him to come home after one of his three-day binges. Then one week before Christmas he vanished, along with every photograph that existed of him in the house; Jackie never saw him again.

It was a tough break but the eight-year-old Jackie was pretty used to them by now, having already seen his sickly elder brother put into the earth and survived a poverty-stricken Irish Brooklyn upbringing. After his father's desertion Jackie didn't hang around the house much to watch his mother soak herself in booze, instead he roamed free with street gangs, fostering a smoking habit aged ten and tasting bootleg gin by twelve. At school he was a prankster, smearing radiators with cheese to stink out his class and releasing a snake into the orchestra pit of a local theatre. He also hung out at a nearby pool hall and got pretty good at the game, skills that came in handy years later when he starred as Minnesota Fats in *The Hustler* (1961) with Paul Newman.

Shortly after Jackie turned nineteen, his mother died. After paying for the funeral he took what little money was left over and caught a train to Manhattan, determined to become a famous comedian. Pretty much broke, he worked as a bartender in a saloon, sometimes sleeping in the back room with the empty bottles. His stand-up act was pretty crummy and he flopped at his first proper gig. Afterwards he consoled himself at the bar with a drink, well maybe fifteen drinks, and when it was time for his second spot Gleason slayed 'em, improvising his nuts off. Arriving for the following night's performance he knew the only way to remember how he did it was to hit the bar and have about fifteen drinks.

Other gigs followed. At one club Gleason was hired less for his comic ability than his street fighting skills. When things got rough, Gleason was obliged to find something heavy and help sort it out. One memorable night he took offence to a heckler and demanded satisfaction outside. Unfortunately it was Tony Galento, contender to the world heavyweight boxing title, who flattened Gleason with one punch.

It was during those long hard years playing the clubs that Gleason forged his reputation for boozing royally, drinking with the likes of Frank Sinatra. It was actually Gleason who introduced Sinatra to Jack Daniel's, a beverage that became synonymous with the crooner.

Married, Gleason acted like a bachelor when he hit the nightspots and had a string of goodtime girlfriends; the missus stayed at home tut-tutting, waiting for him to come in God knew when from some bar or another. Sometimes to make things easier Gleason wouldn't go home at all, preferring to live in a hotel or hang about at Toots Shor's, the Big Apple's most celebrated watering hole and focal point of boozy 1950s Manhattan. Gleason hit it off straightaway with the pugnacious bar owner, who liked to say, 'If a bum ain't drunk by midnight, he ain't trying.'

In any sane world the drink should have been a barrier to progress, Gleason showed up some nights too smashed to even make it to the stage, but he was a comedy juggernaut that couldn't be stopped and he was given his own TV variety show. Harry Crane was one of the writers and arrived at Gleason's apartment to talk about some of the sketches. It looked like Sodom and Gomorrah; a live band, booze and broads all over the place. 'Jackie, we gotta talk about this script.' Gleason waved him away, 'We'll talk Thursday.' Problem was, the show was going out live on Friday. Crane started to panic. Leaving, he was accosted by anxious mothers in the lobby asking, 'My daughter's up there! Is she still alive?' Crane ventured back on Thursday and the party was still in full swing. 'The band is playing. Gleason is dancing steps that haven't been invented yet. No chance to talk script, so I left again.'

Crane had little choice but to knock out the sketches and present them an hour before airtime. Gleason scanned each page for about a minute before handing them back, saying, 'Gotcha, pal.' Crane was gobsmacked, this was a man about to go live to twenty million people; of course he delivered every line perfectly, or improvised better ones, and the show was a smash.

To celebrate his newfound fame Sinatra presented Gleason with his own Cadillac limo. They drove up in it to a baseball game together. Gleason had been drinking all day at Toots' bar and once at the stadium turned his attention to hot dogs and beer. At the climactic moment of the game, with the crowd screaming, Gleason turned to look at Frank and threw up all over him. Adding insult to injury, on the drive home Gleason ordered the chauffeur to pull over to the side of the road. 'Let's throw this bum Sinatra out of here, he's smelling up my limo.'

Gleason would roister with other celebrity pals; bar hop with Bogart, drink with Joe DiMaggio then go and hit balls in Central Park in the middle of the night. He once said about pal Dean Martin, 'Dean and I have been on more floors than Johnson's wax.' His recovery capacity was immense, too. Gleason could get as drunk as a wheelbarrow, go lie down for fifteen minutes and be completely sober afterwards.

Pretty soon Gleason was the biggest comedy player on American TV and the highest paid performer. He spent the money well, on a luxurious penthouse suite with its own live-in bartender and a sprawling mansion in upstate New York that came complete with its own dance hall, pool hall and twelve fully stocked bars. And what did Gleason do for his bosses at CBS? Only create one of the most popular ever sitcoms, *The Honeymooners*, about a working-class couple dreaming of a better life from their bare Brooklyn tenement. Gleason had full artistic control and got away with murder, not only refusing to rehearse, preferring to wing it on the night, but actually drinking on camera live in front of millions, unheard of in the squeaky-clean climate of fifties broadcasting. He drank from a dainty teacup but you'd have to have been a moron not to realise it was full of Scotch. Gleason would wink knowingly at the camera and say, 'Mmmmboy, that's some good coffee!' He also made a habit of mentioning top liquor brand names in skits; afterwards the distillers would send him a case of the stuff.

Incredibly Gleason never actually 'saw' his own success, revealing that he didn't own a television set since he was never at home to watch the damn thing. 'I thought television was something that distracted from my drinking.'

Gleason worked hard and partied even harder. It was an enviable lifestyle that often led to complete exhaustion. When that happened he merely checked into hospital to rest up for a few days' recuperation. One time a colleague went to visit him but was told by the nurse, 'Mr Gleason went home, he said he wasn't feeling well.'

Jackie used to stay with a friend who always wisely kept his well-stocked liquor cabinet locked whenever he had to leave the house. But every time he returned Gleason was always pissed out of his head, yet the cabinet lock remained untouched. How did he do it? With a screwdriver, of course. Gleason would take the back off the cabinet, drink all the contents, and then replace it again.

When *The Honeymooners* was at its peak, Gleason walked away from it. He'd grown bored with the show and wanted fresh challenges. He moved to the west coast and designed yet another mansion, this time with a vast circular bar. Jackie also invented a brand-new bar stool that, no matter how wellied the occupant, it was impossible to fall out of. 'I would have defied any of my old drinking pals like Toots or Bogie to fall off those stools,' Gleason boasted. 'Even W C Fields would have felt safe in them.'

Jackie was soon courted by Hollywood and enjoyed a long film career. In 1977 he accepted a role as a redneck sheriff in *Smokey and the Bandit*. On set star Burt Reynolds watched as every morning at 9 a.m. Gleason yelled to his assistant, 'Mel, hamburger,' and a glass full of vodka was brought forth. After a few days Reynolds asked, 'Heh Jackie, why do you yell "hamburger"?' Coyly Gleason replied, 'I don't want anybody to know

I'm drinking.' Although it was perfectly clear what was going on, the crew were in awe of Gleason and sat enraptured as he regaled them of his drunken escapades.

But even legends die and the first hint of mortality appeared in 1978 when Gleason suffered a heart attack while appearing on Broadway. Incredibly he not only finished the performance but went out for dinner and drinks afterwards, thinking the pain in his chest was merely heartburn. It wasn't, and after being rushed to hospital he underwent triple-bypass surgery. Friends and family hoped this close brush with death might make him ease up a bit on living life full-on, but Gleason was having not a bit of it, stocking his hospital room with liquor for the duration of his stay. 'An alcoholic doesn't know why he drinks,' he told a journalist from his hospital bed. 'I do. I drink to get bagged.'

After checking himself out, Jackie continued to smoke his usual five packs of cigarettes a day and booze it up. Shit, he should've been on the slab long ago, this was all a bonus. 'A safe life isn't a life at all,' noted Gleason. 'Too many people seem to be saving themselves for their wake.'

Then on the set of the Tom Hanks comedy *Nothing in Common* (1986), people noted how gaunt and frail Gleason looked. Taking his daughter out to lunch one day during filming Gleason told her, 'I won't be around much longer.' He was fighting colon cancer and knew he was losing. Hospitalised, when doctors informed him there was literally nothing that could be done Gleason decided to check out, preferring to die at home amongst friends, smoking and drinking to the end, leaving this world on the same terms he'd always lived it.

H

RICHARD HARRIS (1930–2002: Actor)

For Richard Harris the whole point of drinking was to have fun, it was the communal nature of boozing, of going into a pub on his own and by the end of the evening being surrounded by a new gang of boisterous pals. 'Men, not women,' he'd state. 'Boozing is a man's world.'

For years Harris habitually drank two bottles of vodka a day. That would take him up to early evening whereupon he'd break open a bottle of brandy and a bottle of port and mix the two. When it came to drink Harris took no prisoners. In his favourite bar in New York the barman would see Harris walking in and immediately line up six double vodkas. 'People spend the first half of their lives being cautious and the second half regretting it.' Harris wanted no regrets when it was his time to croak it. Collapsing in LA one time in the mid-seventies and placed on a life-support machine, with newspapers around the world compiling his obituary, a priest was rushed to his bedside to administer the last rites. When Harris woke to see the man offer him a rosary bead he said, 'Father, if you are going to hear my confession, prepare to be here for days. By the end of it, I can guarantee you will very much regret your vow of celibacy.' The priest bolted.

He was born in Limerick, Ireland, into a large brood of seven brothers and sisters; often he'd get lost amid the scrum, so learning early on to be a rabble-rouser was the only way he could make his presence felt in the household. Sometimes he'd run away, sleeping rough outdoors; no one ever came looking for him and he'd return meekly to his bedroom. But all this fostered a feeling of neglect and isolation. 'I never got to know my parents and they never got to know me.' School and Harris didn't mix either. He never quite got his head around academia and so hit out instead, getting expelled for setting fire to the toilets and attacking a nun with a ruler.

Apart from being fun, booze was a means of escape for Harris but it unleashed a violent side to his nature that caused madness and mayhem wherever he went. Returning home one night blotto, when his wife Elizabeth made an innocuous remark about his condition, Harris threw a wardrobe at her. It was also not unknown for him to rush into fast-moving traffic on main roads and mindlessly attack passing cars with his bare fists. Terribly mangled late one afternoon, Harris staggered into the bar at Pinewood studios asking for a lift home. Everyone sort of looked at each other hoping someone else would volunteer. One director did and not long after the pair were roaring up the motorway in an E-Type Jag. Harris fell asleep. Stirred from his slumber a little way into the journey, Harris started to look frantically about him, 'Where the fuck am I? Who are you? Where are you taking me?' He started pounding on the windscreen with his knuckles, causing a crack in the glass. The director pulled over to the hard shoulder, threw Harris out and made his way back to Pinewood, leaving the actor stranded, bewildered and no wiser.

When Harris travelled to America to start work on what would be his most famous film, *Camelot* (1967), he and Elizabeth decided to make the journey as romantic as possible so went by ocean liner; Harris's personal astrologer Patrick Walker was a guest, too. It turned into the cruise from hell. At dinner Harris accused his wife of being unfaithful and unleashed every expletive imaginable in her face, shocking fellow passengers. One member of staff later called Harris 'probably the most dangerous drunk I have encountered in forty years on passenger liners'. Elizabeth flew into Walker's room for a bout of sympathy. Minutes later Harris burst in, grabbed the astrologer by his lapels and flung him against the far wall; then slowly and deliberately proceeded to destroy every item in the room. Walker later confessed that it was the most frightening experience of his life.

In Hollywood Harris continued his belligerence, driving back from a party out of his gourd he started destroying the inside of the car, tearing up the upholstery until his hands bled. Elizabeth couldn't take any more and left him. Footloose and fancy free, Harris described his ideal woman as, 'a deaf and dumb nymphomaniac whose father owns a chain of off-licences'.

Besides women, Harris was also a magnet for that kind of person who with a couple of pints inside them wanted to test their manhood against the screen tough guy. Harris probably lost more fights than he won. 'I was dangerous; you'd have to knock me out to beat me. I'd whack you with a glass if it was necessary.'

Lauded as a fine actor and genuine movie star, Harris worked with the likes of Lindsay Anderson and Michelangelo Antonioni and could pick and chose any project. Many an eyebrow was raised when Harris, the Irish nationalist, agreed to appear in a film dramatisation of Oliver Cromwell, the man who had attempted genocide in his country. The paradox was intriguing and the pressure eventually got to him, combined with all the booze he was consuming, leading to a total breakdown. When the time came to shoot the execution of Charles I, played by Alec Guinness, Harris flipped. He woke up in his hotel room at dawn in a cold sweat convinced that they were actually about to cut off the King's head. 'We must give him another chance,' Harris yelled down the phone to the director. 'We must think twice about this.' A nurse was summoned, as was a psychiatrist. Acting uncontrollably, Harris was held down by people kneeling on his chest and tranquillised, knocking him out for a straight eighteen hours.

Marrying again in 1974 to model Ann Turkel brought a bit of stability back into his life but Harris was still capable of getting dangerously hammered. One morning he woke up and there was blood all over the pillow. Scrambling out of bed he stared at himself in the mirror, noticing one eye weeping and closed and stitches in his face. Incredibly, he had no recollection of how he'd got into such a state. Going downstairs he hoped Ann might be able to enlighten him. 'What happened?' he asked. She stared back at him. 'What happened? God, there's a restaurant in Santa Monica and you've wrecked it. And you wrecked it laughing – you weren't even angry.'

To save further restaurants from destruction, and probably prolonging his own life, Harris gave up the booze in 1981. He was hardly a fan of sobriety, though. It was a bore: 'There must be other things in life besides drinking,' he said. 'Though I haven't discovered what they are yet.' At least he was waking up in the morning and actually able to remember what he did the night before: 'Trouble was, it wasn't worth remembering.'

It was a personal tragedy that got him back on the sauce, but only Guinness or maybe the odd glass of wine, not spirits, 'because they were my undoing'. He was attending the funeral of one of his brothers and, having already lost his father, two sisters and two brothers to hereditary heart disease, he began thinking, as the coffin joined the others in the family crypt, what wouldn't his relatives give to rise out of the grave just for five minutes to enjoy a pint of Guinness? Harris searched out the nearest pub and tasted his first pint of stout for thirteen years. 'It tasted better than making love to Marilyn Monroe.' From now until his death Harris enjoyed a daily tipple. 'You need to stay lubricated, just to remind yourself you are still living and breathing.'

Winning a whole new generation of fans playing Professor Dumbledore in the *Harry Potter* movies, after finishing the second instalment Harris retreated to his permanent suite at the Savoy and all but disappeared. After weeks of silence his family broke in and saw an emaciated and weak figure. They immediately called an ambulance. 'When they took him away to hospital,' recalled director Peter Medak, 'the lobby just completely stopped, and Richard sat up on the stretcher and turned back to the whole foyer and shouted, "It was the food! Don't touch the food!" That was typical Richard.'

The diagnosis was Hodgkin's disease, an insidious lymphatic cancer. Despite intensive treatment it was clear that Harris was fighting a battle he simply couldn't win. At peace with himself, Harris had a life to look back on that was the envy of most of us. That he'd boozed most of it away didn't bother him one jot. 'I had the happiest days of my life as a drinker. If I had my life again I'd make all the same mistakes. I would still sleep with as many women, and drink as much vodka. Any regrets would make me seem ungrateful.'

As his body lay in the morgue, Harris's two sons stood by their father pausing for reflection. Thinking it too quiet and sombre, Jamie slipped outside to grab a pint of Guinness. Dipping his finger into the black nectar he moistened his father's lips with it. And that's how the great man went to meet his maker, with the taste of a good pint on him.

CHARLES HAWTREY (1914–1988: *Comedy Actor*)

For a man who played alongside the great English music hall comedians like Max Miller and was a regular in the most successful comedy film series in cinema history, to die a sad, lonely wretched drunk who spent his days arguing with his cat or chatting up rent boys is a national travesty, if a totally self-inflicted one.

By the time Charles Hawtrey joined the Carry On team he was already a comedy veteran, having played in Will Hay and George Formby films. Hawtrey excelled in weedy, put-upon characters, and with his near-skeletal appearance and wire-rimmed glasses resembled a praying mantis made human. He was a unique performer, and an even more unique character.

Born in Hounslow, the son of a London car mechanic, Hawtrey was a quintessential mother's boy. And what a mother! Often she'd accompany him to Pinewood, home of the Carry Ons, where she'd indulge her odd habit of swiping loo paper from the studio toilets. Rumbled once, she flushed the lot away, causing a major plumbing disaster that halted production on *Chitty Chitty Bang Bang*. Henceforth Hawtrey was obliged to keep his mother locked in his dressing room.

In total Hawtrey made twenty-three Carry Ons and he's an utter delight in every one of them. For a while the series producers Peter Rogers and Gerald Thomas tolerated his boozing. Often he came in completely plastered and they'd have to force black coffee down his throat and stand him up between two quite literally supporting actors. Or he'd reappear on set after a liquid lunch a little the worse for wear. Shooting a scene in *Carry On Spying* (1964) he passed out cold. A unit nurse innocently asked, 'Have you tried giving him a nip of brandy?' Kenneth Williams scoffed, 'That's the last thing he needs, dear.'

Making *Carry On . . . Up the Khyber* (1968) on location in Snowdonia, the cast stayed at a local hotel. Past midnight Williams heard Hawtrey ascending the stairs shouting and in a well-gone state, having consumed at the bar two bottles of port and a whisky, and noted in his diary: 'It's not the eccentricity, or the grotesquerie, that puts one off Charlie. It is the excruciating boredom.'

For Hawtrey drinking was a way of life, a momentary escape from the loneliness and depression he suffered. By the end, though, the booze had all but taken over. He played a hopeless drunk in *Carry On Abroad* (1972), swigging back suntan lotion, precisely because he was off his tits the whole time. Why play against type? Made on a shoestring, the Carry Ons were the epitome of team effort; Hawtrey's behaviour was holding up production and could not be tolerated any longer. He was barred from the series in 1972 and his career never recovered. One can argue that the Carry On films suffered just as much, since his presence is sorely missed in the last few entries.

Sadly, Hawtrey looked back on his Carry On years as pure torture; their success had typecast him for ever, making finding other work almost impossible, and he was paid peanuts into the bargain. 'I got bugger all and at the end was shat on very badly.' Hawtrey was reduced to appearing in pantomime. His drinking was so bad now that after each performance the police would lock Hawtrey in the cells overnight to stop him causing a nuisance in the local area. The next morning the theatre manager would fetch him and he'd go on stage, not really knowing where he was or what he was doing and having to be guided through the performance by the other actors.

Hawtrey retired to the seaside town of Deal and lived like a virtual recluse, Kent's answer to Howard Hughes, though Hughes never waltzed along the promenade in a fur coat waving at sailors. Asked if he'd ever slept with a woman, Hawtrey answered that he was sure the experience was nice, 'but not as good as the real thing'. The 'real thing' tended to be rent boys or youths and merchant seaman he'd picked up. Sex for Charlie was of the back-alley type, sleazy and dirty. 'Come on and give it to me, big boy,' he might yell at the appropriate moment to some willing volunteer. 'Slap your bollocks against my arse!' was another expression one has the horrible feeling he used more than once. Other choice gems included: 'Would you like to grease my arse pipe?' And 'Let me consume your cock broth.'

Aside buggery, most of his time was spent drinking. It started at breakfast with five double gins and vermouths, while the evening saw him speed up a bit, downing two and a half bottles of port. Even his cat was an alcoholic, munching on port-soaked sugar lumps and sherry-spiked butter.

For the most part Hawtrey was a liability whenever he stepped out of his front door. In local pubs he behaved outrageously and was eventually banned from every one of his locals. Approach him in the street and ask for his autograph, his two usual responses were 'Fuck off!' or, if he was feeling charitable, 'Piss off!'

Few guests were ever invited inside his domain. Kenneth Williams visited once and recalled the ghastliness of its interior and that all Hawtrey wanted to do was show off his latest male porn mags: *Whopper*, *Campus Glory Holes* and *Touched by an Uncle*. They made a curious pair, Hawtrey and Williams, the campest old queens ever to grace a movie screen. And while Williams was tormented by his homosexuality, in turns fascinated and repulsed by it, 'It's such a messy business,' Hawtrey revelled in it.

In 1984 Hawtrey's house caught fire and, trapped on the first floor, stark bollock naked, he insisted on being rescued by the burliest fireman. Once on terra firma he realised he'd left his fags up there – oh, and a sixteen-year-old youth in his bed.

Thanks to escapades like that Hawtrey made himself a pariah in his community, with few if any friends; even showbiz colleagues began to give him wide berth. Sometimes he'd phone up Carry On co-star Joan Sims and just babble inane utterances. 'He'd be on the line for hours, this meaningless gurgling and sighing. This very lonely sad little man.' He had finally cut himself off from the world, deliberately it seemed, and enjoyed himself immensely while doing so.

In the risible end it wasn't the booze that did Hawtrey in but the fags. By 1988 the arteries in his legs were all but wasted and gangrene was spreading. The stark choice was lose both legs or die. Hawtrey refused the operation. 'I want to die with my boots on,' he said, lighting a fag in his hospital bed, then later throwing a vase at a nurse who had the temerity to ask for an autograph. It was his final act on earth.

The funeral was a quiet, almost non-existent affair. Nine people bothered to turn up. In accordance with Hawtrey's wishes his resting place has no headstone or marker to show that he ever lived.

ERNEST HEMINGWAY (1899–1961: Writer)

The very mention of his name conjures up images of barrels of booze, bar brawls, bullfights and big-game hunting. Ernest Hemingway was like a character from one of his own novels, a lost relic blurring his mind with booze from the realities of a world he hated. Suffering from clinical depression, he found comfort in the bottle and his capacity for alcohol knew no sane boundaries, yet he fiercely denied he was an alcoholic, until his delusions could no longer be sustained.

He was born in Illinois to a well-respected country doctor and a religiously strict mother who dressed him up in girl's clothing and left his hair long and curly. Is it any wonder that Hemingway spent his entire adult life desperate to prove his masculinity. At school he excelled in sports and English and on graduation was hired as a junior reporter on a local newspaper. Impressed by the hard-drinking antics of his older grizzled colleagues, Hemingway took to living it up in bars until closing time, then retiring to his apartment with a bottle of 'dago red'.

In the First World War he volunteered as an ambulance driver for the Red Cross on the Italian front. Legend has it he carried two flasks of alcohol on his belt and was drinking eighteen Martinis a day. While attending the wounded in the trenches a mortar shell exploded nearby and flaming shrapnel tore into both of his legs. Still he managed to haul another man to safety. Convalescing in hospital for several months, Hemingway charmed the nurses into bringing him a steady supply of cognac, Cinzano vermouth, Marsala and Chianti. Later when he was shipped back to the States he made, 'nightly and rigorous assaults on the ship's terrified wine stocks'.

Returning a hero, Hemingway didn't much care for Prohibition

America and moved to Canada, where he could drink like a free man. Drinking for Hemingway was good sport, a test of manhood: 'A man does not exist until he is drunk.' But it was too damn cold in Canada so he left for Paris, at the time home to one of the century's most celebrated literary colonies: you couldn't help but bump into a woozy F Scott Fitzgerald or groggy Gertrude Stein in the fashionable Left Bank. James Joyce was there too, and he and Hemingway often went on alcoholic benders together. Joyce would invariably fall into an argument or a fight with a fellow drinker and due to his poor eyesight, barely able to see his attacker, would yell; 'Deal with him, Hemingway! Deal with him!'

Using Paris as his base, Hemingway gallivanted round Europe covering wars as a roving reporter; sharing a glass of wine with Mussolini, vodka with Soviet dignitaries and sangria with bullfighters in Spain. He soaked up the places he visited, but forget churches or museums; that wasn't for Hemingway. 'If you want to know about a culture, spend a night in its bars.'

Hemingway had grown bored of Paris; one suspects the French capital had had quite enough of him. Certainly he'd alienated much of the writing community there. Gertrude Stein got so fed up with him arriving banjaxed at her house that she put a sign outside her door: KEEP OUT, THIS MEANS YOU!

In 1928, Hemingway moved to Key West, Florida, quickly finding a suitable abode, but more importantly a bar that fitted his purpose, Sloppy Joe's. After beating the local barflies into the ground, he invited round some of his old drinking buddies like Fitzgerald to get loaded with or go out and fish all day. A biographer described Hemingway's fishing boat as 'kind of a floating whorehouse and rum factory'. A typical inventory of necessary supplies for a day's fishing included three coolers of beer, five or six bottles of rum, fourteen bottles of Chateau Margaux salvaged from a sunken ship, plus a stock of pre-war absinthe.

One particularly memorable oceanographic expedition involved a feisty duel with a hooked shark during which Hemingway managed to shoot himself twice in the calf. 'There was no pain at all,' he said, due to the fact he was well anaesthetised.

Just months before publication of *A Farewell to Arms* in 1929, the novel that would seal his literary fame, Hemingway learned that his father had committed suicide. Predictably he turned to booze for escape, since 'it got you through that black-ass middle of the night and let you live until morning'. Worse, Key West went the way of the rest of America and Prohibition arrived. Luckily pal Fitzgerald was stocked with an inexhaustible supply of Canadian whisky and French champagne.

Hemingway had now reached the point in his life where he was more legend than mere man; people flocked to his various hang-outs to watch him in action, as if he were some Victorian side-show freak or an animal in a cage. People saw it as sport to challenge him to a drinking duel; he'd take on all comers, and was rarely if ever bested. Finally, fed up with being gawped at, Hemingway fled Key West. He was sad to go; in his garden he'd erected a fountain fashioned from a urinal from Sloppy Joe's. Hemingway told the owner that as he'd pissed a small fortune into the bowl he should own the damn thing, so ripped it off the wall and carried it off.

Thirsting for more adventure, Hemingway travelled to Africa in the summer of 1933, leaving a young son behind with a nanny and the advice, 'Go easy on the beer. And lay off the hard liquor until I get back.' He adored the savannah, got pally with the white hunters on safari and loved the convivial atmosphere of telling rollicking tales and drinking whisky round the campfire. He was mullocked most of the time, actually, and managed to fall out of a speeding Land Rover.

Maybe thinking he'd be safer at sea, he purchased a thirty-eight-foot cabin cruiser he christened the *Pilar*, crewed by a loyal band of fellow drunks. Off he'd venture on month-long forays into the Gulf Stream. It was a freedom he couldn't find on dry land, where his fame had encroached so much into his world it had become unbearable.

With two failed marriages behind him already, Hemingway hitched up with wife number three and moved to Cuba, purchasing a tropical hideaway where he'd write the classic books *For Whom the Bell Tolls* and *The Old Man and the Sea*. His working schedule was rigid: up at six, pound away on his typewriter till noon, then sally forth to Havana's Floridita Bar to sink double daiquiris.

By 1939 Hemingway was being told to cut down drastically on alcohol.

Gamely he tried to drink just the three Scotches before dinner but pretty soon was back taking tea and gin for breakfast and slugging absinthe, vodka and wine throughout the day. He'd be buggered if any quack was going to tell him how to conduct his life.

When the US entered the Second World War Hemingway came over all patriotic and outfitted his yacht with grenades and machine guns. He even managed to get the thing registered as a military ship charged with patrolling Cuba's shores on the lookout for Nazi submarines. He'd be awarded a medal for his deeds, which largely consisted of marinated joyrides. His wife accused him of using these 'booze patrols' as an excuse to get away from her, go fishing and drink with the boys rather than help win any war. To which Hemingway replied, 'Honey, drinking is war.'

After the cessation of hostilities, Hemingway began to drink even more heavily, at least a quart of whisky a day, scarcely going to bed in a sober condition. According to journalist George Plimpton, who got to know Hemingway well in these later years, the bulge of his liver could be seen protruding from his body 'like a long, fat leech'. But Hemingway was made of stern stuff. He survived numerous car accidents, bush fires, boating mishaps, even a plane crash; in fact two, both on safari. After walking away from the first one, just days later he crashed in the jungle again, managing to sustain himself somehow for forty-eight hours with a ruptured kidney, liver and spleen, a sprained arm and leg, crushed verte-brae, a paralysed sphincter, a burned scalp and major concussion before being rescued by a river patrol. Incorrectly reported as dead, Hemingway enjoyed what few people ever have, that of reading their own obituary.

Combined with his other casualty-ward ailments mostly brought about by booze – ailing eyesight, muscle cramps, chronic insomnia and impo-tency, plus 200 shrapnel scars and a shot-off kneecap – Hemingway may not actually have been of this world. Friend and rival F Scott Fitzgerald spoke mockingly about trying to get rid of him. 'I dropped a heavy glass skylight on his head at a drinking party. But you can't kill the guy. He's not human.'

By the time he reached sixty, though, Hemingway was literally coming apart at the seams, his craggy face resembling a particularly weather-beaten stretch of Norwegian coastline. For years Hemingway had been the maker of his own legend, the macho outdoorsman who could outdrink, outbox and outscrew any rival. In Paris, courting his fourth wife, Hemingway placed a photograph of her husband in the toilet bowl and blasted it with a machine pistol, flooding their room at the Ritz. Eventually it was this need to live up to such myth-making antics, and his growing alcoholism, that rendered him incapable of producing the gifted work of just a few years before. It led to severe depression and paranoia, a conviction that friends were trying to kill him and the FBI was after him. Hospitalised, he was given electro-shock treatment over the course of two months.

Plagued by a slew of demons, Hemingway wanted out. In his last paranoid days he tried walking into a plane's propeller and jumping out of an aircraft high above the Rockies. Finally he looked to his father's example and one morning, just nineteen days shy of his sixty-second birthday, placed both barrels of a 12-gauge English shotgun in his mouth and blew his cranium apart.

'WILD BILL' HICKOK (1837–1876: Western Hero)

One of the legendary figures of the old west, James Butler 'Wild Bill' Hickok was a man of many guises: sheriff, civil-war spy, Indian fighter, frontier scout and one helluva poker player you crossed at your peril. He was also a formidable whisky drinker and gunfighter who put more people in their grave than Rambo.

He was born on a farm in Troy Grove, Illinois, and quickly rebelled against his stiff-shirt Baptist parents by downing whisky, kicking hard against authority and playing around with guns, going into the local woods to hunt wolves. As soon as he was old enough he left home and headed west, finding work driving a passenger stagecoach on the Santa Fe Trail. Often these were seen as easy targets for bandits and young Hickok had plenty of opportunity to hone his sharpshooter instincts.

Disaster struck one trip when his coach broke down, leaving everyone stranded. There was nothing left to do for Hickok but to get stoned on whisky and crash out near some bushes. Dressed as he was in his one and only suit, which hadn't seen a laundry in eight months, its various odours soon attracted the attention of a wild bear that took a sizeable chunk out of his arse.

Unable to find his pistols in the evening gloom, Hickok went after the furry bastard with a knife. The shocking yells and screams woke the passengers who stumbled out of their compartment to see slain on the ground a mammoth bear and a half-grizzled Bill. 'Gimmie all the whisky you've got,' he asked and poured one full bottle over his wounds and sunk the other, before crashing out again.

During the Civil War he and Buffalo Bill Cody held up a supply train and rode off with its cargo of whisky, with a little help from some cavalry troopers, back to their regiment for a mighty booze-up. Cody later wrote: 'It was one of the biggest jollifications it has ever been my misfortune to attend.'

Hickok turned his attention to the more genteel pursuit of gambling. Poker was his forte and one quarrel over cards led to him gunning a man down in the street. Hickok avoided jail by claiming self-defence. Hickok, it seemed, lived in a perpetual world of wild and reckless abandon, one continual round of whoring, drinking whisky in large quantities and playing cards with his pistols, a pair of twin ivory-handled Colt revolvers, nestled in a red sash around his waist, half-cocked in anticipation of trouble. He was a flamboyant figure who wore his hair long and spoke in a way that would have graced any western film. Confronted by outlaws in a saloon, Hickok drew his revolver and yelled, 'Leave or there'll be more dead men around here than the town can bury.'

By 1865 his deeds had earned Hickok the not undeserved moniker 'Wild Bill', and when he arrived in Chicago his reputation had most assuredly preceded him. In one bar, as he accepted free drinks in exchange for a tale of derring-do, his presence attracted the attention of a local gang of thugs, five in total, who ridiculed Hickok's frontier clothing. Bill let it ride for a while until one ruffian asked if every hillbilly bumpkin picked his teeth with a Bowie knife. Bill looked hard on the youth and replied, 'No, but we all know who our mothers are.' The crowd parted, sensing trouble. Deftly, Hickok grabbed a pool cue and reduced the thugs to a broken, bleeding pile on the floor. He then resumed his place at the bar.

Inevitably Hickok became a target for every gunslinger who wanted to establish his own reputation by killing the great 'Wild Bill'. Over his career Hickok claimed to have personally killed 'considerably over 100 men', not counting Indians or Mexicans, of course, making him perhaps the most prolific serial killer of his generation. Hickok himself was remarkably hard to dispatch. Once in Colorado he was shot three times but survived.

Little wonder, then, with such statistics, that Hickok was made sheriff of Hays City, Kansas, the scene of wild brawls and home to hard-drinking ruffians. Hickok was determined to keep the peace; his modus operandi usually involved a bullet. He shot a man through the head during a fracas merely for remarks made against his person. As the dead and the maimed began piling up the good folk of Hays City wondered if the cure wasn't worse than the disease and replaced Hickok. Later he was employed as marshal of Abilene, another tough frontier town, and spent most of his time drinking and playing poker at the saloon, telling his deputies to come and get him if there was trouble. When the bodies started stacking up again, all with bullets originating from Hickok's revolver, the city council discharged him. Tragically, one of the dead was Hickok's own deputy and close friend who got in the line of fire during a gunfight. The lawman openly wept as he laid the body on a billiard table in the saloon. Hickok never killed another man in anger.

For the next few years he drifted from town to town, losing all his money at the gaming tables. Destitute, he decided to trade on his notoriety and tour with Buffalo Bill Cody and his Wild West Show. Poor old Hickok never quite got to grips with show business. For one scene the cast all had to sit round a campfire telling stories and passing the whisky round, in reality cold tea. 'Wild Bill' took a sip, spat it out and threw the bottle to the ground shouting, 'You must think I'm the worst fool east of the Rockies that I can't tell whisky from tea. This don't count and I can't tell my story unless I get real whisky.' While the audience revelled in this glimpse of the real 'Wild Bill' Hickok, Cody got some proper whisky for his friend. After a few drags Hickok got randy and broke character again to pursue the female cast members.

On the road Hickok's reputation brought trouble. At one hotel in Pennsylvania a group of roughnecks on a drinking binge in the bar were determined to take on the western stars. Hickok was all for meeting them head-on but Cody insisted they leave through a side entrance. Out in the street Cody looked round and there was no sign of 'Wild Bill'. Unable to resist temptation, he'd gone to fight the roughnecks single-handed and with a broken chair had laid out five of them and driven the rest out. 'They won't bother us any more.'

Legend has it that a bout of gonorrhoea and increasing alcoholism affected Hickok's eyesight and eventually his shooting skills, and he was forced to leave the show. He then discovered a rival cowboy touring production had hired an actor to play him. Incensed, Hickok turned up for one performance and when the actor in question made his entrance jumped onto the stage and knocked him through the scenery. The stage manager ran on protesting, so 'Wild Bill' grabbed him and threw him into the orchestra pit. Satisfied, Hickok resumed his seat and shouted at the company to proceed with the show, just as the police turned up to arrest him.

Trying his luck at cards again, Hickok wandered the west a drunken gambler, losing all his money and repeatedly arrested for vagrancy. Winding up in Cheyenne, Wyoming, he met and fell in love with Agnes Lake and they married. Following a brief honeymoon Hickok left his new bride to earn enough money through gold prospecting to set them up for a happy life together. The newlyweds would never see each other again.

'Wild Bill' caused quite a commotion when he rode into the town of Deadwood, where fate was ultimately to catch up with him. He set up camp on the outskirts of town to prospect for gold, but spent most of his time drinking and playing cards in saloons, hoping his reputation as a gunfighter would keep danger at bay; Deadwood was a hangout for desperadoes and killers. It worked for a time; Hickok was a marked man but no one had the guts to face him. Then one afternoon a petty villain named Jack McCall walked up behind Hickok as he sat playing poker and shot him in the head. As 'Wild Bill' lay across the table, the cards in his outstretched hand dropped to the floor, showing a pair of black aces and a pair of eights; forever that would be known as a 'dead man's hand'.

ALEX 'HURRICANE' HIGGINS (b. 1949: Snooker Ace)

He's the George Best of snooker, blessed with a God-given talent that turned the sport from a minority game to the favourite of millions. He should have been lionised; instead Alex Higgins's self-destructive behaviour made him a pariah. The booze, the birds and the gambling didn't help much either, they were fatal flaws that cut short what should have been a more glittering career.

He was born on a council estate in Belfast to an illiterate labourer and a mother who worked as a cleaner. By the time he was twelve he'd given up on school, spending most days down the snooker club hustling adults for money. After winning amateur titles in Northern Ireland, Higgins turned professional in 1971 and a year later triumphed at the world championship at his first attempt.

Higgins was a breath of fresh air in the game, sitting in between shots smoking and drinking, something unthinkable today. An anti-hero the public could relate to, with a fierce, uncontrollable temper, Higgins hated authority, any authority, and in his world that meant the people officiating and running snooker. At tournaments he'd say to referees who might encroach on his space, 'Don't come within six foot of me.' He was a blue touch-paper waiting to be lit and audiences flocked to see him play.

His flamboyant style and breakneck speed around the table earned him the 'Hurricane' nickname, an adjective that also easily described his life away from the green baize. Already his drinking was becoming a problem and people in the game voiced concern that if he carried on at the rate he was he'd not make his thirtieth birthday. He carried on regardless, ticking off the decades as they came. 'He'll live to be seventy, that bastard,' said a former manager. He was one of life's survivors, and Higgins knew it, that was part of the problem.

More snooker titles followed, including another world championship win in 1982, but his private life was about to hit the fan. Married with a young family, he'd drink at home in front of the baby. His wife Lynn hated it and soon couldn't cope and left. A reconciliation holiday only ended in a suicide attempt which nearly killed Alex. Lynn agreed to take him back on the condition that he promise to sort himself out. Higgins agreed and checked into a private hospital. When Lynn visited him there she was outraged to find him living it up royally, sending nurses on trips to fetch him lager. After five days Alex left, saying the place was full of nutters and there wasn't anything wrong with him.

Back in the family home Higgins hadn't changed a bit, was probably worse, prone to fits of violence during which he'd smash things up. Christmas 1985 was the last straw. When Lynn refused to have his friends round for dinner, knowing it would only descend into one long drinkathon, Alex stormed off to the pub. Returning late that evening he walked from room to room saying, 'This is what I think of your gold cutlery.' Smash! 'And this is what I think of your Waterford crystal.' Smash! Everything was going through windows. Panic-stricken, Lynn grabbed her daughter and they locked themselves in the bedroom. Alex was outside for three hours trying to break his way in with a golf club. Lynn finally called the police, screaming, 'He's gone mad.' When they arrived Higgins refused them entry, and when they burst in it took three officers to make the arrest.

Understandably Lynn left him for good after that and Higgins's world began to fall apart. In 1986 following a UK Championship match Higgins retired to the players lounge and partook of a welcome beverage. An official approached him asking for a urine sample as part of a random drugs test. Higgins's paranoia kicked in straightaway and he told him to fuck off or he'd lay him out. When the tournament director got hold of Higgins and demanded he take the test, Alex head-butted him. Security was there in an instant but Alex managed to wriggle free and still shaking with anger put his fist through a door and started smashing up the place. He was escorted off the premises by police and later fined and banned for five tournaments.

At the time Alex was seeing Siobhan Kidd, a woman thirteen years his junior. It was another fiery relationship, full of blazing rows. 'Alex couldn't have a stable relationship with his cue, never mind a woman,' mocked racing pundit John McCririck. After one heated argument Higgins threw a glass ashtray at Siobhan. It missed, smashing against a wall. The police were called and Alex spent a night in the cells, and was done for breach of the peace.

Strange things were beginning to happen in the world of Alex Higgins. One night after losing £1,000 at a casino, he returned to his flat, shall we say well fortified, only for Siobhan to lock him in, lest he try to get out again. No problem, thought Alex. He peered out of the window and quickly estimated the distance to the street below as thirty feet. Figuring if he bent both legs and then rolled on impact, like a parachutist landing at Arnhem under heavy fire, he just might make it. Of course the silly bugger jumped, landing painfully on one foot, splintering bone, and falling forward smashed his head onto the pavement, knocking himself out.

Sent to hospital, the X-rays proved he'd broken numerous bones and would be out of action for months. A helpful cop put Alex's many fans' fears to rest; 'He was not seriously injured, luckily enough he landed on his head.' Amazingly, just a few days later Alex turned up at a snooker championship, foot in plaster and hobbling on crutches, the butt of numerous Long John Silver jokes. People wondered if he planned to do pantomime that year with fellow snooker ace John Parrot.

There was trouble again at an exhibition tournament in Plymouth, when Higgins lost and caused a ruckus in the players lounge and was thrown out. Hitting a local nightclub, his evening predictably ended in a brawl. Walking to his hotel afterwards Alex was set upon by a large fella, who used an iron bar to play Mr Piano Man on his knee caps. Higgins crawled a few hundred yards before the sheer pain knocked him out. He woke up in hospital, which was starting to become a bit of a habit. The doctors wanted him to stay on for more days of observation but Alex discharged himself, hobbling out like an earthquake survivor from Guatemala.

Alex's relationship with Siobhan was on equally shaky ground. During one row he threw her out of their hotel room into the corridor, not so bad only she happened to be naked at the time. And then the big one when Alex threw a table across the room and then whacked her with a hairdryer. 'I, to my shame, went a bit mad.' The case ended up in court; the relationship ended up as history.

Never mind, Alex could revel in the company of his new best friend, Oliver Reed; the world held its collective breath. Actually they seemed to do more damage to each other. During one drinking session Reed put Giorgio Armani aftershave into Higgins's Scotch. His face screwed up in painful shock and he was ill for two days. Revenge was sweet when Higgins treated Reed to a Fairy Liquid crème de menthe. 'Ollie was burping bubbles for weeks.'

Higgins enjoyed paying Reed the odd visit at his stately home. One night after several drinks Higgins passed out in an armchair. He was rudely awoken by a jab in the ribs. 'How dare you fall asleep in my presence?' It was Ollie, who'd grabbed an axe and looked like he had every intention of using it. Higgins was chased up the stairs and ran into a room and bolted the door shut. That didn't deter Reed, who began chopping at the solid oak like Jack Nicholson in *The Shining*. It took him just a few minutes to weaken the wood and Higgins saw the tip of the blade peek through. 'I was terrified. I honestly thought I might be about to breathe my last if he got through.'

Other wayward friends included snooker's new maverick Jimmy White. One memorable evening saw an inebriated White driving on a country road with Higgins alongside him in the passenger seat. The rain was coming down hard and White lost control of the car and hit a wall. He shot forward, his chest making painful contact with the steering wheel. Higgins wasn't so lucky: not wearing a seat belt, he sailed through the air like Superman making a quick getaway through the windscreen and disappeared into the darkness outside.

White got out and yelled into the bleak air, 'Alex! Alex!' Nothing. Silence. He tried again. Then he heard something, a slight mumbling from behind a wall. 'I'm all right, James, do not upset yourself.' It was Higgins, he'd survived; of course he bloody had. Crawling over the wall, he clambered onto the bonnet and back inside through the gap in the windscreen his nut had made. As he settled into his seat he beamed, 'I'm born again!'

At the 1990 snooker World Cup Higgins surpassed even himself when he threatened to have fellow Ireland snooker player Dennis Taylor shot. After a match the two engaged in a blazing row in the players lounge during which Higgins spat, 'If I had a gun in my hand I'd blow your brains out.' Later he punched the championship's press officer in the stomach. It was one misdemeanour too far and he was banned for ten months and had all his ranking points taken away. It was the most severe ban ever imposed on a snooker player. But you couldn't say he didn't have it coming: for years he'd regularly been up before the disciplinary board facing one ban or another. Once he came into the hearing with half a dozen bottles of champagne and said, 'Chaps, before we listen to this, shall we have a drink?'

With his professional career in tatters, things weren't progressing very well either on the emotional front with new girlfriend Holly. There were the now customary bouts of drinking and blazing rows. One night it kicked off big time when Holly claimed Higgins whacked her. The drinking continued, as did the brickbats. Then Holly picked up two sharp knives and stuck one in Alex's arm and the other in his stomach. Believing she intended to finish him off there and then – 'I had never seen anyone in such a strop' – Higgins bolted and walked bleeding into a neighbour's house. As he was being patched up at hospital the police arrived for a statement. 'Fuck off, the lot of you,' Higgins yelled, rather uncharitably. 'I'm not pressing any charges. I just want out of here.'

There was more trouble up ahead. On a train bound for London Alex got talking to a girl and before either of them knew what was happening lust had taken over and they'd crashed into the nearest toilet cubicle for a fast knee trembler. Desperate to see her again, Higgins paid a visit to her London flat but was quite perturbed when the door was opened by a rather large Australian geezer. Higgins hurled a few choice verbals and then retired to a pub. After a few drinks he ventured back and when his frantic knocks went unanswered he kicked the door in. Running up the stairs he was met halfway by the Australian and the ruck was on. 'There was only one winner,' said Alex later. 'And it wasn't me.'

Higgins was arrested, charged and banged up in a cell till he sobered up, which took quite some time. He was also told to report to the police station in a week's time. Of course he forgot and was arrested, but managed to get the local coppers to take him out for a liquid lunch, half pints of mild for the officers and several large brandies for Higgins. 'Alex,' one copper said, 'you're an expensive guy to arrest.'

In 1998 Higgins was diagnosed with throat cancer, going under the surgeon's knife and subjected to forty doses of radiotherapy. People naturally assumed it would kill him off quicker than a Moscow pensioner during a harsh winter, but no, the bugger survived. But at what cost? He now looked emaciated, resembling someone who'd been on hunger strike for twelve years; no longer the hurricane, either, more like a slight breeze. People were even more shocked to see him still rolling his own cigarettes. As usual he didn't give a shit. In his own mind he was indestructible.

His hatred of authority hadn't been blunted, either. During an exhibition match for charity in 2007 Higgins touched a blue ball and the referee called foul. After glaring at the official for a few seconds Alex casually walked over and punched him in the stomach. Quite understandably the referee refused to carry on and the match ended in chaos. A witness said Higgins was drinking pints of Guinness between frames and performing the occasional Irish jig at the table. Again it was the sheer unpredictability of the man, as much with a snooker cue in his hand as a whisky glass that has always been part of his flawed genius.

BILLIE HOLIDAY (1915–1959: Singer)

Arguably the greatest jazz vocalist of all time, Billie Holiday lived a life scarred by racism, poverty, abusive men, drugs and alcohol, lots and lots of alcohol. It's all there in her voice, the kind of real heartbreak you can't fake or emulate. She had a remarkable ability to turn even the simplest, banal love song into a poignant piece imbued with passion and raw, almost painful emotion.

Hot-tempered and ready to clock anyone who gave her grief, Billie raced through life like an out-of-control locomotive; it was as if she deliberately chose to reject a normal existence and had a ball doing it in spite of all the tragedies that befell her.

She was born in Philadelphia to an unwed teenage mother and raised in a tough neighbourhood of Baltimore. When her mother moved to New York to find work as a maid Billie went to live with her grandparents in a run-down slum. Beaten regularly by her cousin who lived there, Billie was also subjected to bullying from her cousin's son. After he hit her in the face one day with a rat, Billie took a baseball bat to the little bastard and put him in the local hospital.

Already as tough as old boots by the age of eleven, what innocence Billie had left was cruelly snatched from her when a neighbour tried to rape her. Left deeply damaged and vulnerable, what emerged from the incident was a new rebellious spirit that saw Billie sent to a reform school for wayward girls. Playing truant, Billie ended up not even bothering to go at all, preferring to get smashed on corn whisky.

At fourteen she went to live with her mother in Harlem, staying in a whorehouse and running errands, some of which necessitated her lying on her back. 'I had a chance to become a strictly twenty-dollar call girl and I took it.' Within just weeks of her arrival, though, she and her mother were picked up in a police raid and Billie served four months in a city workhouse.

Throughout these difficult times Billie found solace in music, singing along to the records of Bessie Smith and Louis Armstrong. Back out on the streets and resorting once again to prostitution, Billie also started singing in Harlem speakeasies and nightclubs, whorehouses and reefer pads, just about any place that would have her and served strong hooch and paid well. Quickly she came to the attention of an influential talent scout and her career really took off when the jazz giant Benny Goodman used her on one of his albums. By the end of the 1930s Billie's recordings of songs like 'Strange Fruit' and 'Summertime' had made her an icon.

As someone who'd grown up around speakeasies and within a culture of drinking, Billie could handle hard liquor better than anyone. Her ability to consume huge quantities was breathtaking, as one friend testified after going back to her home following a gig. She'd already taken stimulants to get through the show; now to unwind Billie took some opium, drank, and smoked a couple of joints. Then she took some pills, drank some more, and later shot up heroin in the bathroom. This little cocktail of oblivion might easily have killed a lesser mortal, but Billie's upbringing had given her the armour-plated bodywork of a tiger tank.

Prejudice was something else Billie was familiar with and had learned to handle. Performing in a Manhattan club, between sets she took a seat at a table and ordered her usual drink, a mixture of gin and port wine. Two southern white boys visiting the Big Apple took great exception to this 'darkie' wearing a mink coat. Billie told them to get lost; instead they stubbed out their cigarettes in her mink. Looking both in the eye, Billie told the pair if they had any balls they'd meet her outside in an alleyway. They showed up, and so did Billie, who beat them unconscious with her bare knuckles.

By the early forties her live performances were becoming more and more erratic; sipping Brandy Alexanders before going on stage, she was guilty of sometimes mucking up her phrasing or slurring her words, and there were times when she simply never showed up at all. Still, she remained hugely popular in the jazz world and one of the highest paid performers of the time, $1,000 a week, much of it spent on junk or fleeced by a succession of hustler boyfriends and dodgy husbands. Billie seemed drawn to men who brutalised and humiliated her; her early life as a scion of sadism was undoubtedly part of the reason as she went almost willingly from one fist to the next; a punch bag with a sassy ass. Her last husband, Louis McKay once punched Billie so hard she fell halfway across the street. Managers robbed and roughed her up, too. One friend recalls visiting Billie at her home before a concert as her manager John Levy, characterised by her piano player as a 'sadistic pimp', was just leaving. Sitting on a couch was Billie, her face beginning to sprout big nasty purple bruises. 'I can't go to work tonight,' she said. 'John beat the hell out of me.'

After the death of her mother in October 1945, Billie began drinking more heavily than ever to ease her grief and also upped her heroin intake to such an absurd degree that instead of cooking the stuff on a tablespoon, as most addicts did, she used a tuna can instead. In 1947 Billie was arrested on drug charges and had no choice but to submit to placement in a federal drug-rehabilitation centre, where she stayed for almost a year. A star inmate, she did her chores, she did her time, but she never sang a note, not one while behind bars. Just days after her release she performed before a packed house at Carnegie Hall.

Now a convicted felon, the authorities came down hard on Billie. She was allowed no rehabilitation, no second chance. First they suspended her cabaret licence, thus prohibiting her from performing in New York clubs where booze was sold. Then the police began to hassle her almost round the clock, turning up at gigs, heckling, threatening, and raiding her dressing room.

To get around the ban Billie went on the road, touring concert halls across the country. She also largely ditched her heroin habit, filling the gaping void with yet more alcohol. No one seemed able to save Billie from herself and her addiction. By the 1950s all that hard living had begun to affect her voice, the emotive resonance growing frayed and ragged round the edges, but like a punch-drunk fighter she carried on. Singing had become her life, giving expression to all the pain she'd suffered; it was heartbreaking to hear.

In the end it was the booze that killed her. Collapsing with cirrhosis of the liver and heart failure, she was rushed to hospital where even here the authorities continued to hassle her and she was busted for possession of heroin on her deathbed. With police guards outside her door, there are reports that Billie's doctors were told not to prescribe her effective pain relief, making her last days particularly miserable.

She was allowed the occasional visitor, one of whom was Frank Sinatra. He walked in and there was Billie smoking outside her oxygen tent and asking a nurse to fetch her a beer, defiant to the bitter end. She seemed reconciled to dying, but Sinatra was appalled at her physical state. Her once plump frame was emaciated, mere skin and bones; the booze had rotted everything inside her.

They chatted about the old times, about how much Frank owed and admired her as a fellow performer, then Billie whispered in his ear, 'Will you cut the shit, baby, and get me some dope!' On her deathbed Billie wanted one last fix. Sinatra said he'd try and smuggle some in. For days he asked around, hustling up some heroin from somewhere, until he heard Billie's liver had failed and she'd gone into a coma. Then she was gone.

Horrendously the hustlers, the parasitic promoters and the lousy husbands that had ripped her off most of her career had done such a good job that Billie Holiday died with just 70 cents in her bank account.

DENNIS HOPPER (b. 1936: Actor)

This is a story of enormous potential largely squandered, undermined by self-destructive hedonism and untempered rebellion. Dennis Hopper firmly believed he'd be dead by his thirtieth birthday; he used to take three grams of cocaine so he could sober up and drink more; on *Easy Rider* he didn't change his clothes for six months and punched a hole in a coffee table with a local drug dealer's head. Is it any wonder that *Empire* magazine once said, 'If Dennis Hopper didn't exist, Hollywood would be required to invent him.'

He was born on his parents' wheat farm in Kansas and was barely into his teens when he started snorting gasoline from his grandfather's truck and tripping. That was until he overdosed one day on the fumes and went wild, smashing up the headlights with a baseball bat. Reprimanded, Dennis instead graduated to stealing cans of beer out of the fridge.

Never close to his parents, feeling isolated at home, unwanted, he left and headed out to Hollywood with hopes of becoming an actor. Guest spots on TV shows earned him a contract at Warner Brothers and a supporting role as a juvenile delinquent in *Rebel Without a Cause* (1955). He befriended its star James Dean, they'd hang out together and smoke dope, but when Dean died in a horrific car accident Hopper was determined to be the new rebel in town. Glancing back at the likes of John Barrymore and Errol Flynn, Hopper saw it almost as his duty to raise hell. A head-on collision was inevitable and it arrived when Dennis worked for veteran director Henry Hathaway on *From Hell to Texas* (1958). After walking off the picture three times because he wouldn't take direction, Hopper made a defiant stand on the final day of shooting, point blankly refusing to perform a scene the way Hathaway wanted. It was a battle of wills. Who would crack first? After eighty takes and fifteen hours it was Dennis who caved in, physically and mentally drained. In tears he did the scene Hathaway's way and walked off the set, but not before he heard, ringing in his ears, Hathaway's curse: 'You'll never work in this town again, kid! I guarantee it!'

And he didn't, for seven years, returning in the mid-sixties with a new wife, actress Brooke Hayward, but the same don't-fuck-with-me attitude.

He was also a borderline alcoholic. As a teen Hopper's preferred tipple was beer, but in Hollywood the hallowed brew was deemed uncouth; people drank Martini. 'At first, I thought the stuff tasted awful,' said Dennis. 'It's an acquired taste, I acquired it.'

This being the sixties, drugs were everywhere, but mainly in Hopper's vascular system. Mists of paranoia floated around in his head unchecked. He believed both the CIA and FBI were tracking his movements, so he'd stalk the neighbourhood late at night, gun in hand, in search of government agents. Brooke believed it was the combination of drink and drugs that warped Hopper's personality, made him violent, a loose cannon. She began to fear for her own safety, not least because of Dennis's habit of falling drunkenly asleep in bed with a lit fag between his fingers, causing fires.

With the release in 1969 of his pet project *Easy Rider*, Dennis was hailed as a counter-culture icon, a tag that has never truly gone away. But Brooke couldn't take living with him any more, the beatings, the craziness. Splitting, she put a restraining order on him. When the divorce went through Brooke would have been completely within her rights to claim half of Dennis's money from the profits of *Easy Rider*. She opted to not ask for a thing. 'I didn't want him coming after me with a shotgun.'

Riding high as Hollywood's hottest director, Hopper threw his career down the toilet with his next project, *The Last Movie* (1971). The location shoot in Peru made the final days of Sodom look like afternoon tea at the Vatican. The set was awash with drugs, booze and groupies. Dennis himself was wasted for much of the time, posing for the end-of-shoot photo, bottle in hand, hollering, 'This picture was not made on marijuana. This picture was made on Scotch and soda.'

He also found time to marry actress and model Michelle Phillips, but blink and you'd have missed it: the union barely lasted a week. Just a few days in, Michelle began to have serious doubts about her future happiness when she saw her new husband firing guns in the house, and when he handcuffed her believing she was a witch, that was probably the last straw. In an interview with *The Times* in 2004 Dennis contested Michelle's assertion that he imprisoned her. 'I didn't handcuff her. I just punched her out.' Michelle eventually made a dash for the airport with

Hopper in hot pursuit, driving his car onto the runway in an attempt to stop the plane taking off.

With Michelle gone, Dennis set up his own hippie moviemaking commune in Taos, Mexico. The local populace largely resented them moving in, these strange people dressed in flower beads talking bollocks. It was rather a rough town, too, the last place you'd want to huddle round a campfire with guitars singing 'Mr Tambourine Man'. To protect himself from vengeful locals, Dennis set up machine-gun nests on the roof of his house and armed himself to the hilt. It was like the Alamo.

After the disastrous failure of *The Last Movie* Hollywood didn't want to touch Hopper with a barge pole and he was reduced to appearing in small independent movies. In Australia he starred in *Mad Dog Morgan* (1976), at least that's what his filmography says, and there is actually a film to prove it, too. Just as well, Dennis can't remember a damn thing about it. 'I was out of my mind back then. I was on 150 per-cent-proof rum and had no idea what the hell was going on.'

Dennis was in an even worse state when he arrived in the Philippines to play a small role in *Apocalypse Now* (1979). Taking one look at Hopper, Francis Ford Coppola said, 'What can I do to help you play this role?' Dennis mumbled, 'About an ounce of cocaine.' So the production office supplied Hopper with the drugs he needed to get through the film. His performance as a crazed photojournalist is, well, crazed, and on his last night on location he and Coppola got decimated together, with Dennis refusing to leave until there was no more beer left in the house.

Perversely, Dennis believed his drinking never affected or interfered with his work – as he liked to say, he drank all day and still managed to write and direct *Easy Rider*. But at the time he couldn't foresee himself being able to live without booze. His idea of the perfect retirement was getting the biggest bottle of alcohol he could buy, sit in an armchair somewhere and get perpetually pissed. In the early eighties he did manage to quit drinking for a while. The reason, his father lay dying, 'and I wanted him to see me sober for the last year of his life'. Then it was back to the bottle.

By 1982 Dennis's consumption of booze and drugs was frankly frightening. He really was on course for hell and damnation. At his peak

Dennis was consuming daily, wait for this: a half-gallon of rum, with a fifth of rum on the side in case he ran out, twenty-eight beers and three grams of cocaine; 'lines the length of a fountain pen every ten minutes'.

As the eighties continued it was a miracle Hopper's liver and kidneys hadn't packed up independently from the rest of his body, which remark-ably was in pretty fine fettle. It was his mind that went AWOL. He'd gone to Cuernavaca in Mexico to make a film called *Jungle Fever*, playing of all things head of the US Drug Enforcement Administration. He arrived smashed out of his skull on booze and drugs. Checking into his hotel he convinced himself that people were being tortured and burned alive in the basement. Believing he was next in line, he made a bolt for it, out into the warm Mexican night, stripped himself naked and wandered into a forest. He spent the whole night there, totally out of his mind. He sensed bugs and snakes crawling over and inside his skin, he had visions of an alien spacecraft landing and followed the glowing lights. 'I thought the Third World War had started. I masturbated in front of a tree and thought I'd become a galaxy – that was a good mood!'

By dawn, Dennis's revelries over, he wandered back into town, still naked. Some police tried to dress him but Hopper screamed at them, 'No, shoot me like this! I want to die naked.' It didn't take the film's producer long to conclude that Dennis was in no fit state to take part in his movie and he organised two hulking stuntmen to accompany him on a flight back to the States. Waiting for take-off, Dennis peered outside and in his raddled mind saw the wing catch fire. Breaking free from his bodyguards, Dennis tried to open the escape hatch to get outside. 'I was just totally gone,' he later related. 'But it's always very impressive when you do things like that.'

Back in LA Hopper was sent in the direction of the nearest rehab. When his daughter Marin called, the hospital doctors explained that her father was practically brain dead and they were moving him to an insane asylum. While there he grabbed a pair of hedge clippers and went wild with them until the orderlies put him in a straitjacket. Zonked out on a cocktail of drugs to keep him passive, Dennis wandered corridors looking like an extra in *Dawn of the Dead*. Doctors marched him around to different groups of patients saying, 'How many of you have seen *Easy*

Rider? Well, this is the guy who starred in it. You see what drugs will do to you.'

On his release, Hopper realised his problems were more alcohol than drug related, but his warped strategy to stay off booze was to keep doing drugs. 'So rather than having a beer in the morning, I'd have cocaine.' But thanks to the support of friends Hopper's mind found its natural plateau of normalcy. He knew there was no turning back now; his addictive personality would take over. One glass of wine with a meal, he'd want to know where the vineyard was. A line of cocaine? Bullshit, he'd want to do an ounce.

Dennis was never to touch booze or hard narcotics again. Today he's pretty much Hollywood royalty, not necessarily because of his uneven body of work, but because he survived it all. In the words of screenwriter and friend Tom Mankiewicz, 'I'm so happy that Dennis is still around because he has absolutely no right to be still alive.'

TREVOR HOWARD (1913–1988: Actor)

A hellraiser from the old school, the precursor of Harris and Burton and all the rest, Trevor Howard saw acting as just another job, not high art as Gielgud or Olivier perceived it. He despised showbiz bashes and premieres, preferring to spend his free time downing pints in his local or watching England play cricket at Lord's. He blustered his way through life like one of those old plantation owners, hopelessly undomesticated, never knowing or caring for the function of a fridge beyond its use as an ice cube dispenser for his whisky.

He was born in Kent, but raised in Ceylon at the fag-end of British colonialism with nannies and parents who were coldly remote from their children; his father worked for Lloyd's of London and his Canadian-born mother was a nurse. Spurning her wishes that he become an army officer, Howard latched on to acting primarily because 'there wasn't anything else to do'. He enrolled at RADA where his talent was immediately noted, and worked regularly afterwards on stage in Stratford and the West End. With the outbreak of war he put his career on hold only to be turned down by the RAF and the army. Finally called up into the Royal Corps of Signals airborne division, he was discharged in 1943 for being mentally unstable and having a 'psychopathic personality'. Ironic, since he would play innumerable stiff-upper-lipped English military types on screen.

Howard first brought that military bearing to play in his film debut, as a naval officer in *The Way Ahead* (1944), but it was *Brief Encounter* (1945) that marked Howard out as one of the best film character actors Britain ever produced. What the fans didn't know at the time was his propensity to get totally smashed. On night shoots Howard would sit in his car waiting to be called, just knocking back the booze, then climb out, throw up, go on set and give an immaculate performance.

When rat-arsed, Howard tended to become very loud and boisterous. In Vienna making *The Third Man* (1949), in which he played a British major, he got wildly drunk after finishing work and came to the attention of a real British army officer visiting the set. 'Who is that arsehole?' 'That's Trevor Howard,' replied an assistant. The name drew a blank. 'You know, *Brief Encounter* and all that.' There was a noticeable sigh. 'Oh, bloody actor is he? Well why is he wearing the King's uniform? I've a jolly good mind to report him.' And report him he did and Howard ended up meeting the commander of British forces in Austria. Outside the office hundreds of secretaries and ATS girls lined up for autographs, 'I do apologise for my behaviour, sir,' said Howard as he made his triumphant exit.

Making *The Roots of Heaven* (1958), Trevor and Errol Flynn became firm drinking buddies and there was plenty of opportunity to get sloshed with a truck loaded with whisky following the crew around the jungle location. 'We had a couple of jars on that one,' scoffed Howard. There's one tale of a dainty English theatrical visiting a New York bar when out of a crowded corner booth came the sound of a familiar gruff voice. A closer look confirmed it was his friend Trevor Howard, red-eyed and unshaven, holding court amongst a group of young American actors. 'Trevor, what on earth are you doing? Look at the state of you. How long have you been here?' An evil grin spread across his face. 'Three days!' roared Howard.

Much of the sixties was spent toiling in international productions like *Von Ryan's Express* (1965). Invited to a lavish party thrown by co-star Frank Sinatra, when it was time to leave Howard saw that his hire car was blocked in the driveway by late arrivals. Undeterred, the plastered Howard attempted to extricate the car himself, a big mistake. First he accelerated forward, ramming the vehicle parked in front, which in turn rammed the one ahead. Next he reversed gently, or so he thought, but the car thudded into the one behind, which shunted and damaged the car behind that. The noise brought guests spilling out of the house to watch open-mouthed at the devastation. Luckily as the accident took place on private property the police weren't called, but the cost of replacing the damaged limos made it the most expensive night out of Howard's life.

Throughout all this hellraising there was one constant in his life, actress Helen Cherry, whom he'd married in 1944 in a union that lasted until Howard's death – a real testament one has to say to Helen's almost super-human powers of perseverance as she endured decades of her husband's rip-roaring drinking and serial womanising. Also his gruff manner, ably demonstrated by his role as Captain Bligh in *Mutiny on the Bounty* (1962), was much the same in real life. He used to swagger into pubs and restaurants with a loud, 'Whoooaaa!' It was his calling card. 'When he'd had a few drinks he could be noisy,' recalled actor Harry Andrews. 'If he was really drunk he was a roarer.'

Howard found a willing drinking partner in Robert Mitchum when they made *Ryan's Daughter* (1970) together in Ireland. 'Strange guy, Trevor,' Mitchum recalled. 'The first day I met him, he hit me on the head. Whap! Then he said, "You sweet thing," and he kissed me. Then: Whap! again. We closed a few pubs. Hell of a workout.'

A famed dopehead, Mitchum often passed the odd joint to Howard, though the hoary old thesp still preferred the booze. Pretty soon the film crew could tell immediately if Trevor was on dope or alcohol, happy and easy-going when he'd had a spliff, a cantankerous old bastard once at the whisky.

There were parties most nights, usually at Mitchum's cottage, and Howard was a regular. One evening he was in the kitchen making love to a bottle of Chivas Regal, when there was a loud rap at the door and a woman entered looking dishevelled and bleeding from a head wound. It was Helen; she'd fallen down a ledge while walking to the house. Mitchum put his Pernod down and went to tell her husband. 'Pay no attention,' said Howard, pouring himself another Chivas. 'She pulls these stunts all the time. It's her way of attracting attention.'

It was more serious than that. She'd done some damage to her lower back and the nearest hospital was twenty-five miles away. Mitchum broke the news. 'Right you are, sport,' said Howard. 'Bloody unpleasant trip over the mountain on a rocky road in a Land Rover.'

'It's going to be awfully painful,' Mitchum agreed, 'poor Helen sitting up in a Land Rover with her sore back.'

'Yes, yes, indeed,' Trevor concurred, 'bloody difficult trip, sure to be goddamned uncomfortable. No sense in my going.'

Howard was known to go on almighty benders where he lost all track of time. During a press tour to Germany he was assigned a publicist to make sure everything ran smoothly. At Heathrow airport Howard bought a new watch in duty free, and then popped into the nearest bar to down a few pints. Before the flight Howard needed the men's room and standing at the urinal admired his watch: very fancy it was, could tell the time round the world, the day, the month, that kind of thing.

After two weeks in Germany, where Howard was blotto most of the time, he arrived back at Heathrow and was in dire need of the toilet facilities; darting into the same men's room as before, or one very much like it. The publicist was waiting outside when he heard cries of dread from within. 'Aaargh! Aaahhh! Noooo!' He raced inside and there was Howard standing at a urinal looking at his new watch.

'Trevor! What's the matter?'

'I've been pissing for two weeks!'

Something of a matinee idol in his *Brief Encounter* days, as Howard approached late middle age the booze laid siege to his face, turning it craggy and angst-ridden, as if perpetually on the lookout for a cathedral parapet to perch on. Regularly pickled on his later films, his mood swings could be fairly dramatic. Filming 1971's *Catch Me a Spy*, co-star Patrick Mower was having dinner with some friends when Howard came into the restaurant. 'Invite him over,' said Mower to an actor friend he knew was a great admirer of Howard's. 'Oh, I couldn't, he's too big a star.' In the end the friend was persuaded to approach Howard and invite him to join the table. As he tucked into a small Scotch, Howard was bombarded with questions about his movies from Mower's friend, but he didn't seem to mind, indeed seemed to be appreciative of his knowledge. Insisting on one for the road, Trevor knocked back a double and bang, something changed. The friend was about to ask another question when Howard exploded. 'You've been up my fucking arse since you met me, you fucking little squinty cunt!' It was an amazing transformation. 'The last whisky had taken him over the brink,' said Mower. 'And from being absolutely sober and nice as pie, he suddenly turned into an abusive alcoholic.' The friend was distraught and Mower tried to reassure him that it wasn't personal and that Howard wouldn't remember a damn thing in the morning. He didn't.

As the drinking got out of hand directors eventually sussed out how best to deal with Howard on their films, that was to find the most stunning looking woman on the unit and arrange for her to appear on set, if not in her underwear then jolly close. Howard's eyes would dart about two feet out of their sockets, but she would rebuff his advances, at which he would head for the brown paper bag he always brought with him that contained his booze supply. The girl's job was then to admonish him greatly, smack his hand and say, 'Naughty boy, Trevor,' and for the duration of the shoot he was putty in her hands and behaved impeccably, or almost.

One of Howard's last films was the British comedy *The Missionary* (1983), which saw him perpetually blotto. Filming in Longleat, the cast stayed in a little country hotel and in the middle of the night an assistant heard a godawful scream emanating from Howard's room. He ran in and found that the silly old bugger had got into the wardrobe and couldn't get out.

Right up until the end Howard was a boozer. Just weeks before his death, from cirrhosis, he fell over in his bedroom utterly steampigged and knocked himself out. His wife called an ambulance and by the time it arrived Howard had regained consciousness and was grumbling over the unnecessary fuss as he was lifted onto a stretcher. Suddenly he cried out to his wife. 'I'm here, darling,' she loyally responded. 'What is it you want?' Howard growled at her, 'I want another gin and tonic.'

JOHN HUSTON (1906–1987: Director/Actor/Writer)

John Huston lived the kind of ballsy, macho, outdoors life, unencumbered by convention or restrictions, that if you tried to live today some fucker would probably arrest you. He was a boxer, an adventurer, a gambler, a white hunter and a ladies' man who married five times and kept a veritable stable of mistresses. Paul Newman called him 'the eccentric's eccentric'.

He was born of Scottish and Irish heritage in Nevada, Missouri, a town won by his grandfather in a poker game, or so Huston family lore has it. His parents divorced when he was just seven and the young boy sometimes travelled the vaudeville circuit with his actor father Walter, or criss-crossed the country with his roving reporter mother.

Really he should have died as a kid, diagnosed with an enlarged heart and a kidney ailment. Making a miraculous recovery, he quit school at fourteen and despite a frail lanky physique became an amateur boxing champion, with a broken nose to show for it.

Hankering perhaps to follow in his father's footsteps, he next turned to acting before jacking that in to become an officer in the Mexican cavalry. While in Mexico, so Huston told it, he was challenged to an old-fashioned gunfight. Purchasing the biggest revolver he could find, his plan was to hide and then shoot his adversary in the leg as soon as he rounded the corner. The duel never took place, the young Huston was disarmed – by his mother.

Getting Mexico out of his system, Huston took up journalism before moving to Paris with hopes of becoming a painter. He certainly lived the life of one, starving in a garret and sleeping on park benches completely potless. Returning to America in 1933, Huston tragically ran over a young woman on Sunset Boulevard, killing her instantly. He claimed he was sober at the time. His father, now a popular screen actor and a favourite of Louis B Mayer, appealed to the movie tycoon to use his influence to keep the scandal out of the papers and maybe lean a bit on the LAPD. A subsequent inquest absolved Huston of any blame for the accident.

Now working for Warner Brothers as a screenwriter, the experience gave Huston a thirst to direct, and you can't do better than start with *The Maltese Falcon* (1941). Huston also distinguished himself during the Second World War, heading a photographic unit, filming moments of danger on the battlefields of Monte Casino and others, usually with his trademark cigar protruding out of his always thoughtful face.

A born prankster, Huston once flew over a golf course and dropped 5,000 ping-pong balls during a celebrity golf tournament. He also at one time owned a pet monkey that exasperated his wife, actress Evelyn Keyes, not least because he insisted the ape shared their bed. One morning they awoke to discover the chimp had stirred during the night, had swung on the drapes, opened all the drawers, strewn the place with torn undergarments and, worse, deposited conspicuous amounts of chimp shit everywhere. Poor Evelyn could take no more and gave Huston an ultimatum: 'John, darling, I'm sorry. One of us has to go. It's the monkey or me.' After a somewhat disconcertingly short pause he replied, 'Honey, it's you!'

Huston was always on the prowl and set his sights once on diva Ava Gardner. He invited her and some friends to stay over at his LA home. Much drinking and merrymaking went on before everyone retired to bed. Ava was in a small guest room beginning to undress when, without knocking, Huston threw the door open and stood there beaming like a Cheshire cat on heat. It was obvious what he was after but Ava was in no mood to give it to him. As he made his move, Ava did a swift sidestep and was out the door and hurtling down the stairs and out into the night. 'I was barefoot,' she recalled. 'So he would have to run pretty fast to catch me. And by God, he really was after me! And just as fast and just as fit as I was!'

After several circuits of the garden, she raced back indoors and hurled herself out of the first-floor balcony and head first, fully clothed, into the swimming pool. As she dragged herself out soaked to the skin, Huston stood roaring with laughter. Ava didn't see the funny side of it and woke up her friends demanding to be driven home. Huston went back to the bar to freshen his drink and stood on the veranda waving them an alcoholic goodbye as they drove into the sunrise. 'Poor John,' said Ava's friend. 'He really is very lonely, you know.'

After striking up a firm friendship with Humphrey Bogart during the making of *The Treasure of the Sierra Madre* (1948), Huston made *The African Queen* (1951) with Bogie next. Bogart hated Africa instantly, but Huston revelled in the adventure of the place and was determined to bag an elephant, fancying himself a great hunter. On one occasion he invited Katharine Hepburn on safari with him and inadvertently led her into the middle of a herd of wildebeest, a situation from which they were lucky to escape alive.

As for the drinking that went on, Katharine decided early on to seize the moral high ground and gave a lecture to Bogart and Huston on the evils of alcohol. When she had finished, Bogart smiled and said, 'You're absolutely right, Kate. Now pull up a chair and have a drink.' She stormed off. As far as she was concerned the pair of them were 'rascals, scamps and rogues'.

The cast and crew faced constant dangers including torrential rain, poisonous snakes, scorpions, crocodiles, armies of ants and water so contaminated that they couldn't even brush their teeth with it, let alone drink it. Inevitably everyone came down with malaria or dysentery, save Huston and Bogart, who attributed this to living almost exclusively on imported Scotch whisky. 'Whenever a fly bit Huston or me, it dropped dead,' joked Bogart.

Huston was pally with another great Hollywood star, Errol Flynn, and they often indulged in the odd macho punch-up. At one Hollywood party the two men were so bored that Huston suggested they step outside onto the lawn and indulge in a bit of fisticuffs. 'Whaddya say?' said Huston. 'You're on, sport,' replied Flynn. For the next hour the two men pounded each other senseless until an ambulance arrived to take them to hospital.

Citing 'moral rot' at home with the advent of McCarthyism, Huston left Hollywood and moved to Galway, Ireland, in 1952, falling in love with a land that revolved around pubs, making it his home until 1975. He was already up to wife number four by this stage, who'd borne him two children, including future star Anjelica Huston.

Peter O'Toole was a sometime visitor to Huston's Emerald Isle estate. During one trip the pair planned a hunting expedition but come the morning it was pouring with rain. Huston crept into O'Toole's room to announce, 'Pete, this is a day for getting drunk.' At breakfast they shared a bottle of whisky and ended up on the horses anyway, still in their pyjamas, tearing through the countryside in the pissing rain rough-shooting it. 'John eventually fell off the horse and broke his leg,' recalled O'Toole. 'And I was accused by his wife of corrupting him!'

For much of the fifties and sixties Huston seemed to quite often lose his way artistically, making awful tripe like *The Barbarian and the Geisha* (1958), so pissing off John Wayne during production that the big man eventually lost his cool completely and punched Huston unconscious.

The Misfits (1961) was much better, but Huston seemed to have little self-control, drinking and gambling at local casinos sometimes until five in the morning, resulting in occasions when he'd fall asleep in the director's chair on set. Arthur Miller, then married to Marilyn Monroe, believed Huston gambled, sometimes recklessly, because he wanted to come as close to the cliff edge as possible to see whether he could avoid plummeting over it. One night Miller left Huston at the crap tables some $30,000 behind. He returned next morning to see Huston, a Scotch in his hand, still shooting the dice, but now ahead $35,000.

To placate Huston the studio actually provided him with a gambling allowance, though when his losses exceeded it he'd stop filming to scrounge more money. But gambling was only one of many vices. 'There was women, horses, alcohol and smoking; there weren't too many weak-nesses that he didn't have,' says Michael Caine.

After further barren years and ill-judged projects, Huston emerged in the autumn of his career as a director of distinction once again with the classics *The Man Who Would Be King* (1975) and *Prizzi's Honor* (1985), despite suffering acute emphysema and heart disease after decades of heavy smoking. He directed his last film *The Dead* (1987) hooked up to an oxygen tank, though this didn't stop his nightly shot of tequila.

Huston was a proud eighty-one when he died in his sleep of compli-cations from emphysema. He once recalled his life as 'a series of mis-adventures and disappointments'.

J

GEORGE JONES (b. 1931: Musician)

Imagine waking up in the morning and before brushing your teeth you're sipping a screwdriver, and then spending the remainder of the day downing bourbon. Welcome to the wonderful world of George Jones, country singer and music legend, a guy Frank Sinatra called, 'the second best male singer in America'.

Jones would get into such a state that often he'd be unable to perform; ending up missing so many performances they nicknamed him 'No-Show Jones'. His pitiful life seemed to mirror the defeat and despair of his song lyrics, heavily melancholic, even by country and western standards. Take the opening verse of the classic 'If Drinking Don't Kill Me (Her Memory Will)' about a man knocking them back till four in the morning when the bars all close and he's thrown into the streets. Driving home his head collapses on the wheel and the horn blasts out: 'The whole neighborhood knows / That I'm home drunk again.'

Jones was born in rural Texas, one of six siblings in a hamstrung family always on the poverty line; his father was a labourer and alcoholic given to fits of dark despair and violence when liquored up. As a kid Jones escaped into music, listening to the gospel singing he heard in church and country music tunes on the radio. Given a guitar at the age of nine, he busked for money on the streets.

Fleeing home aged fourteen, Jones supported himself by singing on local radio stations. Fuelled by nothing stronger than Coca-Cola in his early years it was ironic, and horribly prophetic, that his first No. 1 country hit in 1959 was an ode to moonshine liquor – 'White Lightning'.

Overtaken by severe stage fright he started to drink, a habit that intensified with the pressure of fame and relentless touring schedules. 'I never had anything as a kid and all of a sudden I had everything thrown at my feet. It can ruin you quickly.' Jones's life evolved into an endless stream of parties, one-night stands and hangovers in between concerts and fist fights; he once had his head pounded against a concrete floor by fellow country musician Faron Young during a backstage brawl. He was out of control and didn't have any brakes.

The drinking got so bad that Jones would go to any lengths to get his hands on some booze. After a particularly hectic two-week binge his wife was determined to keep him dry by clearing their house of liquor and hiding the keys to all twenty of his cars. Suffering like hell for a drink, Jones had a brainwave, recalling that in his garage was a ten-horsepower rotary-engine lawnmower. 'The top speed for that old mower was five miles per hour,' Jones recalled. 'It might have taken two hours for me to get to the liquor store, but get there I did.'

That lawnmower came in handy again during another of his marriages (there'd be four in total), this one to fellow country and western star Tammy Wynette. One night Tammy woke up past midnight and noticed Jones was gone. Getting in her car, she drove to the nearest bar ten miles away and sure enough in the parking lot outside was the lawnmower; Jones had ridden the damn thing up a main highway.

Jones and Tammy wed in 1968 at the peak of their careers, but the marriage was never going to be like the Waltons'; they fought constantly. One night Jones came home tanked on whisky and chased Tammy through their Nashville mansion with a loaded 30-30 rifle. They divorced soon afterwards, in 1975.

In the 1970s Jones augmented his alcoholism with a nasty cocaine habit that turned him from a mildly dangerous eccentric into a complete wacko. Take the time he pulled out his .38 revolver and ventilated the roof of his tour bus with six bullets, while his band mates were still in it! Or the occasion at a Nashville club when he performed the entire gig in the persona and voice of Donald Duck.

Worse of all was the time he tried to blow out the brains of his best friend. Peanut Montgomery was a well-known songwriter and drinking buddy of Jones who'd gotten sober and come round one evening to tell George how the good Lord had turned his life around. This wasn't what Jones wanted to hear, strung out as he was on Jack Daniel's and Bolivian marching powder. He chased Peanut out of the house and waved his revolver in the air. 'See what your God will do for you now,' he shrieked as he offloaded several bullets at his fleeing friend. Luckily they all missed.

By the early eighties Jones was at his lowest ebb, declaring bankruptcy after a number of show promoters sued him for missed dates and told by doctors that he would only live another couple of days if he continued to drink. Rather urgently he entered hospital and spent four weeks drying out, a procedure that almost killed him. For the next year he'd be plagued by recurring withdrawal symptoms, so bad that he checked himself back into hospital a further seven times.

Jones credits his current wife, Nancy, whom he married in 1983, with helping to turn his life round. At the height of his booze and drug frenzy when they met, she saw a lot of good in a man who seemed intent on destroying himself. She stood by him as he battled with his demons, exercising tough, even brutal love. As a joke Jones hung a sign outside his home's front door: 'Forget the dog. Beware of wife.'

Living in the world of sobriety, the battle against his addiction apparently won, Jones fell off the wagon spectacularly in 1999 when he crashed his sport utility vehicle into a concrete bridge while driving home. 'I wasn't dead drunk, but I was feeling good.' Left in a critical condition, with a slashed liver and punctured lung, Jones died twice on the way to hospital and took a week to regain full consciousness. This was to be the man's last piece of hellraising. It put the fear of God into him and he finally sobered up. As an act of public service the mangled remains of his car were dangled from a crane over a busy main road with a sign bearing the legend: 'Drive Safely.'

K

EDMUND KEAN (1789–1833: Actor)

Few actors can claim to have scaled the heights and borne more significance upon their shoulders for the craft they practise than Edmund Kean. His prodigious acting talent, however, was mitigated by wild and ungovernable behaviour, a volcanic temper and a preference for the bottle, especially if brandy was in it.

Kean's childhood is clouded in mystery, his parentage debatable. It's thought that he was the bastard son of Ann Carey, a part-time actress, and Edmund Kean Sr, a drunk who died insane at the age of twenty-two. Abandoned as a child, the young Kean was raised by an elderly actress who was part of the Drury Lane theatre company in London. Kean soaked up the greasepaint but rejected any notion of trivial domesticity, preferring to live wild and free, skipping school, stealing food and sleeping rough. Discovered one time asleep on a dunghill, he was dragged back home and tied to the bedpost. His wanderings got so bad the old actress put a brass collar around Kean's neck and took him with her to Drury Lane on a lead, tying him up backstage like a dog.

As a teenager Kean was eager to conquer the stage, but was rejected by Drury Lane so he began a ten-year struggle as a strolling player, going from town to town performing extracts from Shakespeare in taverns, pushing a handcart containing all his worldly possessions. Worse, he burdened himself with a wife and two sons. It was a lowly existence that left its fair share of scars, notably a dependency on alcohol, which he used to soothe his thwarted ambition.

Sometimes Kean would be asked to join a touring company, usually in the position of harlequin, a role in which he excelled. One night, after heavily knocking back the brandy, he gave an erratic performance, duly noted by one member of the audience who harangued him forcefully. Kean wasn't standing for this and hurled insults back. The verbal knock-about carried on for several minutes until an incensed Kean informed everyone that he was going home for his sword to challenge the man, now quivering in fear. Running to his nearby lodgings, still dressed as a harlequin, Kean's blood had sufficiently cooled to no longer wish the man dead; instead he bounded up the stairs and jumped through a glass door at the top of the landing, waking up the entire household. Everyone trotted out in their night attire to see a right-fucked harlequin dancing like a wild dervish and then in a single bound leaping over the landlady and disappearing like a ghost into the gloom. Kean was gone for three days, later confessing to his wife that he spent the entire time drinking and searching for that damnable critic.

Arriving on Guernsey during a theatrical tour, Kean returned from the pub that first evening with a devilish grin on his face, telling his wife, 'My dear Mary, I can get brandy here for eighteen pence a bottle! I can drink it instead of beer.' And indeed he did, leading the locals to judge him to be little better than a sot.

While on the island Kean was asked to appear in a leading role at a benefit concert. He steadfastly refused, stating how he hated the role and the play. No amount of persuasion would alter his mind, so he stayed in the pub getting spice-racked. At the last moment he quite fancied the spectacle of watching his replacement in action. Barging into the theatre, he sat in one of the upper boxes and proceeded to applaud, sing or shout, 'Bravo,' and, 'Well done, my boy,' after a particularly good speech. The poor actor stood aghast at this and the audience grew restless, but Kean carried on regardless until he was forcibly removed.

At last in 1814 Kean achieved his dream of appearing at Drury Lane in a major role, Shylock in *The Merchant of Venice*. One wonders what Faustian pact was concocted, since just days after the good news his eldest child died. Kean's performance as Shylock, which borrowed liber-ally from his own chaotic personality, was radically different from the prosaic classical style of acting audiences were used to and thus created a sensation. Kean was quick to exploit his success by enthralling his public yet further with a series of Shakespeare roles. It was then off on tour to America, where he played to rapturous acclaim. Kean was now the most famous and acclaimed actor on earth. Coleridge said of Kean, 'Seeing him act was like reading Shakespeare by flashes of lightning.'

Yet behind the make-up Kean was nurturing an increasingly unpopular public persona. The wildness in his blood often got the better of him and he sank into a pit of depravity. He drank prodigiously, impairing many of his performances; that's when he actually deigned to show up at all. Dining with friends at a tavern, Kean once plain forgot all about that evening's performance. To save face the management told the audience that in a desperate dash to the theatre Kean had been thrown from his carriage and the great tragedian's shoulder was broken. To give substance to this deception Kean appeared a few days later on stage going through the arduous role of Macbeth and Othello with his arm in a sling! One doubts if the subterfuge fooled anybody.

A servant would be on hand at all times in the wings with a tumbler of brandy for his master's various exits so by the time the curtain fell Kean was ready to do the same.

One evening, during a performance of *Richard III*, the manager of the theatre ordered the servant not to give Kean as much as one drop of alcohol. When the man protested, he and the bottle were bundled into the prop room, out of harm's way. Exiting the stage, Kean was soon raging like bedlam for his booze, swearing that he would not step foot back upon the boards until his thirst was quenched. Then like a bloodhound he sniffed the air and muttered, 'Methinks I scent thee now.' Pushing past the manager, Kean threw open the door of the prop room, exclaiming, 'I'll kill you! You'll deprive me of my only support, will you? Where are you? Come forth!' Like a man possessed Kean threw asunder bits of scenery until he discovered his tumbler, drained its contents, and then rushed back to the stage to perform his duelling scene like a mad bastard, much to the delight of the audience.

For exercise Kean slept with whores, periodically catching nasty bouts of the clap, or rode recklessly on his horse throughout the night, returning sweaty to sleep with the beast in its stable. And he kept a tame lion as a pet. A streak of poisonous jealously also coursed through his veins. Kean saw himself very much as monarch of the English stage and resented any rival. He'd hire local yobbos, get them mashed in the Coal Hole public house on the Strand and then send them off with instructions to heckle and generally disrupt rival stage productions. He even saw his own son Charles as a potential future competitor. Back home after a night at the theatre he sat relaxing with a glass of brandy when his wife remarked, 'Do you know he can act?' To prove it she made the boy recite some speeches. 'That will do,' said Kean in black mood. 'Go to bed, and remember, we will have no more acting.' After Charles had left the room Kean spoke: 'He might succeed as an actor, but if he tries, I will cut his throat.'

Despite his obnoxious behaviour, Kean had always managed to win back his audiences with a bit of virtuoso acting. His real downfall began the day he took the wife of a city alderman as his mistress, a nice change of scenery from his usual diet of prostitutes and desperate actresses. She was, he scoffed, a lady at table and a harlot in bed. When their racy letters were discovered the husband successfully sued Kean for adultery and he was pilloried mercilessly in the press. Unable to face the scandal, his wife left him.

Kean was now damaged goods and crowds flocked to see his performances merely to heckle and taunt him. His demeanour changed rapidly, an air of desperation clung to him, he looked bloated and his skin blotched. Friends deserted him. He was pitiful. Leaving the tumult of England behind, Kean sailed to America in 1825, hoping for better fortunes. Alas, his reputation had preceded him and in New York he was pelted with oranges on stage. In Boston the auditorium was packed with more of an angry mob than theatre-goers. Stepping on stage, Kean was hit with cabbages and beat a hasty withdrawal.

Meanwhile, outside the theatre a crowd numbering hundreds smashed their way through the doors and into the auditorium. Fights broke out and some paying patrons jumped for their very lives out of windows to escape the madness. Some ran amok backstage, screaming, 'Kean! Kean!' as if overtaken by animalistic urgings. Kean had wisely legged it by this time, taking refuge in a nearby house. When the mob discovered the actor had flown their bloodlust turned to utter anarchy. Running into dressing rooms and the prop store, they armed themselves with swords and other artefacts of warfare and set about the theatre itself, wrenching down chandeliers, smashing windows and ripping up seats.

Meanwhile Kean was still in hiding, having heard that if the mob got hold of him they intended to tar and feather him. In the early hours of the morning, in disguise, Kean made good his escape, returning to England to all intents and purposes a broken man. His comeback performance in London was a disaster. The play had begun but of Kean there was no sign. He was found in his dressing room weeping and in total despair, claiming to have forgotten the part. Too late to cancel, Kean had no option but to go on. The playwright Thomas Grattan watched from the gallery shocked as his old friend battled vainly with the lines, barely able to get any of them out in a coherent form. 'He gave the notion of a man who had been half-hanged, and then dragged through a horse pond.' When the curtain fell it did so to complete silence and, wrote Grattan, 'I felt, though I could not hear, the voiceless verdict of damnation.'

This kind of performance, sadly, became the norm with Kean. Regret and sympathy extended by the audience to a once great performer would turn to anger and boos and hisses would ring out, drowning Kean's pitiful voice. As his once-great dramatic powers waned, so his health decided to go on a permanent vacation. By the end he was decidedly frail. Kean continued to act, sometimes at his old stomping ground of Drury Lane, but the magic had long ago been snuffed out by his own hands. It was always to packed houses, though, his public perhaps sensing that any performance might very well be his last.

When it was announced that Kean would be acting for the very first time with his son, a great crowd assembled to witness this historic occasion. Complaining all day of an illness, Kean cut a haggard figure in his dressing room, but fortified with a shot of brandy was determined the show should go on. Playing Othello to his son's Iago, Kean was greeted with the warmest of ovations when he walked out, and taking Charles's hand proudly presented him to his public, a gesture that elicited even wilder overtures. It took some moments for the noise to subside and for the play to begin. When it did, it was obvious to those in attendance that Kean was weaker than usual, but he gamely plodded on. Watching from the wings he was heard to say, 'Charles is playing very well. I suppose it's because he's acting with me.'

During the third act Kean was in visible distress, pausing too often for breath and unable to move without the utmost difficulty. Instead of the usual boos and jeering, the audience this time encouraged and applauded these Herculean efforts, sensing it wasn't the demon drink at work. Then suddenly Kean stood motionless, time seemed to stand still, a hush fell upon the auditorium. Focusing in the gloom, he saw his son, advanced a few steps towards him and fell into his grasp. 'O God, I am dying,' the words came out in a hushed faltering tone. 'Speak to them, Charles.' With the assistance of another of the players Charles carried his father off stage. The curtain fell.

Kean was taken to his home in Richmond, Surrey, where he lay in bed for several weeks. Unable to take solids, he subsisted on arrowroot and jelly, mixed with brandy and water. At times his mind played tricks on him and he believed himself once again a strolling player, hawking his talents from town to town, or wallowing in early success at Drury Lane when the world lay open and rosy ahead of him. Or he might indulge in conversation with figures from his past that in his mind's eye stood in the room with him. Once, when the clock sounded midnight, he suddenly leaped out of bed quoting Richard III, 'A horse, a horse, my kingdom for a horse,' before collapsing on the floor. Those were to be his final words. He died the next morning.

L

PETER LANGAN (1940–1988: *Restaurant Proprietor*)

In the seventies and eighties Langan's Brasserie was amongst the most popular restaurants in London attracting a celebrity crowd, real A-listers like Brando, Sinatra and Princess Grace. It wasn't just the food they came for, but the owner, Peter Langan, a real character and eccentric and right royal boozer. He was the enfant terrible of gastronomy.

Not surprisingly for a man who claimed to drink six bottles of champagne a day, he often fell flat on his face in the restaurant and went to sleep amid the diners. It was a colourful feature that one had to step over the proprietor to either get to one's table or to exit the building. It was practically an insult if Langan didn't descend on your table and ruin your meal. His favourite ploy was to go up to the most attractive female customer of the evening and say, 'Show us your tits.' Not quite Oscar Wilde, but it worked one evening and he got an unexpected flash that so embarrassed him he ran into the kitchen.

Langan, in partnership with film star Michael Caine and renowned chef Richard Shepherd, opened his restaurant in 1976 in a discreet side-street off Piccadilly and it quickly gained a reputation for unpretentious British fare with a French twist. Langan's credo for the restaurant was very much like his approach to life in general: make a bit of money but primarily have a good time. But it wasn't just the food people queued up for; Langan was a walking freak show, the cabaret between the courses. Prince Albert of Monaco paid a visit one evening. When Langan spotted him he staggered over to his table to ask, 'You Prince Albert? Your darling mother had great tits.' The heir to the throne of the principality did not return.

Another royal, Princess Margaret, dined there one evening with her cousin the Earl of Harewood. When Langan heard what the Princess had ordered, a mere coddled egg, he approached the table in his usual state of intoxication and asked loudly, 'And how was the fucking egg, then? I'm amazed you'd be bothered to go out, just to eat one of them. Don't they know how to do them at the Palace?' When she left, staff had to physically restrain Langan from giving her arse a really hefty pinch. Unlike Prince Albert, however, Margaret became a regular.

Langan, when sober, was a charming and obviously intelligent man, thanks to a good private education. He cut an imposing figure, always wearing a white suit which unfortunately was never immaculate since he often slept in it for days on end. Michael Caine acquired an almost Holmesian gift of being able to identify the various locations round London where Lagan had dossed down for the night simply by the state of his suit. One time Caine noticed a pattern of blue footprints running across his back and deduced that since the nearby Ritz Hotel was currently being refurbished in that shade of paint Langan had been sleeping in the rubbish tip outside.

Michael Winner recalled dining at Langan's with Charles Bronson and his wife Jill Ireland when the man himself came to sit at their table: 'He slurped, spat, burped and dribbled over us for three hours,' recalled Winner. 'Charlie was far too polite to tell him off.'

Langan revelled in his fame and notoriety; remarkably he was able to be utterly insulting and obnoxious without causing too much offence. One punter named Gordon Copp was known for his rapier tongue and never at a loss for words, except on the occasion Peter told him, 'Your daughter is fat, but fuckable.' However, the likes of Rudolph Nureyev, Andy Warhol, Warren Beatty and, it must be said, a few others did walk out of his restaurant. Most, though, saw Langan for what he was, a showman of a kind. When one diner complained about a cockroach in his food, Langan picked it up, dropped it in his mouth whole and washed it down with champagne. When the designer Emilio Fiorucci arrived for dinner with his pet dog, Langan took an instant dislike to the tatty mutt, got down on his hands and knees and bit it. He also made a habit of crawling under tables to gently nibble on the leg of lady diners.

Out of office hours Langan could be equally destructive. He spent one night on the tiles with a peer of the realm, calling him the following morning to ask, 'Were you still with me when I hit David Frost?'

One inevitably feels sorry for the poor man's wife Susan, for she more than anyone knew the simmering violence and darkness that lurked beneath the veil of drink. He attacked her once with a kitchen knife, jealous about another man. Her injuries required hospital treatment, but still she went back to him, a decision that would lead ultimately to disaster.

Not content with causing culinary chaos in London, Langan intended to do much the same thing in Los Angeles. His dream was to open a US version of his restaurant. The idea struck terror into the heart of Michael Caine, now a resident in Hollywood. 'I got down on my knees, in public, and begged him not to open up in Los Angeles. There was nothing there for him but a good hiding. But he was determined.'

Caine did feel he owed Langan something for the success of the London brasserie so reluctantly agreed to help. First he got together a $1 million deal from would-be investors and arranged a meeting. Langan arrived more bladdered than usual and promptly fell on the floor. 'If we invest in this restaurant,' asked one of the businessmen, 'who's going to be spending our money, Mr Caine?'

It pained him, it really did, but Caine had to answer. 'Well, he is,' directing his gaze to the crumpled, snoring form on the carpet.

'Good day, Mr Caine, thank you very much.' The investors walked out.

Langan immediately sought to make the kind of impression on Hollywood that he'd done in London. It didn't help that he arrived at LAX airport on the baggage conveyor belt looking more crumpled than usual. Out at some glitzy restaurant with Caine, Langan spotted Orson Welles and went over. 'You're Orson Welles, aren't you?' A smile spread across that familiar face. 'Yes,' he said in his amiable growl. Langan pounced. 'I think you're an arrogant fat fuck.' The place went into uproar, the manager arrived and kicked them both out. 'Peter left with some anatomically unfeasible advice to the manager as to what to do with his restaurant,' recalled Caine.

After more embarrassing public displays it was obvious that Langan was sinking into alcoholism. Caine asked a friend of his who was a member of Alcoholics Anonymous to try to pull Langan back from the brink. The friend took great pride in the fact that he'd never had a failure. 'Peter was his first,' Caine recalled. 'And almost drove *him* back to drink.'

Langan's behaviour grew yet more alarming. One day he had a major bust-up with chef Richard Shepherd, grabbed a table and chair and positioned them on the pavement outside the restaurant, scaring customers away. His regular habit of sleeping in the restaurant all night now saw him periodically smashing the place up in a drunken fury.

In 1988 when his dream of opening a restaurant in LA became a reality, Langan had become such an embarrassment that he was banned from his own opening party. Pretty soon his American business partners got so furious with him that Langan was told never to set foot in the restaurant that he'd spent so many years trying to open.

Back in the UK he found he'd got even fewer friends. His antics, once so beguiling in their outrageousness, had over the years grown wearisome and were now just plain pathetic and rude, with an unpleasant edge to them, a sort of desperation. He was banned from his London restaurant too.

A wandering soul, Langan lived in a succession of cheap hotels and crummy apartments, the cliché existence of the down-at-heel alcoholic, though not for him Kestrel lager out of a shopping bag or glugs from a vodka bottle, he still had a modicum of class left, so it was strawberry daiquiris for breakfast.

He decided to go back home to his wife Susan, but she didn't want him either and confessed one night that she had a new lover. Embarrassed in his professional life, Langan faced humiliation in his personal life, too. It was too much to bear. Typically he chose his exit to be as dramatic as possible. Luring Susan into the bedroom, he locked the door and produced two bottles of petrol and a box of matches. Susan was terrified and in desperation jumped naked from the window. It was another fifteen minutes before she saw the bedroom go up in flames; an agonising time during which Langan must have fought with his private turmoil before finally making up his mind.

But he didn't perish in the inferno, clinging on in hospital for seven weeks before the wounds finally claimed him. It was a relief in the end, said Caine, 'relief from the pain of the day and the demons that had been trying to destroy him for so long'.

PETER LAWFORD (1923–1984: Actor)

He's a forgotten man today, his name and face barely managing a flicker of recognition, but in his prime during the 1950s Peter Lawford was one of the most significant showbiz personalities in America, part of Frank Sinatra's Rat Pack and married to John F Kennedy's sister. Lawford was the first actor to kiss Elizabeth Taylor on screen, and the last to speak to Marilyn Monroe before she died. Yet he was a chronic alcoholic, drug and sex fiend whose long spiral to a sad, pitiful end takes some beating, let me tell you.

He was born in London, the son of a First World War hero, and faced a childhood of privilege, with homes abroad and glamorous holidays, but also deep trauma. Aged five he disturbed a burglar climbing through his bedroom window one night and his screams alerted his mother, who appeared in the doorway brandishing a gun and shot the man dead. A traumatised Lawford could no longer sleep alone and shared his parents' bed until he was eleven.

His long love affair with alcohol began early, aged seven, when his mother watched him after a party wander round the room emptying all the glasses left by her guests and smoking their cigarette butts. Learning from the servants that this wasn't the first time Master Peter had done this, after the next social gathering she put emetic tablets in selected glasses and watched him run into the bathroom to be violently sick. 'Such terrible heaving,' she recalled.

Most of Lawford's future hang-ups can be laid firmly at the door of his wildly narcissistic mother, not least her habit of dressing him up as a little girl for long periods and whipping his bare little ass with a leather strap when he misbehaved; the adult Lawford would pay call girls to perform much the same procedure.

Arriving in Hollywood in 1940, Lawford's aristocratic bearing and playboy good looks got him signed to MGM, where he made a number of formulaic pictures without necessarily achieving true film-star status. But he was immensely popular, especially with the opposite sex, and indulged in affairs with Lana Turner, Ava Gardner and Kim Novak before marrying Patricia Kennedy in 1954. When her brother was elected President of the United States Lawford's social position skyrocketed. Already a member of the Rat Pack, performing with the group in Las Vegas and in films like *Ocean's Eleven* (1960), Lawford was a valuable conduit between Hollywood and the political glamour of brother-in-law John's 'Camelot' presidency. He exploited the position for all it was worth, introducing Kennedy to Sinatra and Marilyn Monroe, keeping in the President's good books by acting as a pimp smuggling call girls into the White House, or supplying them at his home when Jack came visiting. The two men were like brothers, drinking and carousing and snorting lines of cocaine together.

Two events in quick succession were to lead to Lawford's pathetic downfall. When White House aides voiced concerns about Sinatra's alleged Mafia connections Kennedy distanced himself from the singer, and it was Lawford who got the blame. He was ostracised from the Rat Pack and Sinatra never spoke to him again. Then came Kennedy's assassination, an event that according to Lawford's son Christopher, his father never got over and was the catalyst to a dramatic and new recklessness with drink and drugs.

This became obvious during the making of *Harlow* in 1965 when he often arrived on set late, still looking as if he was propping up some dingy back-alley bar and fluffing his lines. It was a miracle he remembered where the studio was. Predictably it was his marriage to Patricia that bore the brunt. For years she'd found it hard to tolerate his addictions, combined with a rampant infidelity, mainly with prostitutes, and by 1966 sought a divorce. She still loved him but couldn't exist any more within the train wreck of a life he'd built around himself. Lawford had no compunction whatsoever about sharing his drug supply with his own son, the pair often staying up all night getting smashed together. Tragically, if unsurprisingly, Christopher himself would become an addict, taking twenty years to quit.

The once dapper lady-killer carried his hedonism around with him in his face, looking ten years older than he was. Internally it was even worse. Suffering from stomach cramps, Lawford entered a drying-out clinic, still managing to stash a gin bottle in the toilet cistern of his private bathroom. At the end of his stay Lawford was confronted with the raw truth. His liver was now about the size of the *Hindenburg* and if his lifestyle didn't change he'd be dead in six months. Lawford thanked the doctors for their help and left the clinic. The first thing he did was find the nearest bar and down a Martini.

With a faltering film career, Lawford was still enough of a personality to warrant subbing occasionally for Johnny Carson on his TV talk show. The two men were good friends until the night Carson attended a party at Lawford's apartment, got drunk, smoked dope and went nutzoid. He was so fucked-up that he came within a hair's breadth of jumping off a balcony, ordinarily not fatal, but since Lawford lived on the thirtieth floor, pretty hazardous to one's health. Carson was livid afterwards, convinced Lawford had spiked the grass with LSD, as he'd a habit of doing. Carson refused to see Lawford ever again.

Rapidly running out of friends, and all but disowned by the Kennedy clan, by the early seventies women were walking out on him, too; fed up with his boozing and drug taking, they were more babysitter than lover to him. But despite the wrecking-ball attitude he had to his body, the showbiz professional in Peter never left him. One time he was driven to a TV studio to guest on a game show, completely out of it, but once in front of the camera he changed completely and gave a deft and skilled performance. Driven back home afterwards he reverted to the dribbling, incoherent ruin of earlier.

Lawford married again in 1976. The reception was a disaster, with Lawford knocking back so much vodka and Quaaludes that by the end of the evening he was openly flirting with female guests. The next morning he couldn't remember a damn thing about the previous night, including the fact that he'd gotten married. 'How do I get out of it?' he asked a friend. His bride was twenty-five and they'd only known each other for three weeks. When asked what possessed him to marry her in the first place Lawford replied, 'She's a pusher. She gets me drugs.'

By the early eighties Lawford was in a seriously bad way; according to doctors 75 per cent of his liver was shot. Each day merged into the next in one long groggified haze, he knew he was killing himself, but couldn't stop. Ashamed, he stayed in his modest apartment and wouldn't let any of his remaining friends see him. Liz Taylor arrived one morning and repeatedly banged on the door, but he wouldn't open it. His new girlfriend Patricia Seaton often picked up the pieces. On paranoia over-drive, Lawford was convinced Patricia had another lover, so he calmly walked up behind her when she got in the door and placed a gun against her head, threatening to blow out her brains. She talked him out of it and hours later a sober Lawford had no recollection of what he'd so nearly done. Not surprisingly, Patricia walked out, returning a few months later to see Lawford in a catastrophic state. He'd gone all Howard Hughes – long fingernails, wild hair – and the apartment was unfit for human habitation. With Patricia's help Lawford agreed to go to the Betty Ford clinic, but it didn't start awfully well when on the flight over he got through a trolley full of vodka miniatures and was insensible when they landed in Palm Springs.

Going through cold turkey for a week, Lawford settled into the detoxi-fication programme but one sensed his heart really wasn't in it, since he'd hired a helicopter to fly in drugs for him. He'd take a walk into the desert, meet the 'copter, snort a few lines, and then walk back to the clinic with no one any the wiser.

Lawford's determination to lay off the booze lasted exactly one month. His body was now deteriorating at a rate of knots. The awful stomach cramps of a few years before had returned and he was coughing up blood, never a good sign. He had a bleeding ulcer and was put under the knife sharpish. Almost half his stomach had to be removed. Sensing the end was approaching, Lawford wed Patricia but it was no marriage in the real sense for he was now a virtual invalid, having to be fed through a tube and helped to use the toilet. One day she found him collapsed on the kitchen floor, bleeding profusely. Rushed to hospital, his skin a deep yellow, he was put on a life-support system as doctors battled to clean out the toxins from his body, but he slipped into a coma and remained that way for the next four days.

It was Christmas Eve morning when he awoke alone, trying to raise his body to a sitting position, and blood spurted from his mouth, nose and ears. It was all over. With no money to pay for a proper cemetery plot amongst the Hollywood greats he'd known in life, Lawford's ashes were instead scattered in the Pacific Ocean and washed away, rather like his reputation.

WILFRID LAWSON (1900–1966: Actor)

Although little known to the public at large, Wilfrid Lawson was one of Britain's foremost theatrical alcoholics who, despite an almost permanent state of intoxication, remained a popular figure within the industry and was hardly out of work as a character actor on film, stage and television.

He was very much an actor's actor, or in the words of friend Richard Burton, 'an eccentric, perverse old bastard'. A man who even when he wasn't drunk, a rare situation, looked it, his face resembling a Barnsley fish and chip shop after a gas explosion. And then there was his unusual manner of speech that didn't merely strangle the English language, but killed, cremated and buried it at sea with full regimental honours.

Born in Bradford, Lawson came to prominence on the London stage in the plays of George Bernard Shaw. His performance as the common dustman Alfred Doolittle in the film version of Shaw's *Pygmalion* remains his most recognised role; it won him a short-lived Hollywood contract, but after the war he returned to Blighty and never left.

Hired to perform on a live radio play, Lawson arrived at the studio stone cold sober, a state of affairs that the producer wished to maintain at all costs. Not only was Lawson himself searched for any hint of alcohol, but his dressing room was thoroughly investigated too and, once management was satisfied that it was clean, the actor was locked inside. An hour later when Lawson was requested, the producer was dumbstruck to see his star completely cucumbered. It was a miracle, he thought, a feat worthy of Houdini at his peak; the room had been locked all the time and there were no windows inside. How had the mad bastard Lawson done it?

Simple. Once he heard the producer leave he'd thumped on the walls and floor to grab the attention of somebody – anybody. Upon doing so he'd yelled out, 'Are you bribeable?' To which the unseen voice said he was. Directed to the locked room, the stout fellow saw some money slide under the door with instructions to purchase booze, which Lawson then consumed using a drinking straw through the keyhole.

During another performance, this time live on television, Lawson was muddling through his lines when he suddenly dried. Luckily his fellow actors were able to cover for him and when the scene ended Lawson breathed a huge sigh of relief and said, 'Well, I fair buggered that up, didn't I?' not realising he was still on air.

Such antics endeared Lawson to the kitchen sink group of emerging young actors that came along in Britain in the late fifties, the O'Tooles and Finneys, who idolised him. Lawson even appeared with some of them at London's Royal Court Theatre. In John Arden's *Live Like Pigs*, with Robert Shaw, Lawson was trousered during most performances. In one scene he merely had to get into a bed and would frequently lie there farting loudly.

Lawson was particularly close to Richard Burton. The two men shared many a night of roistering. After a liquid lunch in the West End Lawson invited Burton to the matinee of a play he was appearing in at a nearby theatre. Since he wasn't in the early scenes Lawson offered to sit with Burton in the stalls. About twenty minutes after curtain up Burton started to get rather anxious that Lawson had not yet left to don his costume or make-up, instead just sitting there enthralled by the spectacle. Suddenly Lawson tapped Burton on the arm and said, 'You'll like this bit. This is where I come on.'

Another actor who idolised Lawson was Christopher Lee. In his autobiography Lee talked of being asked to guest star in a new Viking adventure television series being shot in Germany. The prospects looked gloomy until he discovered that his episode would also star Lawson, cast as a great Saxon chief. The day arrived for Lawson to commence his scenes but there was no sign of him on the set; instead he was nicely curled up in his dressing room, asleep. An assistant banged on the door. 'Go away,' came a voice. 'I know you not.' Finally he was persuaded to come out and, looking around in genuine puzzlement at his fellow actors, he declared, 'A little nap, I think,' and immediately went to sleep on a chair. Again the assistant tried to coax him from his slumbers. 'Why are you bothering me,' pleaded Lawson. 'Who are you? Where's the beer?'

Generous amounts of liquid were bestowed upon him as he went through wardrobe and make-up. He was now ready, sort of. The big scene involved the villainous Lee entering Lawson's encampment offering the usual threats, and then a close-up on Lawson's defiant riposte. The rehearsals went fine, although Lee thought at one point he saw Lawson mutter, 'What am I doing here?'

They filmed Lee's speech first, with Lawson grinning like an idiot off-camera. 'Right,' said the director, 'we'll do your close-ups now, Wilfrid.'

The expression was blank. 'I see,' said Lawson, 'Splendid, splendid. Well, how about a beer?'

His dialogue was simple enough: a few grunts, talk of battles won, the odd glare, and then the classic, 'I, I who fought with Ogier the one-eyed Dane, will not bow the knee.' The director called action; Lee did his Saxon dog spiel, but from Wilfrid came there nothing, not a sausage, not a line, not even a flicker of consciousness. Lee tried again, 'You Saxon dog!'

'I beg your pardon,' said Lawson.

'Cut,' yelled the director, holding his head in hands. 'Can we start again, Wilfrid?'

'Eh? Of course, my dear fellow. Hadn't realised.' He began to mumble to himself, 'Now what was it again? I will not . . . no, no, no . . . is that right? No, will not, will not bow the knee, the knee, no, to you. No never. Is that all right?'

The director looked exasperatedly at the actor. 'Yes Wilfrid, fine. Go on.'

Looking mystified, Lawson asked, 'Go on? But I've finished.'

'You've got to talk about the battles you've fought,' the director prodded, while urging his cameraman to keep on rolling whatever happened.

'Ah the battles.' Classic pause. 'What battles?'

'The battles where you fought with the Danes and were a great Saxon chief.'

'A Saxon,' it was all flooding back to him now. 'Oh yes, would not bow, yes. Saxons will never bow the knee. I, I am a Saxon and consequently will never bow the knee to you, you Saxon dog, I beg your pardon, Norman dog.' Pleased with himself, Lawson looked for an assistant. 'Do you think you've got another bottle of beer nearby, dear fellow? I fought,' he was back in medieval mode. 'I did fight with Aggie the one-eyed Dame. Really only one eye?'

'It's in the script, Wilfrid.'

'What script, and when's the next plane?'

Even towards the end of his life, when no right-minded insurance company would cover him, filmmakers still wanted to work with the great Lawson. Bryan Forbes cast him in his comedy *The Wrong Box* (1966) starring Michael Caine. Caine later wrote that, despite being 'bombed out of his mind twenty-four hours a day, Lawson was still one of the most brilliant actors with whom I ever worked'.

Filming on location in Bath, Forbes had taken steps to make sure Lawson at least showed up on set. He got one of his assistants to put Lawson on the train at London and made sure another of his assistants met him at Bath. Couldn't go wrong, that plan, could it? When the train pulled into Bath station there was no sign of Lawson. He couldn't have got off, since the train had been non-stop, but despite an exhaustive search in all the carriages he was not to be seen. With all hope lost the train was allowed to pull out of the station and there, sound asleep on the opposite line, was Lawson, who'd obviously disembarked on the wrong side. With all due haste he was removed from the tracks, just before the London-bound express roared through.

Lawson met quite a bizarre final curtain, suffering a fatal heart attack while having a death mask made for a film. But surely he will go down in history as the originator of one of the most famous and often quoted theatrical anecdotes. On tour with a Shakespearean company, Lawson got wrecked one night with his fellow actors and upon hearing his cue stumbled onto the stage, almost falling head-first into the audience.

A woman in the front row could smell his foul breath. 'My God, he's pissed drunk.' Lawson lifted his head, 'If you think I'm pissed, wait until you see the Duke of Buckingham.'

JACK LONDON (1876–1916: Writer)

The most successful American author of the early part of the twentieth century, famous for such classic man against the harsh elements books as *The Call of the Wild* and *White Fang*, was something of an adventurer himself. London lived for a time as a hobo, took part in the Yukon gold rush and drove wild dogs across the frozen north. He also drank like a fish trapped in a barrel of beer. Little wonder that his credo read: 'I would rather that my spark should burn out in a brilliant blaze than it should be stifled by dry-rot. The proper function of man is to live, not exist.' He did just that, but only for forty short years.

Born in San Francisco, London's childhood was one of blinding poverty and parental turmoil. His father deserted his wife upon hearing of her pregnancy, while she sank into a deep depression and tried to kill herself, first pouring laudanum down her throat and when that failed shooting herself with a pistol in the forehead. Miraculously the bullet glanced off and friends forced her to the ground before she got round to a third attempt.

She quickly remarried a Union Army veteran who accepted the boy as his own, but life remained tough and Jack took to the streets aged ten selling newspapers to supplement the family's meagre income. Jack had little formal education as he was forced to leave school early to find work in a factory canning pickles, the first of numerous manual jobs that included stints in a mill, a laundry and shovelling coal in a power station. It was a past he would never forget, one that fuelled his socialist political leanings that at times were borderline anarchist.

Aged fifteen, London was spending much of his time along the San Francisco waterfront, stealing off drunks and evading the law. Buying his own boat, he took to fishing and in the evenings hung out in the local saloons with fellow sailors, whalers and harpooners, tough sea dogs twice his age or more who'd drink the cheapest rotgut to prove they were men. 'Drink was the badge of manhood.' So Jack matched them, drink for drink; found he was pretty good at it too, able to drink most of them under the table. (It's said he first got arseholed aged five, guzzling some of the beer in the bucket he was carrying to his stepfather at work in the fields, and became dreadfully ill.) After these drinking bouts Jack was sometimes found the following morning unconscious and entangled in the fishing nets on the drying-frames into which he'd blindly stumbled the night before.

By seventeen London was already a veteran boozer, tucking the stuff away quite expertly. 'I drank every day and whenever opportunity offered I drank to excess. I was learning what it was to get up shaky in the morning with a stomach that quivered and to know the drinker's need for a stiff glass of whisky neat in order to brace up.' Once he got so banjoed he suffered alcohol poisoning and almost died. After another particularly heavy bout of boozing London was in a comatose condition for some seventeen hours. 'I shudder to think how close a shave I ran.' He then decided to bum around the country, riding the railways for almost a year. He even got arrested for vagrancy in Niagara Falls and served a one-month sentence in the town's penitentiary.

When he woke up one morning in the doorway of a house after a night on the tiles to find not only his money, watch and coat stolen but also his shoes, London decided to give up the demon drink for good. Seized by a new zest for life, he went gold-hunting in the Klondike, but all he found out there was malnutrition and a nasty bout of scurvy, not much gold. The thrilling experiences, however, dodging avalanches, braving frozen lakes and navigating dangerous white-water rapids, were memories he would return to again and again for his future novels and stories.

Returning home broke, London resolved to never again work as a labourer. Brains paid, not brawn. Determined to be a writer, he faced periods of desperation and hardship; often forced to pawn his own clothes to pay his typewriter rent. And always hovering in the background was the spectre of the bottle. Soon he was in need of a drink before breakfast. 'I achieved a condition in which my body was never free from alcohol.' It got so bad that if he travelled to some out-of-the-way place he declined to run the risk of finding it dry, so always carried with him several quarts of booze. 'There was no time, in all my waking time, that I didn't want a drink.' These were the written symptoms of a die-hard alcoholic.

After three years of economic woe and endless rejection slips, London's adventure stories at last found a wide following and he suddenly became amongst the highest paid and most popular writers of his day. Yet he remained restless for adventure so he built his own yacht and sailed to the South Seas. He also reported on the famous San Francisco earthquake, covered the Russo-Japanese War for the Hearst newspapers and reported on the Mexican revolution. Long before Hemingway, London was a living symbol of rugged individualism.

And yet, despite all the fame and literary recognition, a deep depression clung to him, plaguing his thoughts with suicidal tendencies. He considered killing himself with a gun: 'The crashing eternal darkness of a bullet.' Was this due to the realisation that he was now a complete slave to alcohol? He even supported the introduction of Prohibition, not for altruistic motives but because he saw this as the only way to stop himself drinking.

Married twice, Jack was a rampant womaniser. Every time he returned home after a night away his first wife Bessie locked him out of the bedroom for fear he'd been with prostitutes and might give her the clap. With his royalties he'd managed to purchase a 126-acre ranch in California, filling it with every modern convenience; he even had his own fire engine, which proved singularly ineffective when the place burned to the ground a few years later.

Ultimately this strenuous lifestyle began to take its toll and during the last three years of his life London's health deteriorated markedly as he suffered rheumatism, melancholia, dysentery and headaches. This is a man who not only was an alcoholic but also a workaholic, producing as many as three books a year. Friends noticed that his adventurous spirit was no longer there, the gleam was gone from his eyes. His doctors told him that if he continued to drink he was almost certainly going to die soon. He went on drinking. Sometimes he'd get into bed to read while having a smoke, only to fall asleep and the cigarette roll out of his mouth to start a fire. His wife would have to rush in and douse London and the bed with water. She became convinced her husband was deliberately heading down a suicidal pathway – better to burn brightly than rot.

By the end London was in such extreme pain due to a kidney ailment that he was injecting himself with morphine and heroin. And debate still rages amongst London scholars as to whether the author took his own life deliberately or whether it was an accidental overdose, or whether his kidneys just finally gave up the ghost. Forty is a young age to die, but London packed so much into his life that all you can do is salute a man who actually hired his own bartender to pre-mix Martinis and send them by train in time for one of his parties, and someone who had two signs on his front door, one reading NO ONE ADMITTED WITHOUT KNOCKING and under that: DO NOT KNOCK.

COURTNEY LOVE (b. 1964: Musician)

She has been a delinquent, a stripper, an actor, a drug addict, a rock bitch and a boozer. *Rolling Stone* called her 'the most controversial woman in the history of rock'. It certainly didn't help that her husband blew his brains out with a shotgun, but Courtney Love has tried to make the best of it. In a life already riddled with chaos, more didn't really seem to make much difference. Born in San Francisco, Courtney had as parents the two dippiest hippie shit-eaters that the sixties drug era ever spewed out, with the child-rearing practices of demented apes. Her father was one-time manager of the Grateful Dead, her mother a flake from a wealthy family. 'My mother told me she tried to abort me,' Courtney later revealed. 'And that I was the result of a rape. My dad says my mother was high on acid. I was raised by wolves.' She was also prescribed sedatives for insomnia as a preschooler.

It gets worse. When they divorced, Courtney was only five; her mother won custody after testifying in court that her husband gave his daughter drugs at the age of three, something he's always strenuously denied, although after the death of Kurt Cobain he did make the outrageous comment that he felt sorry for the rock icon 'because he was up against the devil, my daughter'.

For young Courtney there would be brief stays in hippie communes before her mother moved with her new husband and family to New Zealand. Left behind because she was already trouble, Courtney spent years in boarding school and juvenile institutions. She was rarely to speak to either parent again. Arrested aged thirteen for shoplifting a Kiss T-shirt, Courtney eventually escaped to LA, 'to be a rock star and a movie star', working as a stripper to pay the rent. 'I didn't want to sell drugs,' she explained. 'I didn't want to be a prostitute. So I stripped.'

Graduating from taking her clothes off to being an über-groupie, Courtney hung around the periphery of the LA punk music scene, flitting in and out of bands before forming Hole and becoming something of an early nineties role model for dysfunctional youth: a punk Barbie, or 'kinder-slut', as she liked to call herself, adorned on stage in smudged make-up and torn baby-doll dresses. Her lyrics were angry, her music was loud, and she had a messy charisma.

Courtney met Kurt Cobain while Hole and Nirvana were still underground rock acts. At first Cobain wasn't interested, he broke off dates and ignored her advances, but Courtney would not be deterred and latched on to him like a Second World War limpet mine. 'We bonded over pharmaceuticals,' she said. Both were damaged individuals from broken homes who'd found solace from the pain in alcohol and drugs; now they had each other and they'd become the most destructive celebrity couple since Sid Vicious and Nancy Spungen. Courtney was even accused by a *Vanity Fair* journalist of shooting up heroin while pregnant. Indignant with rage, when Courtney spied the journalist years later at an Oscars after-show party she threatened to dent her skull with the nearest available heavy object, which happened to be Quentin Tarantino's best original screenplay statuette for *Pulp Fiction*.

Courtney and Cobain married in Hawaii in 1992, Courtney wearing a dress that once belonged to Frances Farmer and Cobain in green pyjamas, because he couldn't be arsed to put on a tux. Six months later Courtney gave birth to a daughter and Nirvana had become one of the biggest bands in the world. While Cobain loathed the attention that success encumbered him with, Courtney craved it; after being abandoned as a child, fame was her security blanket. Both self-destructive individuals, Cobain was the one who actually stepped over the line and destroyed himself. A grieving widow, Courtney still managed to piss off the greater populace when she read aloud Cobain's suicide note. 'God, he's such an asshole,' she began, and then shouted at the huge crowd who had gathered. 'I want you to all say asshole really loud.' They didn't.

After lying low for several weeks and quietly cremating her husband away from the TV cameras, Courtney then took her band on tour. Mentally she was not in a good place, but at least she had Kurt with her, his ashes tucked away in a teddy-bear knapsack. At an airport, going through security, an officer opened the bag and asked 'What's this?' as puffs of dusty ash flew into his face. 'That's my husband,' replied Courtney.

It was during this tour that Courtney garnered her reputation for being something of a loose cannon. At a music festival in Washington she flicked a cigarette at fellow musician Kathleen Hanna before punching her in the face, boasting: 'I do believe my fist met her rat head and it was orgasmic.' She wound up on probation for that one. On a Qantas flight to Australia she was asked to remove her feet from the cabin wall. 'Go the fuck ahead and arrest me,' she goaded. They did. Then at a concert in Orlando Courtney was arrested on charges that she punched several fans; the judge dismissed the case, ruling that they had been exposed to no more violence than might be reasonably expected at a rock 'n' roll show.

But her continued alcohol and drug use, combined with a volatile, fractured and utterly unpredictable nature meant Courtney remained a woman on the edge. During a photo shoot for Q magazine she poured a bottle of champagne over her head then stripped naked and streaked up Park Lane in Mayfair. 'I'm not a woman,' she declared, 'I'm a force of nature.' She was also vulnerable; one night she needed the fast intervention of Johnny Depp to save her life. At the Viper Room, the Hollywood nightclub Depp used to own, 'off my fucking head', Courtney passed out. When she awoke, the heat throb was giving her CPR.

Things got serious in October 2003 when Courtney attempted to break into the home of an ex-lover and was arrested for being intoxicated and for disorderly conduct. When police searched her home and found drugs the social services were called in and she lost custody of her daughter. It should have been a wake-up call, but although her daughter was returned it didn't curb her outrageousness, which mostly occurred in public, when there was an audience. Appearing on the David Letterman show clearly blotto, Courtney repeatedly bared her breasts at him. 'We're gonna lose our liquor licence,' he jested. Later that night her band played at a club and she was arrested for third-degree assault after hurling a microphone stand into the crowd and clocking some guy on the head with it.

Another assault followed in 2005, at much closer quarters, when Courtney attacked musician Kristin King with a whisky bottle; the provocation was that she'd been in her ex-boyfriend's home. Kristin alleged Courtney also yanked her hair, chipped one of her teeth and violently grabbed a breast. Appearing before judges was becoming an occupational hazard for Courtney, along with anger management courses, community service orders and drug treatment programmes. She was even told to avoid premises that served alcohol. What kind of example she thought she was setting for her teenage daughter God only knows. When the courts threatened to take her away again in 2009 unless she went to rehab, Courtney got her act together, rediscovered Buddhism and redirected all the angst in her life back into her music instead of tabloid-worthy antics. At least she's able to laugh at the circus side-show that her life represented, once joking that she'd like to meet Rolling Stones rocker Keith Richards to compare livers.

M

SHANE MacGOWAN (b. 1957: Singer)

Since the early 1980s the Pogues frontman Shane MacGowan, a sort of bastard hybrid of Johnny Rotten and Brendan Behan, trod a precarious path between addiction and annihilation. His alcoholic intake, not binges since he drank all the time, has earned him iconoclastic status. His tales of drunken debauchery are so gobsmackingly unbelievable that they must be apocryphal. Frighteningly, most aren't. Take the time he fell out of a tour van that was moving at about 50 mph. A mere mortal would have been killed. Shane probably didn't even lose grip on his vodka bottle. Or the tale of him drunkenly walking past a taxidermist in London, seeing a stuffed bison on the street outside and, panic-stricken, finding a phone box to alert the police about a wild animal on the loose.

But out of this whisky-sodden apparition that George A Romero would reject from a zombie film for looking too gruesomely realistic, come beautiful and extraordinary songs about drinking, naturally, leaving Ireland and the reflections of a soul caught between redemption and damnation.

Surprisingly for such a hellraising spirit, MacGowan was born in genteel Tunbridge Wells, Kent, while his Irish parents were visiting relatives. Raised on a farm in County Tipperary, a childhood rich in traditional song, poetry and dance, the family moved to London when Shane was six and he hated it.

One of MacGowan's more mad claims is that he started drinking aged four, tipples of Guinness, much preferring it to that piss Ribena his mum used to give him. He was seven when he first downed a bottle of whisky and got so stoned geese started to indulge in conversation with him. 'It fucking opened my mind to paradise,' he later said. 'I haven't been sober since I was fourteen. I'm not interested in being sober.'

An intelligent kid, Shane won a scholarship to Westminster public school ('it was policy to let in some rough every now and again'), but was expelled for possession of drugs. For the next couple of years MacGowan hung around with the low-life brigade of London's West End, the junkies and the alkies, got in such a state he was sent to a detox clinic aged seventeen after trying to throw himself out of a window. He spent six months there, the longest spell of his life when he didn't take a drink. They let him out thinking he was cured. The silly bugger walked into the nearest boozer and started drinking again.

His rebellious spirit certainly caught the mood of London at the time. Punk was beginning and MacGowan found his perfect outlet in that new and vibrant explosion of music and formed his own band, Nipple Erectors. He was at his happiest during punk; it was a world as chaotic as he was. Surprisingly, the Nipple Erectors didn't make much of a dent in popular culture, but Shane did much better with his next band. Pogue Mahone, Gaelic for kiss my arse, later changed to the Pogues, were a sort of deranged fusion of the Irish folk music of his childhood and the Sex Pistols on acid. Great live, fortified by lagoon-like quantities of alcohol, it was Shane's wild persona that was integral to the band's attraction. He became notorious for performing completely shitfaced. One rock journalist described his on-stage persona as 'looking like a fleshed-out stick-man doodled by a mentally disturbed five-year-old'. The legend of Shane MacGowan had begun.

His drinking reached such epic proportions that the group's tour manager would make Shane stay outside in the street while the band checked into hotels, so they could at least get a room before the management laid eyes on him. The ruse usually worked, except on one occasion when the band were in reception and the doors flew open and there was MacGowan, propped up by two burly stage hands, his trousers down around his knees, and no underwear. There's also the story of his sleeping body being yanked out of the Serpentine lake in London's Hyde Park by a dog; 'I'd had a drink or two,' excused Shane.

Essentially a shy person, MacGowan hated the whole rigmarole of fame, the interviews, attending functions, arse licking record executives, and so he upped the drinking to cope with this social anxiety. He also saw himself very much as heralding from that rich Irish literary tradition of fannied bards like Brendan Behan who were paid in whisky and slept in ditches. It was a tradition he sought to uphold – at least the drinking part, not so much the ditch sleeping. MacGowan has often made the point that his alcoholism is inextricably linked to his creative output.

He was also self-conscious of his Night of the Living Dead visage, and his teeth, well, bloody stumps really, assembled in his mouth much like Stonehenge after a tsunami hit. They were the result of a drunken accident when he hitched a lift on the back of a mate's bike and tried to get off while it was still in motion and rather forcibly kissed the tarmac of the Hammersmith Road.

The boozing increased, not least because it became almost impossible for him to walk the streets of Dublin, London or New York without being dragged into bars by well-wishers desperate to buy him a drink. A journalist for Q magazine in 1988 watched as MacGowan washed down stomach-ulcer pills with port, wine, brandy and a champagne chaser.

Few could believe how much he was able to drink and remain conscious. He was like a mad scientist, mixing things to get the intoxicating effect he wanted. One friend recalls arriving at his King's Cross flat one morning and there he was tucking into a two-litre bottle of wine and a packet of Kraft cheese slices. This was breakfast. There was also the time he was drinking in a bar and his behaviour was so obnoxious he managed to piss off virtually every customer. So the story goes, he demanded another gin and tonic so the barmaid got everyone to spit in the glass and served up the frothy monstrosity smiling to a paralytic Shane. He declared it 'the best gin and tonic I've ever had'.

For a while the members of the Pogues put up with MacGowan's away-with-the-fairies condition, his shambles on stage, being late for concerts or not showing up at all. Supporting Bob Dylan in America, the band flew out but MacGowan was so drunk he was refused entry three times on three separate flights. He missed the shows.

Japan in 1991 was the last straw. Catching the bullet train from Tokyo to a gig in Osaka, Shane drank sake the whole journey and fell off the train as it arrived at the station, smashing his head open, and was unable to perform that evening. It was sayonara Shane, nice knowing you. He was sacked. Ironic really, since the Pogues rose to fame as hard-drinking rabble-rousers and here was Shane getting the boot for living up to that image.

By this stage MacGowan was telling journalists he regularly dropped fifty tabs of acid a day, as well as drinking three bottles of whisky. Luckily he found he had the constitution for it, joking that his liver was regenerating. There was the occasion his long-time girlfriend Victoria Mary Clarke turned up at his flat to find blood gushing from his mouth after he'd tried to ingest a copy of the *Beach Boys' Greatest Hits*. In his deluded state Shane was convinced that the world was on the brink of nuclear annihilation, and as leader of the Irish Republic, he was holding a summit meeting in his kitchen between the superpowers of Russia, China and America. In order to demonstrate the cultural inferiority of the United States he scoffed down a bit of decadent Beach Boys' vinyl.

After this bizarre episode he eased back on the hard spirits, admitting he wasn't particularly nice company on them. 'I would turn into a fucking wanker and then pass out.' Where was the fun in drinking oneself into oblivion? 'There's no kick. I want to appreciate the kick.' So he turned to wine and beer and Martini, a poseur's drink, you'd think, for someone like Shane, unless you drink it by the pint, of course.

In 2000 he was persuaded by friends to go and dry out in the Priory but got booted out after two weeks for continuing bouts of, 'unreasonable behaviour'. Asked how long he stayed sober afterwards, Shane replied, 'As long as it took to get to the nearest bar.' That didn't work, then. It seemed that everyone was worried about Shane's alcohol consumption except Shane himself. 'I was given six weeks to live about twenty-five years ago!' He was an unapologetic boozer, with no intention of slowing down. In 2002 he drank so much before a performance at the Olympia Theatre in Dublin that he stopped singing and threw up over fans in the front row.

Amazingly, in 2007 Shane reached the age of fifty, a milestone in the lives of many of us, a bloody miracle when you're talking about Shane

MacGowan. He put his relative longevity down to his hard lifestyle, 'I party my way through life,' and his generally crap health merely a consequence of very good living. The drinking had subsided a bit; he no longer poured it down his neck as recklessly as before. What was left was an element of playing up to his hellraising image, a clever way of ignoring people he doesn't want to deal with.

He was back with the Pogues, too, touring once again, but with a difference, most of the members having stopped drinking, Shane being the main exception. But Shane always did what he wanted to do, as one of the Pogues admitted: 'He'll probably outlive us all, just to annoy us.'

DEAN MARTIN (1917–1995: Singer/Actor)

Few performers ever built more of a career round booze than Dean Martin. The image he projected to the world was that of the ultimate lounge-bar lizard who lived in a perpetual alcoholic haze. Even his licence plate read DRUNKY. It was a great gimmick, introduced on stage with the line, 'Direct from the bar . . .'

But how much of it was really true, the slurring his speech routine, looking slightly inebriated at the mere thought of another cocktail? 'I only drink moderately,' he deadpanned. 'In fact, I have a case of Moderately in the dressing room.' Or, 'You're not drunk if you can lie on the floor without holding on.' Image and reality was constantly blurred. Was it an act, or did his laissez-faire attitude to drink conceal borderline alcoholism? As fellow Vegas performer Red Buttons said, 'When people ask me if Dean Martin drank, let me put it this way. If Dracula bit Dean in the neck, he'd get a Bloody Mary.'

He was born in Steubenville, Ohio, to Italian immigrant parents and never spoke a word of English until he started school at the age of five. Dropping out in the tenth grade, he delivered bootleg liquor and served as a croupier in a speakeasy. When money was tight, which was most of the time, Dean and a friend would invite people up to a hotel room and charge everyone fifty cents to watch them punch each other until one or the other was knocked out.

Putting his fists to more profitable use, Dean started boxing professionally as a welterweight, proudly declaring, 'I won all but eleven of my twelve fights,' getting a broken nose, a permanently split lip and broken knuckles. Getting his nose fixed, Dean set out to become a singer, modelling himself after Bing Crosby, but despite his smouldering looks and debonair charm never achieved widespread success. That all changed in 1946 when he hooked up with a young comic Jerry Lewis, forming a hit double act that blended music and comedy. Picked up by Hollywood to churn out film after film, Martin and Lewis quickly became the nation's favourite star duo, Dean the suave straightman to Lewis the plain nutball.

It couldn't last, though, and after ten years the relationship had deteriorated to the point where they weren't even on speaking terms. Keen to concentrate on his singing and maybe pursue a dramatic acting career, Martin quit. 'And there was a big meeting with all the heads of Paramount studios and they said, you can't walk out on $20 million, and I said, well, you just watch me.'

Few believed that Martin could succeed without Lewis; instead he forged a new partnership with Frank Sinatra and his Rat Pack, Sammy Davis Jr, Peter Lawford and Joey Bishop. Their Las Vegas performances became the stuff of legend, the hottest ticket in showbiz. The act was like a private party on stage that audiences felt they were eavesdropping on: the boys told jokes, took the piss out of each other, sang – oh, and drank, and drank some more. Or so the audience were led to believe, though actually the booze on stage was apple juice; they had their professional standards, you know. The real drinking took place afterwards when Dean and Frank hit the town, where trouble was never very far away. In a restaurant one time, carousing like teenagers on their first booze trip, they drew the contempt of the people sitting in the opposite booth. When Frank and Dean got up to leave a voice from the booth said, 'There go the two loud dagos.' Frank struck first, and then Dean hit the other guy and threw him against the wall. For good measure Sinatra picked up a telephone and smashed it over the man's skull. For twenty-four hours he lay in intensive care, hovering between life and death. Sinatra stayed with him day and night till he pulled through.

By far Sinatra was the greater drinker, 'Frank spills more than Dad drinks,' said Dean's daughter Gail. But Dino could knock them back all right and his constitution was a marvel, able to steadily drink all day to keep up his high without getting overly blotto. Few colleagues ever remember Dean having been too free with Sir John Strawberry. There were a few public lapses. Making *The Sons of Katie Elder* (1965), Dean and co-star John Wayne joined acting newcomer Dennis Hopper in wild drinking binges, arriving red-eyed for work next morning. One night Dean and the Duke woke up everyone in the hotel by marching up and down the street outside arm in arm, singing at the top of their voices.

Contrary to the public image, Dean preferred the quiet life to hell-raising about town. After work he generally headed back home to his wife and young family for dinner, put his feet up and watched TV and rose early the next morning for a game of his beloved golf. 'If you drink, don't drive,' Martin cautioned. 'Don't even putt.'

That was Dean's nature: quiet, relaxed. His rampant womanising was an aberration (he'd marry three times, all ending in divorce), and his drinking an occupational hazard he loved poking fun at. Once asked why he drank so much, Martin replied. 'I drink to forget.' Sad, he was told. 'It could be a lot sadder,' Martin declared. 'What could be sadder than drinking to forget?' Martin's reply: 'Forgetting to drink!'

For years the Rat Pack ruled Vegas. It was like a big boys' club. Typical of the kind of gag they played on each other was when Sinatra, while everyone was up at Lake Tahoe, got a pal to dress up in a bear costume and when a tipsy Dean walked by he jumped out and chased the terrified crooner into the woods.

But as America picked up the pieces of the Kennedy assassination, Vietnam and civil rights strife, the boys' boozy, happy-go-lucky lifestyle seemed as stale as last week's hangover. Luckily Dean had managed to diversify making movies; he was America's answer to James Bond with the Matt Helm spy series, and had his own top-rating TV variety show, where once again he played up his image as a drunken sot, complete with a miniature bar as part of the set.

By the mid-seventies Martin's health started to fail. He was drinking more; sometimes the apple juice in the whisky bottle was the real thing.

When his TV show was cancelled he began to slowly drift out of the public arena, his particular brand of entertainment seen as passé. Then things started to go badly wrong. He got hooked on Percodan, a potent painkiller that combined with his heavier drinking resulted in Dean getting so laid back he made a corpse seem animated. In May 1982 the police spotted him driving his car erratically and hauled him over. Tipsy, but not legally intoxicated, the problem for Dean was the unlicensed loaded revolver police found in his glove compartment. He was fined and given a year's probation.

Dino's world literally fell apart in 1987 when his beloved son, Dean Jr, was killed in a military jet crash. He never recovered from it, and turned into a virtual recluse with no desire to perform, no desire to live. Sinatra tried to drag him out of his depression by organising a Rat Pack comeback tour: Dino, Frank and Sammy. Dean reluctantly agreed but in the first few shows seemed to be just going through the motions, when he wasn't flicking lit cigarettes at the audience. Things came to a head when Sinatra begged him to come out drinking one night. Dean wanted to take things easy, eat his spaghetti dinner and watch a movie on TV. Exasperated, Sinatra picked up the plate and poured the food over Dean's head. It was the kind of jape they always indulged in during their glory days; now it wasn't funny, at least for Dean. He got up and went into the bathroom to clean up, staying there until Frank left. The next morning he checked out of the hotel and checked out of the tour – he was gone.

Dean finished his life as more a haunting than a real human being, eating alone in restaurants and yearning for those nights when he had his family all around him for those special dinners he never missed. Physically he looked a wreck and could hardly walk or talk. He'd given up smoking, finally, and cut down on his drinking, but by then it was too late. Going into hospital for tests, doctors found that his lungs were riddled with tumours. Told that surgery was needed to prolong his life, Martin refused and walked out. 'It's obvious that Dean has resigned himself to facing death with a beer in his hand,' said his agent Mort Viner.

On Christmas morning, the same day his mother passed away, Dean died of respiratory failure. He was back with his son, at last. As a mark of respect the lights of the Las Vegas Strip were dimmed. It was a fitting tribute to a man who did so much to glamorise the place and its heady atmosphere of boozing and gambling. 'I'd hate to be a teetotaller,' Martin once cracked. 'Imagine getting up in the morning and knowing that's as good as you're going to feel all day.'

LEE MARVIN (1924–1987: Actor)

To give you some idea of the terror Lee Marvin could inflict on a production, this is what Joshua Logan said about him after directing the star in *Paint Your Wagon* (1969): 'Not since Attila the Hun swept across Europe leaving 500 years of total blackness has there been a man like Lee Marvin.'

This is a guy who liked to live and play close to the edge, who at home had a private bar with a bell hanging over it and liked nothing better than to whip out his revolver and fire a couple of bullets into it; if some drinking buddies were sitting close by at the time, so much the better. Lee loved guns. He had a small arsenal of pistols and rifles, even a Gatling gun, until finally his exasperated wife said, 'You're going to have to choose between me and the Magnums.' Marvin gave his guns to Sam Peckinpah, but retained a Hudson Bay axe that lay under his bed every night.

This barfly brawler was actually born into an artistic, middle-class New York family and was a direct descendant of George Washington and Thomas Jefferson. At the age of four he ran away from home and wasn't found for two days. A foreigner to discipline, Marvin was sent to a succession of exclusive boarding schools only to be expelled from practically all of them for such minor infractions as smoking, drinking and throwing a room-mate out of a second-floor window.

Ditching school altogether, Marvin joined the Marines and was thrust into the Second World War, fighting in the Pacific theatre. On the island of Saipan his unit came under intense bombardment and out of 247 men only Marvin and five others survived the slaughter. Taking a Japanese sniper's bullet up his arse, which severed a nerve just below the spine,

Marvin was taken off the battlefield and forced to listen to the sounds of his comrades being massacred as he lay safe on a hospital ship. The helplessness and guilt he felt haunted him for the rest of his life.

In rehabilitation for thirteen months and awarded the Purple Heart, Marvin drifted aimlessly through a score of menial jobs including plumber's assistant. Called out to mend a toilet in a theatre, he stayed behind to watch the actors rehearse and was spellbound. Taking up acting, he performed on Broadway before appearances on numerous TV series and films where his unpredictable, explosive quality on screen naturally gravitated to him being cast as a succession of general-purpose nutters.

Behind this success, Lee was garnering a reputation as one of Hollywood's fiercest boozers. When under the influence it was real Jekyll and Hyde stuff: mad one minute, he was a puppy licking your face the next. Take the time he lay razzled in the back of a limo stuck in traffic. One rather fancy lady recognised him and wound down her window. 'Oh, Mr Marvin, could I please have your autograph?' With a scowl Lee replied, 'Up your ass!' He did this with a number of other people till a colleague informed him that this was perhaps not the best way to deal with fans. Full of remorse, he barged out of the car and walked down the middle of the road flagging cars down. 'Hi, I'm Lee Marvin,' he hollered as they jammed on their brakes. 'Would you like my autograph?' They got it whether they wanted it or not.

There was also the occasion the cops caught him driving like a maniac along an LA freeway, wearing a hairnet, with a bottle of whisky in one hand and a pistol in the other, firing at mailboxes. He was locked up in jail for the day and then unleashed again upon the poor citizens of California. Shooting *Donovan's Reef* (1963) in Hawaii, co-star Elizabeth Allen remembered a smashed Marvin stripping naked and climbing up onto the bar of a hotel to perform a hula dance.

For sure there was a streak of violence in him that reared its ugly head thanks to drink, like the time in a bar he walked over and punched a paraplegic. Or confronted at the barrelhead by a stranger who wouldn't be brushed off, Marvin smashed a handy banjo into his face, breaking most of the guy's teeth. 'The man represented some anxiety that I was working out and he just happened to be in the way,' Marvin excused.

One of his craziest stunts was the occasion he completely wrecked a wrap party for a TV show. He'd been drinking all day and just cut loose, throwing tables over and spilling beer and food everywhere. Grabbing the show's director Sam Peckinpah, Marvin pinned him against a wall, his feet dangling off the ground. A studio nurse rushed over with a hypodermic needle to send old Lee bye-byes. 'Instead I grabbed her by the breast and threw her on the deck.' It took several large fellas to subdue Marvin and escort him out. Is it any wonder that his marriage hit the rocks? After fourteen years of this kind of shit the poor woman just couldn't take any more.

By the mid-sixties Marvin had gone from supporting actor to genuine movie star thanks to his Oscar-winning turn in *Cat Ballou* (1965), although he never had much truck with the concept of fame. 'They put your name on a star in the sidewalk on Hollywood Boulevard and you walk down and find a pile of dog shit on it. That tells the whole story, baby.'

Shooting *The Professionals* (1966) in the desert near Las Vegas, Marvin got himself arrested for one prank too far. Loaded and bored in his hotel room, across the street he spied one of those famous neon signs and armed with a longbow he shot steel-tipped arrows at the damn thing, several missing and landing dangerously near pedestrians on the strip. It wasn't long before the police were knocking on his door.

Director Richard Brooks knew Marvin's reputation as a drinker and imagined there'd be trouble on *The Professionals* – he was right. It was obvious one Friday morning on set that Marvin was stoned out of his brain. Brooks ordered him back to his hotel and it took several crew members, working on a rota system, to sit on Marvin to make sure he was dried out and ready for shooting on Monday. Back on location, Brooks showed Marvin the incriminating can of film of Friday's pathetic ramblings and threatened to show it round Hollywood if his star didn't agree to behave. Marvin promised to buckle under and Brooks burned the negative.

There would always be lapses, though; it was inevitable, really. 'I don't take pledges. I quit drinking every morning and I start again every evening.' Filming *The Dirty Dozen* (1967) in Britain necessitated frequent trips to London boozers. The action highlight of the picture was the destruction of a large chateau built on the back lot at Pinewood studios. Marvin was to drive an armoured truck amid all the chaos with Charles Bronson riding shotgun. With cameras poised, Marvin was a no-show. Tracked down to a pub in Belgravia, drunk as the lord, he was hauled into a car and taken to the studio, where liberal cups of coffee were poured down his neck. When on arrival he fell out of the car, Bronson flipped. 'I'm going to fucking kill you, Lee.' Coming from hard man Bronson this was no idle threat. *The Dirty Dozen* was a blockbuster and although there were times on set, according to producer Kenneth Hyman, 'when Marvin probably couldn't have articulated his own name', audiences were none the wiser.

Hyman actually saved Marvin from getting a pummelling from 007 himself, Sean Connery. It was at a cocktail function when a rather the worse for wear Marvin spied a quaint old lady sitting on her own in the corner. Staggering across, he propositioned her in the most vulgar manner imaginable. So slurred was his speech that the woman had trouble understanding, so innocently asked him to repeat it. Marvin obliged. Alas, the old dear was Connery's aunt and the man himself was making swift movement in Marvin's direction. Hyman saw the danger and desperately leaped into the breach. 'Don't hit him in the face, Sean,' he begged. 'He's got close-ups tomorrow.' Just in time, Connery saw the funny side of it and roared with laughter.

Shooting *Point Blank* (1967) in LA, Marvin took the director John Boorman and some friends out to lunch. When it was time to leave Boorman could see that Marvin was in no fit state to drive back and told him so. 'Fuck you,' said Marvin as he missed with a punch to the director's head. Boorman grabbed the car keys and jumped in the Chrysler station wagon. Like a wild animal Marvin prowled around the vehicle, bashing it occasionally, before climbing up onto the roof rack. Successive pleas for him to come down were met with snarls as he refused to budge. Boorman decided to take a chance and eased the car carefully down the pacific coast highway towards Malibu. After a few minutes there were flashing lights in his rear-view mirror. He pulled over. The patrolman walked purposefully to the car, looked up, looked at Boorman and said, 'Do you know you have Lee Marvin on your roof?'

After another long boozy night of fun Marvin drove home, but felt perturbed when his key didn't seem to fit the lock of the front door. Pounding on it, the door was opened by a complete stranger. 'Who the fuck are you?' asked Marvin.

'I'm Mrs Smith; I bought this property off you three months ago, Mr Marvin.'

'Then where the fuck do I live?' Mrs Smith had no idea, so some quick thinking was called for. Driving over to a stall on Hollywood Boulevard Marvin bought a map of movie stars' homes. Irritated that he wasn't included he gave up his search and slept the night in his car. By morning, hallelujah, his memory had returned.

Marvin and Boorman got along so well on *Point Blank* they worked together again on *Hell in the Pacific* (1968). In Honolulu airport waiting for a flight to Guam, Marvin was sitting in the VIP lounge relaxing after a heavy night of drinking mai tais when a five-star American general sat opposite him. 'Heh, Mr Marvin,' he said. 'What do you think of the Vietnam War?' Lee looked up blearily and his eye was caught by the general's ribbon-strewn hat. 'I think the war is very rude and what's more I'm going to eat your hat.' Marvin grabbed it, bit a mighty chunk out of it and popped it on his head. The officer was horrified and ran for his flight. 'Lee had no time for generals,' said Boorman. 'He stood for the ordinary grunt.'

Then there was the Hollywood producer, later dispatched to the nearest sanatorium for a full frontal lobotomy, who decided it would be a good idea to cast Lee Marvin and Richard Burton together in a film about the Ku Klux Klan. Predictably both stars were stoned for most of the filming of *The Klansman* (1974). When Marvin arrived on location in the small California town of Oroville, he was given the full treatment by the mayor. In the town hall he listened to innumerable speeches from local dignitaries, getting gradually pissed, until as guest of honour it was time to cut the ceremonial cake. Rising unsteadily to his feet, Marvin opened his mouth and then collapsed face-first into the sponge concoction. Staggering back up, dripping with cream, he walked outside to address a crowd that had gathered. 'Cocksuckers of Oroville,' he shouted, 'united we stand.' The townsfolk were not amused and demanded an apology.

The tension between Marvin and Burton, these two macho stars, was so taut that private bets were laid amongst the crew on which of them would knock out the other first. Actually they got quite chummy, often drinking lunch together. Only the courageous or plain stupid ever went with them: lunch might consist of seventeen Martinis each before going back to work.

Straight after this, Marvin made the adventure film *Shout at the Devil* (1976) with Roger Moore. En route to Malta for some location work, drinking in the airport lounge, Marvin was disturbed by a squadron of Japanese tourists wanting to take his picture. With his view of the Japanese nation somewhat coloured by his combat experiences, Marvin suddenly found himself back under fire in Saipan and started throwing these poor tourists around the departure area. 'It very nearly became a diplomatic incident,' remembered Moore.

By the eighties Marvin was remarried, had moved to the relative normality of Tucson, Arizona, and cut back on the booze. Visited on a movie set in 1983 by a reporter surprised to see him slurping Diet Coke he was asked, 'You're not drinking so much these days?' Lee smiled wearily, 'If I were, I'd be dead.'

Marvin always knew he'd been living on borrowed time, anyway. Some part of him perhaps never left those bloodstained beaches, remaining with the ghosts of his Marine buddies who never returned home. When his body finally succumbed to the inevitable – a sudden heart attack was enough – it was only fitting that Marvin was interred at Arlington National Cemetery. He lays to rest near the tomb of the Unknown Soldier.

EDNA St VINCENT MILLAY (1892–1950: Poet)

During the height of the Depression Edna Millay's poetry books sold by the tens of thousands and audiences flocked to her cross-country reading tours as if she were a pop star. And yet not long after her death her verses fell out of favour with critics and the public alike, her name became a blurred memory. Strange, since she led such a remarkable life: the first woman to win the Pulitzer Prize for poetry, the first foreign correspondent for *Vanity Fair*. She was also an actress, playwright, novelist, gambler and master chess player. Most importantly she was one of the voices of her generation, representing the New Woman, helping to shatter society's notion that a woman needed to be a good wife or mother in order to feel worthwhile. Edna blasted that misconception out of the water; she did what she damned well pleased, drinking and hellraising, and society's morals could go hang.

She was born and raised in Rockland, Maine; her mother was a nurse, her father a schoolteacher. When Edna was eight years old her mother Cora kicked out her husband and reared Edna and her two sisters alone, encouraging them in literary pursuits and promoting an independence of will and the freedom to speak their mind. Poverty was a constant companion and the family often lived on the charity of relatives before settling down in Camden, Maine, but in a tough neighbourhood where on Saturday nights drunken mill workers would try and break into the house to rape the girls.

Already a published poet before leaving grade school, Edna attended Vassar College and immediately set about breaking every rule she could, sneaking away from her dorm for days at a time to visit speakeasies in Manhattan, indulging in torrid affairs with several of her female classmates, and organising drinking bouts that invariably ended with everyone running naked and wired to the tits across campus.

In spite of such indiscretions Edna graduated top of her class and moved to New York, where she epitomised the Bohemian lifestyle, living it up in Greenwich Village, flouting convention with a jazz age spirit of mad gaiety. The roaring twenties were a bit of a blur for Edna; as her celebrity soared as one of the most successful and respected poets in America, she partied hard and drank hard. A near permanent fixture in local bars, the legend soon grew of this diminutive lady who could knock them back big style. It became a test of manhood for some men to challenge Edna to drinking contests, and she won more than she lost.

With her flaming red hair and provocative gaze, Edna was a magnet for both sexes and she indulged in reckless promiscuity, carrying on affairs with as many as six or seven men at a time, sometimes sleeping with three of them on the same day. The poor bastards didn't know if they were coming or going and were driven to utter despair. When her mother Cora came to live in New York she enquired, 'Who is Edna killing now? Is he almost done for?' Far from taking a dim view of her daughter's lifestyle, Cora declared that she had been a slut herself, so why shouldn't her girls be.

Finally there came a point when, in the words of one-time lover and literary critic Edmund Wilson, 'Edna was tired of breaking hearts and spreading havoc.' So in 1923 she married Eugen Boissevain, a Dutch coffee importer twelve years her senior. Boissevain was slavishly devoted to Edna, looking after her well-being along with her business affairs, and since she never did anything so conventional as cook, shop or do housework, he took care of all that, too. With children ruled out as an unnecessary distraction, it was also agreed that the marriage be sexually open, but Edna flaunted her lovers under Boissevain's nose, especially her dalliance with the poet George Dillon.

Ultimately the alcohol drive that had fanned the flames of Edna's creativity led to a physical wipeout and she fell prey to a number of illnesses, culminating in what she described in a letter as a 'small nervous breakdown'. She went to Europe to recuperate. This physical deterioration began to affect her work and by the early thirties her poetry was beginning to receive mixed reviews, although critics had always resented her popularity. Fate was also to play an awful hand in Edna's artistic collapse. In 1936 she was involved in a horrific car accident when the door of her station wagon flew open and she was hurled into the street. Left in disabling pain from the injuries to her spine and arms, Edna was placed on morphine and became a hopeless addict. When she predictably went back to the bottle the mix of hooch and pills proved to be a lethal combination, destroying her body and sterilising what creative impulses she had left.

It was a sad decline as she began to withdraw from public life. When poet Witter Bynner paid a visit he noted in his journal that Edna appeared 'a mime now with a lost face, eyes blearily absent'. Boissevain nursed her as best he could, took her to hospitals and rehabilitation centres and even turned himself into a morphine addict in order to better understand her sufferings.

Eventually Edna was able to ease back on her drug dependency but not the booze, downing two Gin Rickeys, one Martini and a beer all before lunch. Her face was beginning to show the effects of her illnesses and the years of alcoholism: it was puffy, saggy, her teeth were discoloured, the beauty was gone and she knew it. Melancholia set in.

Things got worse when Boissevain was diagnosed with lung cancer. Despite emergency surgery during which one of his lungs was removed in a desperate attempt to save his life, he perished and Edna plunged further into darkness and depression, drinking even more recklessly; she only lasted another lonely year herself. Alone at the sprawling mansion she'd shared with her husband she tumbled down the staircase one night, probably in a drunken stupor, and broke her neck. When her body was discovered eight hours later by the caretaker she was still clutching her Martini glass.

ROBERT MITCHUM (1917–1997: Actor)

The genuine article, the Hollywood tough guy as hard-boiled as an egg left for three days on Mount Vesuvius, Robert Mitchum had a unique screen presence, managing to be heroic and fatally sinister at the same time, laconic to the point of catatonia yet still a rugged man of action, with a voice that sounded as though it was laced with bourbon. He was also a self-confessed pothead and dangerous to be on the wrong side of when he'd had a few.

Born in Bridgeport, Connecticut, Mitchum was pretty wild from day one and frequently in trouble, a rebellious streak that was perhaps a result of his railroad worker father dying in a train accident when Mitchum was barely two, or was it just plain contempt for authority? As a teenager he ran away from home and spent time circumnavigating Depression-era America on the road or hopping railroad cars, taking any job he could from coal miner to prize-fighter. He also claimed to have escaped from a Georgia chain gang soon after being arrested for vagrancy.

His life seemed to settle down after his marriage in 1940 to Dorothy Spence, who'd remain with Mitchum right until the end, despite his drunken debauchery and sexual escapades. A move to Hollywood led to bit parts in the movies, which in time earned him a contract at RKO. At first dismissed as nothing more than beefcake, handsome but lacking serious acting credentials, Mitchum began developing his now legendary screen persona of brooding naturalism and laconic cynicism that was first exploited in film noir pictures. Later on he was equally adept at westerns and romantic dramas, or playing heavies in classics like *The Night of the Hunter* (1955) and *Cape Fear* (1962).

After serving briefly in the US army during the later stages of the Second World War, as a medic checking recruits' genitals for venereal disease – a 'pecker checker' – Mitchum's movie career continued to flourish, as did his drinking. Making *Till the End of Time* (1946), the word from the crew was that Mitchum was swigging vodka in his dressing room and smoking dope. Called onto the set, he performed the scene word perfectly and then returned to his lubrication. *Rachel and the Stranger* (1948) saw him star opposite Loretta Young, a devout Catholic who admonished him for drinking whisky. She also disapproved most vehemently about bad language and introduced a swear box onto the set. An assistant explained to Mitchum how it worked: fifty cents for hell, a dollar for a damn, a dollar fifty for shit. Mitchum butted in with a voice loud enough for the whole studio to hear, 'What I want to know is, what does Miss Young charge for a fuck?'

As Mitchum's professional reputation grew, so did his knack for getting into trouble. For such a big movie star it was revolutionary back then to be quite so brazenly open about his marijuana habit, strutting around with a reefer tucked behind each ear. The inevitable happened in August 1948 when he was busted by LA cops for possession. The authorities were determined to rid Hollywood of vice and Mitchum must have felt really deep in it. When the booking officer asked his occupation, Mitchum replied, 'Former actor.' He was then stripped and shackled and left stark naked to be questioned by a psychiatrist.

Sentenced to sixty days in jail, Mitchum served most of it at a prison honour farm. Meanwhile audiences flocked to see his movies and roared whenever he appeared on screen, proof of the public's fascination for rebels. On his release Mitchum told reporters that his stay had been 'just like a weekend in Palm Springs . . . only you meet a better class of people'.

After the drug bust Mitchum was pretty much fair game in the tabloids. One story had him stripping off at a fancy-dress party, dousing himself in ketchup and announcing that he'd come as a hamburger. Mitchum learned to live with such reports; as he once said, 'Booze, brawls, broads, it's all true. Make up some more if you want.'

He also remained a pothead for most of his life, rolling joints of a truly formidable size. Arriving in the Congo to start a movie, waiting on the tarmac for a jeep to take him out to the location, a private plane landed and an Idi Amin-type big bastard in full uniform got out and climbed into a limo. The window wound down and a finger beckoned over Mitchum.

'I know who you are,' said the voice inside the car.

'Is that right?'

'Yes, you are Mister Mitchum, the film star.'

'Right on,' said Bob.

'Do you know who I am?'

Mitchum looked at the ambassadorial plane and limo and replied, 'Looks like you're the Head Nigger round here,' and sauntered over to his jeep and was gone.

A few days later a small plane flew over the location and dropped a parachute. On it was a small package addressed to MISTER MITCHUM – FILM STAR. Mitchum opened it to find two kilos of superior Congolese 'black' hashish, with a note attached: FROM THE HEAD NIGGER.

When Mitchum arrived in London to do the Michael Parkinson chat show, the redoubtable Parky could smell the exotic odour coming from his dressing room halfway down the corridor at TV Centre. 'Hi, kid, wanna smoke?'

'I wouldn't mind a cigar,' said Parkinson.

Mitchum pulled a face as if someone had taken a dump on his grand-mother's grave. 'Do you wanna smoke some shit?'

Never one to stand on ceremony, when Mitchum arrived for an import-ant meeting with David O Selznick, he'd been drinking all day and was completely shitfaced. He sat down in the plush office and the producer made his pitch about this great new project, but Mitchum wasn't listening; his bladder was roaring and he needed a piss, bad. Unable to interrupt Selznick and absolutely desperate, Mitchum unzipped his fly, sort of twisted himself sideways on the chair and let flow a horse piss onto the carpet. Selznick stood aghast and Mitchum made his excuses and left.

Because of his tough-guy image Mitchum was always avoiding bar-room challenges. During the filming of *One Minute to Zero* (1952) in Colorado Mitchum was drinking when he overheard a guy say, 'I can whip that Hollywood fag.' Mitchum turned around to face his challenger and his jaw drooped, 'Holy Christ!' The guy was built like the prover-bial brick shit house, but Mitchum couldn't back down. He ended up knocking the guy unconscious, sending him to hospital. It was later discovered he was a heavyweight boxing champion. Making the war film *Heaven Knows, Mr Allison* (1957) on location in Trinidad, a hundred authentic American Marines were drafted in for the action sequences. Enjoying a drink at the veranda bar of his hotel a group of soldiers aimed to take Mitchum on. 'I can knock you off your feet with a single punch,' said one. Mitchum stared him down, 'OK, take a shot.' He did so, Mitchum remained standing, unfazed. When the soldier let fly with another punch Mitchum ducked, then sent a fist flying into his face. The soldier's pals rushed in, Mitchum dispatched one down the staircase, slugged another in the head and was about to throw a third over a balcony into the swimming pool when his wife clunked him over the head with her high heels. 'Hey, you're supposed to be on my side honey.' 'You were enjoying it too much,' she replied.

Mitchum was tough, no doubt about it. On *His Kind of Woman* (1951) production was behind schedule and Mitchum crawled into the nearest bottle. In one scene he was supposed to be beaten up by a gang of thugs, only Mitchum was so bombed that he switched to genuine fighting mode and sent the stuntmen flying take after take. 'He was like a grenade with its pin pulled,' recalled director Richard Fleischer. After destroying the set and then his dressing room, Mitchum was full of apologies the next day.

But he kept on drinking, couldn't help it, getting fired from *Blood Alley* (1955) for throwing a crew member into a nearby river. Filming *Not as a Stranger* (1955) with Frank Sinatra and Lee Marvin, 'It wasn't a cast so much as a brewery,' said Mitchum. It goes without saying that much drinking was to be had and they ripped out telephones and threw co-star Broderick Crawford off a second-floor balcony. In retaliation Crawford tore off Sinatra's toupee and ate it; a nice act of defiance but then he started to choke and the unit doctor had to force him to vomit it up. Shooting was delayed until a replacement wig for Sinatra was found.

It's safe to say Mitchum didn't conform to any rules, certainly Hollywood couldn't control him. Shooting *The Night of the Hunter* (1955), Mitchum often turned up on set tight. One time the producer confronted his star, telling him to his face that he was in no condition to work that day. Mitch took umbrage at this and walked over to the producer's Cadillac, opened the front door, took out his dick and pissed on the front seat.

On movies you learned pretty fast not to mess with him. One director announced on the first day, 'I have a habit of yelling at actors, but don't take it personally, it's just my way.' Mitchum responded, 'I have a habit of punching directors, which I hope you don't take personally.'

There's the story of Otto Preminger who ordered that not a drop of alcohol would be permitted on *River of No Return* (1954). One day he spied an actor crossing the set with a glass of vodka and went berserk. The actor cowered in front of the legendary director saying, 'I'm just taking this to Mr Mitchum.' The director paused and said, 'Oh, that's different.'

Mitchum had numerous run-ins with Preminger. Playing the lead in *Rosebud* (1975) on location in Corsica, Mitchum arrived on set at 5.30 in the morning, looking bedraggled. Otto was not amused. 'You have been drinking with the Corsicans!' he bellowed.

'Who the hell else is there around here to drink with, Otto?' Mitchum replied.

'You are drunk!'

'Now, Otto, how in hell can I be drunk at 5.30 in the morning?'

Otto's temper rose. 'You are THROUGH!'

There was a second's pause before Mitchum shouted, 'Taxi!' Preminger's jaw dropped to see his star call his bluff and actually walk. When Mitchum heard he'd been replaced by Peter O'Toole he scoffed, 'That's like replacing Ray Charles with Helen Keller.'

Making *Ryan's Daughter* (1970), the editors had a tough job splicing together bits of film where Mitchum didn't look like he was about to fall flat on his face. On a day off he popped into a local Irish pub and was accosted by this short guy who poked him in the ribs with a pencil, 'Hey movie star, give me your autograph.' Mitchum eyed the midget up and down. 'Will you look at the little leprechaun? Wait until I've finished my drink.' But the man persisted. Finally an exasperated Mitchum snatched the paper and pencil and wrote: UP YOUR ARSE – KIRK DOUGLAS. The man was not best pleased and threw a punch, but Mitch just stood there looking at him. 'If that's the best you can do, little lady, you better come back with your girlfriends.' The man did indeed return with some rather hefty mates. Mitchum head-butted one of them, sending him reeling before dispatching the rest.

Mitchum continued to export his own special brand of recklessness globally. In Mexico City he was given a grand tour by the chief of police. At one stop the chief excused himself to go into the lavatory. Mitchum followed and for a laugh stood behind him and urinated all over his uniform trousers.

In 1977 Mitchum came to London to star as Philip Marlowe in Michael Winner's update of *The Big Sleep*. 'He was a wonderful man, Bob,' recalled Winner. 'But a pain in the arse when drunk. I wouldn't call him a heavy drinker, but occasionally he'd go over the top.' One night Mitchum got hammered outside the Savoy Hotel and spotted a German camera crew and chased them up the street, calling them all fucking Nazis.

The climax of *The Big Sleep* was a shootout between Mitchum and veteran actor Richard Boone, another heavy drinker. 'They were both firing these guns in fucking Buckinghamshire somewhere,' says Winner. 'It was like the gunfight at Alcoholics Anonymous. How the fuck we put that scene together I don't know. The guns were going off at the wrong time, they were shooting in the wrong direction; fucking nightmare. But such nice people.'

Into his seventies Mitchum was still drinking and getting into trouble.

In 1983 he grabbed a female journalist's breast, growling, 'You want me to humiliate you?' Promoting a basketball film, a female photographer gave Mitchum a basketball which he immediately threw back with some force into her face. She was obviously injured, but Mitchum didn't seem to care, instead he went off in search of the nearest bar.

In 1984 his family persuaded him to check into the Betty Ford Clinic in a bid to quit drinking. 'What did you learn over there, Bob?' actor Stuart Whitman asked when he got out. 'More ice.'

Mitchum was eighty years old when he succumbed to emphysema and lung cancer; note it took two diseases to fell him. Actually how he'd managed to survive that long is a miracle. His last night on earth saw Mitchum get out of bed restless, go downstairs and sit in his favourite chair to smoke a cigarette and enjoy a shot of tequila before going back to sleep. He never woke up.

Mitchum once said that he drank as a preparation for death. 'When that great day comes, I will be completely inured to it. It will be just one more hangover.' Let's hope it worked.

KEITH MOON (1946–1978: Drummer)

The undisputed king of rock lunacy, Keith Moon's antics have passed into legend. This was a man who once gulped down a horse tranquilliser that put him out cold for two days. The problem with Moon, like a kid given free rein in a candy shop, was that as drummer of the Who, one of the biggest bands in the world, he could do pretty much anything he wanted to, wreck a hotel room then just write out a cheque afterwards and tell the manager to fuck off. It was a licence to live dangerously wild.

Take the time one of the roadies from the Who borrowed Keith's cassette recorder then went to bed. Later that night Moon wanted it back but try as he might couldn't wake this guy up, no matter how hard he pounded on his hotel room door. A solution presented itself that in the mind of Moon made perfect sense. He found a penknife and for the next four and a half hours painstakingly burrowed his way through the wall until he'd loosened enough brickwork and plaster to charge at the thing, which he did, arriving in the middle of the roadie's room in a cloud of brick dust and woodwork. Calmly Moon took his cassette recorder from the startled roadie, walked back into his own room, sat down and listened to his music.

Born in Wembley, north London, Keith was the only son in a respectable working-class family. He was difficult even as a child, due to his hyperactivity; at school he fought to be the centre of attention. Teachers were at a loss as to what to do with him and consequently he flunked all his exams. But by then music had taken over his life. Gravitating towards the drums, though he claimed never to have had a single lesson in his life, Keith played in local bands before his date with destiny, turning up at an early Who gig. The band was on the look out for a new drummer, and Moon stormed onto the stage yelling, 'I can play better than him,' and proceeded to pound away, practically smashing the drum kit to pieces. 'This is the man for us,' was Pete Townshend's verdict.

Moon would become infamous for destroying his drums live on stage, most famously when the Who appeared live on American television in 1967. To get a real prime-time bang at the end of 'My Generation' Moon rather overdid the pyrotechnics; nor did he tell his fellow band members what he was planning. The resulting explosion was like bloody Krakatoa, momentarily putting the network off the air and injuring Moon thanks to a flying cymbal that sliced into his arm. Townshend would claim the incident left him partially deaf in one ear.

That was also the year of the Who's first American tour and the first flowering of Moon's madcap antics, a predilection to jump off hotel balconies shitfaced into swimming pools, buying a pet piranha that he kept in bathtubs. Trouble seemed to follow Moon wherever he went. Flying out of Florida to the next gig, a roadie noticed a Ford station wagon chasing them down the runway. The driver looked thoroughly cheesed off, an observation all too frighteningly confirmed when he produced a double-barrelled shotgun and started firing at the fuselage. Once in the clouds everyone breathed a huge sigh of relief. It was a narrow escape, all thanks to Moon, who'd slept with the guy's under-age daughter the night before.

The tour continued, as did the madness. After a riotous party at a Holiday Inn, the Who were banned from every single hotel in that chain in America. Moon went potty when he heard the news and armed with several fire extinguishers attacked cars in the parking lot, spraying them with foam. Security gave chase and caught up with the loon in the pool area, where he fell in, trouble being it wasn't filled with water at the time and he landed with a fairly audible thud on the tiles at the bottom. There he lay, still effing and blinding but with trickles of blood coming out of his mouth and a front tooth no longer attached to his upper gum. He was carted off to hospital.

More than anything Moon loved to bring chaos and destruction to hotels. Doing a show in Copenhagen, Keith got to his room on the seventh floor and found he'd been lucky enough to get a water bed. He phoned up his personal roadies, 'OK, guys, what we're going to do is pick up this water bed, put it in a lift, send it up two floors and when the lift doors open on the ninth floor the thing is just going to come out and explode.' That was the plan. They managed to get it halfway out of the casing when the damn thing burst; water went everywhere, up to Moon's knees. The next thing it all disappeared, whoosh, the ceiling in the room below had given way, then the ceiling in the room below that. 'So when people say, "Keith, have you ever smashed up a hotel room?" I say, yes, well three in one foul swoop.'

There was also a fixation to superglue things in hotels, like pieces of furniture to the ceiling, or on one occasion a glass filled with his own urine. He was particularly fond of cherry bombs, lethal fireworks that were more like mini sticks of dynamite. At gas stations or eateries on the road, he'd excuse himself, go to the toilet out back, stuff one down the U-bend, dart out and then hear the explosion from the tour bus as it sped away, laughing as he saw a huge fountain of water spurt forth from where the toilet used to be.

The destruction of toilets became Moon's hotel calling card. He really was a nuisance. Blasting music from a cassette recorder in his hotel room one evening, Moon was warned he was making too much noise. Ordering the manager up to his room, he lit a cherry bomb, shoved it down the toilet and shut the bathroom door – ka-boom! As the door rocked off its hinges panting smoke, Moon proclaimed, 'That, dear boy, was noise,' then turning the cassette player back on, 'this, on the other hand, is the Who.'

Of course there was the obligatory lobbing of TVs out of windows. In Australia a manager arrived in Moon's suite with a drenched television he'd fished out of the swimming pool, demanding to know who'd done the deed. 'I did!' Moon yelled proudly, before snatching it back and throwing it over the balcony again.

Once in New York, Moon lobbed cherry bombs out of a fourteenth-floor window, watching them explode sixty feet above the morning rush hour and pedestrians scatter or hit the deck in panic. He'd also secreted cherry bombs in several ashtrays in the corridors and when they went off, the manager thought his hotel was the focal point of a terrorist attack and called the cops. When they arrived in screeching squad cars Moon lobbed out another cherry bomb which detonated above their heads. This was war and the police unit, guns drawn, swooped on the hotel, charging around the lobby and searching rooms. Moon meanwhile had changed clothes and arrived in reception looking like Noël Coward in a smoking jacket and puffing salubriously on a cigarette holder. 'I say, what's going on chaps?' he offered, going down the line shaking hands with each officer, the very picture of innocence.

Moon was not just the Who's clown prince; he was the soul and energy of the band, his manic drumming totally unique and on edge all the time. 'Keith's drumming was an expression of his personality,' said Townshend. 'And his ego and his grandiosity and his ridiculousness.'

Moon loved the materialism of fame. According to pal Alice Cooper he bought a vintage Rolls-Royce, took the back seats out and placed a throne inside with a holder for his golden goblet of brandy. He hired a chauffeur; it was safer that way. 'You would certainly never put Keith behind the wheel of a car,' said Cooper. 'That would be like inviting mass murder.' Amongst the usual sports cars, Moon also owned a milk float and a mini hovercraft, which he once parked on a railway line, disrupting train services for several hours.

And there were groupies, naturally, and Moon was an Olympic champion in that area, despite having a wife, model Kim Kerrigan. Marriage revealed a dark, violent side to Moon, especially when five winos gone. During their years together Keith broke Kim's nose on three occasions and once chased her round his country estate with a shotgun.

The madness turned even blacker in 1970 after a night of heavy drinking at a club in Hatfield. Getting into his Bentley, Keith and his party were surrounded by yobs, kicking and punching the car. Keith's chauffeur Neil Boland got out to remonstrate with them but left the car in drive and it began to roll towards the main road. Panic stricken, Keith and a friend grabbed the wheel, trying to steer it away from the mad mob, but in the mêlée Boland fell under the wheels, was dragged along the road and killed. Breathalysed, Moon was found to be many times over the limit, but the inquest absolved him of any blame. Deep down, though, Moon felt responsible and the incident haunted him for the rest of his life; some nights he would wake up screaming that he was a murderer and that he didn't deserve to live.

Home for Keith was even madder than he was: a large futuristic place in Surrey that had its own pub at the end of the drive. It was a twenty-four-hour party zone, so whatever day or time he arrived it would be full of people, music and mayhem, just like being on the road. Different music blasted out in each room, non-stop Beatles for example, or Tchaikovsky booming out of the open windows with Keith in the garden pirouetting. The guy had no clue, no idea how to lead a normal exist-ence, he needed chaos, and no one was safe. Flying into London on a 747 jetliner, he barged his way into the cockpit with his drumsticks and started playing an impromptu solo on the flight engineer's control panel. The captain ordered security to evict him immediately.

Another time he was due to meet journalists at the Who's office, but was instead downing bevies at his local tavern. An hour late, he had to come up with an excuse pretty damn quick. Finding a chemist, he bought all the tape, gauze and bandages possible and wrapped himself up like a deranged mummy. Ferried to the appointment, Moon hobbled into the office on crutches explaining how he'd been struck down by a London bus, 'Hit me right up the arse and sent me spinning across Oxford Circus.' Christ, they thought. But when the question arose about how Moon's injuries might affect an upcoming Who tour, he jumped to his feet, ripped the bandages off and did a quick tap dance on a table top. The journalists bolted, no longer wishing to be in the same room as this maniac!

Inevitably Moon's endless partying and manic behaviour became too much for Kim and she walked out. His hedonistic lifestyle also began to seriously impinge upon his career. On the Who's 1973 tour, at a gig in San Francisco, Moon took a cocktail of tranquillisers and brandy and was soon flitting in and out of consciousness. Watching backstage, the tour manager sent a doctor crawling out on his stomach to the drum kit to inject Moon in the ankle with something to keep him going. It worked for a while, but in the end he collapsed and was dragged off. Townshend asked the audience, 'Can anyone play the drums? I mean somebody good.'

Moving to LA, Moon was a live wire; friends just couldn't keep up with him. As they began to flag, praying for bed, he wanted to carry on drinking and causing chaos. He was literally 'on' all the time; if he wasn't channelling this hyperactivity through his drums he had to expel it somewhere. Indeed, much of his hotel trashing was as a result of boredom. So, too, his adoption of various guises, such as dressing in women's clothes or as Adolf Hitler, when he goose-stepped into a Jewish restaurant singing 'Deutschland Uber Alles'. He'd tell friends, 'Because I'm famous and rich I can be classed as an eccentric; if I was a nobody they'd class me as fucking mad and I'd be locked up!'

In the mid-seventies Moon found a soul mate in Oliver Reed during the making of *Tommy* (1975). It was a friendship forged in the bowels of hell. Rabble rousing was the order of the day whenever they met up, like the time in LA when they kidnapped film producer David Putnam as a prank. Putnam was leaving his hotel when he was grabbed from behind and bundled into a waiting car, which then sped off. He was terrified; Moon and Reed thought it terribly funny.

It wasn't just the playful side of Moon that appealed to Reed, he also identified with the violent streak that ran through the drummer like fat through bacon. Sitting in a pub one afternoon, Moon whispered gently into Reed's ear, 'I'm going to chuck that table through the window.' Ollie watched as the musician hoisted the hefty piece of furniture upon his shoulders and demolished the entire window frame with it.

Akin to Reed, Moon had become trapped by his hellraising image. People expected him to be mad all the time, to do bonkers things; it eventually wore him out. The drink, too, was beginning to take its toll. A typical breakfast in the Moon household consisted of eggs, bacon and bangers, plus half a bottle of Courvoisier and a bottle of champagne. The drinking terrified his new girlfriend, Swedish model Annette Walter-Lax, as she saw how it literally made him turn into another person, change his voice and alter his face. 'It was like a horror film, very, very nasty.'

Then one night he went berserk and overdosed on amphetamines. Annette ran to her neighbour, actor Larry Hagman, for help. They both returned to the house and it was a shambles: mirrors were broken, glass doors busted and there were holes in the wall. Keith's greyhound puppy had also swallowed some of the pills and crapped all over the place. 'The smell and the degradation, it was really creepy,' Hagman recalled. By this time Moon had returned to consciousness and greeted Hagman with a cheery, 'Hello, dear lad, how are you?' Larry said he was fine, 'But I hear, Keith, you're not doing too well.' 'No, I was wondering if you could take me to rehab.'

Moon spent two weeks in hospital and during that time was visited by little men from space. There was a pile of ash on the floor of his room that he told Annette had been their spacecraft, but everything was all right because the SAS were going to crash through the window and rescue him. You could say Moon was in a seriously bad way. When Annette asked the doctors what the chances of him surviving were, they told her – none.

At the close of 1977 Moon returned to live in London, a physical and mental wreck. Old friends were horrified by his bloated, almost pratical appearance, you half expected a parrot to swoop down at any moment to perch on his shoulder. Repeatedly he tried to clean up his act but fell off the wagon so many times he sported bruises.

Ironically it was the prescription drugs he'd been given to wean him off alcohol that ended up his killer. After attending a party thrown by Paul McCartney, Keith returned to his London flat where Annette found him the next morning, dead in his bed. The post mortem found thirty-two pills in his stomach, twenty-six of which were undissolved. Oliver

Reed was devastated when he heard the news of his friend's passing, but like the rest of the planet couldn't have been very surprised.

JIM MORRISON (1943–1971: Singer/Poet)

Jim Morrison was one of the most charismatic frontmen in rock music history and one of the most drunkenly debauched, he still holds the record for downing mai tais (a rum-based cocktail) in a Honolulu bar – thirty-two in one evening. He was a master at holding his liquor; half a dozen boilermakers would have no effect on him.

Morrison loved to drink, it was that simple. For him it was the thrill of not being fully in control. 'It's like gambling,' he once said. 'You go out for a night of drinking and you don't know where you're going to end up the next day. It could work out good or it could be disastrous. It's like the throw of the dice.'

He was born in Melbourne, Florida, his father a conservative no-nonsense naval officer who'd rise eventually to the rank of admiral. Morrison's early life involved near constant resettlement to different military bases, never able to put down roots or form lasting friendships. He was nevertheless a dutiful and respectful child who excelled at school.

Things changed as he reached adolescence and discovered booze, which fed a burgeoning rebellion first towards his father then authority in general. Most nights while attending college he drank and returned home late. In the college library one afternoon after spending lunch getting drunk Morrison was bursting for a piss so he ducked behind some bookshelves and just let flow. Then in Tallahassee, Florida, he was arrested for stealing a police helmet from a parked squad car and for being drunk and disorderly.

Morrison's father fully expected his son to pursue a career in the military and took it as a personal affront when Jim decided to move to Los Angeles and enrol in UCLA's film school. Father and son never spoke to one another again, and for years Jim propagated the fantasy that his parents were dead. In his mind they were.

After graduation Morrison headed for the bohemian community of artists and musicians who hung around the LA suburb of Venice Beach. Spending his days drinking, smoking dope and writing poetry, he ran into a former UCLA colleague Ray Manzarek, a keyboardist in a small local rock band. Impressed with Morrison's poems, Manzarek wanted to put them to music and together they formed a band, the Doors. For a while they played regular shows at the Whisky A Go Go, until Morrison got them fired by screaming during a set that he wanted to kill his father and have sex with his mother.

Even in the Doors' early days Morrison had a dangerous quality about him which gave his music and image an edge. His bold, sexually aggressive live performances made the Doors stand out from the hippie-love shit their contemporaries were all spouting and got them signed to a major record label, Elektra; in 1967 the single 'Light My Fire' shot them into the stratosphere. By the release of their second album, *Strange Days*, the Doors, with their blend of blues and rock tinged with psychedelia, had become one of the most popular bands in the United States.

Almost as if he was spitting in the face of his own popularity, Morrison courted controversy wherever he could. In December 1967 during a show in Connecticut he was arrested for attempting to incite a riot by telling the crowd that the police had sprayed him with mace backstage. When someone started hurling abuse at him during another gig Morrison spoke into the microphone, 'You know, sometimes I wish this weren't a democracy, because if it wasn't we could take this guy out somewhere and beat the shit out of him.'

This unpredictability was even more explosive off stage. Morrison was a 'try anything once and hope it doesn't kill me' kind of guy. At Hollywood parties there'd be a candy bowl full of pills and Morrison would take a handful, not knowing what the hell they were, and wash them all down with Jack Daniel's. Still very much into the heavy drug scene of late-sixties California, Morrison's preferred poison was booze, it was his way of coping with the fame and adulation, to pour a bottle of whisky down his neck. His tolerance was incredible, he could drink all night and remain calm and coherent, but then at a moment's notice something would snap inside and he'd become a crazed loon. There was the time he was having drinks with a girlfriend and without provocation leaned across the table and slapped her hard across the face. 'He had those angels and demons inside of him fighting for control,' recalled Manzarek. 'And you could never be sure whether the devil or the angel was going to come out.'

And when that 'devil' was out it wanted destruction, it wanted chaos. Attending a Jimi Hendrix gig, Morrison got loaded and crawled onto the stage, wrapping his arms around the guitarist's knees and hollering, 'I wanna suck your cock.' Hendrix continued to play but Morrison wouldn't let go. Watching in the wings was an equally bushwhacked Janis Joplin, who staggered into the spotlight clutching a bottle in one hand and a glass she was drinking from in the other. She cracked the bottle over Morrison's head and then poured her drink over him. Morrison leaped at her, bundling the songstress to the floor, Hendrix swiftly got into the act and the three rock gods were soon writhing around in an embarrassing heap.

Queuing up to get into a club in Vegas one night, Morrison provocatively pretended to smoke a joint in front of security guards. One of them approached the singer and smashed him in the face with a club; Morrison never flinched, just smiled and carried on smoking. Another blow rained down on him, then another and another. Blood covering his face, Morrison still didn't give a shit. When the police arrived it was Morrison who was hauled away. 'You chicken-shit pigs,' he yelled at them as he was thrown into the back of a patrol car. 'You redneck stupid bastards.' At the station the officers made Morrison strip in full view of office workers, including women, and then doused him with roach powder before throwing him in the cells.

Everyone around Jim knew he was killing himself with booze and tried to get him to stop, even hiring professionals and bodyguards to keep him out of trouble; Morrison would instead take them out and get them all drunk. By 1968 it was obvious Morrison was an alcoholic; he knew as much but saw it all as an adventure, part of his artistic make-up. 'I'm not a musician, I'm a poet,' he liked to say. 'And I'm Irish. The drug of Irish poetry is alcohol.' The drinking exploits of literary figures like Hemingway and Fitzgerald also inspired him and pushed him on.

Things changed, however, when Morrison's drinking habits began to affect the band.

He started showing up for recording sessions and gigs wasted, his performances suffering as a consequence. At one concert in Seattle he was so drunk there were gaps of inebriated silence of up to ten minutes between songs. Other times the band would launch into a number and Morrison would just ignore them. In Chicago he incited the audience to rampage, which they duly did, battling with police and storming the stage, wrecking the band's equipment. Morrison and his colleagues had to escape through a back entrance.

If anything by late 1968 Morrison's behaviour was getting even odder. He'd taken to vomiting or urinating in public without any warning, and throwing himself out of moving cars. He'd coax friends to drive him up into the Hollywood hills at high speed so he could leap out onto the hard tarmac.

As always with Morrison the madness was tinged with an element of anti-establishment hatred. One night, driving without a licence and dead drunk, he smashed into an occupied patrol car. Is it any wonder the FBI were monitoring his activities? Morrison's most notorious brush with the law occurred in March 1969 when he was arrested for exposing himself on stage at a concert in Miami and charged with lewd behaviour, indecent exposure, public drunkenness and feigning acts of masturbation and fellatio. When a policeman asked whether he'd actually whipped his dick out in front of America's teenagers Morrison replied, 'I don't remember, I was too drunk.'

These lapses of memory, while not altogether unsurprising, were becoming worrying. Dropped off at a friend's home, Morrison beat drunkenly on the door but no one answered so he slipped into a gentle coma on the doorstep. He was roused an hour later by cops who'd arrived to arrest him for public drunkenness. The home actually belonged to a sixty-eight-year-old woman who in a terrified state had called the police about a mad intruder.

Soon after the recording of the album *LA Woman* Morrison quit the Doors and the showbiz circus he'd always hated and sought refuge in Paris, determined to become a serious poet and also to put a halt to his drinking. In recent months he'd put on weight, his features had become pasty and he'd grown a scruffy beard, not so much the Lizard King as Burger King.

If anything he drank even more in Paris, living on a diet of whisky and scribbling repeatedly in his notebook the phrase 'God help me.' He seemed to be slipping into a self-dug grave. When Hendrix and Janis Joplin died within weeks of each other, Morrison told his friends, 'You're drinking with No. 3.' He began succumbing to respiratory problems, coughing up blood; though he was only twenty-seven he seemed to be suffering the illnesses of a man several times his age.

After a night of full-on drinking Morrison was found dead in his bathtub in the Parisian apartment he shared with his long-time partner Pamela Courson. Over the years conspiracy theories have been rife as to whether the singer drank himself to death or if it was a heroin overdose that brought on the massive heart attack that killed him. Whatever, his corpse was never flown home but stayed in Paris, buried in Père Lachaise Cemetery, where to this day it remains one of the city's most visited tourist attractions.

N

ROBERT NEWTON (1905–1956: Actor)

Bobbie was well known in the film industry for his devotion to any form of liquid refreshment and so was rather wearily regarded by producers and directors, despite his not inconsiderable talent. His antics were many, such as the time he got so smashed that he arrived for work on the wrong movie set. The director was somewhat bemused but managed to utilise the star in four scenes before he was hauled off by his rightful employers. When he was performing at London's St James's Theatre the curtain failed to rise one evening and the audience grew restless and there began the inevitable rumble of slow hand claps. At last the fabric moved to reveal the sozzled figure of Robert Newton. Silence fell upon the auditorium. 'Ladies and gentlemen,' he bellowed. 'The reason this curtain has so far not risen is because the stage manager has the fucking impertinence to suggest that I am pissed.'

Most famous for his portrayal of Long John Silver in Disney's *Treasure Island* (1950), the problem with Newton was keeping the booze away from him. He was a dedicated professional, but somehow always managed to get hold of a drop of something and thus was never quite as fluent in his delivery of lines. 'But that was all part of his charm,' says Michael Anderson, who directed Newton twice. 'That was his performance, that's what he did that made him so great. He was famous for occasionally pronouncing long "aghhhs" in a scene and it was when he couldn't remember a line. He'd look up at the ceiling and go, "Well, I, er, aghhh." He was thinking of the next line. It became a trademark.'

Born in Dorset into an artistic household, his mother was a writer, his father a painter, Newton wanted to act from an early age and worked in the fertile mines of repertory theatre before finding West End success. He was Horatio to Laurence Olivier's Hamlet at the Old Vic, and also appeared on stage with Ivor Novello and performed in Noël Coward's *Private Lives* on Broadway.

Between his stage triumphs, Newton was carving out an interesting career as a film character actor. Not even the outbreak of the Second World War got in the way. Seeing service aboard a minesweeper in the Royal Navy, Newton was occasionally granted special dispensation to work on select films, notably the patriotic *This Happy Breed* (1944) for David Lean. Newton was a strange choice for Lean, known for his puritanical attitude towards drinking. Indeed it was written into Newton's contract that if he so much as touched a single drop of booze during filming he would forfeit his entire salary. Newton crossed his fingers and signed on, and held true to his pledge – until near the end of shooting.

One late afternoon Newton's co-star John Mills was mowing the front lawn at his cottage in Denham village when some distance away he spied a manic figure wavering from side to side. 'Look at that character,' Mills called to his wife. 'He's plastered, and the pubs aren't open yet.' As the manifestation drew closer the full horror of it dawned on Mills: it was Bobbie. 'Hallo there, my hearties, my darlings,' he shouted. 'I've come to visit you.'

Now, Lean lived not fifty yards away and it would surely have been curtains for Newton if word reached the director of his condition. Quickly Mills yanked Newton inside and proceeded to pour black coffee down his neck. At one point he escaped into the back garden and was found with the Millses' young daughter Juliet, who watched wide-eyed as this strange creature plunged his hands into his pockets and threw handfuls of silver and notes across the lawn, yelling at the top of his voice, 'Treasure trove, Juliet, treasure trove.'

After feeding him, Mills drove Newton back home and left him in a coma on his sofa, praying that all would be well the next morning at the studio. It was an early call and as Mills reclined in the make-up chair Newton arrived, looking like shit, but thankfully sober. 'How do you feel, Bobbie?' Mills asked.

'Never felt worse, old darling, but I'll survive.'

That evening a case of champagne arrived at the Millses' cottage with a note. It read: DARLING CHUMS, A FRIEND IN NEED ETC. LOVE ROBERT.

Newton fell off the wagon even more loudly a few days later, not showing up for work in the morning because he was in a cell at Bow Street police station after a hectic night's entertainment that included being thrown out of a restaurant after calling the homosexual director Anthony Asquith 'the first lady of the English screen' and getting into a scuffle with police, resulting in a rather nasty cut on his face courtesy of a truncheon. Lean agreed to his being bailed.

Actually Lean grew extremely fond of Bobbie and used him again as the brutal yob Bill Sykes in Oliver Twist (1948), extracting from him a dark, almost biblically menacing performance. But too often the drink got in the way. It was usually in the afternoons, after lunch, when Newton could be a bit of a problem. If he arrived on the set and wasn't up to scratch, which occurred a few times, Lean would say, 'Bobbie, I think we'll abandon today; you go off home and we'll carry on tomorrow.' When these occurrences increased in number Lean read the Riot Act. 'And by the end Bobbie respected what David had done, that he knew his weakness,' says cameraman Oswald Morris. 'And there were very few directors who had the patience or the ability to handle Bobbie. But if you could get him to do it correctly, he was wonderful.' Unchecked, Newton had a natural proclivity to chew any scenery going.

Sadly there weren't many Leans around and Newton's unreliability and reputation for carousing was beginning to lose him work. But to up-and-coming actors like Richard Burton he was 'King Lush' and many tried hard to emulate or plain keep up with him. One of Burton's earliest films, Waterfront (1950), co-starred Newton, who often gave the eager youngster a lift to the studio in his battered old Bentley. One morning Burton arrived to see Newton unusually the worse for wear, brandy flask in hand and unshaven. It was deep winter and the car refused to start. Newton handed Burton his flask, went back into the house and returned with a horsewhip and began laying into the bonnet Basil Fawlty-style. The ignition was tried again, this time with success.

Drinking all the way to Pinewood, they arrived predictably late.

Newton's dresser was hurrying him along with his costume when the bell rang for the start of filming. Newton dashed for the set, his dresser trailing behind, desperately trying to point out the fact that he wasn't wearing his trousers or indeed any underpants. The set was awash with technicians and actors as Newton arrived. 'Oh, sir, you can't go on like that,' the dresser yelped. 'And why not?' queried Newton. 'Because there's something missing, sir.' 'Missing!' Newton bellowed before looking down at the awful evidence. 'Thank you for pointing it out. Very grateful,' Newton deftly lifted his shirt. 'Make up!'

Hollywood beckoned next, though one wonders if the moguls really knew what they were letting themselves in for. They soon found out as Newton's craving for alcohol knew no sane bounds. 'It was dreadfully sad to see such a glowing talent being destroyed,' said David Niven. 'We all tried hard to stop the rot.' But he was incorrigible. Niven and Bobbie made a film together, *Soldiers Three* (1951), where Newton's time keeping was not of the best: he'd arrive on set just in time for the first shot still in his pyjamas.

The routine was always the same, at the end of each day Newton would corner Niven before he had a chance to leave. 'Dear fellow, a little light refreshment this evening. A tiny tipple on your way home to the old ball and chain.' Niven always made his excuses but come the final day of shooting felt obliged to give in. 'I know a little bistro, dear fellow,' said Newton, his eyes twinkling mischievously. 'It's just around the corner – come, let us away.' The bistro turned out to be thirty-three miles away and an utter dive, occupied by hard-bitten fishermen who looked as if they'd failed the audition for a company touring *Moby Dick*. They looked disapprovingly as the two actors walked in, still dressed in their film costumes of mustachioed members of Queen Victoria's army in India.

Several times during the journey Niven had informed his friend that he'd no money on him. 'My treat, old cock,' said Bobbie. 'I'm loaded with the good stuff.' A rather sullen and worryingly large in stature barman arrived and for the next half hour Bobbie got them in. Then in the midst of discussing hill farming in Wales, Newton spun round on his chair to face this room of Ahabs and burst into verse:

Love in my bosome like a bee,
Doth sucke his sweete:
Now with his wings he playes with me,
Now with his feete . . . !!!

This recital was met with such alarm by the fishermen that they seemed visibly anxious about what might happen next. 'Hey, you, cut that out, willya,' said the barman.

Not a bit of it. Shakespeare was next on the agenda for Bobbie, a choice slab of *Antony and Cleopatra* which didn't go down well either and the barman, none too subtly, told these pair of pansies where to go and how they could get there. Far from being put off, Newton saw such shallow rebuttals as a challenge; he'd win these scoundrels over yet. 'David, I shall deliver to this scum, the Gettysburg Address.' Up and down the bar he strode, giving it full belt, and finishing to a resounding silence.

'Let's go, Bobbie,' pleaded Niven.

'Of course, dear fellow. Do you have any money?'

'No, I told you forty times that I haven't.'

'Ah,' said Newton, genuine concern for the first time appearing on his craggy features. 'We have a tricky situation here.'

Speedily Bobbie came up with a plan; Niven would dash outside to prepare the getaway car while he'd stay to placate the barman for as long as possible. Revving the engine, Niven yelled for Bobbie to get the hell out. Slowly he edged backwards, then at the doorway announced, 'Barman, dear, just put it on my mother's charge account at Harrods.'

Appearing in *The Desert Rats* (1953), Newton shared some scenes with Richard Burton. One weekend they decided to cross the border into Mexico for a night of carousing. Because American citizens were allowed in without visas, unlike Brits, both men assumed American accents. 'We became absolutely paralysed with tequila,' recalled Burton. 'And on the way back we were so stoned that we completely forgot about our accents, and we landed in the pokey for the night.'

As Newton's behaviour grew more erratic fewer directors were willing to take a chance hiring him, causing depression and yet more drinking.

He'd sit up in Bogart's old house on Benedict Canyon waiting for the phone to ring getting pixillated or disappear for days indulging in Herculean benders. Like most drunks, Newton could be absorbing, entertaining company with just the right amount on board, but once he took that one drink too many, 'he changed gear and became anything from unpredictable to a downright menace', according to Niven. Newton's wives, all four of them, and friends tried loyally and desperately to help him. He'd listen, hell he often agreed with them, and there were periods when Newton was actually sober, but then something inside went off and he'd be crawling back inside the nearest bottle.

In 1956 Michael Anderson came up with the inspired notion of casting Newton as Mr Fix, the Scotland Yard detective who chases Phileas Fogg *Around the World in Eighty Days*, but producer Mike Todd was weary and sought his star David Niven's advice.

'Bobbie is a great friend of mine,' said the actor, 'but he does drink a lot these days.' It was a gentle warning, but Todd decided on a meeting with Newton the next day at his office, with Niven in attendance.

'For Christ's sake, Mike, don't tell him I said anything,' begged Niven. 'He'll never forgive me.'

When Newton walked in it was obvious he and a case of Scotch had been bosom buddies for the last couple of days.

'Ever heard of Jules Verne?' asked Todd.

'Ah, dear fellow,' said Newton, 'what a scribe!'

'We're making a movie of *Around the World in Eighty Days*.'

'A glorious piece, old cock.'

'How'd you like to play Mr Fix?'

Bobbie's face changed to one of pure delight. 'Do I understand you are offering it to me, dear boy?'

'I might,' said Todd, then, looking over at a suitably penitent Niven, 'but your pal here says you're a lush.'

'Aah!' said Newton. 'My pal Niven is a master of the understatement.'

Newton was hired on the spot, but not before agreeing to go on the wagon for the duration of shooting, something he found remarkably easy to do, confessing to Niven one day that his doctor had warned him just one more booze bender could finish him off. The two old friends sometimes went fishing on their free days, Niven secretively bringing along with him a bottle of bourbon. Newton spied it one day but didn't admonish Niven for his impropriety, instead asked, 'Just pass me the cork from time to time so I may sniff it. I really do love the stuff, dear boy.'

True to his word, Newton kept off the sauce. 'But when the picture was over,' says Anderson, 'he went on a massive binge and I think it killed him.' Two weeks after the picture was finished Niven and Newton were required for a day's additional shooting. Niven was in make-up when he heard a roar outside in the corridor. 'Once more unto the breach . . .' It could only be Bobbie. Niven was truly alarmed at the state he was in, his face blotched and puffy, all life seemed to have drained from his eyes. Then tears appeared. 'Don't chide me, dear fellow, please don't chide me.' He was dead not very long afterwards from a heart attack, while his wife cradled him in her arms. 'He was a very dear man,' friend Deborah Kerr recalled. 'It was a great tragedy that in the end he destroyed himself through his increasing dependence on alcohol.'

Michael Anderson's abiding memory of Newton was driving back home to Denham village one Christmas Eve and seeing this figure ahead in the road. 'He was dressed in pyjamas and holding a donkey and for a minute I thought, who is that, and it was Robert Newton. I stopped and said, Bobbie, what are you doing, and he said, this little fellow has nowhere to go for Christmas. He was taking this donkey home with him, putting him in his stable. I think he'd had a few drinks.'

O

PETER O'TOOLE (b. 1932: Actor)

Few have loved the social life of being a drinker more than Peter O'Toole, propping up bars in Dublin or London, nattering with saloon-bar poets and philosophers, putting the world to rights. 'But I don't really know what I get out of it,' he once pondered. 'What does anyone get out of being drunk? It's an anaesthetic. It diminishes the pain.'

But amid the gaiety and natural eccentricity which drink merely compounded, there was an undercurrent of violence to O'Toole's boozing. In Paris once he was returning to his hotel after a night on the town and saw two policemen roughing up a prostitute. Outraged, O'Toole was in a nightclub a few nights later when he noticed another policeman, not connected to the incident, but a policeman all the same, and under the cover of a packed dance floor took the opportunity to exact revenge. 'By the time I'd finished with him I don't think he was in any condition to whack any poor old whore around the head for a night or two.'

He was born in Connemara, Ireland, to a mother with a gentle soul who instilled into him a strong sense of literature, and a feckless, corked-up father who was an off-course bookie, illegal before the war. More than once – well quite often, actually – he'd miscalculate the odds and not have enough money to pay off his winning customers, so grabbing his son he'd quickly bugger off through the shrubbery. To grow up with a father who lived so recklessly inevitably led to O'Toole approaching life in a similarly happy-go-lucky way.

Leaving school with no qualifications, O'Toole nevertheless managed to get a job as a reporter on a local newspaper, 'but I soon found out that, rather than chronicling events, I wanted to be the event'. After national service he took up acting and, appearing at the Bristol Old Vic, struck up a friendship with fellow down-at-heel thespian Richard Harris. Cue countless booze marathons. After one mighty bender they returned to Harris's miserable bed-sit totally rat-arsed and starving hungry. In the cupboards there was nothing to be found, but in the fridge was a solitary pork chop; ancient it was, clearly it had been there a long time. They smelled it, looked at it, and thought better of it, so threw it through a window and went to bed. Came the morning they left the squat and under the window from which they'd thrown this pork chop there was a dead dog.

It was at Stratford where O'Toole's reputation as a hellraiser was sealed. At one after-show party he held court on stage sitting on a throne, sustained by two pedal bins on either side of him, one full of beer, the other of hard liquor, into which he would alternately scoop two pint mugs. At another party ex-drama-school chum Roy Kinnear watched O'Toole down a bottle of whisky without pausing for breath. The local boozer in Stratford was the Dirty Duck, where O'Toole broke the house record by downing a yard of ale (that's two and a half pints) in forty seconds. 'You only do that kind of lunacy because there's nothing else to do.' Another night he got so butt wasted on home-made mead he was arrested at three in the morning for harassing a building. In the morning he told the magistrate, 'I felt like singing and began to woo an insurance office.'

Appearing on the West End stage in *The Long and the Short and the Tall*, a play about a bunch of misfit soldiers in the Second World War, O'Toole's routine was to drink in a nearby pub prior to curtain up, and sometimes with only minutes to spare stampede into the theatre, get changed and bound into his first scene. O'Toole's understudy would stew in suspense backstage as to whether O'Toole would make it from the pub in time – his name was Michael Caine. One Saturday night O'Toole invited Caine to a restaurant he knew. Eating a plate of egg and chips was the last thing Caine remembered until he woke up in broad daylight in a strange flat with even stranger looking women. 'What time is it?' he enquired. 'Never mind what time it is,' answered O'Toole. 'What

Errol Flynn lived life to the full, brawling, boozing and womanising because he hated the alternative – mediocrity. Banned by his studio from drinking, Errol took to injecting oranges with vodka and slyly tucking into the spiked fruit between set-ups.

A rebel from day one, when Robert Mitchum was persuaded by his family to enter the Betty Ford clinic in a bid to quit drinking, he was asked when he came out what he'd learnt. 'More ice,' Mitchum replied sardonically.

'Not since Attila the Hun swept across Europe leaving 500 years of total blackness has there been a man like Lee Marvin,' said one of the star's exasperated directors Joshua Logan.

Richard Burton enjoyed boasting that he could drink any man under the table, but not necessarily his wife Elizabeth Taylor, whose own capacity for booze was terrifying. Their volatile marriage contained more left hooks than an Ali–Frazier fight.

Keith Moon took the destruction of hotel rooms to the level of high art, blowing doors off their hinges and detonating cherry bombs in toilets. He also took to jumping off balconies into swimming pools while shitfaced.

Often drunk on stage, Jim Morrison was arrested once for whipping out his cock in front of a teenage audience. He'd also turn up wasted for recording sessions and incite crowds to riot.

Peter Langan was the *enfant terrible* of gastronomy. Drinking six bottles of champagne a day he often fell flat on his face in his restaurant and went to sleep amid the diners.

Paul Gascoigne was a born prankster. His idea of ribald good humour was secreting cat shit into mince pies before serving them up to unsuspecting chums and running his best mate over in his car.

On a state visit to Washington Boris Yeltsin almost sparked an international incident when secret service agents found him outside the White House naked, except for his underpants, trying to hail a taxi to go and fetch some pizza.

George Brown's time in government was openly lampooned by *Private Eye* who created the euphemism 'tired and emotional' to describe his regular condition. Cabinet colleague Barbara Castle recalled that Brown got slaughtered on the smell of a cork alone.

Francis Bacon's boozing wa staggering and he seemed indestruc tible and generally averse to bodil disasters. He once fell down th stairs of a pub and knocked hi right eye half out of its socke – he merely pushed it back in

A walking, talking object lesson in dissolution, Jeffrey Bernard was a chaotic drinker whose stomping ground was the seedy drinking dens of Soho, and beyond. He once spectacularly managed to vomit on the Queen Mother at Ascot.

fucking day is it?' It was five o'clock on Monday afternoon; they'd just a few hours to get to the theatre. Arriving just in time, the stage manager informed them they'd been banned for life by the restaurant manager. 'What for?' asked Caine. 'Never ask what you did,' said O'Toole. 'It's better not to know.' Ah, the voice of experience. After that Caine made a point of never going out on the booze with O'Toole again.

O'Toole did make firm friends with Peter Finch when they appeared in Disney's *Kidnapped* (1959) together and their piss-ups were mighty affairs. One time they indulged in a pub crawl of Irish hostelries but the landlord in their final port of call refused to serve them because it was after closing time. Both stars decided that the only course of action was to buy the pub, so they wrote out a cheque for it on the spot. The following morning after realising what they'd done the pair rushed back to the scene of the crime. Luckily the landlord hadn't cashed the cheque yet and disaster was averted. O'Toole and Finch remained on friendly terms with the pub owner and when he died his wife invited them to his funeral. Both kneeled at the graveside as the coffin was slowly lowered in, sobbing noisily. When Finch turned away, unable to stand it any more, O'Toole saw his friend's face change from a look of sorrow to one of total astonishment. They were at the wrong funeral. Their friend was being buried a hundred yards away.

It was *Lawrence of Arabia* (1962) that propelled O'Toole to stardom and he took his own particular brand of madcap hellraising onto the world stage. There were brawls with paparazzi in Rome and a fist fight with a French count in a restaurant. O'Toole's social life was often in danger of eclipsing his talent. 'I was silly and young and drunken and making a complete clown of myself. But I did quite enjoy the days when one went for a beer at one's local in Paris and woke up in Corsica.'

Filming *The Lion in Winter* (1968), co-star Katharine Hepburn was required to ride along a lake on a barge. O'Toole paddled out towards her to talk about the scene but caught his finger between both vessels. 'Bloody agony it was, took the top right off.' There were no doctors around so O'Toole carried the tip back to shore, dipped it into a glass of brandy for safe keeping and then stuffed it back on, wrapping it in a poultice. Three weeks later he unwrapped the bandages and there it was, all crooked and bent and frankly disgusting. 'I'd put it back the wrong way, probably because of the brandy which I drank.' Professional medical treatment ultimately remedied the situation.

There was always something bizarre or plain bonkers going on when O'Toole was around. Making *Murphy's War* (1971) in Venezuela, O'Toole encountered a missionary called Hank and went back to his shack for a drink. Hank grabbed a bottle that had a worm floating in its neck. 'I'm going to lock all the doors now,' Hank said after they'd shared a couple of swigs. 'Because funny things happen with this stuff, it's mescal.' O'Toole had never tried mescal before, nor would he ever forget the experience. It was near dawn when O'Toole staggered back to his cabin and suddenly sensed that he wasn't alone. 'I turned around and looked; and it was me – only very small. It didn't disturb me in any way. We kept each other company for about twenty-four hours.'

In 1975 O'Toole had the shock of his life. An abdominal irregularity he'd been carrying for years and persistently ignored finally erupted and he was rushed to hospital. Incapable of taking solid food, pure water had to be fed down a pipe directly into his stomach. Tests proved nothing so it was decided to carry out exploratory surgery. Something very wrong was going on inside O'Toole's digestive system and what they found caused such alarm that a major operation was hurriedly performed. Several yards of intestinal tubing were removed, leaving an eight-inch scar.

On that operating table O'Toole came as close to dying as you can do without actually snuffing it. Stomach problems had been the bane of O'Toole's life since the age of nineteen. No one really knew what was wrong with him and so he drank sometimes just to ease the pain: 'Madame Bottle, the great anaesthetic.' But no more. There was now so little of his digestive system left that any amount of alcohol would be fatal to him. It was proven on the set of *My Favorite Year* (1982), where his character woke up in bed with a stewardess and was required to down one of those mini airline-size bottles of Scotch. A whole case of little bottles had been prepared, each one emptied of liquor, washed, filled with coloured water then resealed. Somehow a real bottle slipped through and when O'Toole took a swig it made him so ill he had to leave the set for several hours.

By the nineties booze was back in his life, but only in moderation. When in 2002 O'Toole showed up at the Oscars to receive a lifetime achievement award he threatened to leave the ceremony because of the show's strict no-alcohol rules. O'Toole arrived in the green room and sauntered over to the bar to ask for a drink. 'We have lemon juice, apple juice, still or sparkling,' said the barman. O'Toole gazed at him with alarm. 'No, I want a drink.' The barman shook his head. 'No alcohol, sir.' O'Toole's face went ashen. 'All right, I'm fucking off.' One of the lackeys managed to stop him in time and eventually some vodka was smuggled in. 'I still like a little drink,' he told the press.

O'Toole never once regretted the mistakes in life that he'd made, the boozing that almost killed him. And like his good friend Richard Burton, the accusation has been raised more than once that O'Toole squandered his genius for Hollywood fame and the bottle. When a reporter asked him to counter such claims he replied. 'Assholes!'

Like his fellow hellraisers Harris and Burton, O'Toole never drank out of desperation or loneliness or some psychological problem. 'We weren't all brooding, introspective, addicted lunatics. And we weren't solitary, boring drinkers, sipping vodka alone in a room. No, no, no: we went out on the town, baby, and we did our drinking in public. We had fun!'

OZZY OSBOURNE (b. 1948: Musician)

He's the Queen Mother of heavy metal, but in his prime Ozzy Osbourne was one of the most self-destructive individuals in the music business, which is saying something. He was a self-confessed madman, unable to do anything in moderation: if it was booze, he had to drink the place dry; if it was drugs, he'd take anything and everything, spending $1,000 a week on drugs at one point and overdosing about a dozen times. Ozzy was not a stable person at all.

Take the time in Memphis, 1974; Ozzy woke after a hectic night drinking to find himself in the middle of a busy freeway, cars racing past him from all directions. How he got there, fuck knows, he'd stopped asking himself stupid questions like that years before. Staggering over to a nearby parked car, he started offloading about a gallon of Hennessey five-star brandy, only to realise too late it was a police car. 'This lady cop went apeshit watching this drunken Limey pissing on her wheel.'

He was born in Birmingham to grinding poverty, one of six children, his dad scarcely making ends meet working night shifts in a steel plant. Hopeless at school, discovering years later he suffered from dyslexia, Ozzy took on the mantle of class clown, making himself popular by making people laugh at his wild antics.

From the age of twelve Ozzy was taken into the pub by his dad and sat down with a half pint of shandy. The taste didn't find favour with him at all, but the effect it had on his senses got him hooked. Later drink was an escape route from the sheer drudgery of shit jobs like plumber's assistant and slaughterhouse attendant. Fed up with his lot, Ozzy turned to crime, petty theft and burglary, but he was no Raffles and ended up doing a stretch in the nick, where he famously tattooed the letters O-Z-Z-Y across his left knuckles using a sewing needle and graphite.

Heading down a self-destructive path, Ozzy found a better way of venting his frustration – rock music. 'You could go round Europe in a van with your best mates, drinking beer, smoking dope and screwing chicks.' Music probably saved Ozzy from more stretches in prison, since he didn't want to get a regular job, nor conform to any system. Rock 'n' roll does have this outlaw factor; you can pretty much do what you want.

Hooking up with local band Black Sabbath, Ozzy found himself amongst some of the early pioneers of a new type of sound: heavy metal. Recording their first album in 1970, a proud Ozzy played it to his parents. They listened politely and afterwards his dad pondered it for a while and then asked, 'You sure you're only on the occasional beer?' By then, of course, Ozzy had added drugs to his addiction portfolio: dope, pills and later cocaine. He was starting to come off the rails. In Hamburg, he painted his face purple for a concert, just for effect, not realising it was permanent paint. 'I had to walk around Hamburg for the next three days with a purple head!'

After two more albums and a hit single 'Paranoid', their anthem, Sabbath were huge and on a rollercoaster ride of booze, drugs and sex, but they were disintegrating fast. Everyone was living in isolation away from other band mates, locked in their private world of debauchery. Ozzy's reckless behaviour was seen as the main culprit in the band's slide into disharmony. He'd certainly been sending his wife Thelma round the bend. She'd already carted him off once to a mental hospital after finding him driving the family car round and round in circles in a field all night. Worse was to come. Ozzy was now spending entire days down the pub, and snorting cocaine to keep him going. It got to the point where he couldn't eat, sleep or control his bodily functions. 'That's when I decided I was definitely going fucking mad.' One afternoon, drugged up to the eyeballs, he came back home and killed the family cats, all seventeen of them. 'I went crazy and shot them all. My wife found me under the piano holding a shotgun in one hand and a knife in the other.'

It was obvious that Ozzy was not a well individual; even so he refused medical intervention. Sabbath, though, had had enough and sacked him in 1978. Devastated, Ozzy locked himself away in a dingy Los Angeles hotel room and drank, snorted and generally pigged out for weeks. He was dragged kicking and screaming out of this self-inflicted hell-hole by one of the industry's ballsiest women, Sharon Arden, daughter of Sabbath's original manager Don Arden. Recognising Ozzy's potential as a solo artist she took over his business affairs, as well as becoming his wife in 1982.

Another thing Sharon picked up on almost immediately was the fact that Ozzy was a chronic alcoholic, one day loving and romantic, the next day a wild man, unrecognisable. It was the classic Jekyll and Hyde syndrome. 'Nobody under the influence of alcohol is the same person, otherwise you wouldn't fucking take it,' says Ozzy. 'If you were the same person, why waste your time pouring vats of fucking booze down your throat? You take it to change, but I didn't like the person I was changing into, yet I couldn't stand living sober.'

Sharon urged him to try the Betty Ford clinic. 'They teach you to drink properly, Ozzy,' meaning in moderation. So befuddled was Ozzy's brain at the time that he envisaged the place as having a bar with people in bow ties and evening jackets drinking glasses of Martini with olives. Once inside he approached Betty Ford herself, asking, 'When do we start the lessons?' She looked baffled and replied: 'You're definitely in the right place.'

Once out, Ozzy gleefully reported to the world, 'Sobriety fucking sucks!' and was back soon to his manic best. Signing with CBS Records in Los Angeles, Ozzy was determined to make an impression. He certainly did that. In the limo going to the meeting Sharon presented him with two doves that he was to release into the air as he walked into the board room, then shout 'rock 'n' roll' and give the peace sign. But after drinking a bottle and a half of Courvoisier the concept got a little muddled and instead he grabbed one out of his pocket and bit its head off, spitting it out in a heap of feathers and blood to the revulsion and stricken terror of the record executives. It was several years before he was allowed back in the building.

Ozzy definitely had something against record company executives. Dining with a group of them at a fancy restaurant, Ozzy jumped up onto the table, kissed one of them full on the lips, unzipped his pants and urinated into a carafe of wine.

In 1982 Ozzy hit America on tour; it was an invasion only marginally less destructive than Pearl Harbor. Every night Ozzy would conduct the mock hanging of a midget and pelt his audience with pig intestines and calves' livers. In turn the audience started throwing stuff back. In Des Moines a fan threw something on stage that Ozzy instinctively grabbed hold of and thinking it a plastic toy bit off the head, and then thought, 'Fuck me!!' It was flapping. It was a live bat. There was this warm, gungy type liquid oozing down his throat; he felt the head in his mouth twitch. 'Oh, fuck me. I didn't just go and eat a fucking bat.' Immediately after the concert he was rushed to hospital for a series of painful rabies shots in his arse. When asked what bat tasted like Ozzy replied, 'I can't even remember. I was so full of fucking cognac.'

Things got worse, yes that's right, worse than biting the head off a nocturnal mammal, when the tour arrived in San Antonio, Texas. In an attempt to stop her husband drinking himself into oblivion Sharon took away all his clothes, leaving him stranded in his hotel room in his underwear. Desperate for a drink, Ozzy slipped on one of his wife's dresses and was gone, looking for the nearest bar. After drinking vodka all morning Ozzy wandered down the high street until he was standing before a familiar building, it was the Alamo. Asking someone to take his picture, just like any other tourist, Ozzy suddenly felt a desperate urge to urinate. Not giving a stuff for protocol, Ozzy pulled up the dress and in full glare of outraged visitors pissed like a horse all over the cherished monument. It wasn't long before a squad car pulled up. 'Mister,' said a ranger. 'When you piss over the Alamo, you piss over the state of Texas. You'd be arrested if you pissed on the gates of Buckingham Palace, wouldn't you?' Ozzy smiled. 'I know. I did, and I was.'

Public urination seems to play an important role in the Ozzy universe. Playing a gig with Def Leppard, Ozzy wandered into their dressing room, predictably out of his mind, and took a piss out of the window, spraying some of the people below queuing to get into the venue. They must have thought it had started raining.

In 1984 Ozzy was back on tour, this time with Mötley Crüe as support. It was depravity central, Spinal Tap on speed. 'I don't know how any of us survived,' Ozzy later reported. 'Because after that tour we all ended up in treatment centres – the whole fucking lot of us.' Staying in Florida, Ozzy was in dire need of a snort of cocaine, but no one had any. Unfazed, Ozzy calmly hoovered up a line of ants on the pavement before openly urinating and then slurping it up like a cat does spilled milk. Challenging the Crüe's guitarist Nikki Sixx to copy him, Sixx took a piss but as he bent down Ozzy beat him to the puddle. 'From that moment on,' Sixx recalled, 'we always knew that wherever we were, there was someone who was sicker and more disgusting than we were!'

To say that the Osbourne marriage was combustible is like saying Himmler had an aversion to bar mitzvahs. Booze was the main culprit. Sharon was a heavy drinker but had managed to kick the habit, but Ozzy was still a captive and pouring more down his neck than ever. 'I used to get off stage, drink a bottle of booze, handful of sleeping pills and you could have driven me over a cliff and I wouldn't have given a fuck.'

In 1989, after bingeing on vodka, Ozzy hit rock bottom. For several weeks he'd been suffering blackouts, waking up in places he'd no idea how he'd got to. Sharon was understandably concerned but not prepared for what would happen next. She was peacefully reading in the lounge when Ozzy came in dressed in just his underpants. 'We've come to a decision,' he said matter-of-factly, but with sinister overtones. 'You have to die.' With that he pounced, his hands round her throat in an instant, squeezing tightly. 'He was gone,' Sharon later recalled. 'It wasn't Ozzy.'

Arrested, Ozzy woke up in jail the next day with absolutely no knowledge as to why he was there. Incredibly Sharon agreed to allow him back into her life on the proviso he went through months of extensive drug and alcohol rehabilitation. He came out not quite cured, but with a new sense of purpose and lucidity. Hear the words of Ozzy's wisdom: 'Being sober on a bus is, like, totally different than being drunk on a bus!' Is it any wonder we've taken him to our hearts?

After years in the wilderness Ozzy returned to mainstream consciousness in *The Osbournes*, a TV reality show in which he and his family were the stars. A huge hit, Ozzy was feted as a true original, and even invited to a White House dinner. It was an overwhelming experience; there was Ozzy feeling deeply unworthy mingling with the great and the good, combating his nerves by downing two bottles of wine. A hush settled as George W Bush arrived at the podium: 'What a fantastic audience we have tonight: Washington power-brokers, celebrities, Hollywood stars . . . and Ossie Ozz-Burn!'

Well and truly plastered, when Ozzy heard his name he leaped on the table and screamed: 'Yeeeeeehhaaaaaa!!' There were 1,800 people in the room; everyone went silent. Bush looked at Ozzy; another rallying cry of 'Yeeeeeehhaaaaaa!!' More silence. More stares. 'OK, Ozzy,' Bush finally said, turning to an aide and muttering, 'This might have been a mistake.' Actually the rest of the evening passed off well, even though Ozzy only had vague recollections of it.

It has been a remarkable resurrection, impressive not least because he's still alive to enjoy it, having finally kicked his addictions. But the damage has been done, like a boxer hit too many times to the head. 'Of all the things I've lost,' Ozzy once lamented, 'I miss my mind the most.'

P

DOROTHY PARKER (1893–1967: Poet and Critic)

Tallulah Bankhead called Dorothy Parker 'the mistress of the verbal grenade'. Few could make a more acerbic remark or riposte than Dorothy; she perfected it, and her reputation was built on the talent. Invited to speak at Yale, she shocked the audience by saying, 'If all the girls who attended the Yale prom were laid end to end, I wouldn't be at all surprised.' Once occupying a small, dingy office in New York, she grew depressed that no one ever came to see her. When the signwriter came to paint her name on the door, she got him to write instead the word GENTLEMEN.

In spite of serious concerns that what she did was frivolous and not great art, Dorothy does count amongst the most accomplished feminist writers in history, making an especially important impact on the New York literary scene, although she was also a sad and self-destructive individual who throughout her life struggled with alcoholism and depression.

She was born in New Jersey while her parents were on summer vacation, but reared in well-heeled Manhattan. It was a childhood built on angst and deep sadness. When she was just five Dorothy's mother died and when her father remarried she came to detest him, laying accusations of physical abuse, but her main vitriol was reserved for his new wife, whom she was never able to bring herself to call mother or even stepmom, instead referring to her as simply, 'the housekeeper'.

Dorothy came late to drink, waiting until her twenties to get soaked, but pretty quickly made up for lost time. Working at *Vanity Fair*, she'd while away boring hours taking healthy swigs from her flask of gin and bottles of Ballantine Ale. Her colleagues got used to hearing raucous laughter emanating from her office as the afternoon wore on.

She lived her early working life mostly in grubby rented apartments, refusing to do anything even remotely resembling housework or cooking. She was known to eat raw bacon rather than go near a cooker, and she was lousy with money, determined only to have a good time, going to parties and raving it up. 'I like to have a Martini,' she once said. 'Two at the very most. After three I'm under the table. After four I'm under my host.'

Aged twenty-five, she succeeded P G Wodehouse as *Vanity Fair*'s drama critic and was an immediate hit, notoriously vicious and notoriously funny. 'If you don't knit, bring a book,' she moaned about one particularly dull production. Then, reviewing a performance by the young Katharine Hepburn in a play, she wrote that 'her emotions run the gamut from A to B'.

Dorothy's caustic wit gained national prominence, but it quickly became a burden. 'At parties, fresh young gents would come up defiantly and demand I say something funny and nasty.' Her barbed pen eventually got her into trouble when *Vanity Fair* fired her for pissing off too many powerful producers. Instead she began to write amusing poetry for the *New Yorker*, collections of which sold in their tens of thousands, and book reviews for *Esquire*. Reviewing one author's effort she commented: 'This is not a novel to be tossed aside lightly. It should be thrown with great force.'

During the 1930s and into the 1940s Dorothy was a supporter of civil rights and a vocal advocate of radical left-wing causes, activities that drew her to the attention of the FBI, who compiled a bulging dossier on her. Such pseudo-communist leanings got her in trouble when she went to work in Hollywood as a screenwriter, becoming embroiled in the paranoid McCarthy witch hunts that resulted in her being placed on a blacklist by the movie studio bosses.

Dorothy's love life was just as committed as her politics; she'd marry three times, twice to the same man. While she was on honeymoon Dorothy's editor at the *New Yorker* began pressuring her for her belated copy. She replied via telegram, 'Too fucking busy, and vice versa.'

She also indulged in numerous doomed affairs, one with a married man that resulted in her having to agree to an abortion that led to even more serious drinking and bouts of depression. There followed two suicide attempts: first with a razor, then with drugs. After the second attempt her friend, fellow wit Robert Benchley, told her, 'Dottie, if you don't stop this sort of thing, you'll make yourself sick.' All the time she maintained her wisecracking public exterior, scoffing at her own misery with blasé humour.

Approaching her forties, Dorothy's looks had dissolved. Admitted to a sanatorium, she confessed to having to leave every hour in order to get a drink. Her doctor finally sat her down and warned that if she didn't stop boozing she'd be dead in a month. Dorothy replied with a sigh in her voice, 'Promises, promises.'

As the years passed she grew ever more frail, succumbing to illness because of her drinking and a deep melancholia due to nagging thoughts that she'd frittered her talent away and not lived up to her writing promise. The great novel she'd always hoped to produce never came to fruition and although she desperately wanted to carry on with her writing career she lacked the strength.

Turning seventy, Dorothy was asked by an interviewer what she planned to do next; 'If I had any decency, I'd be dead. All my friends are.' Eventually she succumbed to a heart attack. Bizarrely, after she was cremated her ashes sat on a shelf at the crematorium for six years until they were mailed to her lawyer's offices, whereupon they remained stored in a filing cabinet for over a decade.

SAM PECKINPAH (1925–1984: Film Director)

Speak to anyone who knew or worked with Sam Peckinpah and most will tell you the same thing: the guy was a friggin lunatic, or at best a true son of a bitch. He was manipulative, regularly exploded in fits of temper, and was a cocaine and booze addict, which inevitably drew out the worst in his personality. People who disliked him did so violently. Even his friends thought he was a royal pain in the ass. At the end of principal photography on *Major Dundee* (1965) James Coburn, a close friend and drinking companion of Peckinpah's, shouted at the director, 'Goodbye, you rotten motherfucker!' It is this reputation as a tough talking, hard rollin' maniac that has overshadowed Peckinpah's artistic legacy.

Born in the quiet suburbs of Fresno, California, little Sam was a strange kid. For one, he loved blasting rats to hell in his father's barn, his trembling sister holding a flashlight catching the spectacle of blood spraying everywhere and the rictus grin of pleasure her little brother derived from the spectacle. There was also the time he accidentally slashed his wrists, but instead of calling for help was so obsessed with the sight of his own blood he stood transfixed, hovering on the edge of unconsciousness. His father got him to the hospital just in time.

Every summer Sam went to his grandfather's ranch in Nevada, mixing it with ranch hands, real cowboys who taught him how to drive cattle and brand them and most importantly how to drink whisky. By his late teens the cowboys were taking Sam along with them on benders that might last a whole week, a week of roistering, brawling and whoring. Luckily one of the cowboys had a wagon pulled by a pair of mules with sat nav-like precision. They'd all pile in butt wasted and wake up back home by sun-up.

The son of a respected judge, Sam was fully expected to follow in the family tradition of a career in law but instead gravitated towards Hollywood, working first as a scriptwriter before getting a chance to direct. Quickly he garnered a reputation as a rebel, a maverick who did things his own way and damn the consequences. The booze didn't help. Sam tended to hit the tequila around eight in the morning, nine if the previous night had been a particularly heavy one.

On his first major Hollywood movie *Major Dundee*, a civil war epic starring Charlton Heston, Peckinpah fired at least two dozen crewmen in screaming fits of rage, drank all night and patronised local brothels, paid for out of the film's budget. He was so abusive on set that the normally even-tempered Heston came close to running him through with his cavalry sabre.

It was a rough place where they were filming in Mexico. Actor L Q

Jones recalled that every Saturday night there were massive brawls and drinking orgies. 'It was the kind of town where they would slice your throat for a dime and give you nine cents change. These were not nice people.' They were driving through the main street one night when Peckinpah shouted, 'Look, there's a bar,' and jumped out of the car. Jones and fellow actor Ben Johnson went after him, finding themselves inside one of the meanest, dingiest bars in the world. Sam was already calling for a beer. He tasted it and spat it in the bartender's face; 'Your cow's been pissing in the beer again.' And the fight was on. 'Ten minutes later Ben and I found ourselves in a corner, back to back,' said Jones. 'We're dodging knives, broken bottles, the works; they're trying to kill us. And we look around and Peckinpah's gone. He's just walked off and left us. Not only did he walk off and leave us, he took the car with him.'

The booze did spawn his most creative artistic period, directing in quick succession genuine classics like *The Wild Bunch* (1969) and *Straw Dogs* (1971). Both films sealed Peckinpah's cult status, shattering the taboos of movie violence, depicting it in its raw state, often in blood-spattered slow motion that became the director's trademark.

Peckinpah's drinking got so bad on location in Cornwall on *Straw Dogs* that there were serious questions whether he could actually make the film. Every morning he'd arrive on set with two flasks, one filled with coffee, the other brandy. One night actor Ken Hutchinson was asleep in his hotel room when his door disintegrated. There was Sam with a bottle of brandy in his hand. 'Get the fuck up, we're going to Land's End.' They drove out there and stood on a cliff edge, passing the brandy between them, hearing the raging sea and catching its wild spray in their faces. 'This is fucking great,' went Peckinpah. It was pitch black! Sam caught pneumonia and the film closed down for two weeks.

Film schedules tended not to mean very much on a Peckinpah movie. *The Ballad of Cable Hogue* (1970) was delayed for weeks due to bad weather so Peckinpah and his cast and crew spent the time drinking. When they finally wrapped, the bar bill came to several thousand dollars.

Now in the big league of movie directors, Peckinpah bought a beach-front house in Malibu and entertained friends and colleagues. Parties there could go on for several days. Local teenagers quickly sussed out that quite often they could walk past the Peckinpah homestead, see everyone shit-canned and steal free booze.

Peckinpah wasn't a beer man; his love was for hard liquor, vodka, gin and mescal. He became fond of saying, 'I can't direct when I'm sober.' He knew he was drinking too much, a tumbler of booze sat in a holder on his director's chair refilled all day, and that his habit got him into fights, once breaking three knuckles on some poor sod's face. 'But I don't punch people any more,' he said in 1972. 'My right hand's turned to mush.'

Directing *The Getaway* (1972) with Steve McQueen, he'd literally have the shakes in the morning and be unable to function without a gin and tonic. On set he'd drink all day, then stay up into the small hours, maybe sleep for a bit, then be up at five and back on the booze. He refused to admit he was an alcoholic, proving it by staying sober sometimes as long as three weeks, during which time his personality would be benign and loving. But when he drank he lost all self-control. He got married during the shoot, his third wife; the poor girl filed for divorce after four months, tired of being used as a punch bag.

His work ethic was ferocious; assistants would be fired simply because they couldn't keep pace with him. Despite all that Peckinpah enjoyed great loyalty from his co-workers because they knew the end result was worth all the shit and hassle. As *Straw Dogs*' Susan George observed, 'He'd walk on water for somebody that he loved, but he also would have pushed them under.'

Throughout his career Sam never shook off his rebel gene. He hated suits, Hollywood bean counters more interested in the bottom dollar than art. It reached boiling point on 1973's *Pat Garrett & Billy the Kid*. The studio sent a lackey to spy on the production. Sam would always start practising his knife throwing act whenever the guy tried to speak to him. Sam also carried a pistol in a shoulder holster and enjoyed creeping up behind visiting executives and blasting several rounds into the air, just to watch them jump and scramble for cover.

One time actor Kris Kristofferson took Peckinpah's pistol away because he'd taken to shooting members of the cast, like Harry Dean Stanton. 'He was heavily anaesthetised with mescal or something,' Kristofferson recalled. 'Sam was a good man; he just needed turmoil around him.'

The drinking had now reached epic proportions; his personal assistant took to following him everywhere with a tray of vodka, lime slices and various mixers.

By the end of the day he was literally swaying in the breeze. He looked awful too. L Q Jones arrived on set and hardly recognised his old friend. 'My God, Sam, I didn't realise you'd died.' When rumours hit Hollywood that Peckinpah was having the whirlygigs on the set of *Pat Garrett*, he took out an ad in one of the film trade papers showing him flat out on a hospital trolley receiving a bottle of Johnnie Walker intravenously.

Making *The Killer Elite* (1975), Peckinpah began taking cocaine, becoming too incapacitated to direct some days and his assistant would take over. 'Peckinpah was insane,' recalled star James Caan. 'He'd disappear for days at a time. Sam was just . . . Sam. He couldn't give a fuck less.' Editing the movie he'd arrive promptly at 10 p.m. and the first thing he did was piss out of the office window. Later he overdosed and landed in hospital.

Perhaps his taking cocaine was an insane bid to replace alcohol in his life; instead they ended up perfect bedfellows. Working on *Cross of Iron* (1977) in London, James Coburn recalled Peckinpah falling onto the pavement drunk on the street, uncertain even which city he was in. When the inevitable heart attack struck him down, doctors warned him to lay off the hard stuff, but he didn't listen. The wild man would not be tamed; booking into a hotel with a couple of guns he shot the place up and then hit the roof to fire off several rounds into the sky.

Peckinpah was losing it, suffering from paranoia episodes he started tapping his friends' phone lines and shooting at his image in a mirror with a Colt revolver. He was arrested at Los Angeles international airport for punching a ticket agent, and while staying at the Beverly Hills Hotel he dived into the swimming pool fully clothed to get refreshed after a long drinking session and dropped like a stone to the bottom. Luckily a friend happened to be on hand and fished him out.

Still battering his body with alcohol and drugs, Hollywood turned its collective back on Sam and he became a professional outcast who by the end had resorted to shooting pop videos to make money. By the early eighties he'd finally cleaned up his act but those years of living dangerously finally caught up with Peckinpah and he died of cardiac arrest, his body ravaged, looking as if it belonged to a man twenty years older.

He should have been a cowboy, Sam; he was born out of time, out of kilter with the modern world and its rules. He was lawless, but at the same time appeared to play up to his image as a boozing maverick, the Peckinpah everyone expected. It must have grated on him sometimes. Certainly it ended up killing him.

EDGAR ALLAN POE (1809–1849: Author and Poet)

He was the first of the great American writers to succumb to the ravages of drink. His famous stories and poems seemed to stem from the grim realities of his life, and few people have led such tragedy strewn lives as Edgar Allan Poe. It was as if he walked the earth with a perpetual cloud above his head, haunted by shadows, with mishap and disaster waiting round every corner. The poor bastard never got a break; no wonder he drank himself to death.

Born in Boston to theatrical parents, Poe suffered tragedy from the moment he was born when his father upped and left the family, dying a year later. Plunged into poverty, Poe was no more than three and living in a squalid boarding house when he had to endure the spectacle of his mother sinking steadily into delirium, coughing up blood as tuberculosis claimed her life. Is it any surprise that when Poe began to write, it was the nightmares swirling round his mind that he put to paper.

Fortune at last smiled on little Edgar when he was taken in by a wealthy merchant and his wife, both of whom realised pretty quickly they'd adopted a very strange boy indeed. While growing up, dread and superstition played around in the young Poe's head. As a six-year-old he recalled being 'seized with terror' as he passed by a local graveyard, convinced that the bodies of the dead would crawl out from the sodden earth and give chase to him.

The liquor bottle attracted Poe early in life. His father had been a heavy drinker and as an infant Poe was soothed with bread soaked in gin.

When he enrolled in the University of Virginia he managed to stay shit-housed for much of his semester, maybe to shield himself from the brutality of the place. Only in its second year, the university was pretty lawless, the police were often in attendance and a professor was murdered on the premises. When Poe began to run up large gambling debts his stepfather, who never had much of a relationship with the boy, refused to bail him out; Poe was reduced to smashing the furniture in his room and burning it to keep warm.

By 1832 we find Poe living in Baltimore and at last writing fiction, but also hooked on alcohol. He'd also begun experimenting with opium and laudanum. His frightening behaviour when under their influence was usually enough to send women scurrying back to their mothers, but then he married his thirteen-year-old cousin Virginia, claiming on the marriage certificate that she was twenty-one. To secure money Poe took several positions on newspapers and magazines, but his habit of going on binges, sometimes lasting a week, necessitating several days in bed recovering, saw him regularly fired.

The *Messenger* in Baltimore was one such periodical. Co-workers found Poe kind and courtly, but when drunk, a colleague recalled, 'he was about one of the most disagreeable men I have ever met'. Unable to carry out even simple functions at the office clobbered, the editor sacked him, saying how he would not be at all surprised to hear of Poe's suicide. A few months later a repentant Poe returned asking for his old job back. The editor agreed, provided the booze remained at arm's distance. 'No man is safe who drinks before breakfast,' he said. Sadly, Poe couldn't be trusted where alcohol was concerned and he was once again given notice.

Poe actually wasn't an alcoholic; he didn't drink on a regular basis, and was quite capable of lasting several months without any liquor at all. He was, however, a classic binge drinker who having once started couldn't stop until he ran out of money or passed out, whichever came first. And the more miserable his life became, the more he drank to escape its brutal reality.

After these benders Poe either slept in the gutter or roamed the streets, unsure where he'd been, where he was and probably who he was. More than once he was arrested for public drunkenness. In 1839 a Dr Thomas

Dunn recalled walking home one evening, 'when I saw someone struggling in a vain attempt to raise himself from the gutter. To my utter astonishment I found it was Poe.' Dunn helped the fellow home and the following day Poe was deeply ashamed, as he often was, by his behaviour.

Poe's life was a constant struggle to make ends meet, his poems and stories were beginning to see print but most of the money ended up paying for his booze. He was also his own worst enemy; when opportunity arose he'd knee it in the crotch. In 1842 he secured a meeting with the American president about a government job, but showed up at the White House praying to the porcelain God and in a dishevelled condition. Intercepted in the corridor by an intern, Poe was ejected.

In January of 1842, during a supper party, Virginia was taken ill, coughing violently, blood spattering her white dress. Poe feared the worst, that she was suffering from the same disease that had ripped his mother from life, tuberculosis. The emotional strain of her illness drove Poe to fits of depression and more bouts of excessive drinking. There seemed to be little pleasure in it any more, he'd more than likely down his glass in one gulp, no savouring of the brew, it was for the sheer effect only; 'the desperate attempt to escape from torturing memories', he wrote, 'from a sense of insupportable loneliness and a dread of some strange impending doom'.

His work gradually recognised in literary circles, Poe received national fame with the publication of his poem 'The Raven' in 1845. Since at the time there was no copyright law, the endless reprints brought Poe no recompense whatsoever and he continued to live in near poverty. And drunkenness. One colleague recalled seeing Poe walking the streets 'tottering from side to side, as drunk as an Indian'.

It was a self-destructiveness triggered by the horror show of watching his wife slowly dying in front of him. Poor Virginia must also have been tormented with the realisation that it was her illness that provoked her husband's calamitous drinking bouts. Alas, she continued to decline in health and in 1847, aged just twenty-five, died. Poe was devastated and on windswept nights would wander to her graveside, crying himself to sleep. 'I became insane,' he wrote to a friend. 'With long intervals of horrible sanity. During those fits of absolute unconsciousness I drank, God only knows how often or how much.'

Turning up in Philadelphia at the home of an old friend, Poe looked haggard, with a wild and frightened expression, convinced that men were in pursuit with the intention of killing him. Several days later he turned up at the office of newspaper reporter George Lippard wearing only one shoe and obviously malnourished and potless. Gaining some sympathy, a little money was raised for Poe to continue his journey, but there was something in the way he talked and his general countenance that made Lippard think 'his strange and stormy life was near its close'.

Travelling on to Richmond, Poe met his childhood sweetheart Elmira and they became engaged. Shortly afterwards Poe left her to go on a business trip. He never returned. Arriving in Baltimore Poe simply vanished for five days; no one knew where he was until he was found lying semi-conscious on the street, not even wearing his own clothes, but ill-fitting garments that obviously belonged to someone else. Taken to hospital, he was delirious for several days, talking of seeing phantoms floating around the room. Early on a Sunday morning he regained consciousness and cried out, 'God help my poor soul,' before dying.

The exact cause of Poe's death remains a mystery; was he murdered or did he die of some feverish disease like rabies or cholera? Or did he merely drink himself once again into oblivion, one time too many for his already fragile, battered body? What's certain is that few artists ever died a more lonely or pathetic death. The French poet Charles Baudelaire called it a suicide. 'A suicide prepared for a long time.'

POKER ALICE (1853–1930: Wild West Gambler)

An old west character every bit as colourful as Wild Bill Hickok and Calamity Jane, Poker Alice was a card playing, whisky swilling, cigar chomping, bootlegging hellcat. In an age when women in saloons usually waited for men in upstairs rooms to rid them of the money they'd just earned at the gaming tables, Poker Alice not only fitted right in with the stone-faced sharks who frequented the poker tables of the old west, she regularly defeated them, earning an estimated $200,000 during her career that spanned several decades.

While many biographies place Alice's birth as Sudbury, England, the only daughter of a schoolmaster, it's also been said that she was born in Virginia to Irish immigrants; no woman can drink that much whisky and not be Irish. The family moved to Colorado at the height of its gold rush when Alice was a teenager and blossoming into a beautiful young woman. She caught the eye of a young mining engineer and wannabe card shark Frank Duffield, and they married. Alas, he died not long after in a mine explosion, so Alice had to look for a way to earn a living. She turned to gambling full time and found she was a natural, with an unerring ability to 'read' other players while she herself kept the perfect poker face. Quickly she earned a reputation as the best player in any saloon, using her winnings to buy the latest fashions, in particular low-cut gowns; at important junctures in a game she might lower her neckline to display her ample cleavage, anything to get a man's mind off his deck.

Besides beating the men at cards, she could also drink most of them under the table. Such was her reputation that people simply gave up challenging her to drinking contests. Her poison was neat whisky, chugging down tumbler after tumbler, while chewing on a big fat cigar, which became something of a trademark. She was truly a formidable lady, carrying a .38 revolver in her skirts that she wasn't afraid to use, having done so once already, pumping three bullets into the chest of a man who refused to back down.

Travelling from boomtown to boomtown, happily emptying men's wallets, Alice arrived in Deadwood in 1890, hung out with the likes of Wild Bill and Calamity Jane. While there she met Warren Tubbs, their romance blooming after she shot a man in the arm who'd threatened him with a knife. They married and had seven children. Alice took seriously her motherly duties and never allowed any of her brood to watch her work at the saloons. Ultimately the family moved away to a homestead up in the Black Hills. Strangely, Alice took to the tranquil seclusion and claimed not to miss the hurly burly of saloon life. But tragedy struck when Tubbs died of pneumonia amid a raging blizzard and Alice drove his frozen corpse in a sled forty-eight miles to Sturgis, the nearest town, where she pawned her wedding ring to pay for his burial. Legend has it that after the funeral Alice went into the nearest saloon and won enough money at poker to buy her ring back.

Alice was by this time sixty years old. Time to ease up, you might think, put your feet up and do a bit of knitting. Not for Alice. She opened a brothel and became a madam. It turned into such a thriving business that Alice needed to extend the property and bring in fresh girls to perk things up a bit. To this end she asked her bank manager for a loan of $2,000, stating that she could probably pay it back in two years. She ended up repaying it, with interest, less than a year later. When her bank manager asked how she was able to come up with the money so fast, Alice took a few hefty draws on her cigar and said, 'Well it's this way. I knew the Grand Army of the Republic was having an encampment here in Sturgis. And I knew that the state Elks convention would be here too. But I plumb forgot about all those Methodist preachers coming to town for a conference.'

Between running what was more or less a speakeasy, Alice would make the occasional visit to the saloons of Deadwood to drink and play poker, no longer caring a fig how she looked. No more Paris fashions for her; instead a khaki skirt and a frayed hat, always the dead cigar dangling from her aging lips. Her beauty had long ago faded too; she now resembled something you'd hire instead of a Dobermann to protect your property.

By 1913 Alice's bordello was doing very nicely, not least because the South Dakota National Guard trained nearby. One night a group of soldiers went wild in the brothel and Alice arrived brandishing a rifle and firing off several bullets. Two men were hit, one killed. The police shut the place down and carted Alice off to jail. She was later acquitted of any wrongdoing – the judge happened to be a regular customer – but the law had her number and over the next few years she'd be arrested numerous times for drunkenness and keeping a disorderly house.

Maybe as a two-finger salute to the authorities, Alice took a quick course in producing her own hooch and got into the bootlegging business in time to take advantage of Prohibition. As a consequence of this and repeated misdemeanours, she was sentenced to a term in the state penitentiary, but never spent a day behind bars, being pardoned by the

Governor, who thought the voters might react badly to him sending a white-haired old lady of seventy-five to prison.

Alice's excessive drinking and smoking had by now taken its toll and her health was quickly deteriorating. She underwent gall bladder surgery in the hope of prolonging her life, but it was not a success and she died at the grand old age of seventy-seven.

DENNIS PRICE (1915–1973: Actor)

In the late 1940s Dennis Price, with his devilish charm and Byronic good looks, was a major star of British film, championed by the likes of Noël Coward and the wildly talented film-makers Powell and Pressburger. He had the world at his feet. So why did he die in virtual obscurity a ravaged alcoholic without a pot to piss in?

He had the best of all starts, an aristocratic heritage and a highly decorated brigadier-general as a father. It was probably expected of him to either serve the British Empire by dispatching as many foreigners as possible in hot climes or take up an ecclesiastical existence. He wanted neither and after Oxford University, where he first developed a taste for theatrics, decided to be an actor, which his parents thoroughly disapproved of.

Undaunted, Price made his West End debut in John Gielgud's 1937 production of *Richard II*, but before further advancement could be made Hitler intervened and Dennis joined the army, billeted at Sevenoaks in Kent, which had a reputation for housing 'theatrical pansies'. In other words, it was a bit of a soft touch; no heavy drilling or machine-gun practice down there. Alec Guinness recalls turning up at the place and seeing a pair of sergeants doing their knitting.

Dennis must have approved, but things got tougher later on when he became an anti-aircraft gunner in Northolt, where his decision to bring along his pink-striped pyjamas one evening did not go down well with the commanding officer. Dennis went to pieces, quite literally, suffering a nervous collapse in the spring of 1942 that saw him honourably discharged. For Dennis the war was over, though one could never quite visualise him ever having the gumption to stick a bayonet into a Nazi storm trooper in the Ardennes.

One remains suspicious, though, of the exact nature of Dennis's breakdown since later that summer he was fit enough to perform in a play in London, watched by a certain Michael Powell who cast Price in *A Canterbury Tale* (1944). After that he appeared in several of those wildly overripe Gainsborough melodramas, becoming a minor matinee idol, but their quality was too erratic to sustain any notable fame. His devastating turn as a serial murderer in Ealing's classic black comedy *Kind Hearts and Coronets* (1949), where he bumps off nearly an entire family that stand in his way to a rightful dukedom, should have led to greater things; instead, tragically, it was the curtain raiser to his sad decline.

By this time Price was already a chronic alcoholic as he struggled to come to terms with his own homosexuality that was doing his marriage to actress Joan Schofield no favours. By 1950 she'd had enough. Their divorce was quite acrimonious, and Price lived with the terror of being outed, this during a period in British history when such practices could see you in jail, and almost certainly end one's career. Worse for Dennis, it was a source of personal anguish since he had two daughters with Joan.

His career had also stalled dreadfully, while his post-war contemporaries Alec Guinness and James Mason were achieving international recognition, the quality of work being offered to Dennis was tepid at best in films of varying quality. Dissatisfied, in April 1954 he made plans to kill himself. Wearing his best Savile Row suit, Dennis stuck his head in the oven and turned the gas on full blast. Luckily a cleaning woman passing his apartment smelled it and pulled Dennis to safety.

In a bizarre way this attempt to top himself worked wonders for the old career. He received sackfuls of mail from fans wishing him well, and directors suddenly realised what a loss he might have been to the profession and started hiring him again, mainly in supporting roles in a succession of classic British comedies in which Dennis excelled as an oily cad, notably, *I'm All Right Jack* (1959) and *School for Scoundrels* (1960), where he's possibly cinema's slimiest ever second-hand car salesman.

He was also excellent in the military drama *Tunes of Glory* (1960), in a more serious role but obviously drinking, as John Fraser, a young actor on the film, recalled. 'He lived on Guinness. About a crate of Guinness a day was his consumption, starting at breakfast. He was always drunk, but he never fell over.'

By the early sixties Price's alcohol consumption had destroyed his once glowing matinee looks; his face had become puffy and he was balding. People, of course, knew about his problem, that for years he'd bring his booze to the studio in a little shopping bag, the bottles audibly clinking together as he made his way to his dressing room.

While he was appearing in the play *Any Wednesday*, the director arranged a cocktail party for the cast, including Moira Lister and Amanda Barrie, to get to know each other. Dennis arrived with a gentleman called Marcus, a friend and helpmate. To make small talk the director suggested everybody disclose what they did in their spare time. Dennis shocked everyone when he revealed, 'We do a lot of shooting in our spare time. Actually one of our hobbies is that Marcus shoots cigarettes out of my ears.' Just then Amanda noticed a large piece of sticking plaster on one ear. She nudged Moira and whispered, 'Missed.'

Dennis, it has to be said, did not inspire confidence in his fellow actors. For one thing he arrived at the theatre most nights with his passport in his jacket, in case the pressure got too much and he needed to leave the country. There was also the occasion he sauntered on stage performing the last act when the rest of the cast were still very much involved in act one. Then he had the line, '*Time* magazine says I have the ruthlessness of an eagle,' except it came out as, '*Time* magazine says I have the ruthlessness of Anna Neagle.'

Money and Dennis were never the best of friends. Even way back in his university days he racked up huge debts. This time he owed the taxman rather a lot of money, citing 'extravagant living and most inadequate gambling', and in a bid to escape financial emasculation did a runner, or as he liked to put it, made 'a strategic retreat' to the tiny island of Sark. There he lived as a tax exile, shooting rabbits, growing daffodils and staring out to sea, between bouts of some rather serious drinking. The isolation got to him after a while, however, and he returned to England to face the music and was declared a bankrupt.

At the end of his career it seemed Price was taking whatever was on offer to pay off his debts, resulting in some rather awful kitsch Euro puddings, but also some affectionately remembered British horror films like Hammer's *Twins of Evil* (1971), the terrific *Theatre of Blood* (1973) and the frankly deranged *Horror Hospital* (1973). He made a custom of arriving on set asking, 'How long before I'm needed?' The assistant director would say, 'Ten minutes, luvvie,' and Price would disappear behind a blind with his shopping bag and there would be the unmistakable sound of clinking glasses, a bottle being opened and then 'glug, glug, glug'. He'd reappear refreshed, excusing, 'Just a bit of script revision, dear boy.'

Dennis was one of those people who you expected almost daily to turn up in the obituary column of *The Times*. And he duly did, not from cirrhosis of the liver, according to some accounts, but a heart attack brought on by his generally feeble condition. He'd fallen at home and broken his hip. And it was in hospital that he died, an almost forgotten idol.

R

OLIVER REED (1938–1999: Actor)

The stories of Oliver Reed's antics are legion, eclipsing many other hell-raisers for their sheer lunacy and showmanship. He once arrived at Galway airport lying drunk on a baggage conveyor. When he got plastered in a restaurant and was asked to vacate the premises he then proceeded to parade around the parking lot in the nude. On an international flight he incurred the wrath of the pilot by dropping his trousers and asking the air hostesses to judge a prettiest boy contest. He was banned from every pub where he lived, once for climbing the chimney naked shouting, 'Ho! Ho! Ho! I'm Santa Claus!'

Who else would invent a drink called 'gunk', a ghastly concoction that was served in an ice bucket and comprised every drink in the bar mixed together? When a newspaper reported a doctor's findings that the safe limit for any man's consumption of alcohol was four pints a day, Reed said bugger that and promptly knocked back 126 pints of beer in twenty-four hours and was photographed afterwards performing a victory horizontal hand-stand across the bar. All this led one journalist to say that calling Oliver Reed unpredictable was like calling Ivan the Terrible colourful.

He was born in Wimbledon, south London to a distinguished middle-class family; his uncle was the revered film director Carol Reed. From the word go Ollie was a heavy boozer, going on marathon pub crawls as a young struggling actor. Staggering back home with a mate, Reed sometimes enjoyed testing their loyalty and bravery by making them lie spread-eagled on the road with him in front of oncoming traffic. The first to get up and leg it was chicken.

Because of his menacing features, for years the only jobs Reed got offered were teddy boys in leather jackets who whipped old ladies around the head with a bicycle chain and stole their handbags. It was his role as Bill Sikes in the hit musical *Oliver!* (1968) that launched him as a genuine film star. At the after-show party he got the child actors Mark Lester and Jack Wild drunk by spiking their Coca-Colas with vodka. Lester had to be taken home by his mother and thrown in the bath fully clothed after he was violently sick.

Filming *Hannibal Brooks* (1969) in Austria, Ollie understandably upset the locals when after a drinking binge he tore down the Austrian flag from outside the crew's hotel and pissed on it. Reed was nothing if not a rabid patriot. Walking into a German bar he was dismayed to find it festooned with every national flag in the world save for Britain's. Grabbing hold of the manager he menacingly threatened, 'I'm coming back tomorrow night. If you haven't got a Union Jack by then I'm going to trash this place.' The next evening Reed walked in and still no Union Jack fluttered over the bar. Within seconds he was hurling chairs through windows.

This kind of activity was becoming the norm on an Ollie Reed movie. Shooting *The Three Musketeers* (1973) in Spain, he stayed in a plush hotel in Madrid and as a practical joke one night removed the goldfish from an ornamental pond in the dining room, keeping them in his bath, and replaced them with carrots that he'd methodically shaped into fish. The following morning at breakfast he bade good morning to everyone and then dived into the pond and began devouring what his horror-struck fellow guests presumed were the helpless live fish. The manager called the police and Reed was hauled off the premises bellowing, 'You can't touch me! I'm one of the musketeers!'

Now a world star, Reed refused to leave Britain for Hollywood despite numerous offers (he turned down the Robert Shaw role in *Jaws*). And there was the occasion Steve McQueen came to London to meet him with the express intention of their making a film together. Ollie invited McQueen to Tramp nightclub, where he got dreadfully drunk and vomited over the American superstar. The nightclub's staff managed to find some new jeans for McQueen to wear but couldn't offer him any replacement shoes. 'So I had to go round for the rest of the evening smelling of Oliver Reed's sick,' McQueen complained. Needless to say, Ollie didn't get the part.

Essentially Reed was nervous about going to Hollywood, because he was nervous of being where he didn't feel secure. 'Drinking, of course, is often about insecurity,' said his friend the director Michael Winner. 'He was very shy and he needed the drink to give him confidence.'

So he stayed in England and set himself up as a country squire, buying a mammoth property, Broome Hall, the scene of numerous wild parties, notably the time Reed invited thirty members of his local rugby club over. The evening started off in the pub with them all stripped naked and singing 'Get 'em Down, you Zulu warrior,' cramming fifteen of their party into a single ladies lavatory cubicle and then embarking on a cross-country run to the house in their jockstraps. Once at Broome Hall the real fun began. In all fifty gallons of beer was consumed, thirty-two bottles of whisky, seventeen of gin, four cases of wine and fifteen bottles of Newcastle Brown ale. Then for an encore they smashed dozens of eggs on the kitchen floor to slide around and play mock ice hockey. 'It could have been worse,' Reed's girlfriend said. 'A lot of them were in training and off the drink.'

One of Ollie's favourite haunts of the late seventies was Stringfellows nightclub in London's West End, where he enjoyed a game that he christened 'head butting'. Each player was required to smash his head against his opponent until one collapsed or surrendered. A regular victim was the Who's bass player John Entwhistle, who after being knocked out three times pleaded with the club's owner to either ban the game or ban Ollie.

Reed was at his worst behaved in public, deliberately so. He always required an audience for his antics. At London's Grosvenor House Hotel he turned a soda siphon on himself and other celebrities attending a charity boxing match then climbed into the ring and entertained everyone with his own version of 'The Stripper'. Another time he was in a posh restaurant in Paris with a friend and there was no sign of the waiter. Growing irritable, Reed wanted to leave but was persuaded to hang on. Ten minutes later they'd still not been served. 'Right,' said Ollie.

'I'll show you how to get some service.' He picked up a chair and hurled it through a window. Within seconds an irate manager and five waiters had surrounded the table. 'Ah yes,' said Ollie. 'I'll have some fish soup please.'

By the late seventies Reed's hellraising reputation had severely hampered his ability to find decent work and he was reduced to appearing in puddings like *Condorman* (1981). Director Charles Jarrott won't forget in a hurry working with Reed on location in Monte Carlo. Immaculately dressed in a white tuxedo, Reed's scenes went like clockwork. He was stone cold sober. Jarrott called 'cut' late in the evening and returned to his hotel suite. Walking onto the balcony facing the Mediterranean he noticed a white tuxedo floating away on the waves. 'Looking back up at the hotel I saw Ollie, stark naked, climbing from balcony to balcony. An English King Kong was abroad!'

Reed made headlines in 1985 when he married Josephine Burge who, at twenty-one, was twenty-five years his junior; friends and family were perturbed over the age difference but it was a union that would last until his death. Reed not so much planned the wedding as he planned the stag night, taking over a boozer in Surrey and drinking for three days solid: beer, cider, half-pint mugs of gin and vodka and gunk. Reed, naked but for a kilt, presided over the booze orgy and friends arrived in shifts to replace revellers who had fallen by the wayside. Local villagers kept their fingers crossed that sleep deprivation might render Reed harmless. 'He's in there with a real rough lot,' said one quaking neighbour. 'They could take the village apart.' But come the third day the boozers were still going strong, pausing only for a cuppa, two tea bags in a litre of Scotch heated in a kettle, which everyone had to partake of. Periodically food in the form of sandwiches was sent in from a nearby hotel. The manager placed the tray outside the door. 'I dare not enter because Ollie sees me as representing authority. If he got half a chance he would grab me and I'd never be seen again.' By the end of it all there was but one sole drinker left in the pub, Reed himself.

As the nineties descended, a life on the piss had taken its toll on Ollie's appearance: he was pot-bellied, grey-haired, lined and stooping like an old man. At times he looked like Father Christmas leaving an Alcoholics

Anonymous meeting. It was a long way from the brooding sex symbol of the early seventies. His face was now 'a sad reflection of a dissolute life', as one journalist put it. 'A Hogarthian example of debauchery's perils.'

Reed's death when it came was messy, nonsensical and avoidable. Shooting *Gladiator* in Malta, Reed quickly found the most English bar on the island and was there most days he wasn't required on set. As he was about to leave after a lunchtime session a gang of British sailors burst in. 'Black rums all round,' Reed announced, downing twelve double measures before retreating to his more customary double whiskies. After challenging the sailors to an arm-wrestling contest, he happily signed autographs before they left, then slumped into a chair to rest, snoring audibly. Then the snoring stopped. His wife Josephine noticed his lips were darkening. Something was very wrong. Laid out on a bench, Reed was given mouth-to-mouth resuscitation while someone called for an ambulance. Quick to arrive, it sped off with Reed to hospital but the paramedics couldn't feel a pulse. It was too late. The great man had passed over.

At least one could take solace in the fact that, just like Bing Crosby croaking it on a golf course, what better place for Ollie to die than in a pub? The only bitter irony was that with the huge success of *Gladiator* his career would have been revitalised after years in the wilderness, though he probably would have pissed it all away again.

Thousands of ordinary people turned up to show their respect at Reed's funeral at the tiny village in County Cork that he'd made his home in the last years of his life. After the service family and close friends congregated round the open grave and poured pints of Guinness into the earth with him. It was a fitting tribute and a fitting way to bow out.

WALLACE REID (1891–1923: Silent Movie Star)

Hard to believe that someone who was amongst the most influential players in the silent movie era could be virtually forgotten today. Wallace Reid worked hard, and partied hard, and in his thirty-one short years represented the best and the dirtiest side of Hollywood, ending up dying in a padded room a drink and drug addict. His tragic death became one of Hollywood's early cautionary tales, the handsome, clean-cut boy who, in the words of one journalist, 'went up like a skyrocket and came down like a charred stick'.

Born in St Louis, Missouri, into a show-business family, Wallace performed on stage at an early age with his parents as they toured the country before attending military school where he excelled at sports. Originally intending to be a writer or director, it was Reid's physical prowess and devilishly handsome looks that won him bit parts at a variety of nickelodeon-era studios, later graduating to leading-man status where he exemplified the clean-cut young American.

Already, though, Reid was a heavy drinker, a secret that his adoring public and much of the film industry knew little about. To the whole world he led an incredibly glamorous life, married to Dorothy Davenport, a young actress, and living on Sunset Boulevard in the first movie star mansion with a swimming pool.

His pictures continued to make money as he turned to more heroic roles, usually a dashing racing car driver involved in thrilling chases and exploits that drew huge crowds, predominantly female. He was the victim of stalkers; women literally flung themselves at him. One young girl ran away from boarding school and sold her jewellery to buy a ticket to Hollywood to see Wallace. She stalked the studio and his home, even secreted herself under Reid's bed. She was swiftly sent packing. Then there was the stunning society wife who for a whole year sent Reid a continual stream of pictures of herself naked, along with the key to her apartment. Finally she gave Reid's valet a diamond ring worth thousands of dollars to admit her into Wally's dressing room where the poor bastard had no choice but to submit.

Still drinking, Reid often stayed out all night at some bootleg bar. One such trip to Santa Monica ended in disaster. Roaring back home with an acting chum on the Pacific highway, Reid hit another car. Both vehicles were write-offs. Amazingly Reid walked away with just minor cuts and bruises; his friend suffered a broken collarbone. The inhabitants of the other car weren't so lucky. The driver was dead, his wife beside him seriously injured, so too their three children. Reid was arrested and booked into Santa Monica jail charged with manslaughter. The studio arranged for Reid's bail and also made sure the incident stayed out of the newspapers. Higher strings were also pulled, or favours called in, since Reid escaped any conviction.

It had been a close call, but Reid continued to be a social gadfly, known by everyone in Hollywood as 'good-time Wally'. His home was often the scene of wild parties where a maid wheeled a trolley around filled with an assortment of needles, opium pipes, morphine, cocaine and heroin. The liquor flowed too, and sex was usually on the menu. A young woman was seen sniffing coke before declaring, 'I want the most beautiful man here. I am his.' There was a virtual stampede in her direction. In case the police called, which they had a habit of doing, Reid had a priceless alibi. He'd park his car a few blocks away so when the fuzz arrived he'd nip out the back, then swan up the driveway to angrily denounce the invasion of his home by these uninvited revellers.

As his popularity grew the studio mercilessly exploited him like few other actors in Hollywood. In one year alone he made ten features. Filming *The Valley of the Giants* in Oregon in 1919, Reid was injured in a train crash. In excruciating pain, a studio doctor pumped Reid full of morphine so he was able to finish the picture. He became hooked. Instead of sending him somewhere to be cured, the studio kept him supplied with the drug in order that their most prized asset could still churn out movies for them. Combined with his drinking problem it was a recipe for disaster.

Although Reid kept his habit a secret from his wife for years, gradually she began to notice a change in him, from the happy-go-lucky man she married to a depressive paranoid who had a fear of being left alone. He also suffered chronic insomnia. Most evenings Dorothy would hear him creep down the stairs and go into the dining room to mix drinks. He found whisky usually did the trick and sent him to sleep.

By the time he made his last film in 1922 Reid could barely function, able to stand for only brief periods. It was heartbreaking to watch. He came onto the set and sort of bumped into the furniture, then just sat down on the floor and started to cry.

Reid checked into a private sanatorium, ironically at the same time he was named America's most popular star in Europe. Before going in he'd confided to his friend Cecil B DeMille, 'Either I'll come out cured, or I won't come out.' With no proper drug rehabilitation programmes back then, these sanatoriums had padded rooms containing a solitary light bulb, a sink and toilet, and a small mattress on the floor. Here Wallace Reid spent the last six weeks of his life, his wife barely out of his sight.

Finally recognising his addiction, Reid faced it through clenched teeth, 'We will fight it out now, till one of us is dead.' It was torture day and night as he endured the physical agonies of abstinence. Weak and emaciated, he fainted every hour. That first week he almost died three times. At least his humour remained intact. When given some whisky in his medicine he said, 'What are you trying to do? Get me started again?'

Although he won his battle, cleansing his body of drugs and booze, the ravages Reid had inflicted upon himself over the years meant his immune system was so badly compromised that when he relapsed he'd no stamina left to pull through. He slipped into a coma and died in his wife's arms. He was just thirty-one. Harold Lloyd, Charles Chaplin, Mary Pickford and Douglas Fairbanks all attended his funeral.

As he'd lain unconscious in the sanatorium, fighting for his life, Dorothy went public about her husband's desperate battle against alcohol and drug addiction, in the hope that his story might save others. The news shocked his public, in an age when drug addiction was scarcely heard of. After Reid's death she went on to dedicate her life to waging a war on drugs. She never remarried.

KEITH RICHARDS (b. 1943: Musician)

Once described as 'the world's most elegantly wasted human being', it is the sheer fact that Keith Richards is still walking around the planet, having ingested enough booze and drugs to fell the inhabitants of an African game reserve, that fuels his legend. 'Drink has never been a problem,' he once observed. 'I've written some of my best things pissed out of my mind.' All the shenanigans and tales of excess, fun though they are, merely obscure the fact that Richards is actually one of the greatest rhythm guitarists in rock 'n' roll history, the epitome of rock stadium cool and a vital cog in the juggernaut that is the Rolling Stones.

He was born in Dartford, Kent, in the same cottage hospital where a certain Michael Philip Jagger had been delivered a few months earlier. Hitler took a personal interest in Richards from an early age, sending one of his V-1 rockets over to decimate the row of houses he and his family lived in. But Keith survived. I guess that made him reckless: if he could survive a V-1 attack, what's cocaine, what's heroin, what's 200 gallons of bourbon?

Hooked as a teenager on American rock 'n' roll, Richards began playing the guitar. It wasn't only the music that appealed, it was the whole lifestyle, the freedom it represented, of being responsible to oneself only, authority could go hang. 'Ever since I left school, nobody has ever heard a "Yes, Sir" from me.'

While at art college Richards started playing with a blues band whose front man was that same Mick Jagger. Initially an R&B cover group, the Rolling Stones branched out into original material penned by Jagger and Richards, metamorphosing into a hard-bastard version of The Beatles. Relatively quickly Richards earned a reputation as a tough nut. Flying into Heathrow airport after a concert early in 1964, the band was enjoying a drink in the VIP lounge when some American tourists started hurling abuse because of their dandified, long-haired appearance. Richards promptly knocked one of them spark out and sent the others flying. Touring America later that year, an altercation backstage with a fan resulted in Richards going out and buying himself a revolver, which he carried with him whenever he toured the States.

Things hadn't mellowed by 1967 when they guested on the *Ed Sullivan Show*. When the doorman at the studio failed to recognise our boys and refused them entry, the Stones dispensed with diplomacy and barged their way through, Keith flattening the doorman with a swift right hook as he passed.

Always a boozer, with a particular liking for large amounts of a 'hellish grog' brewed in the hills of Kentucky, Richards had also graduated from grass, to LSD and then cocaine. It wasn't long before heroin made an appearance, for several reasons. 'It was a damn good feeling, for starters.' Add to that the Stones' punishing tour schedules and Brian Jones's death. There was a lot of shit happening in the Richards universe and heroin gave him a sense of space. 'Eventually, I was so far in space, I was almost in the atmosphere.' Pretty soon he was taking two and a half grams a day, 'just to keep normal'. In New York he'd score in the city's Lower East Side, a neighbourhood so dangerous even Shaft stayed away, a place of burned-out cars, few cops and no hope. At least Richards had his gun with him.

When under the influence Keith could get quite whacked out; take for example the time a Stones road crew got him out of bed, bundled him into a car that shot up the M1 motorway to Heathrow, hauled him through security and onto a plane that seven hours later arrived in New York. Richards wasn't conscious the entire time. Legend had it that he was able to keep his body relatively undamaged from the bombardment of drink and drugs by having his blood changed regularly at a private clinic in Switzerland.

One morning ten policemen arrived for a dawn raid on Richards' English mansion carrying off large amounts of drugs, but also a .38 Smith & Wesson, a shotgun and several boxes of bullets. He escaped imprisonment, something that was becoming a regular occurrence in his life, and celebrated the verdict in a hotel, managing to set his room alight during the festivities.

There was also Richards' less than strict adherence to the nation's drink-driving laws, careering round the place in his Bentley or Mercedes, smashed out of his box. Passengers got used to it, sitting in the back saying, 'Oh, I think we just hit a tree.' Invariably accidents occurred because Keith had a nasty habit of falling asleep at the wheel, once with his heavily pregnant girlfriend Anita Pallenberg in the back. Missing a turn at a roundabout the car hit a kerb and smashed down an embankment. A bloodied and dazed, and now probably sober Keith hid his stash of dope before the cops arrived. Anita survived with merely a busted collarbone.

In 1977 things actually got quite serious in Canada when the Mounted

Police found him in possession of twenty-two grams of heroin. Richards faced a prison sentence of seven years to life, but no one was ever going to jail a Rolling Stone so it was reduced to a suspended sentence and he was put on probation for one year, with orders to continue treatment for heroin addiction. He was still in a bad way the following year when the Stones appeared on *Saturday Night Live* to promote their new album. The group rehearsed with Belushi, Aykroyd and the rest but were so intoxicated, knocking back whisky and vodka and openly snorting coke in the studio, that the sketches were dropped. Richards could barely stand, let alone perform comedy or remember the single line he was given. 'It's interesting to be working with someone who's dead,' cast member Lorraine Newman recalled.

Behind all the madness, the rock glitter, Richards is a radically different man, pretty down to earth. 'I'm all for a quiet life, except I didn't get one.' He likes simple pleasures such as watching British war movies, music hall comics and good old shepherd's pie, his daily diet while touring, which no one, I repeat, no one is allowed to touch, let alone sample. One roadie who did found himself staring down the barrel of Keith's loaded revolver.

When he goes on tour the switch designated 'MAD' is permanently in the on position. A favourite antic, which always got a laugh, was to build a brick wall in front of a friend or colleague's driveway, spend all night doing it, so when they had to dash off next morning for an urgent meeting they'd come face to face with a solid six-foot barrier. One evening Richards was drinking with blues guitarist Roy Buchanan, Eric Clapton and Ronnie Wood. Buchanan had been getting on Richards' tits all evening and when he left for the toilet Keith turned to Clapton and said, 'Get your cock out, Eric, we'll be pissing in that fucker's beer.' Sure enough the three of them added a little natural organic juice to Buchanan's beverage.

By the eighties Jagger had long since mellowed and abstained from drink and drugs, and it was left to Keith and Ronnie Wood to fly the flag for rock hedonism. During the Stones' 1981 tour, Keith's cocaine supply was flown in on a private plane once a week. One time he and Ronnie stayed up two solid days song writing fuelled by vodka and cocaine. By Friday it was urgent they rested prior to a gig on Saturday. Wood went out like a light but Richards was still wired and couldn't sleep so had to be given a heavy tranquilliser with enough barbiturates in it to anaesthetise a horse. It knocked him out so well no one could wake him up again the next morning. He was finally brought back into the world of the living by being doused with iced water.

Richards seemed to be indestructible. 'I've had a few brushes with old death; he's kind of a friend of mine, actually.' When someone put strychnine in his dope he collapsed into a near comatose state, but was strangely still conscious of what was happening around him, namely lots of medical staff rushing around shouting, 'He's dead, he's dead!' and there he was thinking, 'I'm not dead!' Perversely, Richards denied that he had a drug problem. 'I've never turned blue in someone's bathroom, I mean, I consider that the height of bad manners.'

During 1982 the Stones were back on tour. At one gig Richards collapsed on stage, fried to the gills, and played a guitar solo flat on his back, still smoking his cigarette. At Wembley, when Richards forgot some chords and an equally zombied Ronnie failed to cover for him, Keith stormed across the stage and punched Wood hard in the face, almost knocking him into the audience. Keith takes no shit on stage. When a fan ran onto the stage at another gig Richards, mid-riff, took his guitar off and aimed a hefty swing at the fucker, just missing his head, but the intent was there and if he'd made contact would've split the guy's skull open. But as Keith explains, 'When a cat gets on your turf, you gotta chop him down.'

By the mid-eighties Keith had given up his decade-long addiction to heroin and mellowed considerably, sustaining himself instead with large quantities of vodka, ganja and the odd snort of cocaine. 'I was Number 1 on the "Who's Likely to Die" list for ten years; I mean I was really disappointed when I fell off the list.'

If it were possible, Richards achieved even more legendary status when Johnny Depp heavily based his *Pirates of the Caribbean* character Captain Jack Sparrow on him. Richards even turned up in the third *Pirates* film, but was so inebriated by the time the production team retrieved him from his trailer that he required quite a bit of propping up. 'If you wanted straight, then you got the wrong man.'

In 2006, Richards made headlines again when he fell out of a coconut tree while on holiday in Fiji and suffered a head injury so bad that he underwent cranial surgery. 'They cut my fucking skull open, went in and pulled out the crap, and put some of it back in again.' But that was nothing compared to the shockwaves behind his revelation that he'd snorted a line of his own dad's ashes. After the old guy had been cremated Richards said he couldn't resist grinding him up with a little bit of blow. 'My dad wouldn't have cared, he didn't give a shit. It went down pretty well, and I'm still alive.' Of course it wasn't true, spoken in jest during an interview, it was picked up by every news outlet in the world. The interesting thing is that everyone believed it was true, it was like; yeah I can see Keith doing that.

Approaching pensionable age, Richards announced that he'd finally given up all drugs, not because of any altruistic motive, but because those bastard dealers and chemists had reduced the power of his favourite narcotics. 'I really think the quality's gone down,' he moaned. As for alcohol, he'd no intention of giving that up, despite numerous medical warnings over the years. 'Not that I want to brag about it, but I've had about three doctors who told me, "If you carry on like this, you will be dead in six months." I went to their funerals.' As a small concession to health, and a nod to saving the planet, Keith made the shift to swigging organic vodka. He was reportedly so drunk at a Stones gig in 2007 that he almost fell twenty feet into the crowd. It was only the quick intervention of Jagger that prevented a disaster.

Richards has never advocated that people follow his hedonistic lifestyle, since few would be able to live through the experience. He reckons his own particular brand of survival is down to a strong constitution. He even claims he's been inundated with requests to donate his body to medical science when he finally dies. I guess doctors want to examine his immune system just to make sure it's actually human.

RACHEL ROBERTS (1927–1980: Actress)

She was unique, a complete eccentric and bawdy beyond measure. Who else but Rachel Roberts would take to impersonating a Welsh corgi when curried and mashed, literally on all fours barking? At one all-star

Hollywood party she crawled over to where Robert Mitchum was standing alongside his wife and, after pawing at his leg, and panting a bit, attempted to open his fly with her teeth.

Yet, behind the bravado and showbiz exuberance, Rachel's dark side was pitch black. Suffering from suicidal depression and violent mood swings, exacerbated by wild drinking, she ended up committing suicide in the most rancid fashion imaginable.

She was born in Llanelli, Wales, the daughter of a Baptist minister. Rebelling against her strict religious upbringing, Rachel came to the bright lights of London to study acting at RADA. Never a beauty, she was nevertheless a powerful and expressive actress who after several years on the stage came into her own with appearances in the landmark British New Wave films *Saturday Night and Sunday Morning* (1960) and *This Sporting Life* (1963), which earned her an Oscar nomination as Best Actress.

Things got even dizzier when she married Rex Harrison and was catapulted into the glamorous world of cocktail parties and homes on the Italian Riviera. But her puritan nature and left-wing leanings could never quite reconcile themselves with the wasted Hollywood life she shared with Harrison. Torn by guilt, she also watched her career go down the pan. As she herself lamented, 'It is very difficult to be taken seriously when you're introduced at a party to somebody as the fourth Mrs Rex Harrison.'

Already volatile and highly strung, as Rachel's career continued to stall she took heavily to drink, which led increasingly to eccentric public behaviour. One night she and Rex attended an after-premiere party of one of their films but grew increasingly irritated that the paparazzi were ignoring them in favour of their guests, Richard Burton and Liz Taylor. Finally Rachel, who'd been drinking all evening, snapped and climbed atop her table screaming: 'We're the stars of this fucking film!' Not getting the desired response she lifted up her skirt and bawled, 'Here's my pussy. Take some pictures of that!' Poor Rex could do little to calm his wife down. 'Don't you talk to me,' she spat out at him. 'You can't get it up, you old fart.' It really was a horrendous evening.

The Harrisons nonetheless remained friends with the Burtons and visited them on their luxury yacht for a Mediterranean cruise. One night they all got roaring drunk, but Rachel uncontrollably so. She lay on the floor barking like a dog, her usual pissed-as-a-fart party trick, but it reached new sordid heights this time when she started to masturbate her basset hound, a sloppy old thing called Omar. How poor old Rex put up with her Burton for one couldn't imagine. 'She wouldn't last forty-eight hours with me.' Rex in fact often found Rachel's wild antics highly amusing, 'but the rest of the world regarded it as distinctly rum'.

Even so, the marriage was combustible, about as safe to be around as a nuclear reactor built on the San Andreas Fault; she once stabbed Rex in the hand with a table knife during a restaurant meal. It was a union in periodic states of crises, not helped by both their drinking and Rachel's frequent suicide bids. When Rex filmed *Doctor Dolittle* (1967) in the tranquil sun of St Lucia, the couple stayed on a yacht which descended most evenings into a combat zone, their shrieks and curses echoing across the bay for all to hear. When production moved to Hollywood they rented a Beverly Hills mansion where their drunken brawling became what Rachel later called a period of 'real disintegration'. She ran off into the night once and got horrendously nuked, the police later picked her up crawling on all fours to get back home. Invited to a distinguished Hollywood gathering featuring the likes of Billy Wilder, James Stewart and their wives, the Harrisons distinguished themselves by Rex singing obscene lyrics about his penis to the tune of 'I've Grown Accustomed to Her Face' while Rachel, sans knickers, performed handstands.

Comedian Kenneth Williams recalled Rachel sitting stark naked once at a party while dinner was being served, much to the astonishment of guests: 'I'm a Baptist minister's daughter,' she cried. 'And I don't come easy.' Actually she did. Rachel was a world-class nymphomaniac. Fuelled by booze and prescription drugs, she'd go to dinner with Rex and friends, then leave to go outside to seduce the chauffeur in her husband's Rolls-Royce. Returning to the table with lipstick smudged and tights all asunder, she'd announce to everyone, 'I've just fucked the chauffeur.' Rex wouldn't bat an eyelid. Such acts, perhaps, were a desperate bid to crave attention, as indeed were some of her 'suicide' bids.

Deep down there was no one sweeter or more lovable than Rachel, but drunk she was a disaster area. While a guest at the Cannes Film Festival, she spied the French starlet Catherine Deneuve walk by. 'I want to fuck her!' Rachel screamed. 'I want to fuck her.' When friends pointed out that she wasn't a lesbian, Rachel shouted, 'I still want to fuck her!'

It really was only a matter of time before Rex left Rachel, unable to cope any longer with her drinking and madness. She stripped naked in a restaurant once to perform what she called the dance of the twenty-two pussies. When he moved in with the ex-wife of Richard Harris, Rachel responded by swallowing fifty aspirin and spending Christmas Eve having her stomach pumped in a London hospital.

Alone and without the addictive and combative relationship she'd shared with Rex, Rachel descended further into drink and drug dependency. It was clear she was out of control. Invited onto Russell Harty's TV talk show in 1973, Rachel stunned the largely family studio audience by calling her host 'a silly cunt' before laying into the feminist movement by announcing, 'All they need is a cock up their cunt or their arse.' Roundly booed, Rachel dived into a rendition of 'The Lady Is a Tramp' as she was escorted away by security. The interview was deemed unbroadcastable.

Relocating to LA, Rachel appeared in the odd film and still performed on stage, even forged a new loving relationship with a Mexican called Darren Ramirez, but deep down she was lonely and lost. She was dangerously capable of tipping over the edge on just the one drink. Meeting respected Hollywood writer Gavin Lambert, she dug her fingernail into his nose unprovoked, tearing off some flesh. After putting on a plaster to stem the bleeding, Lambert accused Rachel of scarring him for life. 'Well,' she replied, 'people have to live with their scars.'

Despite all this drinking Rachel was never less than professional when working. Her colleagues only saw the vibrant, vivacious Rachel, always cheerful and fun to be with; the more astute, however, could see through the act to the emotional train wreck beneath. Her drinking was hectic, to say the least; she'd leave the home she shared with Ramirez on an impulse, go off to God knew where, return days later and tear the place apart in a marinated rage. Friends could see only one outcome and urged her to join AA and attend hospital programmes to dry out. It didn't help;

Rachel continued to drink and drift further into depression, looking back over her life with Rex, torturing herself over why it ended. Rachel never forgot Harrison; she was obsessed with him to the point that she used to call him several times a night, over the course of nine years, driving him and his new wives up the wall.

Finally it got too much and Rachel took her own life by drinking weed killer, ensuring a lingering and agonising death. Still alive, her innards burning, she broke through a glass door in her torment, butchering herself. It was the loss of blood that finally killed her. On hearing the news, few who knew Rachel were much surprised. 'Rachel used to love life,' said Ramirez, 'but at the end she wanted to die so badly.'

In the last eighteen months of her life Rachel kept a diary, harrowing in its soul searching and honesty, a peek into the mind of a woman in the clutches of suicidal depression. The last entry read: 'I'm paralysed. What has happened to me? Day after day, night after night, I'm in this shaking fear. What am I so terribly frightened of? Life itself, I think.'

SECOND EARL OF ROCHESTER, JOHN WILMOT
(1647–1680: Libertine)

After the puritan reign of Oliver Cromwell, Charles II brought a bit of glamour back into the ruling monarchy of Britain. His court was full of libertines and rakes, really quite awful people; by far the worst of a very bad bunch was the Second Earl of Rochester. In his brief life – he was only thirty-three when he died – Rochester led the most scandalous existence as a wit, poet and off-his-nut womaniser of the highest calibre. He once confessed to a friend that he'd been consistently drunk for a period of about five years. As Samuel Johnson summed him up: 'In a course of drunken gaiety and gross sensuality, with an avowed contempt of all decency and order, a total disregard to every moral, and a resolute denial of every religious observation, he lived worthless and useless, and blazed out his youth and health in lavish voluptuousness.'

He was born in Ditchley, Oxfordshire, to Henry Wilmot, a hard-drinking Royalist who'd been given the title of Earl of Rochester for military services to Charles II during his exile. From an early age the little earl astounded people with his intelligence and at the extraordinarily young age of twelve was sent to Oxford University. His tutor Robert Whitehall fed the boy academia but is also understood to have introduced him to the delights of drink and, it has been suggested, the company of whores.

At fourteen, Rochester graduated from Oxford and set off on his grand tour of France and Italy. He returned to England at the age of eighteen whereupon he was introduced into the King's court and made an immediate impact, quickly establishing himself as a mighty drinker and founder of what poet Andrew Marvell dubbed 'The Merry Gang'. This was a sort of Restoration age Rat Pack with a membership that included several dukes and earls. They liked to drink, dally with whores, fight duels and strip naked and preach sermons from tavern balconies.

But it was as a philanderer par excellence that Rochester built his reputation. Such was the legendary prowess of his rod that Charles II hired Rochester to seduce virgins and initiate them in the sexual techniques that the King enjoyed in his bedchamber; nice work if you can get it. Rochester also imported dildoes from the continent, selling them to ladies at court and to various nunneries.

His peccadilloes, however, got out of hand when he was thrown in the Tower of London for kidnapping an heiress. Elizabeth Malet was fair of bosom and hefty of fortune and Rochester wanted to get his hands on both. Their courtship, favoured by the King, was cut short when Elizabeth saw sense and called it off. Infuriated, Rochester and a gang of armed men ambushed her coach as it left Westminster Palace and hurried her off into the night. Luckily the plan was thwarted and the King, distinctly unimpressed, threw Rochester in the Tower for a month to teach him a lesson.

But by far Rochester's darkest deed was when he and fellow rapscallion the Duke of Buckingham rented a country inn with the sole purpose of getting the gentlemen of the area cognacked on free wine so they could seduce their wives. It was a successful ruse, but there lived nearby an old miser recently wed to a delectable young bride. So jealous was he of her that she was kept under strict surveillance by a maid. Reluctant to come to the pub of his own accord, Buckingham personally escorted him there, leaving the coast clear for Rochester. Taking the disguise of a woman, Rochester gained entry to the house, drugged the maid and had his wicked way with the young wife. He also persuaded her to steal the miser's money and run away with him. Returning to the inn, Rochester banged her a second time before handing her over to Buckingham. For a short period afterwards the young wife became their plaything until, tired of her, they both kicked her out with instructions to go to London and become a whore, 'the only trade for which she was now fitted'. As for the old miser, when he returned home to find his wife and money gone he hanged himself. Oh how the courtiers did laugh heartily whenever Rochester told this tale.

Rochester didn't seem to give a damn for the consequences of any of his exploits, even when it involved the King himself. Many times he reaped the displeasure of His Majesty and was banished from court, where many a lesser mortal might have lost his head, but his disgrace was never of a long duration: he was such damnably good company Charlie always wanted him back. But court advisers were dismayed that the King consorted with such a rogue. There was the time Rochester, in the company of his gang of rakes, indulged in a drunken brawl at Epsom races culminating in a mutual friend being fatally punctured by a pike. Rochester did a runner but was later apprehended and would have been tried for murder were it not for the King's favour which meant he was safe from prosecution. Not long after that a cook was stabbed to death at a tavern where Rochester was dining and instant rumour named him the killer.

However, he stepped over the mark after a drinking party with friends in the King's apartments at Westminster. Staggering home, they came across the King's favourite sundial in the privy garden. It was a mighty structure, thrusting into the sky in such a phallic way that Rochester commented, 'Dost thou stand there to fuck time?' before he and his mates smashed the thing to pieces. Stone cold sober the next morning, Rochester realised the gravity of what he'd done and immediately scarpered. So distressed was the King that he left London for a sailing trip and wasn't heard of for two weeks. People feared he'd drowned. In the end he returned to court, as did Rochester, tail firmly between his legs.

Aside from his libertine antics, Rochester was a poet and playwright, but his output was so scandalous that it was not published under his name until after his death. Even posthumous printings of his play *Sodom* gave rise to prosecutions for obscenity and were destroyed. His poems, unsurprisingly, are overtly sexual in nature and ribald. Take this 1673 offering:

> I rise at eleven, I dine about two,
> I get drunk before seven, and the next thing I do,
> I send for my whore, when for fear of a clap,
> I spend in her hand, and I spew in her lap;
> Then we quarrel and scold, till I fall fast asleep,
> When the bitch growing bold, to my pocket does creep.
> Then slyly she leaves me, and to revenge the affront,
> At once she bereaves me of money and cunt.
> If by chance then I wake, hot-headed and drunk,
> What a coil do I make for the loss of my punk!
> I storm and I roar, and I fall in a rage.
> And missing my whore, I bugger my page.

When Rochester finally settled down and married it was, bizarrely enough, to the very heiress whom but two years before he'd tried to abduct. They set up home in Oxfordshire and by all accounts it was a successful union. Rochester enjoyed playing the county squire, but didn't give up his other life raising hell in the taverns and whorehouses of London, where catching the pox was almost an occupational hazard. But by 1676 his body was so ravaged by syphilis that rumours of his death circulated around the city. He wrote to a friend saying he had received 'the unhappy news of my own death and burial'.

Soon the disease had a fatal hold on him, his body became a battle-ground of sores and lacerations, his bones ached, his former good looks were rotting away, and his mind was beginning to tilt towards madness. What else explains the bizarre episode that followed? Bored with life at court, Rochester assumed a brand-new persona – that of Dr Bendo, complete with false beard – and set up business in Tower Hill making medicinal brews and potions to aid infertility and other gynaecological ailments. When women came seeking assistance for various undercarriage problems the matronly Mrs Bendo would inspect them privately; of course this was Rochester himself dressed as a woman.

Eventually bored with his medical pranks, Bendo was consigned to the bin and Rochester returned to court, but his life was running out. In 1678 he fell grossly ill as he entered the final stages of syphilis, for which in those days there was no cure. He was probably also suffering from cirrhosis as a result of his alcoholism. Fearing he was at the 'gates of death', so frightening must the prospect have been that he staggered on living for almost two more years until an ulcer burst in his bladder. On his death bed he made a late conversion to Christianity, after being an atheist his whole life, writing 'that from the bottom of my soul I detest and abhor the whole course of my wicked life'.

MICKEY ROURKE (b. 1956: Actor)

For years the essence of anti-establishment cool, a heart-throb for millions of women, Mickey Rourke suffered one of the most spectacular falls from grace that Hollywood has ever seen. He paid the ultimate price for not respecting the hand that fed him; Hollywood will only take so much shit before throwing you to the vultures. And Rourke gave out shit better than most, pissing off studio heads, directors and producers without a second thought for the consequences, ending up running out of bridges to burn. He was a maverick who thought he could win without having to play by the rules; he was dead wrong. As Rourke would lament, 'You know the song, "I Fought the Law and the Law Won"? Well, I fought the system and it kicked the living shit out of me!'

Rourke was born in upstate New York and as a boy was extremely close to his father, an amateur body builder, whom he worshipped. His life was ripped apart at the tender age of six when his parents separated and his mother took him and his brother to live in Miami. Disillusionment soon turned to anger when his mother remarried; Rourke's stepfather was a retired police detective and major disciplinarian who subjected the young boy to severe beatings. The level of physical abuse we're talking about here can be judged by Rourke later comparing his childhood to *Halloween 3*. In years to come he'd label his stepfather 'the violent cop who screwed me up'. Nor could he ever bring himself to quite forgive his mother for turning a blind eye to his suffering and pain.

All that pent-up aggression that Rourke wanted to unleash upon his bastard torturer, but didn't dare, found its outlet on the streets, running wild with a gang of teenage tearaways. When he could have slipped into a life of crime, Rourke joined a local boxing gym, proving to be a natural, and it seemed a career in the ring beckoned until two severe concussions put paid to that dream and he fell into acting almost by accident.

Moving to New York, he studied at the prestigious Lee Strasberg drama school, then spent years struggling to get noticed, taking low-paid jobs just to survive, including a stint as a bouncer at a transvestite nightclub, 'and back then all the transvestites were on this shit called Angel Dust, so you'd hit them over the head with a baseball bat but they'd keep on coming'.

All of a sudden Rourke was the next big thing in films with appearances in *Diner* (1982) and Francis Ford Coppola's *Rumble Fish* (1983), and then hailed as the new Brando with moody, off-beat roles in *9½ Weeks* (1986) and *Angel Heart* (1987). Problem was, he adopted the rebel personality of the characters he played and stuck his finger up to authority. He carved out a well-deserved reputation as being difficult and came to resent and hate the business he'd conquered, the bullshit politics; he was only too happy to slag off his own films, calling *Harley Davidson and the Marlboro Man* (1991) 'a complete piece of shit'. He's right, of course, but few in Hollywood badmouth their own product.

Rourke started hanging around with gangland figures or turning up on film sets with an entourage of Hells Angels and assorted other mean-looking bastards. A sign on his trailer door read: ALL STUDIO EXECUTIVES AND PRODUCERS TO STAY THE FUCK AWAY. He'd miss early morning calls because he'd been up all night partying. His mansion in Beverly Hills was like Elvis on acid, with a Jolly Roger flag fluttering outside. The neighbours were moving in and out almost monthly.

A lot of Rourke's hellraising was fuelled by booze. His family tree reeked of the stuff, his father drank himself to death at just forty-nine and assorted uncles were also afflicted. Some say Rourke couldn't handle his fame, that the bigger he got the more he seemed to self-destruct and the heavier he drank. His barren childhood had a lot to do with it; 'so when I had some success, I went ballistic'.

There was something else driving him, too, something powerful: sheer, white-hot rage, a rage that he's spent years and a small fortune in therapy trying to control. It perhaps explains why in 1991 Rourke made one of the most bizarre decisions any movie star has ever made, jacking in acting to become a professional boxer. Getting repeatedly pounded in the head might have helped him work out some of his anger issues, but by the time he reached forty Rourke was facing possible brain damage if he carried on. So he quit, his brain still this side of normality, but his face wasn't so lucky: his nose had to be rebuilt with cartilage from his ear and he had to endure several bouts of reconstructive surgery that left him looking like a Batman villain. 'I looked in the mirror one day and went, Holy shit!'

Outside the ring his life was even more screwed. Rourke's first marriage to actress Debra Feuer broke down and his second to model Carré Otis never stood a chance. He was regularly bouncing off the walls and she was a heroin addict. As Rourke said, 'I met someone who was as damaged as me and all hell broke loose.' Indeed, Carré was mysteriously shot in the shoulder by a gun registered to Rourke, later claiming that the gun went off accidentally when she moved the bag it was in. No charges were brought. Rourke also punched a heroin dealer who was selling dope to Carré. 'I hit him harder than anybody in my life. He was out before he hit the ground. I hit an artery and there was a stream of blood that went twenty feet into the air.'

In July 1994 it was alleged he'd used his fists on Carré and he was arrested by police. The charges of spousal abuse were later dropped, but this wouldn't be the last time Mickey would have run-ins with the law. In January 1994 there was a fracas outside a Miami nightclub and Rourke was picked up for resisting arrest. And in 2007 in Miami he was arrested on suspicion of driving a motor scooter while intoxicated. 'Fuck you,

I'm not drunk,' he blasted, and was proved to be just under the legal limit.

Inevitably Rourke and Carré divorced, but the split devastated him, sending him almost to the brink of suicide. At one point it was only the intervention of a priest that stopped him taking a gun and shooting Carré's violent drug dealer before turning the barrel on himself. 'If I wasn't Catholic, I probably would have blown my brains out.'

His life empty of Carré and boxing, it was soon to be void of acting; no one in Hollywood wanted to hire him. He'd now lost everything: his home, a wife, flashy cars, his fortune, his career all gone. Virtually broke, Rourke lived in a rented apartment, an apartment he once managed to set on fire when he left a TV dinner in the oven and fell asleep in the living room. The doorman raised the alarm and managed to pull Mickey out from the smoke-filled rooms. He was desperate, alone, and cracking up. People in the street would stare at him, trying to conjure up exactly who he was. Or some lone nutter, recognising him from his bad-boy days, wanted to take him on; Rourke once sustained a severe knife wound to the arm in broad daylight. It was nightmarish. He was in such a dark place that Rourke has claimed to have deliberately sliced the top of his little finger off, until it was hanging just by a single tendon. He needed hours of microsurgery to sew it back on.

For years the only work on offer to Rourke was minor roles and straight-to-DVD clunkers; that was until *The Wrestler* (2008), his first mainstream starring role in almost two decades. It brought him undreamed-of adulation and acclaim, even an Oscar nomination.

Welcomed back into the Hollywood fraternity, Rourke was under no illusion as to who was to blame for his downfall, namely himself, and that he was determined not to blow it this time. There would be no third chance, you feel. Says Rourke, 'My grandmother always said: "God has a plan for all of us." I should have went along with his, not mine. My plan sucked!'

'BABE' RUTH (1895–1948: Baseball Player)

He was the Pelé of his sport, the Tiger Woods, the Muhammad Ali, a man who so dominated his chosen profession that eventually he eclipsed it. But his wild lifestyle, which personified roaring-twenties hedonism, saw him frequently at odds with authority. For an athlete supposedly in prime fitness, Ruth partied till all hours, didn't give a stuff for team curfews, drank to excess, ate junk food by the tonnage, crashed cars and womanised like crazy. He was an unstoppable force of nature.

Born George Herman Ruth in a tough, working-class district of Baltimore – some would say slum – Ruth was a self-confessed bum as a kid, skipping school, stealing, brawling and throwing rotten tomatoes at police officers. Early on he learned to drink; swilling the dregs of the beer in his father's saloon, and by seven was chewing tobacco. Family members recalled that the young 'Babe' sometimes smoked, drank and chewed tobacco all at the same time.

Exasperated and unable to handle their rowdy son, Ruth's parents sent him to a Catholic school for boys in the hope it would straighten him out. It was there that he picked up a baseball bat for the first time and, channelling all that rebellious spirit, proved a natural at the sport. Leaving school in 1914 to join a local minor-league team, where his youthfulness earned him the nickname 'Babe', he was soon snapped up by the Boston Red Sox of the majors and hitting home runs for fun.

After a deprived upbringing, Ruth embraced his new life rather too enthusiastically. He drove fast and recklessly and thought nothing of stuffing his face with a half-dozen hot dogs, sometimes on the bench during a game. After which he'd take some bicarbonate of soda to belch out the gas. Team-mate Ty Cobb claims he once saw Ruth eat six sandwiches and an entire jar of pigs' knuckles washed down by a pitcher of beer.

'Babe' was one of those drinkers who didn't class beer as booze. Alcohol was whisky, and he drank plenty of both. If you believe his team-mates, Ruth was capable of draining a bathtub full of beer and two bottles of rye in a single session. 'Sometimes I reflect on all the beer I drink and I feel ashamed,' he once said, in reflective mood. 'Then I think about the workers in the brewery and all of their hopes and dreams. If I didn't drink, they might be out of work and their dreams would be shattered. So it's better to drink this beer and let their dreams come true than be selfish and worry about my liver.' The words of a true humanitarian.

Not only could Ruth drink enough for half a dozen men, but he belched like a god and could fart at will. Amongst the many accolades and trophies he won during his illustrious career, Ruth was particularly fond of earning first place in a farting contest. 'Honest,' he'd say to disbelieving visitors, pointing out the trophy. 'Read the writing on it. Boy, I had to down a lot of beer and Limburger to win that one.'

But this exuberance got the better of him sometimes. During one game he punched an umpire he thought was making bad decisions and was dismissed from the game. During another season he was suspended a total of five times for various misdemeanours. He also seemed destined for a head-on collision with his team's owners. On away matches Ruth liked to party all night, returning to the team hotel at dawn. Caught out one time, the tough-minded boss of the Red Sox team confronted him at the ballpark the next day. The argument got so heated that Ruth challenged his boss to a fist fight. But there was only ever going to be one winner; Ruth sat out the next match embarrassed on the bench.

When Ruth left the Red Sox in 1920 to play for the New York Yankees, crowds flocked to see him. One awed sportswriter wrote, 'The more I see of "Babe", the more he seems a figure out of mythology.' As for his reputation for living it up, if anything it increased, with the full complicity of sports journalists, who back then allowed the stars to misbehave without fear of public exposure. There's a story about Ruth chasing a naked woman through a train carriage and a bunch of reporters playing cards nearby not taking the slightest notice.

In each new town after a game Ruth would hit the nightspots and party hard. Once in Miami he got so mothered that chasing a fly ball during the following afternoon's game he ran directly into a palm tree and knocked himself out. Even prohibition didn't stop him; Ruth had a bootlegger in every city. His standing order was a case of whisky, a case of rye and enough beer to fill a bathtub. No one could keep up with him; Ruth was reputed to have never been beaten in a drinking bout.

Some team-mates would go out on benders with him and the next afternoon at the game they'd be sitting in the dugout nursing horrendous hangovers; Ruth would just get up and hit a home run.

In many ways Ruth was a simple man; some judged his rowdy and lewd behaviour as that of a juvenile who never really grew up. But unlike the prima donna sports stars of today, he was a man of the people, literally. He'd no bodyguards or entourage and would just show up in pubs or bars and drink with his fans, happily signing autographs and posing for photographs.

Besides booze and broads, married twice, 'Babe' was a committed womaniser; his other weakness was for speed, buying customised sports cars and invariably wrecking them. Traffic lights were a nuisance for Ruth so he ignored them on his daily drives to the Yankee stadium; police would smile and let him go. One time he was driving the wrong way down a one-way street when he was pulled over by an irate cop who visibly cowered when he saw who the man was behind the wheel and profusely apologised.

But this love of cars almost cost Ruth his life one night. Driving his latest purchase along a rural road in Pennsylvania, he sped too dangerously around a bend flipping the car off the road. The vehicle was a write-off and, miraculously, Ruth crawled out of the smoking wreckage uninjured. However the next day local newspapers reported: RUTH KILLED IN CAR CRASH. He shrugged his shoulders and returned to New York to purchase an exact duplicate of the smashed-up car and carried on much as before. When he was caught speeding for the second time in a year, the judge fined him $100. Nonchalantly Ruth searched in his jacket pocket and peeled off a single note from a wad of bills. Outraged by such frippery, the judge demanded he spend the day in jail.

By this time Ruth was earning the highest salary in professional sports, peaking at $80,000 in 1930, this in the midst of the Great Depression. Asked by a reporter if he deserved to get more money than the President of the United States, Ruth said simply, 'I had a better year than he did.'

For a relatively uneducated guy Ruth had a neat turn of phrase and an infectious sense of fun. He loved to play practical jokes. A favourite was hiring the biggest room in a hotel to host wild parties and wiring one of the chairs to give the sitter a mild electric shock. Other jokes included dropping lit cigarettes into team-mates' pants as they were putting them on and stuffing the smallest member of the team into a locker as the players left to enter the field. One team-mate recalled taking a shower after a game once and feeling a strange hot sensation on his back; it was Ruth pissing on him.

This penchant for practical jokes perhaps went too far when he prepared a small explosive device and placed it inside a friend's car. Alas, Ruth used too much gunpowder so instead of the mild bang he'd anticipated the blast nearly wrecked the damn vehicle.

By the mid-twenties various bouts of illness, injuries and his roistering lifestyle had begun to slow the great man down a bit. When he collapsed before a game a London newspaper reported that he'd died and even printed an obituary. But he was soon hitting home runs again, and misbehaving, to the consternation of the Yankees' team manager Miller Huggins, whom Ruth always ribbed mercilessly. One tale has him grabbing Huggins by the heels and hanging him upside down off the back of a moving train.

Towards the end of his playing days, thanks in large part to a diligent second wife, Ruth eased back on his fine living, particularly the booze. But at thirty-four his remarkable physical prowess was on the wane. His body had taken a severe battering over the years and was now creaking and rusting like a once great locomotive. Every game he seemed to get slower, swing and miss the ball a little more often. Home crowds sensed the end was only a matter of time and in 1935 Ruth retired, clinging to a dream he'd had for years to manage his beloved Yankees. Diligently he waited at home by the phone for the call that never came. He was devastated; the game he'd given his life's blood for had spurned him. Maybe it was payback for all those hellraising antics.

Those last few years for Ruth were times of sadness and frustration. He tried to play golf, did a bit of travelling, but it was obvious that he was an empty shell, all his passion for life had been sucked out. In one last bid he wrote a letter to the Yankees owner, pleading to be made their manager. When the reply arrived it was another rejection. Ruth put his head in his hands and just cried; everything was gone. That's when the depression started and he began drinking heavily again. It reached the point where he contemplated suicide, locking himself in his room and threatening to jump out of the window. He was finally coaxed out but the episode haunted his wife from that day onwards.

It was cancer that got him in the end. 'Babe' was only fifty-four. His legend lives on, though; it echoes around every baseball stadium in America. It's his records that every hotshot player wants to break. But it's not just the number of home runs he hit, sometimes more home runs per season than an entire team managed, but the sheer distance of them. At one exhibition game Ruth hit one ball out of the ground and into a neighbouring farmer's field. People joked that when it finally came down it was covered in ice.

S

BON SCOTT (1946–1980: Musician)

A role model for every tattooed, bare-chested rock hellraiser since, Bon Scott lived the clichéd boozy rocker's lifestyle to the hilt as lead singer of AC/DC, stuffing a sock full of sand down the front of his pants before going on stage, telling a crew hand, 'The chicks love it, mate.'

His formidable constitution was a source of wonder for years, able to consume industrial quantities of booze while still managing to hoist the lead guitarist onto his shoulders and parade him round the stage. 'It keeps you fit,' he once said. 'The alcohol, nasty women, sweat on stage, bad food – it's all very good for you.' He had it all – the voice, the demeanour; everything was primed for stardom when he had the misfortune to literally drink himself to death on the eve of AC/DC attaining the worldwide recognition for which they had worked so tirelessly. It's one of rock's great ironies.

Born in Kirriemuir, Scotland, Bon was six years old when his family emigrated to Australia, settling near Perth. His affinity for music derived from his father, who played drums in a local Scots pipe band. But a lifelong distaste for authority led to him dropping out of school at fifteen and becoming something of a wannabe Ned Kelly. Aged sixteen he spent several months in a juvenile institution after being charged with unlawful carnal knowledge and stealing petrol. On his release he attempted to join the Australian army but was rejected for being 'socially maladjusted'.

So, perfect credentials for a career in rock music. From the mid-sixties onwards Bon was in a number of successful local bands, notably the Valentines, a bubblegum pop band for teenage girls, until their squeaky clean image evaporated in 1969 after a drug bust and they disbanded.

Bon was as fiery offstage as he was on, a rebel living an exaggerated lifestyle. Mainly it was about the music, but having as good a time as possible ranked pretty high. Being 'straight' was a state to be liberated from. Prog rockers Fraternity were his next band, who dubbed him 'Road Test Ronnie' as he was generally the first to try any new type of acid or weed. 'He seemed able to cope with any drug that science or nature could come up with,' recalled one band member. Only Datura knocked him out for a few days, so the others wisely avoided it.

Bon's next group was Mount Lofty Rangers, but that didn't last very long. Relations were strained and during one rehearsal a drunken Scott had a raging argument and stormed out. Throwing a bottle of Jack Daniel's on the ground, he hopped onto his brand new Suzuki 550 motorbike and screamed off into the distance. He didn't get very far. Next thing his friends heard he was in hospital, close to death after colliding with a car. He was smashed to smithereens, his jaw wired, most of his teeth knocked out, a broken collar bone, busted ribs and deep slashes across his throat. Bon remained in a coma for three days.

Miraculously he survived and was back looking for work in the music biz. By 1974 Bon was in Sydney as a roadie for a newly formed band called AC/DC. When lead singer Dave Evans fell out with the group Scott was the obvious replacement, and as their new front man AC/DC quickly established themselves as the most popular rock act in Australia. But while the other musicians enjoyed a quiet rest after gigs, Bon partied till dawn, downing Scotch and bedding groupies. There were so many girls around the band you had to beat them off with sticks. Bon was indulging one of them in his dressing room when there was a loud rap at the door. 'Fuck off! I'm having a fuck.' It was the girl's father and a friend, who smashed their way in, tenderised Bon like he was a steak, smashed out his new front teeth and threw what was left of him outside into a rose bush.

He embraced the rock lifestyle a little too earnestly, coming perilously close to dying plenty of times from booze, drugs and living on the edge. On tour in America Bon hooked up with some guys in San Francisco who distilled their own alcohol and the band didn't see him again for three days. While staying at a motel in Melbourne he emerged onto the balcony completely koalaed and dived into the swimming pool – from the second floor! And there was the time when he arrived at London Airport, three days late, wearing only his pants and a pair of sunglasses – no shoes, no shirt, just pants – and not knowing how he'd got there, or indeed where he'd come from or what he'd been up to.

But he took his duties as the band's elder statesman seriously by making sure the other guys from AC/DC did not follow his bad example. His advice to them was, 'Whatever I do, you don't!' Sometimes it was difficult. On tour in the wild Australian outback Scott arranged to have some stranger he'd just met supply the band with booze at their motel. This guy duly turned up with a crateload of bottles, unfortunately all stolen from the other motel rooms. The police arrived, sirens blazing and a voice on the megaphone – 'We've got you surrounded. Come out!' Scott grabbed guitarist Angus Young's famous school cap and walked out totally starkers into a searchlight beam, 'Hello, officers!' he called. It turned out this stranger Bon had met was on the cops' most-wanted list.

In 1979 AC/DC finally cracked the international market with the album *Highway to Hell*. On tour in America, Bon really let rip. After a show in San Antonio, Texas, he was so incapacitated that he polished off an entire bottle of aftershave in a single gulp, mistaking it for whisky.

At the height of his powers, Bon's drinking was getting out of control, taking him over. He'd be as organised as a pile of coat hangers before gigs, unable to string two words together backstage, but then in front of the audience he could sing coherently and word perfect. There were also problems back home with the Ozzie excise men chasing him for an estimated eleven years of back taxes.

In London for a few days enjoying the night life he got so jackassed one evening he passed out and a friend, Alistair Kinnear, drove him back to his digs in East Dulwich. Unable to wake the rocker, Kinnear left him in the car to sleep off his hectic night of partying. The following morning Kinnear found Scott's body curled horribly around the gear stick. Rushed to hospital, Scott was pronounced dead on arrival. For years fans debated whether it was alcohol poisoning or the classic suffocating on his own vomit that killed their idol, or merely a mundane case of hypothermia. The coroner had no compunction in announcing the cause as 'death by misadventure'. Bon was just thirty-three. I wonder what he would have regretted more: the actual act of dying or having done so in a parked car in East Dulwich.

Scott was cremated and his ashes interred in Fremantle cemetery, which became something of a pilgrimage site for fans who liked to sit at his grave and have a beer near the great man.

Scott's death left a gaping hole in AC/DC and for a while the other members contemplated disbanding to honour his memory. In the belief he'd want them to continue they did just that, hiring new vocalist Brian Johnson and recording *Back in Black* which became one of the biggest selling albums of all time, placing AC/DC amongst the pantheon of rock bands; too late for Bon.

GEORGE C SCOTT (1927–1999: Actor)

With his tough-as-nails face, a nose battered flat in bar-room brawls and intense acting style, George C Scott was regarded as one of the finest American actors of his generation. But he was from the very beginning a maverick, shocking Hollywood in 1971 by becoming the first person ever to refuse an Academy Award, for his performance in *Patton* (1970). Scott had his fair share of inner demons you could say. Combined with a bestial temper that gave vent to physical violence, he was sometimes a dangerous man to be around; he half-pulverised Ava Gardner when she refused to marry him. This is a man who once hired a bodyguard not to protect him from stalkers or fans, but to protect other people from him! He was a brute, a falling-down drunk, a one-off.

Born in Virginia, he was just eight years old when his mother died; he was raised by his father, an automobile-company executive. Graduating from high school in 1945 he enlisted in the US Marines, spending most of his time burying bodies in Arlington National Cemetery, depressing work that led to a solid drinking habit he'd never manage to shake off. 'You can't look at that many widows in veils and hear that many Taps without taking a drink,' he later said.

After his discharge Scott took up acting, spending the obligatory lean years on Broadway before picking up notable film roles in *The Hustler* (1961) and as the demented bomb-loving US General in *Dr Strangelove* (1964). By the time he made *The Bible* (1966) in Rome he was married to the actress Colleen Dewhurst and an international star, someone used to getting into trouble, and used to getting his own way. His co-star was Ava Gardner, who found herself responsive to his charm and intelligence. That's when he was sober; ginned-up was a different matter: 'He'd go berserk in a way that was quite terrifying,' reported Ava. Despite the warnings she began an intense affair with him.

Shooting one highly charged scene Scott, who'd been drinking all day, suddenly went bananas and ripped off his costume, throwing the torn remnants on the floor and storming off the set in his underwear. 'Why?' thought Ava. 'God only knows.' After another night of drinking Scott decided to take his anger out on Ava's face. She'd tried to leave the room after a heated argument but he'd flung her against the door and punched her so hard she hit the floor. His fists rained down on her defenceless face one after the other. The next morning she arrived on set with bruises and a black eye.

The Bible's director John Huston was so appalled that he hired three tough-looking Mafiosi-types to act as Ava's bodyguard for the duration of filming. If Scott ever appeared threatening or about to strike they moved in and quietly, but firmly, put him inside a car and drove him away.

When the film wrapped Scott followed Ava to London and the Savoy Hotel. Hearing him banging on her door, she hid in the bathroom while her female assistant tried to get rid of him. Scott wasn't taking no for an answer and pushed a broken bottle at her throat. Somehow Ava got out and alerted security. Scott was led to his own room and told to behave. He did no such thing, smashing the place to pieces. Charged with being drunk and disorderly, he spent a night in the cells.

You'd think that might have been the end of it, but no, Scott had left his wife for Ava and wasn't taking no for an answer; he was certainly persistent, you have to give him that. Back in LA Ava was staying in a private bungalow at the Beverly Hills Hotel when in the early hours of the morning someone put their fist through the back door. She knew who it was. Stinking of whisky sweat, the hulking figure of Scott loomed out of the darkness, pleading with her to come back and marry him. The ultimatum was clear: if he couldn't have her, nobody would. Ava stuck to her principles and pleaded with the brute that it wouldn't work between them. That's not what he wanted to hear and Scott smashed her across the face, followed by more blows. Breaking a bottle, he waved the jagged edges in front of Ava's terrified face. 'Marry me, do you hear what I'm saying?' Not the most romantic proposal ever. The threats and beatings carried on for hours until Ava managed to call a doctor who came over and gave Scott a sedative. A mutual friend arrived with him and when she saw the damage Scott had wrought – Ava had a detached retina in one eye and heavy bruising – rushed to the fireplace to get a poker to pummel the fucker with. 'Don't, he'll kill us both,' Ava screamed.

Just then Scott got up and walked through the broken back door and was gone. Ava never saw him again, though for years if a movie of his appeared on TV she'd start to shake and have to turn the set off.

After the madness of Ava, Scott joined Alcoholics Anonymous; probably a good idea. He also returned to Colleen Dewhurst and they remarried. But it didn't last and they divorced for the second time in 1972.

Scott would marry a total of five times. In between movies and weddings he was dedicated to the theatre and often appeared on stage, but his drunken behaviour terrified his co-workers. During a Broadway play he punched a mirror in his dressing room, 'probably because I didn't like what I saw in it', cutting his hand so badly he had to finish the play wearing a rubber glove that was full of blood by the end. 'My violent behaviour is some sort of aberration,' he once said. 'A character defect I'm not particularly proud of.' The guy was a tough bastard, no question, and didn't take kindly to intrusion from the press, regularly beating up paparazzi and nosy journalists.

Backstage during another play he trashed his dressing room, then broke one of his hands hitting some scenery because he couldn't stand one of his co-stars. There's the time he got so off his pickle and realised he was in no fit state to perform that evening so he simply didn't show up at the theatre. During rehearsals of *Plaza Suite*, Maureen Stapleton confided to director Mike Nichols: 'I'm so frightened of George I don't know what to do.' Nichols replied: 'My dear, the whole world is frightened of George.' He once spectacularly leaped off stage mid-performance to run after a woman who had taken his photograph.

Scott called his heavy drinking 'an addiction', confessing to a fellow actor that he downed a quart of vodka a day, washed down by beer. As for pubs, they were 'a very necessary part of my life'. As were bar-room brawls. With his reputation as a hard man there was always someone eager to take him on, and Scott often obliged, busting his nose at least five times in fights. To say that Scott was a complex man would be like saying Albert Einstein had a good Mensa score.

Back in the cinema, Scott played his most famous role in 1970, General Patton, but fought continually with director Franklin J Schaffner and sat out two shooting days with a bottle for company. 'I got fed up, exhausted and frustrated, so I'd go out and get loaded.' It was this kind of behaviour that eventually affected the kind of work available to Scott and by the late 1970s he'd become a faded grand actor.

Making *Hardcore* (1979), an unsettling drama abut a father looking for his daughter caught up in the porn world, some scenes were shot in the red-light district of San Francisco. As the crew set up, Scott sat alone in his trailer getting wasted, then wouldn't come out when they were ready for him. No one could budge him. Finally, he demanded to see the director, Paul Schrader. Walking inside, Schrader saw Scott sitting in his underwear, a big bottle of vodka cradled in his arm. 'This movie's a piece of shit,' Scott blasted. Oh dear, thought Schrader, this is going to be difficult. 'Well, George, we're all ready. All you have to do is put on your wardrobe, say your two lines and you can go home.' After a sullen silence of considerable length Scott agreed, on one condition. 'What's that?' asked Schrader. Scott leaned forward. 'You must promise me that you will never direct another motion picture again.'

Schrader had no choice, he dropped to his knees: 'Mr Scott, you're right. I'm a good writer but a terrible director. I promise you here and now that I will never direct again.' Scott slapped Schrader on the shoulder, 'Good! Good. OK, let's go and do that shot!'

Scott was the first to acknowledge he'd caused maximum chaos around him over the years. In his late fifties he gave up drinking but then hit the bottle again on his sixty-third birthday, not sure now if he ever could go back on the wagon. 'And I'm not worried about it,' he said defiantly. 'What I am is a functional alcoholic.'

He did mellow in his later years; the odd heart attack helped to slow him down. His last marriage, though, to actress Trish Van Devere, followed the same tempestuous path as all the others. The final straw had been a cruise where they fought constantly. At one of the ports Trish mutinied and refused to get back on board. After a trial separation they agreed to get back together but decided it was best to live a continent apart: one would live on the west coast, the other on the east.

Scott continued to drink right up to the end, dying from a ruptured abdominal aortic aneurysm. As suited his personality, he allegedly refused surgery that might have saved his life because it meant he would have had to quit drinking.

ROBERT SHAW (1927–1978: Actor)

Like most of that hellraising generation of British actors – Burton, Harris et al. – of which he was part, Robert Shaw took his drinking very seriously and had the constitution of an ox. When he started, few if any could match him pint for pint or stay the course. He was also one of the most competitive individuals ever placed on this earth. After he made *The Sting* in 1973 he invited its director George Roy Hill over to Ireland for what turned into a two-day pub crawl. 'I think we must have hit every pub in West Ireland,' said Hill. 'And I made the serious error of trying to keep up with him drink for drink.' Back at Shaw's home Hill collapsed exhausted into bed only to be woken up by the sound of screaming. Downstairs in the games room Shaw was stripped to his shorts, pummelling an opponent into submission at ping-pong yelling, 'One more game, you son of a bitch, one more game!'

He was born in Westhoughton, Lancashire, but grew up in the harsh wilderness of the Orkneys where his father was a doctor and a fearsome drinker. When his boozing got out of control his wife took the children away from what she called his 'disruptive' influence. And although they did reconcile, he informed her one day that he was going to kill himself, to which she replied, 'Don't do it in front of the children.' He promptly swallowed a bottle of poison and was dead. Robert Shaw was just twelve years old.

After his father's death, Shaw was taken to his mother's native Cornwall, where he grew up to be a keen sportsman. Admitting to bouts of laziness at school, he was good enough to earn a place at Cambridge but instead went to RADA determined to become an actor, although his teacher tried to warn him off, saying he was too rebellious to succeed in such a cut-throat business. She was certainly half right. At Stratford he won the admiration of John Gielgud, but scared him to death at the same time. Shaw knew he was a trouble maker. 'I was always against authority. As a young man I had no charm. I was all aggression.'

Now married with a young family, Shaw was forced to take menial jobs to supplement his income as a struggling actor. His big break arrived when he won the lead role in the swashbuckling TV series *The Buccaneers* (1956–7), and appeared in the hit play *The Long and the Short and the Tall* with Peter O'Toole. He made even bigger headlines when he ditched his wife and stole actress Mary Ure from the *Look Back in Anger* playwright John Osborne. They married in 1963, the same year Shaw hit screen paydirt as the blond assassin out to kill James Bond in *From Russia with Love*.

Then came a spurt of big Hollywood movies, playing a Nazi tank commander in *Battle of the Bulge* (1965), and an Oscar-nominated turn as Henry VIII in *A Man for All Seasons* (1966). But behind the facade of the movie star was a mighty drinker who once boasted that he downed more booze than any of his hellraising contemporaries. 'Drink? Can you imagine being a movie star and having to take it seriously without a drink?' asked Shaw. 'I agree with Burton that drink gives poetry to life.'

He arrived once heavily tanked up for the Johnny Carson show to announce to the watching millions that he had syphilis. In fact he was playing Randolph Churchill in a film at the time, who died of that disease, so maybe his raddled brain had got confused. 'But I never hit anybody over the head with a bottle or punched anybody in the mouth,' he'd say of his drinking. 'There was never any violence.' A consummate artist, Shaw was a sensitive man beneath all the bluster. He once read a graphic account of a man dying of cancer and felt convinced he had all the symptoms. He went around London asking friends, 'Do I reek of death?' He was quite definitely a man's man, though, and didn't take any nonsense from anybody. Walking home one night he saw a group of men insulting a woman. Grabbing the largest of the yobs, Shaw threw him hard against a brick wall and dared his dozen buddies to take him on.

So he had a temper, that's for sure, and he and Mary had fiery rows; she'd throw things at him and he was known to take a swing at her. It was a combustible marriage; Mary had been the bigger star when they first met and resented now taking a back seat to Shaw, sacrificing her own career to raise children. She appeared in the odd film, notably co-starring with Burton and Clint Eastwood in *Where Eagles Dare* (1969), but not much else. Shaw was an old-fashioned husband and insisted he be the main breadwinner. It worsened her own drinking problem that had begun when she was with the adulterous Osborne. Sometimes her drinking resulted in bizarre behaviour. One night Shaw woke up in their New York apartment to find Mary gone. Fearing the worst, he searched the city, finally finding her wandering naked around Central Park.

With money rolling in Shaw moved to rural Ireland to escape the draconian British tax laws, as far removed from the false glitz of Hollywood as you can imagine. He loved it, spending much of the time down the local pub, sometimes serving behind the bar when it got busy.

In quick succession Shaw made two films that elevated him to superstar status. He was Paul Newman's choice to play the villain he and Robert Redford con in *The Sting* (1973), and then Steven Spielberg cast him as the maverick shark hunter in *Jaws* (1975). When Shaw first read the script he called it 'a piece of shit'; it was Mary, as she'd earlier done with the Bond film, who talked her husband into taking the role.

Shaw's trouble with alcohol was a frequent source of tension during filming, especially those weeks working in a cramped boat on the ocean. In later interviews Roy Scheider described Shaw as 'a perfect gentleman whenever he was sober. All he needed was one drink and then he turned into a competitive son-of-a-bitch.' Most of his hostility was directed at co-star Richard Dreyfuss. It all started the day Shaw poured himself a large whisky while bemoaning, 'I wish I could stop drinking.' Dreyfuss said, 'OK,' grabbed the glass from his hand and threw it out of the porthole. 'He didn't forgive me for that,' said Dreyfuss. Shaw went on to provoke the young actor from that day on, baiting him sometimes with anti-Jewish remarks. It was his way of creating a feeling of antagonism that their screen characters shared, but it was tough. Shaw offered Dreyfuss $1,000 to climb the boat's seventy-foot mast and jump into the sea. When he refused, Shaw called him a coward. Another time he drenched him with a fire hose. 'That's it,' hollered Dreyfuss, 'I don't want to work with you any more, go fuck yourself,' and he walked off set for the day.

At home things weren't going so well with Mary; she was becoming more reliant on drink and prescription drugs as she saw her career go to hell and her husband cheating with his secretary. Determined to return to the stage, she was cast in a pre-Broadway tour of *Love for Love*, but was sacked after only a few weeks; replaced by her understudy Glenn Close. Mary was devastated; 'It seemed to her to be the end of everything,' said Shaw.

In 1975 Mary found another engagement, this one on the London stage. Anxious about the opening night's reception she took some sleeping pills to calm her nerves but still managed to engage in a blazing row with Shaw, who went to bed leaving her to sleep on the sofa. The next morning he left for the location of a film he was making in the capital, noticing Mary hadn't stirred yet. Returning that afternoon with a bunch of newspapers full of praise for her performance, he found Mary in the same position, stone cold, dead. Incredibly, Shaw informed the relevant authorities and then returned to work, completing that day's filming. 'Then I collapsed and cried all the tears in my body for three days.' The coroner's report later stated that death had been due to a lethal combination of alcohol and sleeping pills. Rumours persisted it may have been a suicide. She was just forty-two.

Mary's tragic death sent Shaw reeling. Plagued by nightmares, he'd wake up screaming in the middle of the night, sit up and instinctively touch the space beside him, thinking Mary was there. He could only comfortably return to sleep with his children in the room. Consumed by guilt that he hadn't been there for Mary when she needed him, he dealt with it the only way he knew how: drink, and lots of it. 'My grief was such that I tried to drown it with floods of vodka.' He managed to pull himself out of it for the sake of his children, and also remarried.

Capitalising on his *Jaws* success, Shaw made *The Deep* (1977), teaming up with another notable drinker, Nick Nolte. Unsurprisingly they got on well, sitting up every night drinking vodka and reading novels aloud. Shaw knew the film was formulaic schlock, telling Nolte, 'It's a treasure picture! A treasure picture! Let's drink some rum!'

One day they were shooting on a boat. Rain began to fall, not giving up for hours as the cast and crew sat around. Shaw turned to Nolte, 'See that bottle of whisky over there?' Nolte glanced at it, 'Yeah.' 'Let's have it.' The two started drinking; the more the rain came down the more they kept drinking, cracking open another bottle. Finally at five o'clock a little ray of sunshine broke through the clouds. 'Let's get the shot!' shouted director Peter Yates. Nolte jumped up all eager, also very blitzed, desperately trying to pretend he wasn't. 'No, no, let me handle this,' said Shaw, walking to the front of the boat where he promptly fell flat on his face. 'Oh my God, he's drunk!' said Yates. Shaw then proceeded to roll off the side into the water, where he climbed into a little dinghy, started it up and headed across the bay. 'Everybody was terribly frightened to go get Shaw,' Nolte later recalled. 'So I got elected since we were friends. So I go across the bay, to this house where he is. I look through the window and I see him sitting in a chair with another bottle. So I crack open the door and say, "Bob . . . ?" He turns to me and says, "What took you so long?" That was Shaw.'

He made no secret of the fact that he was now making movies purely for the money, describing 1978's *Force 10 from Navarone* as a 'genuine piece of shit'. It was a war picture, and Shaw was embarrassed 'to be running around a mountain in Yugoslavia with a machine gun' at his age. Its director, Guy Hamilton, knew Shaw was an alcoholic, surmising that the illness was somehow fated. 'His father died at an early age of alcoholism and Bob Shaw was absolutely convinced that he was going to follow in his footsteps. And did everything to prove it. I was deeply fond of Bob, but I think he was an unhappy man and there's nothing you can do with a true alcoholic.' What happened with Shaw was, two beers and he'd be drunk, but the terrifying thing was it took two or three days before he was compos mentis again. You'd simply go round and say, 'How many fingers am I holding up, Bob?' and until you got the right answer they couldn't shoot with him.

Shaw took his fragile physique onto his next film *Avalanche Express* (1979). His voice was so weak and his delivery so shaky that the producers had to hire another actor to dub the soundtrack. By the time the film opened, Shaw was dead. Driving in Ireland near his home with his wife, exploring the countryside as they liked to do, Shaw complained of severe chest pains and stopped the car, hoping to walk it off. He'd only taken a few steps when he collapsed by the side of the road, it was a massive heart attack. Fifteen minutes later he was pronounced dead and cinema had been deprived of one of its real characters.

FRANK SINATRA (1915–1998: Singer/Actor)

Widely held to be the greatest singer in American pop history, Frank Sinatra's incredible rise and fall, and rise again and continued legendhood was fuelled by whisky and not an awful lot of water. His favourite tipple was Jack Daniel's. He swore by the stuff. 'I'm for anything that gets you through the night, be it prayer, tranquillisers or a bottle of Jack Daniel's.' He could polish off a whole bottle at one sitting. It helped lubricate the vocal cords, but also unleashed a monster so ferocious that people just backed off and waited for the hurricane to pass, then surveyed the damage. You tended to have a better chance at staying alive that way.

Sinatra arrived on this earth in a slum area of Hoboken, New Jersey. Actually he almost didn't; he was still-born, but thanks to quick thinking by his grandmother, a former midwife, the infant was doused with cold water and survived. From good Italian stock – his father hailed from Sicily – Sinatra decided on a singing career in the footsteps of his idol Bing Crosby, and after years of hard graft in clubs emerged in the early 1940s as arguably the first modern pop star, his appearances provoking the kind of mass hysteria that wouldn't be eclipsed until Elvis and The Beatles.

Even as a young star Sinatra had a mean hankering for booze; he and some mates would hire a hotel room some weekends and just get blasted. 'I woke up one morning and found myself wrapped round a mailbox in the street,' Frank fondly recalled years later. The abuse he heaped upon his body was such that doctors feared it might kill him, and he wasn't even thirty yet. 'Alcohol may be man's worst enemy,' Sinatra once quipped, 'but the Bible says love your enemy.'

By the early fifties Sinatra's star had not so much fallen as plummeted, his singles failed to chart and no one went to see him at the movies. He grew disenchanted and it was now that his drinking binges turned him into a seething mass of rage and resentment. At a party he overheard someone call another guest a 'Jew bastard'. Sinatra knocked him out cold. Walking up to the bar, he poured himself another drink, downed it, then belted the guy again as he was being stretchered out. At another party he got plastered and hit someone over the head with a bottle.

He was married to Ava Gardner at the time, and she estimated that every night Sinatra drank four big Martinis in a champagne glass, had wine with dinner, then it was off to a nightclub where he'd hit the Jack Daniel's. 'I don't know how he did it.' Both heavy drinkers, alcohol informed that marriage like few others and eventually tore it apart. Sinatra's lush pad in Palm Springs, complete with piano-shaped swimming pool, was the scene of many a violent fight; one of the bathroom basins still carries a crack from a champagne bottle that Sinatra hurled at the actress. When they divorced in 1957 Sinatra was on the rise again, no longer a bobby-soxer's wet dream but the embodiment of the hard-drinking, hedonistic swinger who had his pick of the women. A regular user of prostitutes, Sinatra also dated some of the most beautiful women of the era. He went out on a date with Grace Kelly but turned up drunk and kept lamenting about his split from Ava. Although a huge friend of Humphrey Bogart – they went boozing and carousing together – no sooner was the actor in his grave than Frank was banging his old lady, Lauren Bacall. Most bizarre of all was Sinatra's marriage to ingénue Mia Farrow: she was nineteen and he forty-eight. Dean Martin wisecracked that he owned a bottle of Scotch older than Mia. The marriage barely lasted two turbulent years.

Sinatra's evolution from forties crooner to the sophisticated swinger of the fifties and sixties had much to do with his rowdy entourage, the infamous Rat Pack. Shooting *Ocean's Eleven* (1960) in Vegas with Dean, Sammy and the gang was more like one long party than actual work. 'The idea is to hang out together, find fun with broads, and have a great time,' said Sinatra. And that's what they did: drank till dawn, showed up late on the set, started drinking again, performed their scenes in as few takes as possible, preferably one, and then hit the Vegas stage for a show that evening.

It was Sinatra's association with another Vegas phenomenon that almost proved his undoing – gangsters. Throughout much of his career Sinatra would be hounded by rumours that he fraternised with killers and mobsters, notably Sam Giancana, the mafia boss of Chicago. But despite the FBI amassing the largest file on any entertainer in US history, Sinatra was never impeached. Hoover and his agents got close a couple of times but Ole Blue Eyes' friendship with successive presidents (Kennedy, Nixon and Reagan) made him untouchable.

Sinatra is known to have paid favours to the mob, from playing shows gratis to maybe even money laundering, and in return they helped him out in various ways. When Jackie Mason started making wisecracks in his show about Sinatra's marriage to Mia Farrow the comic began to receive phone calls threatening his life. Mason refused to change his act. Six days later three bullets were fired through the door of his hotel room in Las Vegas. 'I don't know who it was that tried to shoot me,' Mason quipped on stage a few nights later. 'After the shots were fired all I heard was someone singing: Doobie, doobie, do.'

The death threats kept coming; stop making cracks about Sinatra or else. It was late in the evening when Mason was sitting in his parked car outside an apartment building in Miami when a masked man yanked open the door and smashed him full in the face, breaking his nose. 'We warned you to stop using the Sinatra material in your act,' the attacker said before leaving. Fuck artistic integrity, thought Mason, this was getting serious; he dropped the Sinatra jokes.

This mob connection did eventually lead to the dissolution of Sinatra's relationship with John F Kennedy, when his administration began cracking down on the Mafia and the President was advised to keep as clear from Frank as from herpes. Expecting a visit from JFK, Sinatra installed a helicopter pad on his Palm Springs property. When the President decided to stay instead with Bing Crosby, Sinatra went nutzoid, demolishing the helipad with a sledge hammer.

By the sixties Sinatra flaunted his boozy image, his drinking habit a secret so public that the *Washington Post* nicknamed him 'The Bourbon Baritone.' Whenever the Sinatra household held a party a flag was hoisted bearing the Jack Daniel's logo. 'I don't trust anybody who doesn't drink,' he once said. 'There's something wrong with them.' Whether or not Sinatra was a full blown alcoholic is a moot point; certainly he was a functioning alcoholic, able to resist the demon drink in the weeks leading up to cutting a new album, to save his voice. Like a bullfighter, though, Sinatra always insisted on sex before a recording session, believing it made him sing better. What's amazing about Sinatra is that for someone who drank as much as he did, and smoked untipped Camel cigarettes for most of his life, his voice was never destroyed; if anything it was enhanced, marinated. When he sang in that battered, world-weary way of his the songs were made richer, hitting a peak of emotion few other performers could reach.

Still he hadn't been able to tame the dark side of his personality that the drink triggered. 'When he was sober, Frank was a pussycat,' said Hollywood agent Swifty Lazar. 'When he was drunk, he was the meanest son of a bitch that God put on earth.' Friends offered simple advice when Sinatra was drunk: get out of his way. Staying at a hotel, Sinatra felt hungry at 1 a.m. and called reception for something to eat, but went ballistic when told the kitchen was closed. To appease him the manager personally showed up at his suite with a complimentary bottle of champagne; Sinatra punched him out. At dinner one evening a drunken Sinatra turned venomous on fellow guests, including Lauren Bacall and Swifty Lazar, then ripped off the tablecloth and threw food over everyone before storming out. There was something deep within the Sinatra psyche that actually craved this aggro. He'd be sitting bored in a hotel room and suddenly want to take a walk, so outside he'd go into the predictable mêlée of waiting fans and paparazzi, get a few yards then be forced to turn back, punching and fighting his way inside.

Vegas was still his playground but as the sixties dragged on the players on the board changed and Frank didn't like it. He'd been king at the Sands Hotel but now the place had been bought by Howard Hughes and the new management refused him credit. Sinatra went nuclear-nuts, stamping on tables and threatening staff. It was hoped by the following morning he might have calmed down a bit – Sinatra, calm down? You're joking! Driving a golf cart, with Mia beside him, he revved the machine up and headed straight towards a plate glass window. Crash!! Into the lobby he went, where he tried to set the curtains and other furnishings alight. The amazing thing was no one interfered; no security or police were called. After this show of anarchy Sinatra demanded to see the casino hierarchy. After hearing nothing he pounded on the door of the communication office, terrifying the female telephone operators. When a security guard turned up Frank threatened to take his gun and shove it up his ass. Finally, a meeting with the Sands vice president Carl Cohen was arranged. Frank tried to stay calm and composed, and he did, for at least five seconds; after that every expletive known to man was hurled towards Cohen, followed by the table. A big man afraid of no one, Cohen responded with a swift right hook that removed Frank's two front teeth.

Sinatra's final years were relatively quiet, though he could still sink a bottle of bourbon a day well into his seventies. He continued to perform sellout concerts round the world, with only the occasional glimpse of the old Frank, as when in Australia he caused uproar by describing local journalists aggressively pursuing his every move as 'fags', 'pimps', and 'whores'. He was forced to apologise, through gritted teeth.

Suffering from senile dementia, Sinatra eased back on public appearances, then disappeared altogether after a heart attack in 1997. He was eighty-two years old when he finally passed away. His final words, spoken as doctors tried desperately to stabilise him, were 'I'm losing.'

Befitting a man who lived his life within easy reach of a tumbler of bourbon, Sinatra was buried with a bottle of JD slipped into his coat pocket.

NIKKI SIXX (b. 1958: Musician)

Few bands have left such a blitzkrieg-style trail of destruction in their wake than Mötley Crüe. Their talisman Nikki Sixx stared death in the face so many times he started to actually believe that he might be a god. How he survived a lifetime of rock hedonism and debauchery maybe even he doesn't know; he sure had fun doing it. 'If you've crashed a sports car worth $300,000 while getting blown by a Playmate, you've just about done everything.'

There wasn't a pill he didn't pop, a drug he didn't snort, a bottle of Scotch he didn't crack open. In the depths of his depravity he was shooting up cocaine and heroin and when he ran out of drug supplies he'd shoot up Jack Daniel's instead. 'I used to sit there and think, well, it's about getting high, it's about blowing your mind. Let me find the closest thing to my mind; so I used to shoot it up in my neck.'

He was born Frank Carlton Serafino Feranna, Jr., in San Jose, California and raised by his party animal mother when his father abandoned the family when the boy was barely out of diapers. To say that Nikki came from a dysfunctional household is like saying Jeffrey Dahmer had a slight attitude problem; he was smoking marijuana with his mother at the age of seven.

Farmed out to his grandparents, Nikki raised hell as a young teenager, shoplifting and slashing car tyres with a buck knife. Sent back to his mother, the delinquency continued: he'd break into the homes of neighbours and got expelled from school for selling dope. Running away from home, he headed out to Los Angeles and worked odd jobs, usually ripping off his employers. While working at a liquor store he stole enough booze to open up his own premises, and was fired from a record shop after being caught stealing from the till and punching the one-armed owner. He was a loose cannon with no direction or centre; when he tried to find some stability by contacting his father he was cruelly rejected out of hand.

The only thing really for Nikki was music and a crazy ambition to have his own rock band; he'd stolen his first bass guitar aged fourteen. In 1981, along with friend and drummer Tommy Lee, Sixx formed Mötley

Crüe, but the early days were tough with no record company insane enough to sign them; instead they'd sit getting half-cut on cheap wine and vodka in an alleyway with the winos and drunks of Hollywood, depravity a close ally. 'Once we had taken clothes from a homeless girl, there were no taboos,' Nikki once remarked.

Mötley Crüe's mission statement was simple: 'To destroy everything that came in our path.' Boy, did they achieve that! Their first gig at a West Hollywood nightclub pretty much set the pattern for Crüe's savage assault on the rock world. When someone in the audience spat on lead singer Vince Neil he jumped off stage and put the guy in a vicious headlock, then Nikki smashed his bass hard onto another punter giving them lip, while Tommy joined in hitting him between the eyes with a drumstick.

The fuel for these shenanigans was booze, bourbon mostly. 'I hate things that are diluted,' Sixx once declared. 'I mean, you don't mix Jack Daniel's with Coke. That's a sin!' The band would turn up groggy for radio interviews sporting various facial injuries from a night's brawling. Meanwhile Nikki, logic clouded by too much whisky and not enough ice, brought his own special brand of pyrotechnics to Crüe's early gigs, like setting fire to his stiletto boots during songs.

When Crüe's manager Allan Coffman, a former Vietnam vet, tried to get them all to curb their alcohol intake, Nikki for one took little notice; turning up for a gig at the Whisky A Go Go fully loaded, upon hearing someone make lewd remarks about his personage he smashed their head into the bar. The rest of the night was equally memorable; Sixx found Vince after the show severely comatose under a car and had to drag him back to their digs, where he discovered one of Tommy's groupies hand-cuffed to his bed.

The madness of Crüe was certainly infectious, even Coffman himself succumbed. When the band signed to record label Elektra they cele-brated big style and Coffman got so monkey-arsed he thought he was back in 'Nam dodging Vietcong bullets. Being driven home, he suddenly rolled out of the car in the middle of an intersection and crawled on his belly across the tarmac commando-style.

After one gig Nikki and Vince got into a fight with a motorcycle gang after they'd made improper advances towards their girlfriends (what gentlemen). When the police arrived Sixx was so busy fighting for his life he never even noticed, he just saw this huge fella rush at him so punched him hard in the face with a bicycle chain. It was a cop who pulled out a gun and waved it in his face. Suitably subdued, Sixx was savagely set upon by the patrolman's colleagues and smashed seven times in the face with a baton, breaking a cheekbone. The next thing Sixx knew he was in jail facing a five-year rap for aggravated assault. The band managed to bail him out as they'd a gig that evening, then returned to the police station with the money they'd earned to make a deal with the cop to drop the charges. He was only too happy to comply. 'Who says you can't find justice in this country any more?' mocked Sixx.

Run-ins with the cops would become a feature of Crüe's musical career. Taking a break from recording an album one night, Nikki and Tommy were hassled by a couple of policemen as they enjoyed a few drinks in a bar round the corner from the studio. When they left the Crüe guys took their revenge by pissing through the open window of the patrol car before running off.

As the Crüe's reputation for general debauchery grew their music almost became of secondary concern to general onlookers; really, any band that comes up with a song called 'Girls, Girls, Girls' has no right to be taken seriously. There was madness at almost every gig. When a bottle was hurled at Nikki on stage, slicing open his hand, he spent the remainder of the concert spraying the front row with his blood. He also managed to get the band sacked as touring support for Kiss when he and Tommy were caught having sex with Kiss drummer Eric Carr's girl-friend behind his drum kit as he was playing live. Nikki's pyromaniac tendencies hadn't gone away either. On stage in San Francisco he walked over to a candelabra and ignited his leather jumpsuit during a bass solo. Within seconds the local fire department had raced onto the stage to put him out.

The fun didn't stop off stage. Back at their hotels furniture would be hurled out of windows, landing on top of parked cars outside, and flare guns unleashed, burning down rooms. Drinking in his hotel suite, Nikki ran into the corridor and doused a door with lighter fluid and set it alight, thinking it was a band mate's room; instead, behind it were a father and son who were terrified to see their door turning into a prop from *The Towering Inferno*. Sixx ran off, laughing.

Things took a dark turn when Nikki and others in the band started taking drugs, cocaine being the main culprit. At a party Sixx was snorting lines of coke and skipping in and out of a jacuzzi with the predictable phalanx of naked females. Displaying a grain of common sense, their manager locked all the doors in the house so no one could leave in their narcotised state. Nikki would not be imprisoned, so broke out and scaled the walls to drive off naked in his Porsche. At 90 mph he came in contact with a telephone pole that smashed through the windshield, coming to a rest in the passenger seat. Shaken, he got out and hitched a ride home still stark bollock naked.

From cocaine Sixx graduated to smoking heroin and taking speed-balls. Hopelessly hooked, he used his body rather like a chemistry experiment, combining varieties of drugs in search of the perfect high. And he was still drinking heavily. But it was the drugs that were killing him faster. His veins were starting to collapse; he even once resorted to injecting heroin into a vein in his penis. Deep paranoia had also set in: he'd taken to patrolling his house looking for intruders with a loaded Magnum, swore Mexicans and midgets were running about the place. A couple of times neighbours saw him crawling naked around his garden with a shotgun.

There were desperate nights alone when he considered blowing his brains out as a preferable alternative to carrying on living, then very nearly got his wish when he overdosed at a drug dealer's house in London. When he couldn't be revived by stuffing ice cubes down his underpants the dealer took the novel approach of beating the life back into him with a baseball bat. When that didn't work he thought a dead rock star would be too much of an inconvenience so he dumped the body in a nearby skip. Amazingly Nikki came to of his own volition and lived to inject another day.

In the summer of 1987 the Girls, Girls, Girls US tour kicked off and few rock extravaganzas have been as depraved. On stage Nikki and Tommy poured Jack Daniel's down their throats to such an extent that the company actually issued a promotionally labelled Mötley Crüe bottle. One night the band lined up their dicks on a bar and poured bourbon over them and set light to their pubic hair. Travelling from gig to gig in a customised Gulfstream jet, no sooner were the band on board than obliging stewardesses had laid out drugs and drinks on their meal trays; white wine and zombie dust for Nikki.

Things got even more manic in Japan. Taking the bullet train back to Tokyo after a gig in Osaka, Nikki and Tommy downed fifteen bottles of sake then poured Jack Daniel's over the heads of their fellow passengers. When their promoter Mr Udo asked if they'd please settle down Nikki threw a Jack Daniel's bottle at him. It missed and instead connected with the head of a Japanese businessman who fell screaming to the floor with blood pouring from a large gash. When the train pulled into Tokyo the riot squad were waiting and Nikki was hauled off to the cop shop in handcuffs; all in a day's work for a Crüe boy, I guess.

All this mania had to end eventually and that time came a couple of nights before Christmas 1987 when Sixx performed arguably the greatest feat any rock star can hope to achieve: he actually died. When his dealer shot him up with some Persian heroin Sixx was wiped out and turned blue. No amount of pounding on his chest could revive him. When the paramedics arrived and wheeled him out into an ambulance they covered his face with a sheet. Within minutes rumours flashed across Los Angeles that Nikki Sixx was dead; radio reporters broke the news, his band mates were informed. Sixx was indeed dead, albeit for only two minutes; in the ambulance they'd almost given him up as a lost cause when one of the paramedics had another go, pumping a double-dose of adrenalin into his system that brought Nikki rudely back into the land of the living.

Waking up in hospital, tubes up his nose and in his veins, Nikki tore them out and discharged himself. After learning of the reports of his death he changed the message on his answering machine to, 'Hey, it's Nikki. I'm not home because I'm dead,' then found a stash of spare heroin in his bathroom and shot up yet again, collapsing in a heap. He woke up in a pool of blood with the needle still dangling out of his twitching arm.

Even Nikki realised this was the signal that he needed rehab fast.

He came out clean but with worrying withdrawal symptoms; in a strange way losing his addictions felt like a major part of his being had been amputated, that he wasn't Nikki Sixx any more. Of course there were the obligatory lapses. When Nikki and Tommy went for dinner one night, a glass of wine with their food ended with the whole bottle being drained and the next thing they knew they were in a recording studio carving swastikas into the walls.

Amazingly still sane and still coherent, Nikki has been clean, or at least relatively so, since that last overdose. In 2007 he became the first member of the rock world to speak on Capitol Hill for NAADAC's 18th Annual National Alcohol and Drug Addiction Recovery luncheon. Senators and Congressmen waited in line to meet Nikki and show their appreciation for his enormous efforts on drug and alcohol awareness. It took him a while but the guy finally saw sense that with alcohol and drugs the only way out is to die young or quit. Come to think of it, Nikki Sixx did both.

T

CAPTAIN EDWARD TEACH aka BLACKBEARD
(1680–1718: Pirate)

Described as 'The embodiment of impregnable wickedness, a nightmarish villain so lacking in any human kindness that no crime was above him,' Blackbeard was by far the maddest, baddest, most notorious pirate in the history of seafaring. He drank rum by the cask and indulged in whores three at a time; the rest of his day was spent killing perfect strangers. And when he wasn't instilling sheer terror amongst the general populace, he was committing barbarous acts upon his own crew to maintain discipline and discourage mutiny. He once shot his own first mate, saying, 'If I didn't shoot one or two crewmen now and then, they'd forget who I was.'

A native of Bristol, Teach was probably the first recorded juvenile delinquent, wanted for robbery and other misdemeanours. Bolting from good ole Blighty, he joined the navy at the age of twelve as a merchant seaman and served in numerous colonial wars and campaigns. Following hostilities, like many of his fellow sailors, Teach found himself out of work and drifting into piracy. He and his gang of unreliable cut-throats captured a 250-ton French slave ship, renamed her the *Queen Anne's Revenge* and, armed with twenty-two guns, brought a wave of terror to the Caribbean that lasted years. He plundered merchant ships mainly, allowing the crews safe passage home if they peacefully gave up all their valuables and liquor. Those who resisted he marooned and sent their ship to the bottom of the ocean.

When it was time to go into battle Blackbeard was better armed than the Terminator: six cocked and loaded pistols strapped to his back, a cutlass on each hip, knives across his chest and a dagger in each boot. He was also known to use rum bottles filled with gunpowder as grenades. If all that wasn't bowel loosening enough, Teach stuck lit cannon fuses in his hair and beard. Sometimes the very sight of Blackbeard was enough to make most of his victims surrender without a fight.

When drunk, Blackbeard was just as dangerous to his own crew as the enemy. He loved to play drinking games; a particular favourite had him inviting his officers into his private quarters to down a cask or two of rum, then blow out all the candles and yell 'duck' before firing his pistols into the blackness. The game finished when someone was either hit or Blackbeard got bored.

Following another drinking session Blackbeard carolled some crewmen to come down to the munitions lock-up with him. Once there he sealed all the hatches and set fire to several pots of brimstone. The objective of this game was to see who lasted longest in the hellish smoke. Blackbeard won, of course. Afterwards he proposed, 'Next time we shall play a game called gallows and see who can swing the longest on a rope without being throttled.' Whether they ever got lathered enough to do so is unrecorded.

Pirates of the time usually partook of a drink by the name of rumfustian, a potent heavily spiced blend of beer, gin and sherry. Blackbeard's tipple was rum and he had an incredible tolerance level, unmatched in his day. When he walked into a tavern all eyes fell upon him. Ever the showman, on one occasion he impressed the tavern regulars by mixing gunpowder in his rum, setting it on fire and guzzling down the explosive concoction.

Pirates were not just expected to drink, it was part of their DNA; indeed Daniel Defoe, writing about the pirate creed, claimed, 'Sobriety brought a man under suspicion.' Certainly, Blackbeard kept his crew well lubricated, learning quickly that to be a successful pirate captain you had to keep everyone happy with endless supplies of booze, and when stocks ran out things could get quite tricky, as this entry from Blackbeard's own journal testifies: 'Such a day, rum all out – our company somewhat sober, a damned confusion amongst us! Rogues a plotting – great talk of separation. So I looked sharp for a prize – such a day took one, with a great deal of liquor on board; so kept the company hot, damned hot, then all things went well again.'

Along with a hold brimful of rum, Blackbeard usually took to sea with a new wife, growing tired of her eventually and giving her away to a crewman as reward for good service. Little wonder that over the course of his pirating Blackbeard got through fourteen wives! His last bride was a mere sixteen years old, and there are distressing stories that he invited several of his brutal companions to take it in turns to ravage her as he watched.

It didn't take long for the British colonial governors to grow weary of Blackbeard's piratical incursions and Lieutenant Robert Maynard was instructed to seek out and destroy the scoundrel. The hunt lasted for months, until one night Maynard got his man. Blackbeard had gone ashore to get plastered and upon his return to the *Revenge* Maynard was lying in wait with three war ships. He attacked, and although Blackbeard managed to blast two of Maynard's vessels out of the water his own ship ran aground. Maynard demanded the pirate captain's immediate surrender. Blackbeard smiled, 'I'll give no quarter,' he answered, raising a glass of rum. 'Nor take none from you.'

Maynard went in for the kill. The battle was ferocious; witnesses later described the ship's deck ran ankle-deep with blood. By the end of the carnage only Blackbeard remained alive from the whole of his crew, though barely – he'd been punctured by five musket balls and stabbed and slashed twenty times, yet still the bastard stood defiant as Maynard brought his cutlass down upon his neck, taking two blows to remove the foul head. Legend has it that when Blackbeard's headless corpse was thrown overboard it swam several times round the vessel before catching a hold of a shark's fin and riding the creature down to Davy Jones's locker.

Credited with plundering over forty ships during his dastardly career, Blackbeard's death virtually represented the end of an era in the history of piracy in the Caribbean. His head, stuck on a pole as a grim warning to other would-be pirates, was eventually taken down and according to myth the skull fashioned into a silver drinking chalice.

DYLAN THOMAS (1914–1953: Poet)

There was the Dylan Thomas of the magical phrase and the musical voice, the darkly seductive bard of the Celtic moon. Then there was the unkempt, unshaven train-wreck Dylan Thomas who got off his nut, fell down stairs and was more familiar with his own vomit than most people have a right to be.

Dylan was his own worst enemy. His poetry, beautifully crafted though it was, came second to his image as a pissed man of letters. He revelled in this romantic image of the drunken poet; was it the lifestyle of the drinker that appealed to him more than the indulgence itself? 'I hold a beast, an angel and a madman in me,' he once wrote, and few who came into contact with Dylan would argue with him on that score.

Born in the Welsh seaport of Swansea, Thomas grew up the son of a schoolmaster and thwarted poet. Certainly Dylan inherited his love of words from his father but spurned the chance to go to university when at sixteen he quit school to work as a junior reporter for a local newspaper, where he got his first taste for booze, touring the town's multitude of pubs with his fellow journos. Getting plastered and throwing up in alleyways was a sign of masculinity, acceptance almost.

Soon he took to writing poems and in 1933 headed for London, hoping for literary fame. Here his outlandish manner and wild appearance could not be ignored, nor his capacity for beer and propensity to bed friends' wives. Indeed, his drinking became such a serious problem that colleagues sometimes took him off to secluded places in Cornwall and Ireland to remove him from temptation. But the drink was ever prevalent, despite his best efforts to cut back: 'When I come to town, bang go my plans in a horrid alcoholic explosion that scatters all my good intentions like bits of limbs and clothes over the doorsteps and into the saloon bars of the tawdriest pubs in London.'

As usual with drunks, it was the partner who bore much of the brunt. Thomas's wife Caitlin MacNamara had more crosses to bear than most, putting up not just with her husband's boozing but also his brazen infidelity, generally potless situation and domestic uselessness. Take the time she asked Thomas to make her a cup of tea, generally not too difficult a task. He returned with a concoction not dissimilar to swamp water, explaining that he could not find a top for the pot, so had covered it with half a pound of cheese.

Caitlin could more than hold her own in the booze league, being wild and reckless herself, performing cartwheels after a few drinks, usually when wearing no knickers. They were once described as 'a matched pair of dipsomaniacs'. They met in 1936 in, where else, a pub and it was love at first sight, booking straight into a hotel where they drank solidly for five days, apparently without eating. Twice their wedding was delayed after spending the money put aside for the event on alcohol. 'We became dedicated to pubs and to each other,' said Caitlin. 'Ours was not only a love story, it was a drink story.'

It's amazing that during this mad, tempestuous marriage Thomas managed to sire three children. During one birth Dylan was nowhere to be seen. He was found several days after the event just south of bejesus in a public house in Fulham and dragged to the hospital unwashed and unshaven, in an old dressing gown and slippers. Things were even rougher for the newborn back at the couple's Chelsea flat, where empty beer bottles and cigarette packets jostled for floor space with the playpen. Worse, the couple repeatedly left their kids alone every evening to go to the pub. Dylan loved the ambience of bars; they were a stage to him, a captive audience to show off to. Caitlin was bored by them; the endless hours of sitting there watching Dylan live up to his reputation.

Rows were common, physical violence too, as Caitlin herself grew promiscuous with a carnal taste for rough trade. At least their fights were a communication of sorts; Caitlin loved a good scrap and couldn't think of anything worse than someone who was indifferent to her. But such was the emotional chaos they created that a jealous husband once fired a sub-machine gun at the holiday bungalow they were staying at with their children.

One wonders how many of Dylan's antics were just that, antics, or the actions of a drunkenly deluded mind. There are tales of him slicing off companions' ties with a razor blade, and staying with friends only to take some of their furniture to the nearest pawnbrokers. He and Caitlin also had a habit of arriving on the doorstep of a relative's house when it was difficult to say no, requesting food and shelter. Thomas responded to the inevitably strained and resentful atmosphere by once pissing against a living room wall and taking a dump on the carpet.

There's also the occasion he was an honoured guest at an Oxford poetry society which served only select wines. Thomas demanded a beer jug and went around filling and refilling it with each successive vintage wine, mixing it up with a teaspoon.

Sanctuary was Laugharne, back in Wales, where he had a cottage in which he could write in solitude, when he wasn't visiting the local ale house. At one point he even managed to cut his daily beer intake to ten pints. Actually Dylan's beer intake wasn't that prodigious, it didn't take much to make him merry, and then he tended to nod off. Spirits were a disaster, he couldn't really take them, describing one hangover thus: 'I have the villain of a headache, my eyes are two piss holes in the sand, my tongue is fish and chip paper,' unlike Caitlin, who could drink a half-bottle of whisky without it having much noticeable effect on her.

From the mid-forties Thomas began appearing on BBC radio reading his poetry. Once he arrived so stewed for a live broadcast he was still soundly snoring in front of the microphone a mere twenty seconds before he was due on air. The drinking was evident in his physical appearance, too. Friends were shocked; his nose looked as if it were in training for a W C Fields lookalike contest and his face was bloated and pale, as if he'd been dragged out of the Thames after a month. He was not in good shape and nor were his finances. In spite of his growing reputation Dylan's poetry brought little money. Sometimes he was literally starving and would go on the scrounge, sending begging letters to friends. He became quite accomplished at it, putting, one suspects, almost as much effort into a request for funds as in a piece of poetry. Richard Burton often lent him money, though invariably he'd use it to buy booze.

To bolster his funds Thomas engaged in college lecture tours to America. On his first night out in Hollywood he was introduced to buxom Shelley Winters, who asked the poet why he'd come to the movie capital. 'To touch a starlet's titties,' he said. 'OK,' said Shelley, 'but only one finger.' Shelley was captivated by the poet and invited him to Sunday lunch at the flat she shared with the young Marilyn Monroe. Throughout the meal Thomas drank profusely, first half a pitcher of gin Martini prepared by Monroe, then a bottle each of red and white wine, followed by six bottles of beer.

After the meal Thomas revealed another desire, to meet Charlie Chaplin, and once again Shelley obliged. One afternoon they took a friend's car and drove up the Hollywood hills to Chaplin's opulent pad. Shelley drove as Thomas was quite out of it, looking, in her words, 'like a stoned leprechaun'. He'd been drinking all day and during the drive pulled out a pint bottle of cheap gin from his jacket pocket and knocked back the loathsome gutrot, somehow managing to stay upright as the car hurtled round bend after bend. As they neared Chaplin's place the car got a little more out of control so Dylan grabbed the wheel, pulling them away from the intended driveway and instead right into the neighbouring tennis court, demolishing the net. A few yards more to the right and they would have ended up in Chaplin's swimming pool. Thomas seemed unperturbed. 'Come on, girl,' he yelled. 'I want to meet the greatest comic genius of our century.'

Inside the house a party was in full swing featuring the great and the good of Hollywood, most of whom Shelley was terrified of introducing to Thomas. Instead the poet wandered aimlessly round the room holding a large brandy glass that he filled from any leftovers he could find. Chaplin, playing at his grand piano, eyed the intruder with less than charitable eyes. Finally, he'd had enough and brought his fists crashing down on the piano keys. He stood up. 'Even great poetry cannot excuse such rude, drunken behaviour.' Thomas knew the game was up and left in as dignified a manner as could be mustered. From outside there came the sound of him heavily pissing into a potted plant on the porch.

In the final year of his life Thomas's health deteriorated dramatically; he'd complain of acute chest pains and regular blackouts. Arriving in America in late 1953 for another series of poetry readings, it proved a conveyor belt of disasters. First he got drunk and fractured his arm falling down some stairs on his way to the theatre, then caused such a disturbance during the performance he was thrown out. During rehearsals for a production of *Under Milk Wood* Dylan couldn't stop vomiting. Still, he toured the bars of Greenwich Village with his lover, the poet Liz Reitell, who could only watch the sad spectacle night after night. 'There was no great muse that made Dylan drink,' she remembered. 'He drank because he was an alcoholic. He had all the devils, and some of the angels, too.'

Finally he sought medical advice and was told to stop drinking, and for a time that's what he did, telling friends, 'I've seen the gates of hell,' and, one presumes, hadn't much fancied them. But it was already too late.

Staying at the Chelsea Hotel, Thomas spent the day in bed drinking beer and whisky, and by the evening had some kind of mental collapse. The following morning he left the hotel telling friends he badly needed a drink. He returned an hour and a half later uttering the immortal words, 'I've had eighteen straight whiskies. I think that's the record.' He only lasted a few more days.

He was complaining of breathing difficulties and a doctor attended him several times, during one visit pumping his body full of morphine. The problems persisted. Dylan began showing signs of delirium and speaking of abstract hallucinations and when he finally fell into a coma he was rushed into hospital. Caitlin flew in and was taken by police escort to the ward, where she asked the nursing staff theatrically, 'Is the bloody man dead yet?' Reality soon hit home and she went nuts and had to be restrained and carted off to a psychiatric unit.

Dylan never regained consciousness. His body was returned to Wales and buried in Laugharne, his spiritual home. He was still a year short of his fortieth birthday, and one wonders if Thomas, like many of those who die young, had a death wish. Caitlin believed he held the view that all the best poets snuffed it before middle age and that he himself would never make forty, 'and there were times when he almost seemed to live his life by that'. On his final trip to New York, Dylan was already referring to Caitlin as 'my widow' and held a conversation with a friend about dying young. 'But who wants to die?' said the friend. 'Oh, I do,' said Dylan. 'Why?' replied his puzzled friend. Dylan smiled, 'Just for the change.'

HUNTER S THOMPSON (1937–2005: Writer)

One of the most revolutionary writers of the twentieth century, a hero of the counter-culture, Hunter S Thompson is best remembered for his booze- and drug-raddled reports for *Rolling Stone* magazine and for creating his own style of journalism, 'gonzo'. From these articles the reader was left in no doubt as to the unpredictable and downright eccentric nature of the author. Thompson was unquestionably the most catastrophically self-destructive person of his generation, which took some doing. He drank day and night; every trip to the liquor store was like buying for a wedding reception. A walking chemical laboratory, he took every drug that was invented, and some that weren't. 'An evening in his company,' mused one journalist after meeting him, 'could result in being wanted by the authorities or having your head kicked in.'

Born in Louisville, Kentucky, Thompson's rebellious streak was there from a relatively young age as he drifted into crime and drinking. 'Ever since I was a teenage criminal, I've always been doomed, a person clearly headed for hell.' He couldn't even make it to his high school graduation because he was in jail.

Inspired by Hemingway and Fitzgerald, Thompson took up journalism but money was tight as he tried to get a break on magazines; many times he had to choose between liquor and food and, well, the bottle usually won. Eventually he landed a job at a small newspaper in Pennsylvania but fled after wrecking the editor's car. In 1962, during an assignment in South America, Thompson started taking drugs for the first time when a bout of dysentery necessitated he lessen his alcohol intake. He ingested so many stimulants that his hair fell out.

During this period Thompson lived mostly in California, for a time in San Francisco, where he dropped acid, bought a gun and hung out with the Hells Angels. When a group of religious fanatics moved in next door Thompson nailed the head of a wild boar to their front door and smeared its entrails in their car. They left.

Gonzo journalism really took off when Thompson began writing for *Rolling Stone*, arriving in their offices to offer his services drinking a six-pack and ranting non-stop for an hour with the magazine's publisher

Jann Wenner. Their long relationship would be best described as combustible; one night Thompson blasted Wenner in the face with a fire extinguisher for falling asleep to a Joni Mitchell record. Another time he blew a mouthful of fuel over a lighted Zippo in the direction of his editor. Luckily Wenner was fast on his feet, lest he be engulfed in a fireball; at worst he was slightly singed.

Sent to Rhode Island by *Rolling Stone* to cover the world's most prestigious sailing regatta, the America's Cup, Thompson attempted to spray-paint the words FUCK THE POPE on the side of one of the competing yachts but was spotted by security guards. Firing a distress flare, he set fire to a boat and in the ensuing panic made good his escape. You could say he was out of control, if indeed he'd ever been fully in control. Pulled over by the cops once, he had a loaded .44 Magnum in the glove compartment and a bottle of Wild Turkey open on the seat beside him.

In 1971 Thompson set off for Las Vegas armed with enough drugs and booze to fell an elephant. His resultant misadventures became the book *Fear and Loathing in Las Vegas*, an overnight success that confirmed his cult status. Years later it was made into a film with Johnny Depp, who hung around Thompson's presence for several weeks, soaking up those vibes.

Very few deadly substances failed to pass through Thompson's lips, and yet somehow he always survived. 'I never thought I'd make it past twenty-seven. Every day I'm just as astounded as everyone else to realise I'm still alive.' Some feat considering he occasionally employed a giant-sized medical syringe to inject a pint of gin directly into his stomach, and admitted to loving the thrill of driving on a highway at the dead of night on a motorcycle at 120 mph high on acid, 'Just to see how far I can go, how weird I can get and still survive.'

In the summer of 1972 Hunter was in Washington for *Rolling Stone*, covering the then current Watergate scandal. He attended a politico shindig and offered to take a few guests home, including US senator Gary Hart and actor and political activist Warren Beatty. Thompson was smashed, driving his rented car while balancing a bottle of bourbon between his legs and at one point running a police car off the road. Unconcerned by the entreaties of his passengers to let them out, Hunter threw the whisky bottle out of the window and hit the gas, ramming his way through suburbia until the cop car was but dust in the rear-view.

In 1974 Thompson went to Zaire to cover the now legendary Ali–Foreman fight, the 'Rumble in the Jungle', again for *Rolling Stone*. He never delivered the story, instead selling his fight tickets to buy drugs. 'If you think I've come all this way to watch two niggers beat the shit out of each other, you've got another think coming.' He buggered off instead to the hotel pool with a bottle of whisky and a big bag of grass.

Hunter, it seemed, always lived close to the edge, bursting with wild energy and bad blood, 'I like to be the craziest man in the room usually. There's great comfort in knowing that nobody else is as crazy as you are.' Crazy, but with the endearing gene of the born prankster, as when he met for the first time fellow writing guru Tom Wolfe. The pair were on their way to eat at a plush restaurant when Thompson darted into a marine supply shop, emerging minutes later holding an anonymous brown paper bag. Throughout lunch Wolfe couldn't take his eyes off the parcel, which sat on the table. Curiosity finally won out. 'What's in the bag, Hunter?' he asked. 'I've got something in there that would clear out this restaurant in twenty seconds,' replied Thompson, and opened the bag to reveal a small tin. Thompson unscrewed the top and pressed down hard. 'There ensued the most violently brain-piercing sound I had ever heard,' Wolfe recalled. The whole restaurant froze in abject terror as Hunter slipped the can back into the bag. It was a marine distress signalling device, audible for twenty miles over water.

As tales of his wild behaviour permeated the culture, it was Thompson's image rather than his writing that made him a public figure and drew people to him. 'Somehow the author has become larger than the writing. And it sucks.' So he chose to live as a virtual recluse in a fortified compound up in the Colorado mountains, a few miles outside the resort of Aspen, along with an undetermined number of large Dobermanns trained to kill. It was called Owl Farm. The place was peculiar to say the least; visiting reporters noted a living room decorated with animal skulls and, rather unnervingly, a machine gun resting against the side of a TV. Thompson obviously took his privacy seriously. 'If people believe they're going to be shot, they might stay away.'

On one occasion a teacher and his English literature students were invited out to visit Thompson at Owl Farm. Joint in one hand and a glass of whisky in the other, Thompson ordered the class to prop the books of his they'd brought along with them against a tree. Then he pulled out his .45 Magnum and blasted bullet holes through the text. 'Next,' he yelled after each shot, sometimes followed by a primal scream that turned the scene closer each time to something out of *Deliverance*.

Thompson had a typical American's obsession with firearms, the proud owner of a vast collection of handguns, rifles, shotguns and handmade explosive devices. Had he wanted, he could have equipped a small South American country to wage a civil war. To celebrate the twenty-fifth anniversary of *Fear and Loathing*'s publication, Thompson didn't attend any snobbish literary event, no; he invited a few ole boys round to Owl Farm and in the sprawling backyard strapped a propane tank and a sex doll to a stationary tractor. He took aim and fired – Boom – the whole thing went up like a gas station in Dresden.

Thompson liked explosions, liked blowing things up. He once pushed his car off a cliff, 400 feet down to the ocean, setting it on fire just before it went over the edge. And only Thompson could invent a game called shotgun golf, the purpose of which was to shoot your opponent's golf ball out of the sky with a well-aimed 12-gauge. He was convinced the game would take America by storm. 'I see it as the first truly violent leisure sport. Millions will crave it.'

Even the relatively simple act of going fishing usually ended for Thompson in a scene of mass destruction. Down in Key West, Florida, he was getting out of the boat when he slipped, his hand hitting the throttle as he fell onto the dock. The boat sped off, careering round the harbour and then like a heat-seeking missile heading back for Thompson. It smashed up several boats before vaulting up onto the dock and across the lawn and into the country club.

By the 1980s Thompson's fame was so omnipresent that Hollywood craved his company. Befriending Jack Nicholson, Thompson drove to the top of a creek overlooking the movie star's property and offloaded a few friendly bullets while booming out a tape of what Nicholson's then girl-friend Anjelica Huston described as 'terrible dying-animal cries'.

Thompson then placed a frozen elk heart on Nicholson's doormat, causing blood to seep into the living room. All very funny, and typical of Thompson's sense of fun. What he didn't know was that Nicholson had a stalker at the time and thought his number was up that night, what with the gunfire-and-death overture blasting in the wind. He shat himself till dawn and alerted the FBI.

Towards the end of his life all that was left of Thompson was the legend; as a writer he was adrift, oceans away from the acerbic swipes at modern America that informed his best work of the seventies. But he could still cause mayhem. Turning up at his favourite eatery in Aspen only to find the place knee deep in well-heeled tourists, Thompson lobbed a smoke grenade into the bar and waited for the moneyed rabble to flee in terror. Then he casually walked in, took a seat and enjoyed a peaceful drink. On another occasion at the Aspen Country Club, well tanked up, Thompson missed an easy putt so took a shotgun from his golf bag and blasted the green until it resembled the Somme. He was banned for life.

Things turned dark for Thompson in 1990 when he was accused of sexual assault and six investigators from the District Attorney's office turned up at Owl Farm with a search warrant. After eleven hours of opening cupboards and looking behind the sofa they'd found cocaine and marijuana, thirty-nine tablets of LSD and a few sticks of dynamite. Thompson was surprised they didn't find more.

Such run-ins with the law only increased Thompson's diabolical fame and made him even more appealing to the current crop of Hollywood hot rods like Sean Penn and Johnny Depp. Don Henley of the Eagles had a house nearby and the actor John Cusack recalled being invited out to Owl Farm and, as a test of friendship, being told by Thompson to steal Henley's car. 'So right off the bat it was grand theft auto,' said Cusack. They got quite pally after that. One of the last times Cusack saw Thompson was in LA. He and Johnny Depp picked him up in a car and he had this inflatable doll with him that he insisted on calling Ling Ling. 'We drove around Hollywood and he kept beating the doll,' recalled Cusack. 'He'd take her out into the street and say, 'You bitch,' and you'd see these cars swerving. He was always ready for a show that was beyond any sense of decency and went into some absurdist land that made your head spin.'

For all the japes and drugs, first and foremost Thompson was a mighty boozer, able to drink from the moment he woke up to the time he went back to sleep late, very late, into the night. His constitution was remarkable; many people tried to match him drink for drink and failed. He also liked to offer guidance and advice to his fellow imbibers. 'Have an objective to give your bender a theme. For instance, stalking and killing a wild pig with a bowie knife.'

One *New York Times* journalist arrived at Owl Farm to witness a groggy wreck of a man stumbling out of bed in the mid-afternoon; Thompson was then in his mid-sixties. But as the night drew on Thompson partook of a steady stream of drugs, cocaine, pills, marijuana, all washed down by brandy, white wine, chartreuse, tequila and whisky. While most normal humans would have been whacked out by this, it had the opposite effect for Hunter: the bedraggled creature of a few hours before was now in full bad-boy mode, ranting and raving and waving a shotgun in the air.

Thompson behaved like a madman until it wasn't fun any more. Fed up with his deteriorating health and the world in general, Thompson sat in his favourite chair in the kitchen one night, put a pistol in his mouth and pulled the trigger. His son and grandson were in the next room and heard the shot.

Determined to be just as gonzo in death as he was in life, Thompson wanted his remains to be blasted into the atmosphere courtesy of an artillery cannon. He got his wish. The cremated Thompson's ashes were loaded into ten mortar shells crammed with gunpowder and then packed into the waiting 'supergun' atop a fifteen-storey tower. Present at the private celebration at Owl Farm were guests such as Johnny Depp, assorted rock bands, blow-up dolls and plenty of hard liquor. With 'Mr Tambourine Man' blaring from the sound system, Hunter S Thompson was blown into the sky, grey flakes of bad boy raining down on the revellers. There was a sense of peace after the ashes settled, and everyone got drunk.

RIP TORN (b. 1931: Actor)

Rip Torn was originally earmarked for the role that eventually launched Jack Nicholson to fame, that of the druggy lawyer in *Easy Rider*. That was until he and Dennis Hopper almost knifed each other to death. The duel took place in Peter Fonda's New York town house one night when Hopper stormed in and barracked Fonda for getting pissed with Torn instead of working on the *Easy Rider* script. Hopper was angry, having just come back from Texas scouting locations and hearing that hippie kids with long hair were being sheared with razor blades like sheep. 'Take it easy,' said Torn, who hailed from that neck of the woods. 'Not everyone from Texas is an asshole.' Hopper pushed him away. 'Sit down, you motherfucker.'

Things then got very serious when Hopper claimed that Torn pulled a knife on him. Torn would recall the event very differently, saying it was Hopper who grabbed a steak knife and waved it menacingly just inches from his head. Torn disarmed Hopper, knocking him back against Fonda, who fell on the floor. 'There goes the job,' thought Torn. And there went his career, too, pretty much, or so Torn claimed when Hopper's version of the knife incident spread an image of him around Hollywood as being something of a nutter; this in spite of Torn successfully suing Hopper for defamation. But as we shall see, Torn's reputation as one of the most accomplished Hollywood hellraisers of his generation, with a prodigious appetite for alcohol and a temper to match, is very real, culminating, just shy of his seventy-ninth birthday, in his arrest for allegedly breaking into a bank drunk as the pope and in possession of a firearm; some going for a pensioner!

Elmore Rual Torn, Jr, grew up in central Texas, farm country, in a close-knit family and studied acting at the University of Texas before moving to New York to join the Actors Studio, launch pad for Marlon Brando and James Dean. Making his debut in the 1956 film *Baby Doll* and appearing in the original Broadway cast of Tennessee Williams's *Sweet Bird of Youth*, Torn was viewed as a promising character actor but saddled with a volatile personality – both onstage and off. He was said to be difficult (though what great actor wasn't, he asked), also potentially violent, suggestions that hurt him. He did his best, however, to abide by the spirit of his father's mantra: 'You never start a fight, you finish it.' There was the occasion a fellow actor kept pushing him around in a scene until Torn lost all patience and punched him in the ribs. Actress Stella Stevens couldn't stand him when they starred together in *Slaughter* (1972). Sharing a trailer with him, she emerged one morning to see Torn grinning ear to ear. 'Oh, I love to hear you pee,' he said.

Torn's career continued to suffer because of this unwelcome reputation ('I've never hit anybody who hasn't clocked me two or three times'), not helped much when he attacked novelist Norman Mailer with a hammer. Shooting an independent movie together, *Maidstone* (1970), Torn played an assassin out to kill Mailer's character but took the method technique a little too far by actually trying to brain his co-star. The two men fought furiously on the ground, cameras still rolling (the footage exists, it's a hoot) with Mailer diligently defending himself by trying to chew off Torn's ear. The bite marks were still there forty years later.

There are hints of paranoia, too, that his career was always 'a scramble for existence' because the American government considered his politically outspoken views as too radical. After he denounced the Vietnam War on the Dick Cavett chat show in 1970 Torn claimed a bullet was fired through the window of his New York home.

Weirdly, it wasn't until the nineties that Torn hit mainstream popularity with his role in the *Men in Black* movies and the HBO series *The Larry Sanders Show*, in which he starred as a tough-as-nails talk-show producer. Finally established and successful, it was now that Torn's private life started to periodically hit the buffers. In 2004 he was arrested after crashing his car into the rear of a New York taxi in the early hours of the morning. Station cameras caught the whole arrest procedure, with Torn fairly ripping into his persecutors: 'Go to hell, you guys,' he raved. Barely able to keep upright, more vindictive couplets emanated from his cultured thespian gob. 'Take these cuffs off, let me take a piss.' Arthur Miller couldn't have written a better line. 'I'm a movie actor. You have to pay the fucking price to film me,' he admonished after spying the camera, and then insisted, through barely discernable gibberish, that he'd only partaken of one and a half drinks. He also point blank refused to a sobriety test. Despite being shown this video footage, a jury acquitted

Torn of drink-driving. 'This is one of the great events in my life,' the seventy-three-year-old said after hearing the news, 'to be in the hands of this wonderful jury. I love New York.' He then shook each of the male jurors by the hand and planted kisses on the female ones.

Just two years later Torn collided with a tractor trailer in New York State. Arrested, he again refused to submit to a blood-alcohol test but in the end pleaded guilty to drink-driving and was banned for ninety days and fined. In 2009 he was given probation after being convicted of drink-driving after police spotted him tootling along in his Subaru estate with a Christmas tree strapped to the top, in the breakdown lane on a main highway. Slurred of speech, Torn was asked to perform a sobriety test; this was where any hint of a possible defence came crashing down as Torn could barely stand, let alone walk in a straight line and turn round again. Indeed, he failed to turn round at all and carried on walking. He later excused his failure to perform the test on the fact that the ground was not sufficiently level. All this was becoming horribly familiar, as indeed it was to the judge who ordered Torn to enrol in an alcohol education programme; one doesn't imagine he needed much education on that subject.

Then in 2010 the big one, and what must surely go down as amongst the most bizarre arrests in Hollywood history. In the middle of the night police were sent to investigate an alarm going off at a bank in the sleepy town of Salisbury, Connecticut, and discovered inside a blitzed-out-of-his-mind Torn prone on the floor clutching a loaded revolver. Torn hadn't suddenly gone all Dillinger on us, he'd no intention of robbing the bank, no, not at all: the pissed-as-a-wheelbarrow star had simply mistaken the bank for his own home; of course he did, we've all done it, haven't we? He even left his hat and boots by the door. Then, dumbfounded that his key failed to work on the lock, he'd broken in through a rear window and promptly passed out inside. So much for growing old gracefully.

Taken to the police station and thrown in the cells, Torn was charged with carrying a firearm while under the influence and without a permit, first-degree burglary and criminal mischief and trespass. In theory he faced the rest of his life behind bars. It was a humiliating scene indeed, watching the veteran shuffle into court, handcuffed like Harrison Ford in *The Fugitive*. 'The history here is clear that there's an alcohol issue that needs to be addressed,' said Torn's defence attorney, obviously a master of stating the bleeding obvious.

SPENCER TRACY (1900–1967: Actor)

If ever there was a case of drink turning someone from Jekyll into Hyde, it was Spencer Tracy. Perhaps the greatest actor of his generation, named the best movie actor of them all by Laurence Olivier, Tracy was kind and courteous on film sets, but a sheer lunatic after a booze binge. He doted on his brother Carroll, for example, loved him dearly, that was Tracy sober. Tracy drunk hated the little bastard, hated him so much that one night the manager of the Beverly Wilshire Hotel broke into Tracy's room to see the star throttling his brother and trying to throw him out of the sixth-floor window.

Tracy differed from other Hollywood hellraisers like Flynn and Marvin in that he didn't socialise; he drank on his own mostly. He also took his job seriously and was, for the most part, utterly professional while working. That's when he turned up. Tracy was famous for going AWOL; he'd be missing for days, sometimes weeks, hole himself up in some hotel and drink himself stupid, smash the place up, then return for work again and turn in a mesmerising performance.

He was born in Milwaukee, Wisconsin, to a truck salesman. A tough kid, he habitually skipped school to roam the streets with fellow urchins, getting into fights with neighbouring gangs. By the time he reached high school he'd started to knuckle down and achieved adequate grades to get into college, where he fell in love with acting. Landing only a few small roles on Broadway, Tracy supported himself working as everything from a bellhop to a janitor before being spotted by director John Ford and signing for 20th Century Fox in 1931.

The great tragedy of Tracy's life was that he was fully aware of his alcoholism and fought desperately to overcome the affliction, but never won. Worse, he simply couldn't hold his drink; just a small amount would send him off, 'and I'd go into blackouts and wake up in some goddamn distant city'.

Tracy's binges soon became legendary in Hollywood circles but were kept secret from the public. They usually lasted a week, with Tracy simply buggering off from the film he was working on and heading to New York. Checking into a hotel, his only luggage a suitcase filled with whisky bottles, he'd go up to his room alone, strip naked, climb into the bathtub and stay there for a whole week just drinking. He wouldn't even get out to take a piss or a crap. Finished, he'd clean himself up and go back to Hollywood.

These binges usually occurred at a time when Tracy was at loggerheads with the studio, disagreeing about a script or being forced to make a picture he thought was crap. And then there was his marriage. Tracy drank predominantly because he was a tormented person. A devout Roman Catholic, he was nevertheless driven to acts of often depraved sexual promiscuity, he often went to prostitutes and there was an alleged affair with Judy Garland when she was only fourteen. It was guilt that drove him time and again to the bottle.

In 1933 Tracy was driving erratically on Sunset Boulevard. Pulled over by the cops, Tracy was clearly vulcanised and began snarling like an animal and throwing punches. In the end he had to be restrained with handcuffs and leg irons. Thrown in jail, he was sprung by a penitent Fox. Tracy's drinking often landed him in trouble with the law. In a hotel in Yuma, Arizona, he got stinking drunk and began smashing furniture. After complaints were made the police arrived and when they burst into the room Tracy threw a chair at them.

For the most part Tracy was a professional on set and never drank. One of the exceptions came on the aptly titled film *Dante's Inferno* (1935). Turning up on set dizzy as a coot, he blasted the script as a sack of shit and chased the director around the set until, exhausted, he collapsed on a couch and fell asleep. Quietly the director ushered everyone outside the sound stage and locked Tracy in, hoping he might soon calm down. Big mistake. Awoken, Tracy was like a grizzly bear with a melon up its arse, smashing up the scenery and sets and then starting on the equipment; hugely expensive arc lights were pushed over and smashed. The destruction lasted for an hour, with cast and crew outside all listening. Finally spent, Tracy collapsed and then security ran in, put him in a straitjacket and hauled him away. Amazingly he returned and finished the movie. But Fox, quite rightly, didn't want anything more to do with Tracy and he was fired.

Hollywood weren't surprised, but they were shocked when just a few months later Tracy signed to MGM. That's when his career really took off, co-starring with Clark Gable in *San Francisco* (1936). They became fast friends and often drank together. On one occasion they were drinking after a polo match at the Riviera Country Club and then completely vanished. No one could find them for three days. They were eventually found holed up in a Tucson hotel room, absolutely smashed.

Tracy cemented his stardom with back-to-back Academy Award-winning performances in *Captain Courageous* (1937) and *Boys Town* (1938). He was then thrown into a long-running series of romantic comedies with Katharine Hepburn, which led to one of Hollywood's greatest ever true-life love stories. Their affair was intense, but carried out in secret. And as a Catholic Tracy vowed he could never divorce his wife, even though they now lived apart.

The drinking continued, as did the guilt, and when he was made exempt from military service in the war due to his young family, the personal shame pushed him into wanting to serve with the United Services Organizations, who put on morale-boosting shows for the troops. But on three separate occasions when he was booked to go overseas with them he went AWOL. On one occasion he was found suffering so severely from DTs after a binge he was put in a padded cell.

By the late forties Tracy's boozing had begun to slacken off, thanks largely to the benign influence of Hepburn. She insisted he see a doctor, which resulted in surgery – 'My plumbing has deteriorated,' he told a friend. And when that compulsion to go off on a wild bender raised its head, Hepburn was sometimes forced to tie Tracy to his bed. She worked as a virtual slave, catering to his every whim, sometimes sleeping outside his locked hotel room as he drank himself into a stupor over several days, then coming in to loyally scrub him clean. On at least one occasion this mothering was rewarded by Tracy's fist making contact with her face; she forgave him this, as she did every-thing else.

That Hepburn extended his life there is no question, but there were lapses, oh yes indeed. Filming *The Mountain* (1956), Tracy was at the bar regaling co-star Robert Wagner and others with tales of Hollywood, gradually drinking himself insensible. Just as it appeared that Tracy had drunk so much he was about to pass out, he suddenly picked up his glass and threw it at the face of an approaching waiter. Wagner instinctively put his hand out, catching the glass, but it shattered in his fist, slicing two fingers to the bone. There was blood all over the place. Tracy was carried off back to his room, utterly oblivious to the chaos he'd caused.

When it came time to leave the alpine location to fly back to Hollywood, Tracy went off the rails again, drinking more than he should at the location wrap party. Driven to the airport, Tracy was drinking beer after beer and throwing the empties casually out of the window. At the airport there were a few hours to kill before the flight, time Tracy spent well pouring wine down his throat. On the flight he abused the air hostess for not bringing his drinks fast enough and ended up swallowing the plane's entire stock of booze. His behaviour was so outrageous that when the plane landed in LA it was ferried to some remote part of the airfield to let him off. But Tracy still wasn't done and hit LA's nightspots three evenings in a row, hiring a mini orchestra to play music wherever he went, boozing until he literally collapsed.

There was another incident filming the screen adaptation of Hemingway's *The Old Man and the Sea* (1958) when Tracy and Hemingway got so goggled they demolished a bar in Havana. The owner wanted $150,000 in damages. Jack Warner was so incensed he threatened to throw Tracy off the picture. In the end the studio paid up and Tracy stayed.

In declining health, Tracy became reclusive in his final years. The ever loyal Katharine was always there to nurse him, by his side day and night, almost. When Tracy refused to allow her to sleep in the same room, she diligently stayed next door holding a cord attached to a bedside buzzer.

Early one morning she heard Tracy get up to make himself a coffee in the kitchen, and then there was a loud crash. He'd suffered a massive heart attack. She ran through the door like Jesse Owens and was soon cradling the dying Spencer in her arms.

U

MAURICE UTRILLO (1883–1955: Painter)

Few painters have captured the essence of Paris better than Maurice Utrillo, his poetic interpretations of the streets and squares of Montmartre contributed substantially to popularising a Bohemian image of that quiet artist's quarter. But apart from an echo of loneliness amid the brush strokes, there is no sign in his paintings of the raving maniac Utrillo was, not at all averse to swigging cologne and fuel alcohol when the real stuff was unavailable. Is it any wonder that throughout his life people were herding him in the direction of the nearest mental asylum.

His is an incredible story. Befitting an artist, Utrillo was born in Paris and born a bastard to Suzanne Valadon, one-time circus acrobat and nude model for both Renoir and Toulouse-Lautrec, and later a painter herself. Utrillo was a highly neurotic kid, whose grandmother used to soothe him as a child with strong red wine, a ruffian and a failure at school. He'd much rather play hooky and get flushed, aged nine, with local labourers and ditch diggers than attend lessons. By adolescence he was a sodden, wild-eyed dipsomaniac and being carted off to a loony bin.

A physician urged Suzanne to encourage her son to take up painting as therapy, an emotional route back to sanity. Instead it unleashed his hidden genius. His subject would be the area he lived in: the cafés, streets and houses of Montmartre, canvases of deterioration and decay; as one critic said, 'They have the odour of piss.'

Such was his drinking habit, eight litres of wine a day, that Utrillo regularly traded a freshly painted canvas to settle his bar tab, paintings that later rocketed in value. Wine merchants would often shut him in their back room with a blank canvas and paints, plus a generous supply of wine, and not let him out again until he'd produced a masterpiece.

In an effort to curb his addiction, Utrillo resorted to asking friends to lock him up, out of temptation's way. He'd go through the tortures of hell and scream and wail like a banshee until they could stand it no longer and were forced to release him, either that or he'd smash his way out. Intermittently he'd enter institutions to help restrain his drinking and his mental disorder, but he'd escape from there, too, or simply walk out uncured.

At least his fame as a painter had begun to grow beyond the café culture of Montmartre and in 1910 he held his first exhibition. One night drinking with Amedeo Modigliani, the two men fell into a debate about which of them was the better artist.

'You are the world's greatest painter,' said Utrillo.

'No, you are the world's greatest painter,' answered Modigliani.

'I forbid you to contradict me.'

'I forbid you to forbid me!'

'If you say that again, I'll hit you!'

And so it went on until the only recourse left to them was physical violence. After receiving several blows from the other they reconciled their differences over several more bottles of wine in a nearby café, whereupon it began all over again, like a *Monty Python* sketch. The fists flew once more, leaving both men in the gutter, where they fell into unconsciousness. Waking up at dawn, the demented duo realised they'd been robbed.

Utrillo was prone to violence, often picking fights in bars and frequently being arrested for assault or drunk and disorderly behaviour. He became such a fixture at the local nick that he kept a paintbox and easel there. Arrested one time for vandalism and handcuffed, he urinated on the leg of his captor while exposing himself to several horrified passing women.

The sight of women on the streets distressed him enormously, and he'd chase them off. Pregnant women especially got his goat. He enjoyed whipping out his cock at inopportune moments and waving it at passers by, shouting, 'I paint with this!'

It got so bad that various civic and religious groups campaigned to have Utrillo imprisoned.

Staggering from bar to café in search of the next drink, Utrillo was easy prey to local thugs and bounders. One time he was set upon in a café by hooligans who badly beat him and stubbed out cigarettes on his ears. He was rescued by a friend who dragged him to hospital, and it was there that Utrillo awoke, barely conscious, heavily bandaged with a swollen eye. Instead of thanking his rescuer Utrillo spat out blood and cursed him for having interrupted his drinking. 'That ungrateful son of a bitch,' said the friend, leaving disgusted. 'The next time he can rot in the sewer where he belongs!'

Between the spurts of creativity Utrillo suffered numerous alcoholic relapses, combined with self-destructive tendencies. In 1924, the same year that saw his work exhibited in one of Paris's grandest galleries, he attempted suicide by continually slamming his head against a wall. It took the intervention of the police to stop him.

These waverings might have destroyed a normal man, but Utrillo's mother always looked out for him, a gentle but firm jailer. And while the amount of booze he'd poured into himself had failed to pickle his genius, the disease grew more wretched with each passing year and it took the sanctity of marriage to finally break him free of it. His possessive mother didn't see it that way and, devastated at losing her son, retreated into isolation and died of a brain haemorrhage within a few short years. Unable to cope with his mother's death, Utrillo did not attend the funeral but instead shut himself up in his study for a whole year.

After the love of a good woman had enabled him to win his battle against alcohol addiction, Utrillo became extremely religious and latterly the grand old man of French art, rich and respected living in a villa on the French Riviera. Amusingly, a London museum, in its catalogue, stated that the artist had perished a victim of excessive drinking. Utrillo took them to court and won, arguing that he was still very much alive and sober.

Considering his alcohol intake and mental imbalance, Utrillo must be applauded for managing to reach the age of seventy-two before croaking it. He was buried in his beloved Montmartre, his funeral cortège watched by 50,000 people.

W

JOHN WAYNE (1907–1979: Actor)

In 1958, President Eisenhower invited Nikita Khrushchev to America and was intrigued when the Soviet premier asked to meet the all-American John Wayne. Khrushchev, it turned out, was a big fan and had pirated copies of Duke's movies. For Wayne, the number one commie hater, it was an odd meeting of minds. The encounter occurred at a formal function and, weary of the crowds, Wayne led the special guest to a private room to make use of the bar. 'I am told that you like to drink,' said Khrushchev through his translator. 'And that you can hold your liquor.' Wayne smiled, 'That's right. I hear much the same thing can be said about you.' There followed a keen discussion about the merits of Russian vodka as opposed to Mexican tequila, during which several shots were downed, Wayne and the Soviet premier matching each other drink for drink. At one point Khrushchev said something with a broad smile on his face. Wayne asked the interpreter for a translation. 'He said, he is the leader of the biggest state in the world and will one day rule the whole world.' Duke roared with laughter and asked the interpreter to translate the following, 'Tell him I'm gonna knock him on his sorry fucking ass.'

In the end the booze contest was deemed a draw. A few months later Wayne received a large wooden box at his Hollywood office. Inside were several cases of premium Russian vodka and a note that read: 'Duke. Merry Christmas, Nikita.' Genuinely touched, Wayne shipped over to the Kremlin some cases of his favourite tequila.

Born Marion Morrison in Iowa, the older of two children, Wayne excelled at high school both academically and on the football pitch. But already he'd a taste for alcohol that would reach legendary proportions, as he and his pals would buy bootleg whisky every weekend and get smashed.

Winning a football scholarship to the University of Southern California, Wayne left early to work as an extra in the film industry, slowly climbing the ladder before landing his first leading role in *The Big Trail* (1930). It was on this film that Wayne began to forge a reputation as a fearsome drinker. Boozers comprised much of the cast and most nights' revelries descended into drunken orgies. Rumour has it that Wayne showed up for work some mornings so out of it that he had to be wired to his horse to keep his body from keeling over in the saddle.

Duke did most of his drinking with his male friends, it was a macho thing. His favourite tipple was Wild Turkey bourbon and he drank it neat, without ice, 'To hell with the ice,' he'd yell at bartenders, 'it just dilutes good liquor!' There's a story that in the early thirties Wayne and drinking buddy Ward Bond punched holes through nearly every door in the Hollywood Athletics Club in a drunken contest of physical strength. Duke also frequented drinking spots on the Sunset Strip. One night a press photographer asked Duke if he could take his picture. 'You wanna eat that camera? Then don't point it in my direction.'

In 1934 Ward Bond, Henry Fonda and Wayne sailed down to Mexico on John Ford's yacht, fishing and drinking beer and tequila. It was a riot; Ford got so plastered he was convinced he'd seen 'a green slimy vicious' sea serpent. They landed at the town of Mazatlan and spent the day drinking in bars and visiting whorehouses. At a hotel Fonda collapsed non compos in a chair. Duke got the owner's pet boa constrictor and placed it in Hank's lap. When he awoke he had the fright of his life. As the day went on the roistering got too much for the authorities and they were all thrown in jail and politely asked to leave town.

Throughout the thirties Wayne toiled in low-grade movies, mostly westerns, until John Ford rescued him from possible obscurity with his role as the Ringo Kid in *Stagecoach* (1939). It made Wayne a star, but didn't put a dampener on his drinking. After one party friend and frequent co-star Maureen O'Hara drove a totally poleaxed Wayne home. En route Duke demanded she stop, yelling, 'I need a drink!' He got out and picked a house at random and pounded on the door. A startled woman opened it and invited him in. He stayed for a while, drinking and happily chatting, before heading homeward.

Wayne was married three times. His second wife, Esperanza Díaz Ceballos, nicknamed 'Chata', was the most memorable, though for all the wrong reasons. She was sexy and feisty, a minor Mexican actress, but it was a rocky union from the moment they tied the knot in 1946. 'Our marriage was like shaking two volatile chemicals in a jar,' Wayne said. Quickly the marriage developed into a predictable pattern that carried on for years. Chata drank but couldn't hold her booze; she went on benders and there'd be terrible rows, followed by reconciliations and then the whole thing would repeat itself. She was also insanely jealous, for good reason; Wayne had a wandering eye and had bedded Marlene Dietrich amongst many others.

In 1948 Gail Russell starred as John Wayne's love interest in *Wake of the Red Witch*. Gail was a beauty but an incredibly fragile creature so overcome with nerves before going in front of the camera that she'd throw up in her dressing room and began taking to the bottle for courage. Duke nursed her through the film. Chata was convinced Wayne was carrying on an affair and when he returned home late from the cast party she aimed a gun at him as he walked through the door and pulled the trigger. The bullet barely missed his head.

The next morning she was all forgiveness, uncontrollable tears for days. Duke submitted and gave her another chance. But the lure of the bottle was too strong and she went back to drinking, often with her mother, who lived in the same house. Duke finally kicked them both out and demanded a divorce. When Hedda Hopper asked Duke to sum up his marriage to Chata he replied, 'We had a pretty good time together, when she wasn't trying to kill me!'

As for poor old Gail Russell, she was never to curb her dependency on alcohol, which drastically affected her career. By the early fifties she was in a downward spiral, there were a few cases of drink driving charges and then the big one: at four o'clock in the morning she ploughed into a restaurant on Beverly Boulevard, pinning the hapless janitor under her new convertible. 'I had a few drinks,' she informed the police. 'I had two. No four. Oh, I don't know how many I had. It's nobody's business anyway.'

She tried desperately to give it up, joining Alcoholics Anonymous and spending a year in a drying-out clinic. Her end was pitiful, dying alone in an apartment surrounded by empty liquor bottles. She was only thirty-five.

Wayne meanwhile continued to drink and roister with the boys. During the making of *Sands of Iwo Jima* (1949), some of the young actors cast as Marines were determined to match Duke drink for drink, but they couldn't hack it, turning up on set the next morning hungover as hell, while Wayne was as fresh as a daisy. He even formed his own drinking club in Hollywood; the club's charter was that members had to be, in Wayne's words, at the very least 'a gutter-orientated drunkard'.

Duke wasn't an alcoholic in the truest sense of the word because he could go for weeks without touching a drop. But when he drank, boy could he put it away. His son Michael recalled seeing his father once down a bottle of tequila before dinner, then a bottle of brandy afterwards. Ronald Reagan, a close family friend, once said of Wayne's infamous intake, 'He drank enough whisky to float a PT boat.'

Making *Donovan's Reef* (1963) in Hawaii, John Ford tried unsuccessfully to keep Wayne and co-star Lee Marvin apart. Away from filming, the pair got roaring drunk together and caused chaos. Returning to his hotel one night totally smashed, Wayne saw a group of Catholic priests and launched into a vitriolic attack against the Catholic Church. Guilt kicked in almost immediately and Duke made a donation to a church charity on the spot.

Rumoured to smoke six packs of cigarettes a day, in 1964 Wayne was diagnosed with lung cancer. He was fifty-seven years old. Fearing that his image would suffer, Wayne kept it secret from the press as he underwent two huge operations that left him with a twenty-eight-inch scar across his chest. His left lung was removed. Only after surviving the ordeal did he go public, saying how he'd 'Beaten that son of a bitch cancer.' It only enhanced his mythic status.

Not long out of hospital, Wayne made the western *The Sons of Katie Elder* (1965) and was spotted between takes swallowing vitamin pills, washed down with a hefty swig of mescal, 120 per-cent-proof liquor.

He'd then shake himself like a bison stiffening itself against the cold before thundering, 'Goddamn! I'm the stuff men are made of.'

Sadly, by 1978 the cancer was back, this time in his stomach. He was in desperate pain. In a nine-hour operation almost his entire stomach was removed. Incredibly, he came out the other side, beating the big C again, but little of the real Wayne survived this time. He could only eat bland food and, worse, could no longer touch alcohol. He must have thought, what was the point of living. A year later he was gone. Legends do die, after all.

HANK WILLIAMS (1923–1953: Country and Western Singer)

Often touted as the father of modern country music, responsible for bringing the genre out of the honky tonk backwoods and into the mainstream, Hank Williams was also the progenitor of that elite squad of crash-and-burn rock stars that included Janis Joplin, Jimi Hendrix and Kurt Cobain, who lived fast and died young, a romantic notion for some, though it always ends the same, cold meat on a slab.

He grew up poor in rural Alabama, the son of a disabled First World War veteran and a church-going dominant mother, who would later manage his career. Every bit as strong-willed as Hank, she rarely lost an argument and was a formidable force. She once ended a disagreement by knocking Hank through a plate-glass window.

Given a guitar as a kid, Hank sang in the street for loose change to help his family out. By his early teens he was writing his own songs and entering talent shows. Quitting school as soon as possible, determined to pursue a music career, Williams landed a regular spot on a local radio show, but his teenage years were already blighted by a worrying dependency on alcohol, a problem that started when he took up drink aged ten, sipping beer and moonshine.

The radio exposure created a demand for Williams at dance halls across Alabama, where he frequently got tanglefooted and into fights, or provided an interesting encore to his performance by smashing his guitar over a fan's head, necessitating the purchase of a new instrument just about every week.

In 1944 Hank met and fell in love with Audrey Sheppard; they were married by a justice of the peace at a gas station on the way to a gig. He also entered a hospital to treat his alcoholism, the first of numerous visits. Actually, Hank was more of a binge drinker, going on three- or five-day benders, then not touching a drop for months, only to get stoned on his butt again 'and be foaming at the mouth like a goddamned mad dog', claimed band mate Sammy Pruett, which didn't take much doing since he'd a low tolerance of alcohol.

After years of constant touring with his band the Drifting Cowboys, Hank finally won a recording contract and so began a steady stream of hit records that lasted till his death. But his personal life was a mess: he and Audrey regularly fought over his worsening drink habit. He was getting smashed with increasing frequency. One reporter remembered getting out of an elevator at a Nashville radio station and seeing Hank lying comatose on the floor. Like so many that were close to him, fellow country singer Roy Acuff could see Hank was heading for oblivion and tried to warn him off the booze, saying, 'You've got a million-dollar voice, son, but a ten-cent brain.' Hank didn't listen, or didn't care. His drinking reached such a point that Audrey filed for divorce, calling his behaviour 'unmanageable'. In the end she didn't go through with it and returned to Hank, giving him a son that brought some much-needed stability into his life.

An established star by 1950, Hank was uncomfortable with fame and all the incumbent crap that came with it; he felt exploited, like a piece of meat. The touring got harder and so did the boozing. Soon it began to affect his performances. At one gig in Louisiana he stumbled on stage and asked the crowd, 'I bet y'all drove a long way to see Hank, didn't you?' The crowd responded with a huge cheer. 'Well, now you've seen him,' with that he dropped his guitar and stalked off without playing a single note.

To make sure he went on stage sober the tour manager took the unusual step of hiring a detective, who told Hank to his face that if he ever caught him drinking he'd lay him out cold. Sometimes it worked, sometimes it didn't. One night Hank bribed the stage hands to bring in small airline booze bottles and he stashed them in the toilet cistern in the men's room.

When shitfaced, Hank would get up to all sorts of pranks, mainly in hotels during his tours. One night he sat with a gun spraying the walls and ceiling with bullets. Another time cops found him chasing a lady wrestler completely naked up and down the corridors.

The band were growing increasingly narked at Hank's behaviour and drinking, seldom knowing if he was going to show up for a gig sober, or show up at all. At one concert he kept a crowd waiting for four and a half hours; it had taken that long to sober him up. Devoted fans would forgive him anything, even the time he fell off the stage into the audience; others booed and jeered, many walked out.

A tour of Las Vegas was a particular toil. By the time the concerts were over Hank was so smashed that he had to be carried to the tour bus and frisked for hidden booze. 'He looked like any old derelict you'd see on skid row,' said band member Jerry Rivers. It was getting so bad Hank would drink anything; some band members believe on that trip he tried to pour anti-freeze down his neck.

If anything, the band's tour of Canada was even worse. Playing Ontario, Hank was hopelessly pissed, barely managing to scramble onto the stage and get to the microphone. Once there he sang the same line of the song repeatedly, then fell over and had to be dragged off while the crowd bayed for his blood. Furious, a large portion of the audience laid siege to the theatre, intent on getting at Hank. The local Mounties had to be called in to escort the band out of town.

Then his marriage collapsed. The last straw came when Hank burst into the house after a wild night out and fired at Audrey four times. She left, never to come back, despite his pleas that without her he wouldn't live longer than a year, words that would prove horrifyingly prophetic.

Hitting the bottle with renewed vigour, friends and band members deserting him, Hank was at a low ebb when he invited singer Faron Young and his nineteen-year-old girlfriend Billie Jean Jones to his house for a party. Hank began the evening by opening a large suitcase full of guns, .38s and .45s. Hank was a keen gun collector and was known to take them to bed with him. On one occasion, while examining a new acquisition – a .357 Magnum pistol – Hank pulled the trigger and the bullet whistled just past his ear.

As the evening progressed Hank felt himself drawn to Billie Jean. The impulse was so strong he led Faron outside and pointed a pistol at him. 'Well, boy,' said Hank, 'I don't want no hard feelings, but I think I'm in love with your girl.' Nonplussed, Faron replied, 'You can have that girl. You can put that gun back in your pocket, cuz I ain't gonna die for her.'

So Billie became Hank's girl and very soon his second wife, but the newlyweds had little time together as Hank passed through sanatoriums in a bid to dry out. Suffering from an old back problem he'd also begun to take morphine combined with the sedative chloral hydrate; add alcohol to that mix and there's really only one place you're going to end up. Friends grew concerned at how frail and old he looked, staring out at the world through mournful, dead eyes. Barely thirty, it seemed he'd already experienced and seen enough of life. Asked once how he was able to write all those mournful heartbreak songs, Hank replied, 'Hell, boy, you've gotta live it, man; you can't fake it, you gotta live it.'

Scheduled to perform a New Year's show in Canton, Ohio, Hank woke up during a restless night on 29 December to inform Billie, 'I think I see God coming down the road.' On the morning of New Year's Eve Hank sat in his baby blue Cadillac, a nineteen-year-old at the wheel, destination Canton. He never got there. After driving for hours, the weather turned nasty so they booked into a hotel in Knoxville, Tennessee, to wait out the storm. While there, Williams took sick. A doctor was called and gave him a vitamin injection and morphine to control his convulsions. The doctor later described Williams as 'very drunk' and noted there were pills in the room.

Outside the storm clouds quelled and it was decided to push on and try to make the show. In no fit state to walk himself, hotel porters carried Williams to his car. Driving through the night, Hank slouched in the back; the car was stopped by a patrolman who took one look at the singer and proclaimed, 'That guy looks dead.'

In the early hours of New Year's Day, almost a year to the day since Audrey walked out on him, the young chauffeur grew concerned that Williams hadn't moved in the back seat for hours. Pulling over, he touched his passenger's face; it was cold and already turning blue. Quickly he raced to the nearest hospital but it was too late, Hank Williams was pronounced dead on arrival. The official cause of death was heart failure. Rather eerily, since he died alone in that back seat on some desolate stretch of desert highway, his final single was titled 'I'll Never Get out of This World Alive'.

JOHN WODEHOUSE, FOURTH EARL OF KIMBERLEY
(1924–2002: Landowner and Politician)

Considering the corpulent decadence, the corrupt and pig-trough mentality of so many politicians over the years, it really is a damn fine achievement to end up as the most alcoholically ravaged and most married peer in modern British history. A genuine eccentric, who might have been left to froth at the mouth in a bedlam in less enlightened times, for Wodehouse a quick fumble was very rarely off his brain. When he wasn't chasing skirts or falling down after too much champagne he liked nothing better than shark fishing and looking for UFOs.

Like much of his aristocratic brethren, Wodehouse spent a largely soulless and lonely childhood, with a reserved mother and largely absent father; draughty school holidays were spent mostly with the family nanny. Cold and severe Eton must have come as a godsend, then. Frequent trips to London whetted his appetite for the good things in life and his career as a self-confessed sex maniac began when he 'paid a few quid' for a knee-trembler from an aging Soho scrubber.

At the age of seventeen Wodehouse inherited the family's vast estate when his father was killed in a German air raid. Academically gifted, he went up to Cambridge but his studies were cut short when he got seriously hammered one night and accidentally enlisted in the Grenadier Guards. 'Helping to liberate Brussels in 1944 was the beginning of my downfall,' he later wrote. Capturing a large supply of Champagne, Wodehouse's tank was a veritable drinks cabinet on wheels, 'and I spent much of the war tight and when it was over I couldn't stop'.

To sponsor his now rather insatiable drink habit and proclivity to gamble away a bloody fortune, Wodehouse began selling not just the family silver but its bricks and mortar, assets that had taken a century or more to accumulate, including the historic Kimberley Hall and its 4,250 acres; 'All I could think about was getting a new Aston Martin.'

His appetite for the opposite sex didn't come cheap, either. Like Henry VIII, he went through six wives. I shan't list the details of all six marriages here – there is only so much forestry in South America – simply select the highlights, *Match of the Day* style. Wife number one was Diana Legh, the daughter of Sir Piers Legh, Master of the King's Household; they met on a blind date at the Ritz Hotel. Their marriage was a royal star-spotter's delight, held just after the war at St George's Chapel in Windsor and attended by King George VI, the Queen and the Princesses Elizabeth and Margaret. Walking down the aisle, Wodehouse knew the whole thing was a bloody mistake, 'but I couldn't stop it because the King and Queen were there, and I was in my best uniform'. The honeymoon was about as romantic as cold porridge in your underpants, with Wodehouse later confessing that he had more fun trying to seize hold of the mice scur-rying round the floor of the bedroom than his bride. The marriage lasted barely a year, with Wodehouse terminating the union in a brassily novel way: 'I gave the butler a note to give to her saying that it wasn't going to work out, and that since her mother was sailing for America that night why didn't she go too? That night I found a lovely girl and realised what I'd been missing not having a proper romp. After that, I never stopped.'

Footloose and fancy free, Wodehouse gambled and shagged his way along the Côte d'Azur. 'Sex. I just couldn't think of anything else.' But his lifestyle wasn't without its dangers; he was once caught by an irate husband naked in a hotel cupboard. Back home he ran with London's high-society crowd including Lord Lucan, a frivolous playboy existence that often landed him in the gossip columns; an occupational hazard: 'If you were as drunk as I was, it was hard to avoid.'

Skip to wife number four, a twenty-three-year-old fashion model, Maggie Simons. Both drank and indulged in 'fearful fights', so that didn't last long. His final marriage was to Janey Consett, a former masseuse he had met on a beach in Jamaica some years earlier.

Hard to believe that Wodehouse managed a professional career amid all this, but during the fifties and sixties he ran a successful public rela-tions business that had numerous film-star clients including Gregory

Peck, David Niven, Robert Mitchum and 'that bald bugger' (Yul Brynner). He was also a member of the British bobsleigh team from 1949 to 1958, though this probably had more to do with spending time in St Moritz than a yen for the sport. His other pursuits included playing championship tiddlywinks and breeding prize pigs.

So, quite an active life, considering his hectic love affair with the bottle that made him a positive hazard on the highways and a frequent guest in magistrate's courts up and down the country. He once ran over and killed a pedestrian in Piccadilly. By the 1970s his health was so badly affected that he joined Alcoholics Anonymous and later became vice-president of the World Council on Alcoholism. He confessed to still drinking a bottle of wine a day, but that was a vast improvement on the years when he counted himself an insane boozer. 'After all,' he reasoned, 'no normal person would try to drive a car up the steps of the Grand Hotel in Brighton.'

A member of the House of Lords, Wodehouse stood up before the 1979 general election and urged party supporters to vote Conservative, not a good move when you're the Liberal Party spokesman in the Lords. He was sacked forthwith, and moved across to the Tory bench, which you'd have thought his more natural home and where he took a stance just right of Genghis Khan. 'Queers,' he declared, 'have been the downfall of all the great empires.'

Wodehouse never really actively pursued a political career, though he once bravely admitted in a 1980 debate in the Lords that he was an alcoholic. The problem was, he was never that popular. In 1999 when the governing Labour Party drastically reduced the number of peers, Wodehouse put himself up for election but few if anyone bothered to vote for him. He blamed his exclusion on 'that little sod Blair. I would assassinate him tomorrow.'

Wodehouse died of kidney failure aged seventy-eight; not a bad innings, you might say.

Y

BORIS YELTSIN (1931–2007: *Statesman*)

There can't be any better example of the functioning alcoholic than Boris Yeltsin. After all, this guy was running the second most powerful country in the world bollocked to the eyeballs, a bit unnerving when you think his shaky finger was on the button that could have launched 500 ballistic missiles at the Western world.

For years his drinking and general buffoonery on the world stage was regarded as a joke in his own country. They looked away in embarrassment at yet another slurred speech or important occasion when he needed physical support to stay upright. More seriously, as the years went on Yeltsin was viewed as an increasingly unstable leader, with the very real possibility of him snuffing it at any moment leaving a power vacuum in Russian politics and also sending several vodka distilleries out of business.

If there is a place that is the arsehole of the world, the village of Butka where Yeltsin was born would be the dried fleck of shit hanging off it. Yeltsin hailed from a long line of drunken peasants. Even the priest conducting Yeltsin's baptism had fallen asleep in a vat of vodka and dropped baby Boris in the baptismal font; he was too whacked to pull him out so Mama had to do the rescuing. The priest is said to have muttered, 'Well, if he can survive such an ordeal, it means he's a good, tough lad.'

Certainly he was tough and exhibited a rebellious streak early in life. Unruly at school, Yeltsin was always getting into fights and the instigator of pranks, once persuading his whole class to suddenly jump out of the window and scarper in the middle of a lesson. Another time he broke into an army storage area and nicked a grenade. While he was attempting to disassemble it the grenade went off in his left hand, blowing off his thumb and forefinger.

Yeltsin followed his father into the construction business and joined the Communist Party in 1961, quickly rising to the top of his regional organisation. His record as a tough and effective administrator attracted the attention of Russian premier Mikhail Gorbachev, who in 1985 made Yeltsin effectively the mayor of Moscow. It was here, in August 1991, that Yeltsin came to the attention of the world when high-ranking conspirators sought to gain control of the Soviet state in a coup and overthrow Gorbachev's era of glasnost and perestroika. Gorbachev was held prisoner in his summer retreat near the Black Sea. The whole of Moscow was at the plotters' mercy. But they hadn't bargained on vodka-barrel Boris. In those never-to-be-forgotten scenes of him mounting a tank outside the Russian parliament building Yeltsin became the symbolic centre of resistance to the coup and virtually single-handedly repelled it, rallying the people against the conspirators. The coup collapsed and Yeltsin was the natural successor to the neutered Gorbachev. His aim was to push forward towards democracy and bury communism once and for all.

Yeltsin's 'struggle' with alcohol first came to international light during his visit to the US in 1989 for a series of lectures, when journalists reported on his inebriated condition. He'd discovered a liking for American bourbon and could drink a quart and a half of it at night. There was also a bizarre incident when he travelled by car to meet an old friend at a village outside Moscow, but turned up dripping wet from head to foot. Yeltsin's memory was a blur but he later managed to piece together what happened – just. He'd dismissed the driver and decided to walk the final stretch alone; then as he crossed a bridge he either fell accidentally or was pushed into a canal. Rumours flew around Moscow that this had been a failed assassination attempt. Either that or Yeltsin was just plain drunk.

In September 1994 after a G-7 summit meeting, a gruelling trip during which Yeltsin abstained from booze, he let his guard down disastrously on the flight back home. Yeltsin was scheduled to stop over in Ireland to meet with the Irish Prime Minister, but when the plane touched down at Shannon airport there was an ominous lack of activity. The aircraft merely stood on the tarmac, silent, no sign of life, let alone Yeltsin. An hour later, with Irish dignitaries still waiting, Russian officials announced that Yeltsin was 'unwell' and too tired to meet the Irish PM, leaving commentators to arrive at no other conclusion than he was insensible.

By the mid-nineties Yeltsin's drinking had become worse. Because of his bulky physique he'd been able to consume large quantities of vodka and other hard liquor with very little obvious damage. Nor did his habit seem to adversely affect his work. He'd always known when to stop. Now that ability and that self-control began to evaporate. He was drinking at lunch time and dinner, drinking before receptions and during, looking well fortified at important functions. Not least in August 1994 in Berlin, at a ceremony marking the departure of the last Russian troops from Germany, when he snatched the baton from the conductor of the Berlin police orchestra and took over his duties while jigging about like an embarrassing dad at a Christmas party and blowing kisses to the audience.

It was now obvious to the eyes of the world that Yeltsin was a walking Smirnoff processing plant. He was even ridiculed on *The Simpsons* in an episode where Homer takes a breathalyser test at Moe's Tavern; his alcohol level passes from 'Tipsy' and 'Soused' to 'Stinkin' Drunk' and – at the top of the range – 'Boris Yeltsin'.

Of course the Kremlin tried to cover up the lapses, saying he suffered from an unspecified neurological disorder that affected his sense of balance. Others preferred to refer to him as a man of the people. Indeed, many Russians were quietly proud of the fact that their leader could drink more vodka than the average Muscovite; quite a feat. The West looked on sceptically; the CIA reported during the 1990s that Yeltsin was an alcoholic, subject to occasional binges that kept him out of action for days at a time and led to sudden cancellations of meetings with key foreign visitors.

Perhaps Yeltsin's biggest fall from grace came in 1995 while a guest of the residing Clintons at the White House. On his first night there he embarked on an almighty booze bender that almost resulted in an international incident when secret service agents found Yeltsin standing – well, barely standing – outside the White House dressed in his underwear trying to hail a taxi. When confronted, the Russian President in slurred speech barely decipherable explained that he was hungry and wanted a pizza.

The following evening Yeltsin again partook of a few too many vodkas, eluded his own bodyguard and stumbled around the White House, ending up in a basement area and being mistaken for an intruder by security guards.

Re-elected President in 1996, Yeltsin's oath of office speech was so alarmingly inarticulate that people surmised that either he was extremely ill or he'd been replaced by an animatronics hired from Disney and the batteries were running low. There was further agitation when a few days later he disappeared altogether, raising suspicion that he might actually be dead. The Kremlin came under enormous pressure to produce a body, breathing or not. When Yeltsin finally made an appearance for the world press it provided precious little reassurance. He didn't look as fried as he'd been for his inauguration, yet his speech remained stilted and he looked more corpse than corpus. What no one knew was that Yeltsin had just undergone a quintuple heart by-pass operation. That he was alive at all was a minor miracle. He'd been on the verge of death so many times even his doctors scratched their heads that he was still walking and talking. He'd suffered strokes, giant ulcers infected his stomach, his heart was hanging in there by one solitary ventricle, yet he continued to wake up in the morning.

Now taking drugs and continuing to drink to relieve the pain that racked his whole body, Yeltsin returned to the world stage. On a visit to Stockholm in 1997 he mumbled a few incoherent syllables and then went on to tell his bemused audience that Swedish meatballs reminded him of Bjorn Borg's face. He then lost his balance and almost fell off the podium after drinking a single glass of champagne. Then there was his 1998 meeting with Pope John Paul II. As His Holiness tried to bring the audience to an end, he was forced to retake his seat when Yeltsin announced loudly: 'Holy Father, we haven't finished yet.' At the subsequent banquet, Yeltsin eulogised about his 'boundless love for Italian women'. You have to hand it to the old goat, he certainly made politics fun to watch.

Yeltsin died of congestive heart failure aged seventy-six. Although his tenure at the Kremlin was blighted by years of turmoil in Russia and economic hardship, his legacy is intact as the man who finally consigned communism to the dustbin of history, and to have done it while four sheets to the wind is an achievement deserving of our respect.

Select Bibliography

The following books proved most useful with miscellaneous stories:

My Wicked, Wicked Ways by Errol Flynn (William Heinemann – 1960)

Confessions of an Irish Rebel by Brendan Behan (Hutchinson & Co – 1965)

The Moon's a Balloon by David Niven (Hamish Hamilton – 1971)

Wild Bill Hickok by Richard O'Connor (Remploy – 1972)

Bring on the Empty Horses by David Niven (Hamish Hamilton – 1975)

Dylan Thomas: The Biography by Paul Ferris (Hodder and Stoughton – 1977)

Tall, Dark and Gruesome by Christopher Lee (W H Allen – 1977)

Marvin by Donald Zec (Hodder and Stoughton – 1979)

Up in the Clouds, Gentlemen Please by John Mills (Weidenfeld and Nicolson – 1980)

Sing a Sad Song: The Life of Hank Williams by Roger M Williams (University of Illinois Press – 1981)

Some Sort of Epic Grandeur: The Life of F. Scott Fitzgerald by Matthew J Bruccoli (Hodder and Stoughton – 1982)

Wired: The Short Life and Fast Times of John Belushi by Bob Woodward (Simon and Schuster – 1984)

Dark Star: The Untold Story of the Meteoric Rise and Fall of Legendary Silent Screen Star John Gilbert by Leatrice Gilbert Fountain (Sidgwick and Jackson – 1985)

Spencer Tracy by Bill Davidson (Sidgwick and Jackson – 1987)

Louise Brooks: A Biography by Barry Paris (Alfred A Knopf – 1989)

Ava: My Story by Ava Gardner (Bantam USA – 1990)

Best of Times, Worst of Times by Shelley Winters (Frederick Muller – 1990)

Select Bibliography

Break on Through: The Life and Death of Jim Morrison by James Riordan and Jerry Prochnicky (Plexus – 1991)

Peter Lawford: The Man Who Kept the Secrets by James Spada (Bantam – 1991)

What's It All About? by Michael Caine (Random House – 1992)

Tired and Emotional: The Life of Lord George Brown by Peter Paterson (Chatto & Windus – 1993)

Hammer of the Gods: Led Zeppelin by Stephen Davis (Pan – 1995)

Bogart: The Biography by A M Sperber (Weidenfeld and Nicolson – 1997)

In the Footsteps of Alexander the Great by Michael Wood (BBC Books – 1997)

Montgomery Clift by Maurice Leonard (Hodder and Stoughton – 1997)

Peter Cook: A Biography by Harry Thompson (Hodder and Stoughton – 1997)

Behind the White Ball by Jimmy White (Hutchinson – 1998)

The Life and Times of Sam Peckinpah by David Weddle (Grove Press – 2000)

Charles Hawtrey: The Man Who Was Private Widdle by Roger Lewis (Faber and Faber – 2001)

The Dirt – Mötley Crüe: Confessions of the World's Most Notorious Rock Band by Neil Strauss (HarperCollins – 2001)

Robert Mitchum: Baby, I Don't Care by Lee Server (St Martin's Press – 2001)

Trevor Howard: A Personal Biography by Terence Pettigrew (Peter Owen – 2001)

Blessed: The Autobiography by George Best (Ebury Press – 2002)

It's Not a Rehearsal by Amanda Barrie (Headline – 2002)

Old Gods Almost Dead: The 40-Year Odyssey of the Rolling Stones by Stephen Davis (Aurum – 2002)

Ozzy: Unauthorized by Sue Crawford (Michael O'Mara Books – 2002)

Adventures of a Suburban Boy by John Boorman (Faber and Faber – 2003)

Buffalo Bill and Sitting Bull: Inventing the Wild West by Bobby Bridger (University of Texas Press – 2003)

The Pythons Autobiography by Monty Python (Orion – 2003)

Mr S: The Last Word on Frank Sinatra by George Jacobs (HarperCollins – 2003)

Scoring at Half-Time by George Best (Ebury Press – 2003)

A Drinking Companion: Alcohol and Writers' Lives by Kelly Boler (Cardoza – 2004)

Errol Flynn: Satan's Angel by David Bret (Robson Books – 2004)

Gazza: My Story by Paul Gascoigne (Headline – 2004)

John Wayne: The Man Behind The Myth by Michael Munn (Robson Books – 2004)

Bix: The Definitive Biography of a Jazz Legend by Jean Pierre Lion (Continuum Publishing – 2005)

Calamity Jane: The Woman and the Legend by J D McLaird (University of Oklahoma Press – 2005)

Sinatra: The Life by Anthony Summers (Alfred A Knopf – 2005)

Ava Gardner by Lee Server (Bloomsbury – 2006)

The Life of Kingsley Amis by Zachary Leader (Jonathan Cape – 2006)

The Lives of the English Rakes by Fergus Linnane (Portrait Books – 2006)

Peter Cook: So Farewell Then by Wendy E Cook (HarperCollins – 2006)

Alice Cooper, Golf Monster (Aurum – 2007)

Eric Clapton: The Autobiography (Century – 2007)

From the Eye of the Hurricane by Alex Higgins (Headline – 2007)

Patrick Mower: My Story (John Blake – 2007)

Raising Hell by Tom Wright and Susan Vanhecke (Omnibus Press – 2007)

Wallace Reid: The Life and Death of a Hollywood Idol by E J Fleming (McFarland and Company – 2007)

Wonderful Today: The Autobiography of Pattie Boyd (Headline – 2007)

Drinking for England by Fergus Linnane (JR Books – 2008)

Loving Peter: My Life with Peter Cook by Judy Cook (Piatkus – 2008)

My Word Is My Bond by Roger Moore (Michael O'Mara Books – 2008)

Outlaw Journalist: The Life and Times of Hunter S. Thompson by William McKeen (Aurum – 2008)

AC/DC: Maximum Rock & Roll by Murray Engleheart with Arnaud Durieux (Aurum 2009)

André the Giant: A Legendary Life by Michael Krugman (Pocket Books – 2009)

I Am Ozzy by Ozzy Osbourne (Sphere Books – 2009)

Shooting the Cook by David Pritchard (Fourth Estate – 2009)

Warren Oates: A Wild Life by Susan Compo (University Press of Kentucky – 2009)

I'd also like to thank the staff of the British Film Institute library and the Westminster Reference Library for allowing me access to countless books, magazine and newspaper articles.

Picture Credits

Plate section 1

George Best © Daily Mail, Rex Features
Frank Sinatra and Ava Gardner © Getty Images
Frances Farmer © Bettmann / Corbis
Talullah Bankhead © Time & Life Pictures / Getty Images
Ernest Hemingway © Time & Life Pictures / Getty Images
Brendan Behan © Daily Mail / Rex Features
Kingsley Amis © Getty Images
John Belushi © Everett Collection / Rex Features
Serge Gainsbourg © Sipa Press / Rex Features
Courtney Love © Albert Ferreira / Rex Features
Shane MacGowan © Denis Jones / Evening Standard / Rex Features
Dean Martin © Rex Features

Plate Section 2

Errol Flynn © Michael Ochs Archives / Getty Images
Robert Mitchum © Sipa Press / Rex Features
Lee Marvin © Getty Images
Richard Burton and Elizabeth Taylor © Getty Images
Keith Moon © Getty Images
Jim Morrison © Michael Ochs Archives / Getty Images
Peter Langan © Richard Young / Rex Features
Paul Gascoigne © Rex Features
Boris Yeltsin © Sipa Press / Rex Features

Index

Index